Mark Richardson
Aimée Vanstone
Claire Tupholme
Annabel Cook
Donna Samworth
Heather Killingray

First published in Great Britain in 2008 by:
Forward Press Ltd.
Remus House
Coltsfoot Drive
Peterborough
PE2 9JX
Telephone: 01733 898101
Website: www.forwardpress.co.uk

HB ISBN 978-1 84418 474 3

Memories Are
Made Of This

*A poignant collection of
verse to take you down memory lane*

Foreword

A look, a smell, a place. The smallest of things can be powerful
enough to evoke a memory. This enchanting collection shows how
memories are made of this, and so much more.
From fond recollections of childhood hi-jinks and holidays, to poignant
musings of bitter-sweet times gone by, 'Memories Are Made Of This'
allows the poets to guide us on a trip down memory lane.
This inspiring anthology will become an edition to treasure, alongside
those precious memories. It provides a constant reminder of what we
should value and give thanks for in life as it beautifully captures the
essence of what memories are made of.

Memories Are Made Of This

Contents

Memories Are Made Of This

Memories Are Made Of This

Memories Are Made Of This

Memories Are Made Of This

Memories Are Made Of This

The Poems

Memory Lane

How things have changed

The green land where we ran the course
Now lea land thick with burs and gorse
The public house where old men sat
And told their tales and coughed and spat
Now haute cuisine - at what a price
(Although the food is very nice)
The villa where I passed teen days
Under my parents' loving gaze
Is now a sad tale of neglect
No gates to welcome or protect
The driveway overgrown with weeds
Who knows inside who does what deeds
What rites of passage there unfold
It's best not to return, I'm told
To try to live the past unwise
I now live under Midland skies
Where peace of mind's the greatest worth
Best drive my car and travel north
And leave behind this place of youth
Where memory does not match the truth.

Jill Hudson

Prize-Winning Poem

Congratulations Jill,
your heart-warming and reminiscent
poem has been selected as the best in the
collection and wins you a luxury gift hamper.

(May vary from picture shown)

Iona – Canterbury Peace Pilgrimage

We are just a band of pilgrims
Against the nation's might.
Our message is of love and peace
To set the world aright.

We set off cycling down the road
To spread our message true.
Dear island where Columba lived
We drew some strength from you.

Here friendship, love and peace survive
And blossom like a tree.
We set off cycling from your shores
To set the whole world free.

We do not know what we will face.
We hope we're not too late.
Our message is that love and peace
Can drive away all hate.

We go in friendship to all men
Its bombs we would destroy.
We want to build a better world
For all men to enjoy.

We're just a band of pilgrims
Who know this world's unfair.
We want to change it for a place
Where all men have their share.

Margaret Harrison

Memories Of A Beloved Siamese

Ming was the gentlest of Siamese
Tiny, svelte, a lover of knees
Her brown-cream body pressed close to mine
And azure blue eyes that looked divine
Enquiring, devoted a look that seemed to say
Come on mistress, let's have a play
I will always remember my Siamese Ming
With all the joy that affections can bring.

R Candlish

The Arrival

The month was September, the weather was fine,
my spirits were soaring, I knew it was time.
The waiting was over, preparations complete,
the house was made ready, this baby to greet.
We set off at speed, the car wheels took flight,
and arrived at the hospital on the stroke of midnight.
It seemed that this child was arriving in haste,
I was quickly made ready, there was no time to waste.

But nature decreed that this wasn't to be,
it would be a long wait for baby and me.
The hours that followed passed by in a dream,
I seemed to be part of some unearthly scheme.
Ghostly white figures were coming and going,
like a boat lost at sea I was ebbing and flowing.
Faint sounding voices were urging me on,
then there was calm and total oblivion.

I awoke feeling tranquil and strangely complete,
my thoughts became clearer then my heart missed a beat.
My eyes searched the room there was no one but me,
where was the baby I so longed to see?
I was soon reassured and experienced great joy,
being shown only briefly my beautiful boy.
We had weathered the storm and come safely to rest,
in the harbour of life we had given our best.

Plans for the future would just have to keep,
as we both closed our eyes in a long well-earned sleep.

M Wilson

Just A Bud

Unseen, and so silently that is how he comes to me,
My first love but only in memory.
Dark hair, brown eyes, he has haunted me in disguise
False happiness ending in tears
I have experienced over the years.
At the church gate we met, long years ago
But his love I was not to know.
We were both sixteen
Other people came in on the scene.

We strolled the lanes and over the fields
Enjoying life which only youth yields.
When we drifted apart, he held part of my heart.
Later someone else came into my life.
On the morning I was to become a wife
Came a letter to remind me of bygone days.
The boy with brown eyes the parting of the ways
But that book was closed, a new one to start.
On the brink of marriage, where was my heart?
In life we can only go one way
Further onward, every day.
From maiden days, twice I changed my name
In the Autumn of life, happiness came.
No longer around, the boy with brown eyes
I met a reminder, not in disguise, dark hair, brown eyes.
Now my winter is here, I am bereft
Long ago this world they both have left
Maybe I'll join them when or where
I'll just rest assured I am in God's care.

Doris Huff

Poignant Memories

May I be excused for going back to a time that I hold dear
The first sighting of the fragile bluebells in full bloom
An unforgettable walk through the local woods each year
With potted meat sandwiches and a big bottle of lemonade.

We would set off early on our special day, me and my dad
A short bus ride we were soon in the countryside to wander
Chattering, enjoying every minute, what a good time we had
Each bird and tree, we'd try to name as many as we could.

Spotting the rabbits that darted from the dense hedgerow
Passing fields where horses and ponies peacefully grazed
A peep at the little pond where the fishers for minnows go
Then over a stile and up the steep incline of the grassy bank.

There it was before our eyes, a carpet of pure heavenly blue
We never ceased to hold our breath at the gorgeous sight
In that shaded dell where in abundance the flowers grew
Within nature's own garden the beautiful perfect bluebell.

Now into the soft far distant haze of time it has gone
Yet the beguiling memory still poignantly lingers on.

Dawn Prestwich

Lest I Forget

I heard the crows calling across the trees
Echoing high above the barren land.
I remember it like it is today
As it was over the centuries.
What has that dead oak witnessed
Although now it silently slumbers?
Its friends watch over him and
They remember his strength and tenacity.
The winter's storms seem much the same
As they sting and bite the traveller's face
Scurrying along homewards.
I remember getting soaked yet
Admiring the ferocity of nature and
Thrilled by clouds racing across as always.
Slowly the thoughts ebb and pass by.
I think of dead friends who have faded.
I also think of stories that have preserved deeds.
What does God remember in His annals?
Does His spirit still hope for love and joy?
Will it rekindle the world as He intended?
I remember the weeping at Gethsemane.
When will His promise be more than a memory?

Barry Broadmeadow

We Should All Trust In Our Memories

(To Merna, my very dear mother, with all true love and affection)

Without a single solitary shadow of a doubt
This is indeed wholly true
For these 'haunting refrains' very easily
Come and go as they please.

No only to some of us
But much rather to all of us.

At all times of the days and nights
Do they keenly remain totally beholden to both
The passing, and the forthcoming truths
Of ordinary and extraordinary lives together

Collectively, they are jointly and singularly lamentable
Joyful, and even in-between.
But good and bad,
They are each still entirely unforgettable in themselves.

M D H Crossley-Stalker

A Special Place

A field where the wild poppies grow
And long tall grasses gently blow
The bees and butterflies abound
As I stood and gazed around.

I used to play there all the time
It was a moment so sublime
And, although I was only seven
I felt so very close to Heaven.

I lifted my eyes up to the sky
As the war planes thundered by
Oh how I wished it all would cease
Then once more we could have peace.

The poppies and the grasses sway
On that most perfect summer day
I close my eyes and I can see
It was so very real to me.

I still recall that perfect day
As I go along my way
It was a very special place
Because it was so full of grace.

Janet Towells

The Nastursium Roses

(Dedicated to my surgeon Mr Patterson and staff of Ward 64 Glasgow Royal Infirmary to Jean, Francess, Pauline, Sarah, the two Marys, Terry and Joyce)

Though memories fade into the past
Not going away completely the reflections last
I saw beauty shine from roses
A beauty that encouraged me
A beguiling beauty
That my heart could see

The deep peach colour enriched by the shine
And softness of petals
A beauty sublime
A stillness enlightened by the sun that shone
So vibrantly this I focused on
I knew that I would bloom again
And just like the roses I would shine

My memory of the patients in Ward 64
I know they suffered so much more
Kindness and love flowed for one another
So I dedicate this poem one to another
May God bless you and make you shine
Just like the roses with beauty sublime.

Ruth McIntyre

The Greatest Memories On Earth

The greatest memories on Earth are staged by kids
Every antic they got up to gave us a laugh
Pot lids, for shields when they fought the foe
Chairs set in a line, a train to go to and fro.

Mud pies, polishing stones, skipping ropes, laundry basket car
That took us on journeys which were very far
Old sheets for wigwams, lace curtain a bride's veil
Dolls' christenings, the 'font' an old tin pail.

Crowning ceremonies, the golden crown of dandelions
Hobby horses with knight's faces showing defiance
The damsel, safely rescued by the gallant knights
Ghosts 'n' ghouls dressed in sheets - faces painted white.

Schools, pantomimes, a circus by kids and pets
Soldiers wounded, nurses cared for them in tents
Bandages on heads, arms, legs, sweeping brush crutches
Mum's long black skirts and shawls, now a coven of witches.

Yet, it's true, kids in days of yore, made their own fun
There were no televisions, streets were free from knife and gun
The only noise was the laughter from the old and young
I know it's true, as eighty-two years ago, I had that fun!

Maisie Roberts

Memories Are Made Of This

The first thing I remember? Now that takes me back
I peeped out of the old front door, was only open a crack.
The snow was deep and white, cold 'n' crisp 'n' even
Then I saw my mum, she was home with baby Steven.

I didn't want a bruvver
He made me cross and frown
I just wanted a puppy dog
All furry, fluffy and brown.

By the time he'd grown into a fine young boy
We'd fight and argue over every toy
But he was my bruvver and he was the best
Grazes on his knees and dirt on his vest.

Then Dad brought home a cardboard box
What could be in it? Was it a fox?
My dream had come true, at last my dog
After that, the rest is a fog.

To London town we moved with hope
Getting away from the army folk
We had so much fun, you had to laugh
Saturday nights out came the tin bath!

But finer things were still in store
We did still move, just once more
Dunstable we went at last
All fields 'n' trees 'n' nice green grass.

I finished off my schooling there
With mini skirts and long blonde hair
I met a lad, had motorbike
It was his earring Mum didn't like.

Soon we bought a house and then got wed
Many a tear that day was shed.
We have two children of our own
Since then, how the years have flown.

The kids have grown and flown the nest
They are great, just like the rest
Cats 'n' dogs I now have loads
With muddy paws and a nice wet nose.

This is where my story ends
With lots of good memories and many good friends
Twenty-six years married, I haven't done bad
A better husband, I couldn't have had.

It's been great so far, but still lots to do
At forty-six I'm only halfway through
What's still to come, we will wait 'n' see
As the next chapter begins, I smile with glee . . .

Pauline Freeman

The Year That I Was Eight

That year I was eight.
The world was me, and friends
And family. And in the summer,
Freed from school, we were a noisy boisterous lot
Let loose upon an all-too-much suspecting neighbourhood.
We ruled the streets, the park, the distant woods
Like ancient kings, or despots out of time,
Fearing little but the brutish gangs
From down the road, whom we had fought
From time to time, to keep our 'territory' safe.

Each day was play; our time was gauged in moments only.
We neither knew nor cared what lay beyond,
But filled the instant with our childhood sports.
(A tennis ball sufficed for almost all our simple needs).

One day - I need no prompting to recall -
Our play came to a sudden halt.

From out a clear-blue western sky
Black dots appeared that soon turned into shapes;
A bee-like distant drone became a thunderous roar.
Wave on wave of deadly planes -
Lancasters or Wellingtons, I can't be sure -
In tight formation, rank on rank,
Formed black-edged patterns in the sun,
Dappling the sky, troubling the trembling earth beneath.

People by the dozen scurried from their homes into the street,
Began to wave their arms and shout and laugh for joy,
And cries of 'Give 'em Hell' echoed down the alleyways.
And we, not slow, began to shout the same.
To see these massive monsters as they rumbled overhead
Was awesome to us all - such might and lethal power
Held in check etched deep into our childish minds.

But when the sun revealed itself again,
And planes were dots across the eastern sky,
We turned back to our play. It was our task
To learn to live; we gave no further time
To those who flew the planes that day.
So many went, so few returned.

I never thought - not then, at least -
That they were learning how to die,
For I was only eight.

Jay Whittam

The Bluebell Wood

I remember a very long time ago
Walking through woods where bluebells did grow
So many flowers as far as the eye could see
Primroses too, in abundance under each tree
Such a beautiful sight to see on our way
I shall never forget the scene to my dying day
The countryside was full of fields of green
Against skies of blue that you have ever seen
This was England at her very best
A sight to behold far better than the rest
The peace and tranquillity of those days
I remember in so many ways
The world today is a different place
Nobody has time to sit and contemplate
Of all the beauty that surrounds us still
I don't suppose they ever will
But we realise how much we have lost
Also how much this has cost
We can relive these memories still
As I guess we always will

Enid Skelton

Childhood Memories

I was seven years old and full of questions,
as I walked with my uncle down the old bog road.
It was high summer and the honeysuckle was alive
with the buzz of bees, dog daisies grew along the hedgerows
sharp-toothed ferns cascaded onto the lane.

A noon-day sun shone from a cloudless sky
I was aware of nature's sensations
and wished that I could fold it all within my arms.
But my uncle was in a hurry, he had turf to gather,
things to do, while I was time wasting
listening to a blackbird's song.

Still, he was a kind-hearted man
as we sat together on an upturned barrow
drinking cold sweet tea, eating chunks of cheese
with home-made soda bread.
I often long for those treasured memories
the call of the curlew,
the tabby cat who came with us to chase rabbits.
Sometimes when I close my eyes and think of summer
it all comes back and I am seven years old
walking with my uncle down the old bog road.

Rosaleen Clarke

Having Fun

Never knowing the going
Stopped glowing with growing
And that adults
Can only reach in
We ate tripe, we ate rusks
We were home before dusk
And reached out to the world
From within.

There were cowboys and pirates
And perfect princesses
We'd scrapes on our elbows and knees
A competent climate
Tooth-stealing fairies
And a man in a moon
Made of cheese.

There were trolls beneath bridges
Wolves in the woods
And a bogeyman under the bed
There were wizards and witches
Some bad and some good
And everyone's parents
Were wed.

There was no pride
There was no shame
There was no vanity yet come
Came in the tide with autumn rain
Came winter snow
And summer sun
There was no lust, there was no greed
There were no jealous nets yet sprung
Strife had yet to plant its seed
And life was
Having fun.

Mark Noble

Times We Knew

As time goes by
And twilight years are here
We can still recall to mind
The days of starting school
The friends we made
The times we shared
Those carefree days of childhood
But then came darker days
Of troubled times and war
We think of those times we knew
And many childhood friends
Ones we see no more
With some we still can share
And bring to mind those days
Of our lives along the way
Some times were hard times
From which we learned a lot
But now it is only memories
And thankful for the blessings
And the good things we have got
Sometimes memories fail us
As we go our way
And try to think of ones we knew
To whom we have said 'goodbye'.

L E Davies

Dance Of Devotion

(In memory of a young woman's baptism)

Whirling and twirling
Like a butterfly on the wing,
She danced so gracefully
For our saviour and king.
She gives her all
In this dance of devotion,
Fluttering and twirling
With devout emotion,
Such grace, such beauty
Brought tears to my eyes,
As on bended knee she mutely
Submits to the Lord.

R E Downs-Thurley

Ode To The Gift Of Memory

Our memories come crystal clear,
Of happy times and sad;
Occasions unforgettable -
Which we are glad we've had.

A passing word
A crucial hour
An unspoilt week
A span of years.

Some memories from long ago -
Racing at school in sports;
But others come from later years -
When true love filled our thoughts.

A dream fulfilled
A friendship sealed
A goal achieved
A sorrow eased.

All come to us like precious stones -
Though some we may have lost,
Yet they reveal the life we've lived -
Thank you - whate'er the cost!

Beryl Dunning

Memories

Some time in days of long hot summers
We ran together through long grassed meadows
Plucking sweet flowers and chasing bright butterflies
Held grasshoppers in our cupped hands
Releasing them into long hopped flights.
A time that must go on forever
And we, inseparable, took the blade and cut
With trembling hands a finger on each hand
Which held together the bright blood flowing
Would bind us together for eternity.
But time spins on, years slip away
Increasing rapidly until the spiral
Brought us face to face again.
Older? Wiser? A long lost hope -
A recognition - brief greeting only a nod
Then a passing on our separate ways.
Times not forgotten but shelved
And brought out like a favourite book
Then shelved and locked away again.

Patricia Battell

Reflections

(This poem is dedicated to the memory of our late mother Iris Sefflyn Gabriel Williams June 12th 1911 - 1998)

Memories of our lives together
Where do I begin?
You nourished, protected and cherished us all
For our comfort and joy nothing was too great or small
You gave us your all.

I still wonder how you coped
In spite of the tears and fears
You survived and carried on
You worked so hard and yet you still
Had the time for those who needed you
You seemed so strong.

The mornings I cherished with coffee and toast
We gossiped and dreamed to the annoyance of most
Our Sundays we all dined with laughter and jokes
Great-gran, brothers and sisters
Cousins and babes, uncles and aunties
Had to sample what you baked
Then later out came the bottles of wine
For you that was divine.
Now you are gone, I feel so alone
But you gave me the strength to endure to the end
The memories are priceless, your love endless
So we will carry on to complete the task you began.

Colleen Leslie

School Gloom

In mem-or-y, I still can see,
That laughing stream below,
The water splash and the wellies flash,
In the fleecy layer of snow.

With morning gloom, to meet my doom,
There I went against my will,
To that horrid house of horrors,
The schoolhouse on the hill.

Miss Sharples fetched some apples,
For the juniors in her class,
The only snag, she left her bag,
Where the seniors had to pass.

Ed said, 'For a joke, let's nick the poke.'
Then a rain of apples fell.
Miss tried to sus, which one of us,
But no one dared to tell.

MacShane, the head, then up and said,
'Let the guilty face the wall,
Or I'll find the thief, I swear by grief,
When I trounce you one and all.'

There all dumbfound, we stood around,
Looking glum and sad,
Though the apple fruit was in dispute,
Since Adam was a lad.

Some screamed in pain, as she wield the cane,
And reddened to the throat,
Though she split that cane, she came again,
Bloodthirsty like a stoat.

There was no excuse, for such abuse,
I mean, to put it mild,
But, the rod I fear, she didn't spare,
Though I was seldom spoiled.

I used my brain and dodged the cane,
When I wet my eyes with spits,
'Twould be insane, to suffer pain,
For a few old Granny Smiths.

Big Ed who said, 'Let's nick the poke,'
Was the kind you couldn't hurt.
And we all knew well the one who'd tell,
Would later bite the dirt.

James Baxter

Oaklands Park

Each soldier lines up,
Excitedly forming a queue,
Patiently awaiting
His execution:
To sit at the top
Of the metal slope
And slide.

Or join the navy,
Sit astride
The wooden ship.
In unity
They ride the waves,
Then back,
Again and again.

The airmen in flight
Up in the air;
Over the rooftops
They soar
Then swoop
Over the ants
On the ground below.

The squeals of delight,
The chattering crowd,
And rustle of leaves
Or packets of crisps

Are drowned
By the sound
Of the enemy -
The shriek
Of fear
As the unleashed dog
Is called back
To his master.

Anne Lever

My Godmother, May

Yellow slanting eyes,
Thirties-fashioned profile.
I watched fascinated
As she stepped from the pages of *'Vogue'*
Rattling up our path
In shiny patent shoes, cloche-hatted;
Frothy lace handkerchief
Cascading from the breast pocket
Of her sharp tailored suit,
Black as her ebony hair -
Eton-cropped, shiny as a jackdaw.
A thin red line of lipstick
Accentuating her smile.
Feline; lounging on the settee;
Long amber cigarette holder
Held in long aesthetic fingers.
Leaving the house
With an armful of tea roses.
Then, there were the photographs -
Perched on a breakwater,
'Sunshine girl' with a parasol;
Dancing in a smart hotel
Flashing an arched brow
At the leader of the band;
Sitting on a mountain top in Switzerland
With a mysterious stranger.
Always the fine-etched profile
Which my childish hand
Longed to outline with a pencil.
With the war, came a Polish airman
Who slowly broke her heart;
For a time her sparkle waned,
The yellow eyes clouded with bewilderment
Which I could barely understand.
In time, she married a cosy man
Retired to the country.
A comfortable pussycat
Curling under the trees
Purring on the counterpane -
Leaving her friends behind
To become an exciting memory . . .

Veronica Charlwood Ross

30

Childhood Days

The days of my childhood are ever so clear
There are so many things I can remember and are ever so dear
We used to sit by the fire and watch the shadows of the night
The flames were flickering looking like birds in flight.

Going to the bathroom for a wash
Seeing the icicles you did it as quick as a flash
Making the porridge on the fire as there was no gas to be had
Trying hard not to notice the taste of smoke
Just to have a breakfast you were glad.

The winters were so cold in the morning
The windowpanes were full of frost
And as far as the eye could see
There was snow, you could easily get lost
So white and so high, so crisp and so cold
We would go out and make snowballs as big as one could hold.

Mum would say, 'Go out to play, don't forget your gloves.'
Go out on your sled, go as fast as you can
Making snow into sludge.

The snow stayed for ages, making playtime fun
Or maybe it just seemed that way as we were ever so young.

Then summer would come seeming ever so long
We would come inside for meals and then we'd be gone
Just playing outside having so much fun
We'd kick up our heels and just run, run, run.

Going to the corner shop to spend a penny or two
Having so much choice, it was hard we knew
Mischievous night would come and sneak up the path
Then ring the door bell
Waiting for someone to come then we'd run like hell.

Along came Bonfire Night and a penny for the guy
It was all so safe then staying out late
Seeing the stars in the sky
I can remember it all now looking back to the past
It all seemed to go by so very, very fast
But even for the hard times, not realising then
If I could get it all back I would so love to do it all again.

Marie Lowe

Metamorphosis

When I could walk, and barely talk,
I saw upon a low-set wall
a fascinating creature,
which I couldn't name at all.

I watched in disbelief
its graceful undulation,
as it headed towards a leaf,
in hungry anticipation.

I sought for words I didn't know,
and heard a passing lady say,
'That's called a caterpillar -
now it's your turn to say.'

It seemed to match a word I knew
so I said, 'Caterpillow.'
But she said, 'This is alive and new
and nothing like a dormant pillow.'

She stood beside me, until
I repeated the word correctly.
Then soon I could, at will,
copy her pronunciation exactly.

I was like a caterpillar,
newly emerged in life,
now I've passed through its stages
and become a widowed wife.

Suzanna Boulos

Motherspeak

Do you remember Mother
those far-off days of childhood?
When you told me potatoes grew out of dirty ears.
How I scanned the mirror for months after.
Watching and waiting.
Scared stiff I would emerge as the star of some Hollywood horror film.
When I squinted into the bright sunshine
You warned me that should the wind change course
I would turn into a perpetually, demented, grimacing gargoyle.
The wet, unboiled face flannel
was another watchword in life's dictionary.
Its slimy surface harbouring a multitude of unspeakable horrors.
Do you remember Mum
the far-off days of Motherspeak?
Those wonderful golden nuggets of nonsense
so precious to me now you are on the verge of leaving me.

Maureen Reynolds

Dearest, Remember . . .

In the palm of my hand, three living blooms,
Orange blossoms fit for brides and grooms.
Scented flowers on the threshold of life,
Bonding forever husband and wife.

White flowers ensconced in green foil,
Echo of times, a life-long of toil.
Three throbbing little flowers,
A sharing of precious glorious hours.

Within my heart an open door,
Feelings awakened of sharing before,
A wedding, a courting, a couple in love,
A language spoken, a cooing of dove.

Within the bosom of my sleeping soul,
A void, a vacuum, an empty hole,
Remembering with sadness all we two shared,
The time when you loved and deeply cared.

These three blooms in the palm of my hand,
Carrying me back to a priceless land,
When my life with you encompassed my world,
I never was hungry, nor ever was cold.

Three blooms of orange you placed on my head,
A circlet of gold, enhancing my hand,
Sadly recalling those happy days,
The happiness we had in different ways.

All this happened so long ago,
Now my heart in silence cries, no!
No to years that vanished so fast,
No, to the love which did not last.

Yet deep within, inside of me,
A mirror filled with pictures I see,
These lovely blooms in the palm of my hand,
Now makes me accept and understand.

With gratefulness I lock the enceinte door,
Protecting the treasures I keep in my store,
In the palm of my hand, three living blooms,
Orange blossoms fit for brides and grooms.

Shula Bailey

Discipline In School

School nowadays is different from years ago
Pupils obeyed their teachers when they said yes or no
In the classroom whatever a teacher would mention
The class had to keep quiet and pay attention
If a pupil was caught eating sweets or chewing gum
They could be called to the front of the class to do a sum
One fact in school that was known to be true
Is that this is a task no pupil ever liked to have to do.

School in the past was more strict that it is today
Pupils were careful at what they did or would say
The teacher had full control of the class
And in a friendly way each day would pass
Sadly today this is not the case
The way some pupils act in school is a disgrace
The government should never have abandoned the cane
Because pupils were scared of getting hit and suffering pain.

School years ago still had some time for leisure
The pupils could go with their teachers on a walk for pleasure
They were happy with the walk or to just play in the playground
There were no machines like computers in the shops to be found
Pupils could still be taught and learn their subjects each day
If they needed help they knew all they had to do was say
Whether it was in the past or the present, many people were a fool
They did not realise that the best days of life were those spent at school.

Robert Doherty

The Colliery Lampman

I sit outside
The sun beats down upon my form
As though to say, remember when

You thought you chose
Your family relied on me
To give the world
The black diamonds
Way, way, way below your feet
My siblings were the lamps
For which you cared, so preciously
In the pit head lamproom
Where you spent your time
Ensuring that my glow did light
The Black Diamond seams of yesteryears
You ventured there
And family of generations five
Did disappear each day
Below the moon and stars
And also me
There's nothing left but memories
And heaps of spoil
Which soon maybe a park
For me to view and think of you
My friend, the lamproom man.

Roy Harvey

A Wedding In February

The day burst open with a winter's feel
Cold winds tempered by occasional sunshine.
The surrounding love of family and friends
Brought warmth to this your wedding day.
Today you promised to love and cherish
We watched your union with love in our hearts,
So sure in your knowledge of love for the other
We felt your emotions mix with our own.
Two people who love one another
Blessed by us all who stand here with you
And from me, your mother,
Many memories, of happiness and tears,
Shared with our love over these past years.
A few tears shed today for your passing childhood
That can never return,
A smile for your happiness today and forever,
A pride in a daughter I love more than life,
A trust in the man who makes you his wife.
Today your life is with another,
But always remember my darling child
I'm here for you always, ready to share
Your joys, your tears, all of your fears.

Caroline Nash

Memories Are Made Of This

Some Memories Recalled

When in quiet contemplation, myriad memories spring to mind
Of days of yore, of childhood, some coloured in a rosy hue,
Perhaps you'll find
You meander through so many thoughts, of happy hours gone by
Seemingly endless days of summer sun, hopscotch, football
Flying kites on high
Visits to the seaside, crabbing, paddling, looking about for shells
To place around your sandcastles,
Trailing seaweed with its salty seaside smells.
Time for some refreshments, sandwiches, cake and pop
Then plead for another paddle in small waves
With a jump, a skip, a hop
Wondrous anticipation at Christmas, shops full of toys
Their windows all aglow
Bulging Christmas stockings, packed full of small gifts
Some fruit, some nuts, new pennies in the toe
Small lanterns lit on Christmas trees,
Pretty baubles, holly and mistletoe
Peering skywards through the windowpane,
Looking out for Santa's sleigh
Full of lovely parcels, pulled by red-nosed reindeer
Hoping soon to have their hay
Carols, sheep and shepherds, the eternal lovely story of the nativity
The aroma of Christmas cooking,
Spicy fruit cake, mince pies and turkey
Schooldays, friends and family, your thoughts appear to take wing
Tears of sadness for a broken toy
Mum's loving arms, for comfort as you cling
Snug and warm, tucked up in bed, a story then your prayers
The soft glow from a night light, a sudden creak upon the stairs
A teddy bear, our favourite doll, a golliwog or car
Placed for company upon your eiderdown, or on a bedside chair
Sorrow at the loss of someone you held most dear
Memories recalled bring happy smiles or perchance melancholy tears
Years slip by, your wedding day, furnishing of your first home
Early disasters with your cooking,
Quick consultation with your recipe tome.
Holidays, escapades, mishaps, jolly japes
Dressing up for Hallowe'en, false teeth and long black capes
The wonder of your children's birth, your overwhelming love
Memories, so many memories recalled,
Pray and give heartfelt thanks to our Lord above.

Marjorie Leyshon

Memories Are Made Of This

The Past Or Where I Would Be

Summers were always long and hot in childhood days
Nights in close quarters, with siblings, breathless with the heat
As tiny windows hung with ramblers, stopped the air.
Sheets tied to knobs on bedposts, brass and gnarled
Made tents exciting, heard of only in the magic of an Arabian tale.
Paddling in streams and rivers as yet unpolluted by detergents' foam
Only the green of sharp-leaved watercress as the waters babbled by.
Dragonflies hovering, darting over stagnant ponds
Small lizards easing out from under sandy stones.
Days to lay back on stubbled straw
Watching the birds soar timelessly above thick meadow green.
But Winters, winters biting cold as frost and snow combined
Stomping to school in wellingtons
Through passages forged through solid snow
Arriving just in time for milk, thawed against the pot-bellied stove
Still with lumps of ice in glazed bottles.
For sport, snow thrown in balls or slip-slides made on paths
A peril to our elders.
Then, canals froze over and became our skating rinks
When in balmier days the horse-drawn barges had passed us by.
These were the days when 'winter sports'
Cost nothing more than an old wood tray,
When injuries were treated with a good swab of tingling iodine.
And summer's cost was an elasticated suit in blue or red
Stretched to its utmost in the river or the stream.
But Spring and Autumn too had their just place.
Seasons *were* seasons in our youth.
In spring, boys bird-nested in the hedgerows
Our clout could not be cast, not even on the mildest day
Until the month had passed, of May.
Though we fast approached the longest day.
Autumn, the time of Harvest Festivals and Thanksgivings
Bonfires with Guys and collecting wood and twigs for winter fires.
Then home was the warm place of cooking smells and pots of jam
Where Mother reigned supreme, her offerings glazed with *Love*.
Home was complete when Father bent his head to enter
After a long day of toil, he said the grace and carved the meat
Then later read or told wild tales of his exciting youth.
This is the place where I would be
Memories do not need storage space, nor shelf room,
Only a quiet corner with a comfy chair, where all my friends may come
To be with me at no great expense to travel, only the desire to be there.

Pamela Campbell
The Painter in Words

In The Summertime

Long ago in a romantic past
When I thought it would not last
It was summertime
I remember it well
A wonderful summer I had been want to dwell
The fields had been ripe with corn
Happy birdsong from morn 'til dawn
Dark clouds had not gathered then
Thought of war was all around
Our only thoughts why or when
Listening to the chimes of Big Ben
The city streets and crowds swarming then
In the summertime
Laden with fruit we picked the apples and plums
In the schools we did our sums
So happy and full of fun, but war clouds had begun
The wild parsley in full bloom
And forgotten all too soon
A knock at the door, a favourite song no more
Our favourite themes, forgotten dreams
In the summertime
We could have got out if we could
Romantic dreams squashed in the mud
Spoils of war in hearts of men
Deep in the dust of forgotten fields
In a foreign country where we dug our heels
And we must learn to forgive
But not to forget
And learn the mistakes not to pass on.

Joan Hands

Looking Back

When I was six I had a cat,
With sleek black coat and eyes of green;
By day he was a playful friend,
At night he was a stranger.
For after tea when light was lit,
Upon the window sill he'd sit,
And tell me in his regal way,
He'd things to do, he could not stay,
He had to see to this and that;
For after all, he was a cat.

Then lightly on those velvet paws,
He'd hover by the window edge;
I'd watch him jump, I'd hold my breath,
But knew he would not falter.
Then landing on the dustbin lid
And turning as he always did,
I'd see him spring as though in dance,
Then disappear without a glance,
And I would wonder what desire
Enticed my cat to leave the fire?

'Where does he go?' I'd ask my dad.
'He hunts for mice in yonder field.'
'I wish he'd stay at home with me.'
'He will, when come the winter.'
But could he be a witch's cat?
All dressed in cloak and pointed hat,
While every night they'd ride the skies
To take the planets by surprise.
And did they visit Merlin's house
Or turn a frog into a mouse?

When I was six I had a friend,
With eyes so green I hardly could believe them.
I thought he was a magic cat,
Yet, when he'd seen to this and that,
He'd wander home a weary soul
To look for breakfast in his bowl;
Then on my bed this cat of mine
Would snooze, and purr, till dinner time.

Alma Shearer

Lullaby

Night plays strange games
With sounds which are quite ordinary
In the light of day.
Water in the pipes
Gurgles and coughs.
Sending huge sound waves
Through its copper channel.
The radiators splutter and creak
And make sounds which are quite
Inaudible by day.
The clock on the landing window sill
Still ticks away the precious minutes.
Cars rush past on the highway
In the distance
Leaving a trail of humming engine
Long after they are engulfed
By the large black
Gaping howls of night.

Soon my lids grow heavy
And my limbs relaxed
And I sink into my warm cocoon.
The sounds continue
In and around the house
But they no longer
Hold a sense of fear
As I am drowsy.
Slam - a car door wrenches
Me from my sleep.
High-pitched voices
Screech goodbyes
And goodnights not once
But a thousand times.
The excited chatter
Rises to a crescendo
Then falls away.
I am almost oblivious again.
I am gone.

Nina Woolf

The Steam Train

Walking along the country lane
We heard the whistle's call
And we glimpsed the rounded puffs of smoke
As they breasted the farmhouse wall.

Youngsters all and fleet of foot
We sped to the railway track,
Childishly anxious not to miss
The swirling smoke from the stack.

We floundered and tripped and fell up the steps
Of the bridge which straddled the rail
Just in time for us all to confront
The Monster of the Vale.

The engine coughed from under the bridge
And heaved such a terrible sigh
That the smoke rose up and enveloped us all
While the smuts in our eyes made us cry.

But smutty, smoky, smeared, content,
We bounced on the bridge in delight;
For one gasping, hurtling second in time
We had shared in the Monster's flight.

Pauletta Edwards

Memories

The sun is shining
Blue skies
Clouds go fleeting by
Leafy lanes
Raindrops glistening
Ears are listening.

Bombs are dropping
Best forgotten
Children's voices
Balls on bats
Horses hoof beats
Ears are hearing
People cheering!
Memories are made of these.

Pamela Gormley

Yorkshire Born And Bred

Rows of terraced houses kept clean and neat,
These were our homes on a much-loved street.
Gas-lamps to see with, donkey-stoned steps,
Memories of a child, Yorkshire born and bred.

Washday on a Monday, strung across the backyard,
Mum busy at the mangle, working ever so hard.
Coalman delivering fuel in dirty old sacks,
Shiny black lumps stacked in the shed at the back.

Rag and bone man haggled with horse and cart,
Wended his way homewards long after dark.
Corner shop stocked everything - open all hours,
Sold firelighters, bread and potatoes, sweets and flowers.

Milkman delivered with milk straight from the churn,
Even in bad weather he got round everyone in turn.
We watched the firelight flicker round our cosy room,
At night-time shutting the curtains on winter's gloom.

In the summer all the kids went to play in the park,
No need to be frightened if coming home in the dark.
No muggings, no shootings, no vandalism to face,
The world was a much happier and safer place.

Going to town with Mum and Dad was a special treat,
Sitting upstairs on the tram in the bay-window seat.
And a trip to the seaside was the highlight each year,
With sandcastles, seashells and a walk on the pier.

Schooldays weren't my favourite, they were quite a shock,
Packed off with my satchel, polished shoes and white socks.
But we learnt discipline and heeded what the teacher said
And any badly behaved pupils got a caning from the Head.

Mum was always there when I came home from school,
Women were homemakers then and didn't work as a rule.
Families sat round the table and talked to each other,
Ate meals together - Mum, Dad, sister and brother.

I think back to those days when we felt safe and secure,
When children were children, all innocent and pure.
Today family values and respect are sadly long dead,
But memories remain of a child, Yorkshire born and bred.

Susan Richardson

Birthday Memories

Birthday memories of years gone by
Jelly and ice cream, oh what a sigh!
Sausage rolls, pineapple and cheese
Oh what a treat, were all of these.
Triangle sandwiches, fish paste or egg and cress
Mind how you eat! Don't make a mess!
Little bridge rolls filled with luncheon meat
Chocolate fingers or perhaps a candy sweet.
The lights go off, I wonder what's next?
I look around at my friends' faces -
Quite worried and perplexed!
Out of the shadow, comes a great glow
Wow, it's a birthday cake with candles to blow.
Next come the party games
Blind-Man's Bluff, Musical Chairs, Postman's Knock
Hey, who's watching the clock!
Pass the Parcel is always fun
Because there's a prize for everyone!
Oh no, look it's nearly time to go
Never mind, we've had a great time
Don't forget your coats
Cheerio!
Was it really that long ago?
How the years slip by, it's frightening, I know.
Although we're older now, it's good to look back
At times gone by and the fun that we've had.
The years may keep adding, but memories stay
Each one year by year
A happy birthday!

Shirley Sewell

A Mother's Pride

We accept changes happen, but when did they all start?
Once you were the precious baby of my heart.
Too soon came the schooldays with a future so clear,
My happiness complete, when you were near.
Then that wonderful day, a beautiful bride.
My eyes filled with tears, only tears of pride.
When did it all happen, the changes came fast.
The years rolled by and nothing lasts.
Now I see you, elegant and full of grace.
A loving smile beams from your beautiful face.
From baby to womanhood, each change played their part
All now sweet memories stored in my heart.

Margaret Meadows

Going Back

Please give our children back those yesterdays
Wherein we trod our childhood ways
Running in air so full of fun
In wind and rain and summer sun
No thought of hiding from the light
Playing with joy from early morn till night
Such happy times had we, but then
A spiteful darkness spoiled this youthful yen
We who remember childhood years
Those days and nights absent of fears
Give these our children back our yesterdays
And give them in their hands our summer days
Little heads bent on learning
My older head so full of yearning
To make my generation see more sense
And so protect their innocence
Hide-and-seek and lollipops
Mummy's hand when going to the shops
Paper planes that looped the loop
Rabbit stew, tomato soup
Cocoa at night before our bed
And stories that dear Daddy said.

Lawnmowers on Sunday
Then school on Monday
Washing day
Bubble and squeak
Summer holidays long
Seemed only to last a week
There was no rain, just endless sun
Friendships ne'er lost through all these years
Leave us but with memories; tears
Would that we could give our children that
And feel it's not so bad
This going back.

Dai C Davies

That Was Then, This Is Now

Looking back on days back then, I can always remember when
There were good times to be had; I was a right little Jack the lad
Neighbours saw me so carefree and happy, saying,
'There he goes the cheeky chappie.'
Always being home on time, a ball in a garden was my only crime
When my neighbours came out, my blood ran cold,
'Keep this ball from my garden,' my neighbour did scold.
On my return home Mother did say,
'You'll have a place of your own one day.'
'What happens now will all make sense
When you're on the other side of the fence.'
'So don't look on with saddened eyes,
Just go next door and apologise.'
I apologised as Mother said, I knew that was how to move ahead
Brought up to respect and be polite, I always knew wrong from right.
And now that I am fully grown, I now have a place of my own
But it is now plain to see why Mother taught those things to me
A ball hits my window and falls on my land
From this side of the fence I now understand
Just what annoyed my neighbours so,
When I was a young lad all those years ago.
But politeness and courtesy you rarely expect
Because there is so little respect
No friendly apology when they knock on your door
The heartfelt sincerity isn't there anymore
But I heeded my parents and I grew up well
And those childhood days many tales I could tell
Now I am older but still carefree and happy
And I can still be that cheeky chappie
But things have changed, it's different somehow
But that was then and this is now.

Dave McFadden

46

A Day To Remember –
The First Of September

Wasn't it the greatest party?
Everyone will always remember
Held at Ash Road, Canvey Island
Saturday the First of September.

The first guests started arriving
A little before one
Full two hours early
Before the event actually begun.

But when I saw their excited faces
I could not turn them away
So they were directed to the bouncy castles
And off they went to play.

The barbecues were lit on the park
And pretty John started cooking
Carried on with true grit
And we sat for a few minutes looking.

After Harold was transported back in time
When his beloved Spurs came along
Thinking of all his yesteryears
As he sang the Yiddo's song.

Knock on the door bought the karaoke man
As all the kids rushed to the door
To see Mick unload oki coki van
And drop his equipment on the floor.

We saw a river of people gliding in
As the dam reached overflowing
We wondered how on earth we'd fit them in
But Harold's eyes were glowing.

He was greeted as if a Mafia Don
As the presents and cards were piling
You'd think it was Santa's Grotto he looked upon
Face almost splitting through smiling.

Then the celebrations started swinging
With Paris singing herself dry
Voices started winging
Looks of joy in their eye.

Then all too soon it was over
With friends and family drifting away
We thank you for your time and looking pretty
Though you probably felt dippy the next day.

Sharon Beverly-Ruff

Gramps

A shared love of music, singing and playing Chopin,
hearing him play Rachmaninov.
Seeing him conduct the Male Voice Choir he founded.
Waltzing with him at the choir's annual dinner dance.
Fascinated, as he renovated and tuned pianos.
Smell of glue and French polish in his shed.

Trips out in the car, both in Wales and the Cotswolds.
Me, as his back-seat driver, watching the speedo.
Wearing his suit on the beach in Caswell Bay.
Holidays in the caravan in Aberaeron,
both sneaking an extra honey ice cream, from the *Hive on the Quay*.
Seeing the love for his Welsh homeland in his eyes.

Telling me about his hard days in the mines,
he moved his family to the Cotswolds,
where he'd play the piano in the cinema at night.
Working at Smith's Industries, I'd look out for his parked car
when passing with my dad.
Finally, delight at retiring home to Wales.

My Grampy.

Beth Buckley

Days Long Gone

No more the Ploughman plods,
Behind his faithful pair
And never looking back.
No more straight furrows shaped
By Human skill and care
Along Pride's chosen track.

No more the Sower, goes forth to sow
With measured stride and rhythmic throw
No more the scythe, with timely swings
Reaps barley, wheat and rye
No more the sheaves, shall stand like kings
In Autumn air to dry . . .

All is Mechanical . . .

Save only the weather.

M R Mackinnon-Pattison

Return To Bluebell Wood

Lay me down in this field of blue
Where trees are shady, tall and still.
Where May-time spreads her morning dew
And tuneful larks can chant at will.

Comb my hair with sunshine's fingers
As she weaves her gold through green,
Where scent of bluebells' fragrance lingers,
Reminding me of sweet sixteen.

Close my eyes so that I can see them,
Bare legs running through the grass.
Watch her as his arms enfold her,
Brushing bluebells as they pass.

Oh field of blue
With fragrant air
Enclosed the lovers lying there.
Sunshine threaded
Heart to heart
Entwining souls that could not part.
Dewdrops moistened
Each sweet kiss
Fuelling youth's eternal bliss.

I left my heart in this field of blue,
Beneath our names carved in that tree.
Bluebell Wood, I return to you
This foolish girl that I used to be.

Lesley Elaine Greenwood

Memories

The farm I knew so fresh and green
Where I could sit and tend to dream
The oak tree stretched with arms open wide
Sheltering the cattle that grazed by her side

The whispering corn as it shook its head
Dropping the grain so ripe it shed
Blackberries in clusters, jet-black and sweet
Eager hands reaching to pick them to eat

The warm breeze that blew across open space
Far, far away from the human race
No sound to hear but the drone of a bee
Homing in to nectar on an overhanging tree

But now I wonder where did you go?
For all I can see are bricked up plots
The fields lost forever under concrete blocks.

Doris Hoole

A Country Footpath

I still recall that winding footpath
Opening out onto country fields;
I still recall that netted fence
Melting into summer grass.
And then, there were those childhood strolls
Along the path to where, halfway down,
A windmill stood with circling sails,
Overlooking flower-starred meadows
And fields rich with rolling corn
And wheat. I well remember the day
When, in my pram, my ice cream melted
All over me; and I well remember
Those walks farther down the country path
To where an old crab-apple tree stood
Shading me with its clustered leaves
As I bent down to taste the sour green fruit
Lying in the grass. Then - farther down
To where the footpath opened out
With thick grass verges flanking several fields;
A pastoral paradise of green
Merging into golden yellow beyond.

Those golden memories are as fresh as ever;
And those distant fields of rolling corn
Still unfold their kaleidoscopes
Of chessboard parquetry. Part of the fence
Is still there, netted with newer wire
And overgrown with weeds and brambles.

But the windmill has gone; and, farther down,
A new straightened footpath now overlooks
Crews Hill's famous conservatories.

Some change is for the better,
But it's good that some things never change.

Robert D Hayward

Memories Are Made Of This

The Ghost Of Christmas Past

What happened to the old-fashioned Christmas
With family and friends round the fire,
Sipping mulled wine and eating mince pies,
Whilst carols were sung by a choir?

We'd gather around the piano
While Mum played all the old songs,
Accompanied by Dad's tuneless whistling.
The rest of us all sang along.

The air was always crisp and fresh.
Snow drifted by the windowpane.
Clothing the earth in a silent white shroud.
Will it ever be like that again?

Now it's computers and video games.
iPods and DVDs.
Music's no longer harmonious,
And violence fills the TV.

The meaning of Christmas has disappeared.
There's little spirituality left.
Commercialism has taken its place.
The 'Christ' being replaced by an 'X'.

Can we turn this tide of materialism
Before it engulfs us en-mass?
Or just look through rose-tinted glasses
At the spectre of Christmas past?

Carole Revell

Willen Lake (Revival)

A sunny day spent at Willen Lake
And, as in those old familiar seaside days,
Grown-ups through children's eyes were charmed
By the ebb and flow of the rippled waves.

Fond thoughts of being at the coast long ago -
Like the buckets and spades, walks along the pier
And watching boats sailing distantly at sea -
Were memories once so far away, but now so near.

This truly was a moment for me to savour
And looking up towards the heavens that be
I recalled and remembered a childhood
Hidden somewhere deep within me.

Kevan Beach

Our Garden So Grand

The garden at our council house,
Was a magic wonderland,
The years of unattended grass and brambles,
Were our childhood dens and castle grand,
Scratched arms and legs to get to the very end,
Was a little stream some called a ditch,
Yet armed with wellies and jam jars on string,
We entered a childish world of bliss,
A world of tadpoles and minnows, the joy of paddling,
We fought our way to make a gap,
Next to our wildly overgrown cherry tree,
It allowed us to enter this other world,
Where we played until Mam called us in for tea,
The field just beyond our stream,
Was a jungle where lions and tigers lived,
And as we grew older, it became a secret den,
Where we tried smoking Woodbine, oh was we sick,
They were happy times where we all felt safe,
No computers or videos, the word can I was banned,
We watched Lost In Space on a Saturday night,
Unless someone spotted the licence van,
So it was back to play, skipping or ticker chalked on our path,
While Mam and half the neighbours struggled hard,
To hide their telly in the bath,
Today as I sit on that same doorstep,
Of my mother's ex-council house,
The garden is neat, a patio built and flowers all set,
The gap we fought our way through has gone,
Replaced with climbing ivy and various other plants,
Where's our magic garden gone, thirty-five years on?
Our beloved stream with its trickling sound,
Is hidden by a wall and neatly trimmed hedge,
It's covered now and cannot be found,
I suppose it's called progress and to keep the children out,
After all, we must not let them play outdoors,
There's strangers and perverts lurking about,
I feel a tinge of sadness sitting here,
At forty-seven thinking back,
Of my sister and me, our pals and our dog,
All wading through water like an orphaned pack,
Our own young ones lack imagination for games that were free,
They must be indulged with the latest fads,
But I would never have swapped our magic garden,
Poor but happy, no time to be sad,
But time ticks away and things change forever,
Our memories are all that is left,
Of our magic kingdom to invest a new game each day,
Filthy and grubby with jam sandwich in hand,
Fighting your way through our back garden so grand.

Kathryn Evans

Memory Lane

I wandered down memory lane today, for just a little while
And you were standing there with your loving smile.
It brought back lots of memories of how it used to be
When life was so carefree and you were there for me.
You had your faults like any other, but I loved you from the start
But to walk down memory lane would once have broken my heart.
But I hear your voice in the hedgerows
Your sigh is the wind that blows,
Your dear face in the clouds above
Your kindness and your love.
You were my guiding hand, you taught me right from wrong
You installed in me a belief that was always very strong.
As I walk down memory lane, the pain and tears have gone
And I can remember the happiness that will go on and on.
So I'll never be afraid to walk that way again
For my dearest dad, I'll always know, I'll find you down Memory Lane.

Glenys Harris

Instow

Little boys played with their toys
And rampant dogs
Chased sea-blown winds
As the jazz unlocked the claw of the lobster pot.

Marion blown
And balling through
Poetry rang
Down at our thatched pavilion.

Building castles
In oiled dunes
Beside the rotting wreck
When crossing our bar
The old would be seated down
At The Wayfarer.

Ringing chimes
And watered voices
Would sound
Chapel voices
Rippling

On ferried tides
Complete with steams
And the cycling wheel of
The policeman's whistle!

Andrew Fry

Memories Of My Schooldays

I've aye been a country quine
For me it suits ma lifestyle fine.
Knaven is a district in the countryside
Known the country far an wide
Atween Mormond Hill an' Bennachie
For miles aroon the eye can see.

A leather schoolbag on oor backs
Ower oor shooders we twa straps,
Alang the road we walked tae school
Missing the potholes wis the rule
Got up in time, wir niver late
We learned tae write upon a slate
In my class were three James', Margaret and me
There were times we did not all agree.
Oor first reading book wis Tom an' Ann
Sounding A N K P S T H D
We repeated the letters every day
After sixty years they are there tae stay.

We afen fell an skinned oor knees
Rinnin' on dykes or climin' trees.
There wir evacuees frae Glesga toon
Some didna like being a country loon.
The picnic in June wis tae the seaside
I mine eence getting a donkey ride
We waved oor dads' hankies tae men in the park
They war hyowin neeps tae the song o' a lark
Tae be awa in a bus we felt afa gran'
Took oor pail an spade tae mak castles we sand
We got ice cream an a bradie tae eat
To us at the time, was a special treat.

At playtime we skipped an played wi a ba
Or slid on the ice if there wis sna
We swapped hens' rings, scraps an bools
Usin wir hands, we hid nae tools
We wore a pixie, hummel doddies, coat or jacket
But nane o this designer racket
Sandals an frocks in the summer days
An aye cast some layers a claes.
On the wye hame frae school if we needed tae pee
We sat doon ahin a dyke if there wis nae a tree
On a foggy day we saw spiders' webs
Like a crochet pattern on the hedge.
We got milk an orange juice
I looked forward tae them
Bit the taste o' cod liver ile I canna explain.
At the weekend we got a bath an a scrub
Water heated on the fire poured in a zinc tub
We wore the same claes for a wik

Abody else did it unless they were sick
The same navy knickers we were for gym
Duncin' an jumpin' tae keep us trim
The nurse she cam tae check oor hair
Tae see there were nae beasties there
Oor nails an teeth she also looked
Ain wrote the findings in a book
We kent the soun' o' the thrashin' mull
As it puffed an chugged gaun up the hill.

At the school Christmas party we ate jelly and fruit
Later Santa arrived wi his sack o' loot
We got an apple, balloon an' game
Then played an' sang or we got hame.
Gym an' knitting I didna like
Bit quickly learned tae ride a bike
For shewin we got a bit o' cloot
An drew half hapennies roon aboot
It wis fite threid sewn on blue
I can picture it in ma min jist noo.
The school it hid concerts an' dances as well
An' sometimes folk drinkin' stuff stronger than ale

I min on haein measles, chickenpox an' mumps
An got a row for scrattin' the lumps
At school we ate broth, stewed rabbit, tatties an' peas
Apple pie, sago, semolina, macaroni an' cheese
Older folk in my youth said, 'Fit next will they dee?'
If they looked up noo fit wid they say or see?

Gwen Dunbar

Working Life

When I left school with no children or wife
That was the beginning of my working life
I went down the Labour and gave them my name
All I wanted was a job and wasn't looking for fame
They gave me a list of jobs I could see
But honestly there wasn't one that suited me
I tried all the factories and some building sites
At one the foreman wanted me to work nights
As the years went by in my working life
I even ended up with a lovely wife
The jobs came and the jobs went
That's how my working life was spent
Now the work was becoming hard and I came home tired
It was time to sit down and think of the day I retired
Sitting in front of the fire looking back over the years with my wife
Taking everything into consideration, it wasn't a bad working life.

Eddie Owers

Sweet Carefree Moments

At four years old, watching the crimson sunset
As the sun sank slowly in the west
The year was 1944.
My nightdress pulled over my knees as I sat
Warming my feet on the outhouse slates
Just under my bedroom window.
The moment was mine, all mine, I hugged myself with awe.
Later that year I wetted my socks
As my piece of plank which my brother said would float
Sank with me on board.
My brother was six, he knew it all,
But I'd remember forever his views were poor.
Tramping through pine woods with squirrels darting about
Rolling down hills with a laugh and a shout.
Being told by the gamekeeper who appeared with his gun
We'd strayed too far, so we made off at a run.
Cows father told us were perfectly safe,
Always be sure to shut up the gates,
But that was proved wrong when off at a run
With head down a cow ran at us
When crossing its field, we ran under barbed wire
And were glad of its shield.
We were told not to stray as gypsies would take little children away,
But we didn't meet any!
The sirens wailed at times, but we were safe, no aircraft assailed.
At night we were brought down for safety,
As bombs fell and aircraft flew low overhead,
But we thought it an adventure as Mum and Dad
Sat and pegged a rag rug and did not go to bed.

Rosemary Whatling

Live Inside (remember), This Madspace Origami

All the road through the saltmarsh
Focus on the construction of the
Intricate obsession concerning triality
Focus on the luxurious nature
Around the home, built from the illuminated manuscript
A construction from those other minds . . .

Michael Soper

St Paul De Vence

The Colombe D'Or
With upturned thumb,
Points to the perfect sky
A sign for us all to reach for
As we crawl each routined day
Towards that fateful call.
Where artists' wares are on display,
Triumphs of inner means,
In narrow, middle-aged corridors of stone.
Where we both sat you and I
On our panoramic bench
Pigeon-infested with our daily bread;
And talked of higher things
Of celestial visions and journeys to come.

And close by, limpet-like,
The sand-coloured homes
Clung to the ascended hill;
Where film stars and artists of yesteryear
Drew their inspired fill,
Of beauty in a game of boule
Or just lounging, glass in hand,
Over a luncheon meal.
Is this not a fleeting paradise
Here on this fragile Earth
In this simple sight?
And when we take our final leave
And look back in old age
To this bygone holiday,
Can we then perceive
As if strung like pearls
Along our own destined life,
These were the times
That return to remind us
Of how precious those hours were spent
In this hallowed place of contentment.

Where the church bells rang
To call our souls to peace,
Over cobbled works of art,
To show us the way it ought to be,
A small piece of Heaven
Built over the centuries;
Now framed in pictures on the wall
Where Picasso's white dove
In St Paul De Vence,
Stands sentinel over all of us.

Peter Corbett

My Baily Love

One day I found the Baily rocking in the wind
Its wheels were buried in the sand blistered by the sun.
It rusted just a little bit and peeled a bit here and there
But I fell in love with Baily. And I couldn't leave it there.
Baily just spoke to me like a Baily caravan.
I just had to buy it and get it back to the country roads.
Two days later I struck it lucky. I found my country love
And would you believe it, his name was Baily Love.
And that's why I bought the Baily and I've got two in one.
Three weeks later I'm living in a Baily
I'm travelling in a Baily caravan.
Baily is my bubbly, he makes me laugh all the time.
And that's why I bought the Baily.
I share the Baily with Baily my love
We get a rocket of a time, moving from place to place on the Baily line.
When we see the sunshine, it's on every sunny shore.
And when we pull over we walk the sunny shore.
I couldn't do without my Baily and my Baily caravan
Our music rocks the Baily
Our Baily caravan.

David Rosser

Fifties' Memories

Autumn's cool crisp breath tingled on my cheek,
'Rags and bones', the plaintive cry of a wizened old man,
with an aged piebald, trotting by his side,
with eyes so sorrowful, so bleak.

Mum's knuckle-white fingers gripping the tarnished handle
of an old mangle in the yard.
'Laundry of the Gentry' - stark white sheets
sliding through soapy bubbles in an old tin bath.
This daily toil, to earn a few extra pennies, not a pleasant craft.

Winter so cold; icicles sparkle from the glint of a watery sun,
casting shadows on a shingled path.

At the end of the drive, horse chestnuts screen the house
with a decadent pose, foamy white tips swaying gently in the breeze.
Childhood memories treasured in your heart,
to search at your leisure whenever you please.

Heather Lynes-King

A Day In My Childhood

When the bad news came one morning in September,
I was only nine years old but I'll always remember.
My mother looked at the telegram held in her hand,
She saw the words, 'Killed in action' and could barely stand.
Her screams and moans made my blood run cold,
'My only son, John, just twenty years old.'

Our next-door neighbour, Mrs Kitchen, came round
With a tot of brandy for Mam to calm her down.
My father and sisters were all out at work,
So I stayed with my mother until their return.

I picked up my prayer book from where it was kept,
As I held my mother in my arms and wept.
The Lord is my Shepherd, the 23rd Psalm,
Was the only thing I thought of to comfort and calm.

When the rest of the family were told John was dead,
My father stood still, shaking his head.
My mum went quite crazy and my sisters just cried.
I went to my bedroom, wanting to hide.

Now sixty-three years later, I think of my brother
Caring, loving, gentle like no other.
I wonder what he would look like now,
Had he survived the war.
Was it necessary, really, for him to die for?

Dylis M Letchford

Wilfred Lambley

Today we would have celebrated another year on Earth
A special day together, so I could tell you what you are worth
I always loved you Father, you meant the world to me
I put you on a pedestal and my heart shone with glee
You held my hand while walking I felt so safe in your hands
You played silly tricks on me that I didn't understand.

Until I reached an age where I was just like you
The joker of the family, the brains and beauty too
So now the only gift I can bring to you
Is my presence at your graveside, my love I pour out to you
I can still see your face smiling back at me
I sometimes sense you walking by my side
I look, I see nothing, but I still hold out my hand
And sigh . . .

Sharon Lambley Dzus

Memories

For decades they lie buried under mounds of dust,
Hidden, ignored, old photographs encased in rust.

Like wispy clouds moving before a storm,
Too quickly to be noticed, lacking form.

Entrails entombed, the key long discarded,
Who would want to dig so deep, without a lamp, unguarded?

Silence creaks open these rusty seams,
Images float by, similar to waking dreams.

A child's anticipation on Christmas Eve,
Trudging through chilling snow, with snot on my sleeve.

An older sister's warning, sliding on ice,
Creating guilt for exuberance is not very nice.

Leaving notes in my first flame's hallway locker,
Spinning a bottle, who will mock her.

My purple graduation suit, more beautiful than any,
Pomp and circumstance marching, a prelude to many.

My mind wanders, rambling on a path shrouded in mist,
An invitation arrives, my name on a previously forgotten list.

Anticipating opportunities to retrieve from the cracks,
Recorded events sitting in the forgotten stacks.

Distance is crucial to an expanding view,
Putting recent events behind in the queue.

Memories reside in a mysterious land
Ready or not, to be at hand.

Yes, I reply, I will attend,
Reunions may bring a long-lost friend.

Honora G Simon

First Date From Four Points Of View

Will she love me, will she eck
With her arms wrapped round me neck
On leaving the house last mirror glance
And head for village hall disco dance.

What's this long-haired scruff
Doing with my daughter
Bringing him home is quite enough
Crossing our threshold of bricks and mortar.

Hubby and I fretted and wailed
No advice or heavy hand
Or threats of boys are banned
It's our daughter that we have failed.

And so my braveheart hero takes me home
Like some gladiator from silver-screened Rome
Yet softly spoken, civilised
Greets parents open-handed and tries to re-enact
Romeo and Juliet under Shakespeare's Dome.

Vernon Ballisat

Past Charms

Breath like whispers catching air so thin,
Frosty, feathery furrows lighting up windowpane.
Stretching the sheets to cover my chin,
Whilst quietness descended the length of the lane.

Wall shadows danced as the room grew dark,
But come morning I'd be up with the lark.
The usual rush to get to school,
Where we all had to follow the golden rule.

Crimson, autumnal leaves laid thick and deep,
The excitement of crunching them into a heap!
Chestnuts roasted over an open fire,
Mouth all watering, filled with desire.

Chimney pots spitting grey spirals of smoke,
Smut-splattered washing covered in coke!
Women campaigning to get rid of the smog,
Personal shopping from a catalogue.

Summer days playing in the street,
Leapfrog, hopscotch, all manner of game(s).
No worries about strangers - life was sweet
If only, it was still the same.

Carole McKee

Remember The Olden Days

When we were young we did as we were told,
And everyone was put in their place,
Eat all your food up before it's cold,
But before we could eat we said grace,
Don't leave the table till it's all gone,
Then we were free to go and play,
It was every day the same old song,
And no way could we have our own way.

We dressed like a lord or lady,
No boyfriends till we were of age,
We dare not sit and be lazy,
Or show our temper in a rage.

Now all kids today do what they want,
No one sits at all at the table,
They dress anyhow and find it true,
To run wild and be that unstable,
They have not heard of going to church,
For other things are greater than that,
They just sit around on their own perch,
And they eat junk food till they get fat.

Margaret Burtenshaw-Haines

Football Blues

I remember when I was at school
to escape football lessons I couldn't
afford to be a dreamer,
And to get out of a game I hated, one
had to become somewhat a schemer;
While all the others a leather bag of wind
around a field they'd kick,
The powers that be thought with me to
crack a nut they'd use a brick;
So for punishment to the garden I was sent,
For refusing to play football, to dig and hoe
this would give me good cause to repent;
But under the trees outstretched leaf borne
limbs and shrubberies shady bowers,
Oh! how I revelled and basked in rapturous
delight dancing with the flowers.

Peter Morriss

Childhood Memories With My Dad

I remember the great times with my dad
I remember his Welsh rarebit cheese on toast
Cheese on toast with sliced tomato on top
Just always remember that he used to love it
I loved it then and love it now
I remember my dad was the best
I loved him, he loved me
We had many, many great times
I sadly lost my dad when I was ten
But I know he keeps a watch on me from Heaven
But I know he doted on me
He has left me for sure with many very fond memories
Those little things that we loved and treasured
I remember also a big yellow teddy my dad made for me
He was big, four feet plus yellow teddy
The Welsh rarebit cheese on toast
Indeed he was the best dad
Indeed he was a man amongst the best
He was the best dad in the world
You are always remembered Dad
And my memories of great times with you
My memories of all the things you made me and brought me
My yellow teddy, yes, my big yellow teddy
All my toy cars, yes, I had a lot, I mean a lot
Well Dad, thank you for all the great times
All the great memories with you
My dad, yes, was and is the best.

David J Hall

Stella

When I served in Egypt we drank cold Stella beer,
But after drinking two bottles my legs felt very queer,
They just felt like rubber, I was drunk when I hit fresh air.
This was then in '53, when we didn't have a care,
We had to leave Egypt, when General Nasser made a coup de'etat,
He replaced General Neguib and that my friend was that.
We then moved on to Germany in 1954,
A mile away from Belsen - which we had never seen before,
There were massive graves dug there, two-fifty bodies at a time,
Then I suppose the bodies were covered up with lime.
I was demobbed in 55 at the age of twenty-two.
I still have many memories of Egypt, in my heart I hold them here,
Though I'll never forget the first time I drank cold Stella beer.

James Ayrey

Watery Pleasures

Living quite close to a river meant -
The life that we lived was often spent
On the river itself, a small sailing boat too
Sailing, fishing, swimming the thing to do
My husband and I spent our honeymoon there
When our family arrived, two sons did share -
The fun and joy of beauty around
Nature's watery movement, especially sound.
Water lapping round our feet as we walked -
To our dinghy and then reach our sailing boat
At night the watery reaches, glistened with phosphorus
Every movement by our oars on the water thus -
Sparkled with glistening life in the river
The wonders of our 'Lord God the Giver'.
As the moon rises over the water and beyond -
Waterfowl calling on a nearby pond
This is the time that we loved the best
When most of life, was really at rest.
Seaweed aroma, when warm breezes blow
Ruffling our hair, now we were on show.
Sounds of trees, leaves rustling in our ears
This was so familiar to us, we had no fears.
We found, we were not alone, as we headed for home
Other folk also were enjoying the evening
A small fire and singing, a picnic too
There was nothing we could not do -
But joined in the party and the ring
These are the moments when life is at its best
When most of life's traffic is at rest.

Dorothy Parish

Beauty At Your Fingertips

Flights of fancy
For the dream
And living it
Count your blessings;
Idle thoughts, changing skies
Shifting skies, tales from the north
East, south and west
Love in words is captured in words
And a life shared is a life lived
Whether or not it's beyond the staircase
Pure verse, for the love of you
Whether or not you're on a bicycle made for two;
Helps us to enjoy tranquil moments
And poetical reflections awaken the soul
Through the mind, when emotions are running wild
The path of destiny upon this earth
Could be catching the sunshine or amidst
Images in the mist
But if you picture a place with your minds in focus
You too will remember setting the scenes
For Cupid's embrace and a moment's clarity
For these are some of the mysteries of the world . . .
And still the birds sing
Yet, we're still a world apart.

Colette Breeze

Red Admiral

I dreamt I was a butterfly
As I bobbed upon the breeze
So light and soft a fragrance smelt
It almost made me sneeze.

I fluttered into each garden
The happiest I've ever been
And the sun shone on each flower
They were the nicest - dream I've seen.

Colours of lilacs and reds - mustards and creams
Lavenders and heathers tempted me
My Red Admiral wings, stretched wide in flight
The browns and oranges adorned - nature's light.

Lifting, lifting peacefully
And then a graceful stand
My wonderful warm dream of butterfly land.

Carole Morris

An Anniversary Poem For My Father

(Dedicated to Mum & Dad in Heaven with love forever xxx)

There is a distant hill where I see my dad
That leads to Heaven, I visit him there
Alone with kindly flowers where
I show my love for my family I have
Cherishing memories, a moment not sad
But eternal glowing, growing to care
The love I have in the bible's truth I dare
I kneel beside him, recall as a lad
I amble sonnets for Dad written
I pray quietly as I gently enter
The cemetery imagine Mom smitten
Beside me with her quick step to centre
Upon that distant hill her true love
The road that leads to Heaven above.

Edmund Saint George Mooney

Children Of My Heart

Do not weep for me children of my heart,
For the world is full of tears,
Listen instead, to my laughter on the breeze,
Cherish me with your compassion for others,
Remember your innocent years,
Let the touch of another loved one, be mine
Upon your shoulder, in the dark times,
Let my former words of wisdom, heal your pain,
Remember me again and again!
For in your memories, I will live!
In everything you ever do, I will be there!
In time my smile will be mirrored,
In your loved ones eyes,
In your children, I will be reborn,
To bring you joy, so live your life,
Let all these things come to be,
Then you will never be alone,
I will be with you all your life.

Linda Bedford

Feathers

Going to write
A simple tune
About a lad
And moon, June
And spoon
If not so
Remembering
Over
Summer nights
Clement weather
From curtained
Window bower
Her Ivory Tower
Maid did write
To croon
Lofty lady full
Bosom baby
Curd the afternoon
When I did espy
Jealousy in my eye
Her suitor climb
Whatever
Daunted, I lost
So cruel, the cost
A certain white dove's
Feather.

Robert J Collins

The Horse-Wash

Many an hour I lightly spent
At the horse-wash to watch the display
Of heavy horse with the brew'ry gents,
Being groomed and harnessed to the drays;
Legs a-dangle o'er the pier wall,
I would carefully choose with my friends
The horse we thought most handsome of all,
And after, giggling, would gaily wend
Our way to where the ferry berthed,
Mid the bustle of travelling ranks
Of road-stained cars within its wide girth,
Setting sail to the far misty banks.
And those days the sun always beat down,
Glinting on the slow-moving river
Like spangles on a glittering gown,
While smells drifted on flighty weather.

Gwendoline Douglas

Law Abiding

Happy memories of childhood days
When the Law Hill was a must
For regular daily visits
Where solo flying was simply on trust.

Fired with enthusiasm
Muscles toned and ready
Being young and fearless then
Our nerves were steel and steady.

Trenchcoats acted as wing spans
To trap a breeze or gale
At other times school blazers
Sufficed to blaze the trail.

Gliding gradually progressed
From the nursery slopes
But soaring from the summit
Was the hope of all hopes.

Aerobatics soon followed
With loop-the-loop, spins, freefall
Vertical take-off, nose-diving
And the unexpected stall.

A flying club - milk-top - medal
Was awarded to the best
While others graduated with wings
On passing the gliding test.

Now as I come to reflect
On those post war years
Did we invent hang-gliding
Were school children the pioneers?

Monica Docherty

Impressions

As we follow the imprints of life we are born to follow as others before
Those imprints are there just as plain as life's open door

The door of life gives you a span of years
And as you go through life with laughter and tears

Only the impressions you make and the imprints you leave
Will be damned or blessed by others with those laughters and tears

With your partner in life and the child she will bear
Will also leave imprints on life with the love you will share

To them will be given the imprints of life
If your imprints are clear in return their own imprints
Will be returned year after year

And as you look back through life's wide-open door
Wondering if you could have just given a little bit more

As the years pass you by and the hours tick away
You try to give back till fate takes your hand

It's then that the impressions you made
And the pathways you trod
Can only be measured by others that follow yours
Through that door of life's span
As you recount those impressions of life that everyone can.

Peter L Carvell

On Getting A Hole In One

Last week at golf, I kid you not
I scored a hole in one
I was going round with Charlie
And Charlie said, 'Well done!'
I play off twelve, not very good
But Charlie plays off scratch
I bought the drinks there at the bar
And Charlie had a Scotch.
'Just a bit of luck,' I said
As my whistle it got wetter
But Charlie gave me good advice
On how I could get better.
'You'll find that something happens
If it hasn't happened yet
The harder that you practice
The luckier you'll get.'

Martin Harris Parry

The Body Beautiful

A very pleasant memory of mine,
Happened when I was past my prime,
A young girl of about seventeen,
Had occasion to undress and be seen.

She was of medium height with dark hair and pretty face.
She undressed at a leisurely pace,
No hint of false modesty,
She was as natural as she could be.

Her skin was soft, a creamy white,
She really was a lovely sight.
On her Mount of Venus she had soft and curly hair,
The rest of her body was beautiful and bare.

Long shapely legs, a firm moulded bum,
Slender arms and a rounded tum.
Her breasts were perky and a good shape,
A vision of beauty, she did make.

I was privileged to see her standing there,
Tried so hard not to stare.
Filled with envy, but I've had my time,
Hope her life will be as fruitful as mine.

Olive Young

Nostalgie De La Bone

A wooden bird in a plastic tree came down to me
In its beak a message about the hour
The song it sang repeatedly was
Look at you, once brand new and now so old
Remember when happiness was a ball of string and a kite
But still you envied others with their spinning tops
That hummed a nursery rhyme
In that enchanted forest made up of memories so very long ago
Sitting now as you do beneath the cuckoo clock you feel so lost
Yet let's not forget in this world so synthetic
You can be prophetic
As anyone ever manufactured love!

Vann Scytere

Memories Of My Great-Grandmother

Like a candle burning freely in the wind,
So wild was your spirit and for that I honour you.
You were a daring soul, so strong, so passionate,
Yet quiet and respecting like we all should be.

I admired your grace and the tender words you spoke,
Like any woman, gently, caring, honest.
But you had this edge of flare, of power,
Keeping you as powerful as you always were.

Everything from the silver hair on your head,
To your beautiful, soulful eyes, was remarkable.
It was you who inspired these words to come,
To escape my mouth and settle on this sheet.

If you had never been there, I doubt to think that,
Without your encouragement, that I would have ever written.
So I would like to say, thank you and may you be blessed,
I hope you are happy and watching over us now from the sky.

I have no regrets in meeting you,
Being with you, spending time with you,
Every moment was a perfect one, full of radiance and contentment.
In letting you go, my heart may weep, but I will not despair,
For I know we can meet again,
And I can see your gentle smile once more.

Not a day goes by where my eyes do not cry for your memory,
And many seconds of them are filled with your musical laughter.
Wait for us and make sure our families remain safe,
May your forever merry spirit rest in peace, Beatrice.

Samantha King

Ode To Despo

We sat in our pyjamas
Eating raw bananas
When she held me tight and sighed
'I love you truly, oh my dear.'
She looked at me and smiled.

'What's that funny smell?' I cried
'I love you truly, oh my dear
I love you truly, have no fear.'

'From my bottom to my heart
My love for you is bottomless
Most especially when I fart.'

Raj Mohindra

The Treasured Bicycle

My cousin Kenny, beaming with pride
Brought me a bicycle round to ride.
It's yours to keep, he said with a grin,
No excuse now for stopping in.

That sit-up and beg gave me hours of pleasure,
I travelled for miles with freedom and leisure,
He said he had made it especially for me,
And said that the make was an ASP.

I spoke the name of my bike with pride,
And soon learned the wrong and the right way to ride.
After getting stuck fast in the tramlines one day,
I swiftly learned how to keep out of their way.

I thanked cousin Kenny for being so kind,
And asked him to tell me, if he didn't mind.
Just what the initials of ASP meant,
But 'all spare parts' gave my ego a dent.

But my ASP bike meant the world to me,
As I cycled in freedom, the country to see.
But came the day that it fell apart,
Leaving me with a broken heart.

P E Langton

Remembering

There are some happy memories
That come to mind each day,
One early morning comes to mind
A newborn came to stay.
So tiny and yet so fragile
Premature I was told,
For all the pain and worrying
She's worth her weight in gold.

My baby grew to be a lass
A beauty to be seen,
And in my eyes she had to be
No princess but a queen.
As years go by and she grew up
She married her childhood friend,
And once again a baby born
Which I did love and tend.

The magical wheel that piles so much joy
Bring memories back of our girl and boy.

Clifford Jones

Flower

You were born on a summer's breeze:
A young bud,
Ready to flower.
Like petals, your eyelids slowly opened,
Revealing sky-blue irises
That held me in a trance.
Your face, shone in beatitude.
Radiant as the sun,
Graced with a smile.
I cradled you lovingly:
My being, absorbing yours.
Now winter,
Lays my garden bare
And you, my flower, have gone.
The angels, now cradle you.
The years have passed and I grow old,
But to my bosom, a flower clings.
And in my memory,
It reminds me, of you.

Jack Lanigan

Chain Of Memories

I have a chain of memories I wear with constant joy
The first a doll called Topsy my very favourite toy
I got her from a charity, my dad was unemployed
And all the children of the poor a yearly toy enjoyed
My second was at six year old, I left my brother's bed
I had a room all of my own, it went right to my head.
The next gem on my chain is flawed, stained with the sin of pride
But oh, what joy to carry the flag, when I was top girl guide.
The war came then and memories changed from diamonds into pearls
To represent the tears I shed for England's boys and girls.
A large and sparkling diamond came next with peace declared
And all God's children knelt and prayed, gave thanks for being spared.
A special gem came next in line with love my life was blessed
He loved me too, we married and together built a nest.
There are some cloudy beads of course, for woes I can't forget
The loss of dearest loved ones and deeds that I regret.
Most treasured of my memories give me continued bliss
My children and my grandchildren are all that I could wish.

Dorothy Beaumont

At Christmas Time When I Was Young

At Christmas time when I was young
We were sent to bed early, 'for things to get done'
But whatever did they have to do
Surely Santa, it was all left to you?

I warned my brother, he would get nothing at all
He was told not to climb and he fell off the wall
Mum says he is cheeky and really quite rude
He never gets washed and gobbles his food.

I'm so sorry Santa, for sneaking Gran's sherry
But Mum told me it was making her merry
I have left some for you and a nice mince pie
I know that you have a long way to fly.

I would like some skates, so I don't have to walk
And a whip and top with some colourful chalk
A musical box, with a ballerina inside
And a Sindy doll, dressed up like a bride.

I'll go to bed early and try not to peep
But last year, I could not get to sleep
My brother kept talking and pulling my hair
And I looked out the window but nothing was there.

I think that you must have lots of money
And you know that we don't, isn't that funny
Maybe next year, we will get to meet
But thank you Santa, from the kids in our street.

Elizabeth Ann Crompton

The Photograph

I talk to you and see you smile
if only for a little while.
I think I almost see you laugh
but then - it's just a photograph.

Your eyes follow me wherever I go
and yes - you are dead - I know.
Some may say I'm daft
talking to this photograph.

But through the valley of the shadow of death
the aftermath
My rod and staff
your photograph.

Jean Beith

Memories Are Made Of This

Carrie Elizabeth Low Donald

Baby Carrie now you are here
Filling us with lots of cheer
You are loved that's clear
To us all, you are so dear.

You have got a dad and mum
They will be your chum
Even when you're wet and 'hum'
They are so pleased you've come.

Grandmas you have two
A couple of grandpas too
They four so special for you
Even if they bill and coo!

For you it must be queer
To see faces at you peer
Give a smile, they will cheer
It's only wind you try to clear!

Today you are a tiny tot
But you will grow a lot
Drink your milk while it's hot
With this you'll grow up like a shot.

You'll learn to cry with might
On, on through the night
Dad and Mum walk the floor, left, right
Till you go out like a light.

Peace will reign once more
Do not slam that door
Still dear Carrie you they still adore
Your loving parents, oh how they snore.

I'm your auntie, Erica is my name
To you I'll never be the same
For I am special, so I claim
I love you lots, I'm glad you came.

Of the future I know not
Still for you God has a slot
He loves you such a lot
From when you were a tiny dot.

So dear Carrie take heed of your aunt
Life is one big jaunt
Mind you'll often get a 'dunt'
But you will never be in 'wunt'
God bless you precious one.

What is your name again?
Oh yes, Carrie Elizabeth Low Donald.
Erica Menzies

75

Memories Are Made Of This

Where Do They Come From?

What is this mysterious faculty
Sleeping, until aroused
By sight or smell or sound?
Warm pine needles, breeze stirred
Returns me to a Himalayan childhood.
Lavender . . . and I dive into a linen cupboard
In an aunt's loved ancient cottage.
A pansy's face tells a story
Of the Passion, learnt when very young.
Photographs bring a smile, a heart wrench
Or frustration at forgotten names.
Looks and antics of a growing child
Bring reminiscences of their parents.
Baking bread, a farmhouse kitchen
Where dogs and children crowded in.
Seaweed's distinctive tang
Recalls days of rockpool shrimping.
Vivid sunsets begin a journey
Over oceans to other far-off lands.
Even a burnt finger requiring sucking
Awakes a disregarded 'Don't touch!'
All these from my personal database
Accumulated unknowingly over years.
Time to gather may now be shorter -
But I am grateful for all that I have stored.

D Bagshawe

The Nations They Need Healing

The nations they need healing
This world is in a mess
We need the touch of Jesus
His love, His peace, His rest.

And now we must get talking
To the leaders of this world
And ask them what they're going to do
To put the world at rest.

I think the answer to them all
Is put their trust in God
And pray one day, that we will see
An end to want and war.

Mary Turner

Eggie

I was nine years old,
new in the neighbourhood,
lonely,
watching forlornly
as the boy next door
and his older brother
played Eggie

They noticed me,
invited me to join them;
the ball was thrown high
to a shout of Eggie;
arcane rules were followed;
I felt included,
less alone

Later
we became friends,
played Eggie, Leggie, Kennekie
in a school essay
I wrote he was
the most ordinary boy
known to me

Recently
I saw his obituary;
he was the more distinguished,
a public benefactor,
in a far country,
not ordinary
after all

Late in his life
did he remember Eggie,
the boy next door,
Leggie, Kennechie,
cricket, football, other games,
the mongrel dog he loved
called Yankee?

Neville Davis

Our Pleasures Were Simple

Our pleasures were simple when I was young
No need to use sunscreen when out in the sun
On our bikes we'd cycle for many a mile
Or ramble through fields and over a stile
We were all taught 'the country code'
Shut all the gates, take care by the road
Don't litter to mar the sights
Remember, others too have rights
With a jam jar and bread we'd fish in a stream
And savour the wonder of what we had seen
Catch tadpoles with a cup of the hand
And as it came by, we'd follow the band
Marching along to the beat of the drum
And when it's all over, come home to Mum
At tea we'd get a big hunk of bread
Piled with jam, a sticky sweet red
Dressing up was a lovely game
Or pretending the dog was not really tame
With a line of chalk our boundaries were made
Our plain old road would turn into a glade
Sometimes a castle is what it would be
Or a pirate ship upon the high sea
Oh yes, sirens then were part of the norm
And the coming of aircraft they'd wailingly warn
So into the shelters we'd hurriedly scurry
What it was all about, we'd not even worry
And even there we'd have a sing-song
Just to usher the waiting along
What a wonderful childhood I look back upon
With the tender protection of my dad and my mum.

Stroma Hammond

To Bournemouth

Thanks Terry for taking the strain
Off our break so long awaited
With your plans so uncomplicated
For our five nights stay by the sea
With all our needs anticipated.

Thanks to Simon Fox and his crew
The Queens Hotel became our home
Set near to the stunning ocean view
Of Bournemouth's cliffs, sand, waves and foam
That thrilled and pleased us all.

Here Woods fortunate tour fared well
From menus made to enthral
With fresh foods, as clean plates should tell
And civil service beyond compare
By 'Miss World' look-a-likes who care.

Thanks to Woods and Queens for our stay
God willing, we will return another day!

Ronald Rodger Caseby

Serenity – To Granny

Hazel eyes shine clear and calm
From her pretty round face.
Her smile shows all the wrinkles
In skin, dry as paper, which
Once bloomed like an English rose.

Quietly, she sits in her favourite chair,
Gnarled hands, knowing gentle ways,
Resting on her lap:
Remembering . . .
All she has learnt, and loved, and lost
In eighty-nine years.

She radiates peace and joy
To all those in her thoughts.
We shall not see her face light up again,
But her blessing is with us always
And her love still flows through our veins.

Clare Masters

Tricks

Whole decades disappear down the culverts of a lifetime.
Perhaps unconsciously we blot them out
and scoop up from the pool of thoughts the handfuls we prefer,
an attempt to sort ourselves, make sense of things.
You remember bits of childhood better than what you began
to conjure up, or tried to, from last year; no doubt,
those happier times stay with you and the snows of yesteryear
will never melt, no matter what life brings.
I remember every name and face of schoolmates in my clan,
and my teachers, even what they talked about,
and brown-paper-covered books we'd devour without demur:
the excitement of discovery, new experience, still clings.
End-of-lesson party-pieces: 'Give me a nail and a hammer . . .'
Ray's tremolo ripples; Mary's dusky 'Amor, Amor' adds 7-year-old glamour.

The mind is a chimaera, a free agent,
a Will o' the Wisp that plays about the lips of time,
dabbles in tricks-of-the-trade with memories,
disorientates your flow of thoughts, of dreams.
It peoples a vast immortal pageant
with faces known, unknown - no paradigm
to guide you neatly through, no summaries
like a contents page, no clear-cut schemes.
Your train of thought derails, veers off at a tangent,
leaves you agog, like a Dickson-Carr crime,
or stays clear-cut in the head, or buries
itself in oblivion, while frustration screams.
However much the romancers endeavour to explain,
there are mysteries in these labyrinthine alleys, that remain.

Adrian Brett

Evening

Golden sun sinks in the west
Singing birds fly home to rest
Asleep on Mother Nature's breast
Folded in Mother's wings
In nests which out of reach clings -
High above among the eaves
Little birds sleep while Mother sings.

A child's evening prayer is said
On Mother's breast pillows head
Love light shining in her eyes
Mother carries her to bed.

Barbara Kerby

Mr Romance

He grabs you and chastises you
He haunts you and taunts you,

Pursuing you with great devotion,
Propelling you in a delirious swirl of endless motion.

He aspires to kiss you and caress you,
To hug you and to love you.

He'll shower you with gifts,
Lifting your spirits, taking you to the highest limits.

Roses and romance, music and laughter,
I wonder what's going to happen the morning after?

He's sweet and unique and will have you dancing at your feet,
So when you wake and when you sleep,
When you smile and when you weep,
He'll be there waiting for you to meet.

Your sunshine and your moonbeam,
Your angel in your daydream,
Catch him if you can,
Cos he's your number one fan.

George Makasis

The Good Old Days

Freezing winters - fingers raw.
Chilly lino on the floor,
Steamy washdays, 'bubble and squeak'
Half a crown to last the week!
Dad on Sundays mending shoes,
Silent films to cure the blues,
One day trips to see the sea
(Holidays were not for me!)
Sharing bed with older sister -
Swapping yarns in midnight whispers.
Local Bobby on the beat,
No traffic in our quiet street,
Aunts and uncles by the dozens,
'Hand-me-downs' from wealthy cousins,
Christmas time with piled up plates,
And dancing round to '78s'
Here, in the comfort of my home,
My thoughts of past years often roam,
And now that I have time to spare,
I know that I'm a millionaire!

Joan Leahy

Days Gone By

How well I remember the days gone by
Things that happen today make me want to cry
Childhood memories spring to mind
Some I can never leave behind.

I well remember the days of the war
When food was rationed and what is more
All lights in the house had to be blacked out as the sirens sounded too
As the enemy planes came over one was not sure what to do.

The catch could be heard as the bombs were released too
There was no special target - anywhere would do
But the biggest dread of all was the 'Doodlebug plane'
The drone as it passed over nearly drove us insane.

As long as there was a noise from its tail - aflame with fire
We knew we were safe - as the flames went higher
But - when the noise stopped we knew trouble was in store
And listened to the explosions going off by the score.

These are memories I can never erase from my mind
And those who lost loved ones 'the special kind'.

Marjorie Ridley

Family

On a Christmas morning
Our mum's stocking
Filled with what they could afford
Always struck the right accord
Squeals of delight
Told Mum and Dad
Santa had called in the night
Christmas Eve shopping
Bought late in the day
Market prices down
Matched our mum's half a crown
Into our home Dad did bring
A drop of port
As he thought, he ought
Same was left with a mince pie
It was the time
That Santa heard the midnight chime
With children content
Dad's dole money well spent
With family love, we are
Into Heaven sent.

F Baggaley

Nell

My family from far foreign ground
May come to see me soon they say.
Wheelchair bound I here must stay,
No freedom now to get around.
These cataract eyes and rheumy knees,
Stop me going where I please.
But of my eyes the doctors say,
I must not linger in dismay.
They can be mended, not the knees.

Oh take me to the bluebell wood
So I can take one final look.
Where under every flowering shell,
My mind can see a Tinkerbell.
Now share the picnic basket round,
As you sit upon the ground.
I sit here in my wheelchair,
I see my life before me, clear.
My precious family, very dear.

As mind pirouettes on lichen track,
I feel the years peel softly back.
A young girl in the bluebell wood,
Where courting, George and I once stood.
From lady's maid to grocery store.
From mother, grandmother and more.
Four female generations stand,
United by a loving hand.

As I drift back to present time.
I look around, my eyes are fine.
If you can mend the Queen Mum's hip,
Why can't you make another snip?
So I implore you, doctors please!
Can't you do something with my knees?
I'm only 98 you know.
My mind can skip around a tree,
I'd like to take the rest of me.

Karen Knight

Memories Of A Man

(Mervyn - died 21st June 2007)

How suddenly you were taken from me, a deadly disease
Saw your life's blood drain away, a blood-red dust blew
Down out of the sun and shrouded us both.
A game of tennis, a bruise and you were gone with the
Suddenness of the sun at sunset slipping behind a hill.
Blood and stone
You saw not my partially disabled body, but me, your Jennifer
Your butterfly; you had given your life to me to enable
Me to live mine again.
We languished, we loved, we laughed together,
In the beauty of the world hid a secret
You gave me the strength I thought I had lost.
In that silent room, I kissed the veins in your hands
Warmth was there, but the pulse of life had gone forever
I'm left bereft, not knowing whether to struggle on
My soul tormented, sad and lost without you next to me
Protecting me always.
When I weep I feel you close, before I sleep
I reach out for your beautiful face and wonder
Could the blood of many ultimately be exacted for the vision
Of a single flower, behind the shadowed veil of our love.
Will I make it, I do not know.
Have I had my time, it is as it should be, my decision.
Life and death are one, as are the river and the sea
Shall I fight the mighty current or just drift away
Like flotsam on the ebbing tide.

Jennifer Fox

My Memories

I sit and think as on the firelight I gaze
And ponder on long ago family days
I remember how we sat on special occasions
Poised with forks and bread to take up our stations
Each jockeying for prime position to find the best places
Then waiting, anticipating with smiles on our faces
Our crusty browned toast when piled high with butter
Was munched and crunched with the occasional splutter
As we stuffed it down quickly to make room for another
Mother and Father, sister and her greedy brother
Then stuffed to the gills we told tales by the score
Which made us all laugh and was never a bore
Then Mother with ghost stories would fill us with dread
As we climbed apprehensively the stairway to bed.

Royston E Herbert

Ode To Miss Pilkington

(My school's teacher of dance)

Miss Pilkington, Miss Pilkington,
Who taught us how to dance:
Who taught us 'ballet', taught us 'tap' -
Used pretty words from France -
We left the form room, left the desk
And learned to do an 'arabesque',
To 'plié' and to pirouette' -
Names that we will not forget -
And then we changed our ballet shoes
For bright red slippers tied with bows
With metal taps 'neath heels and toes -
It needed different words for those!

This time we 'flapped' around the floor
And made a happy clapping sound
We hopped and slid and be-bopped round
And practised 'Time Step' more and more.
Then came the day we went on 'pointes'
- This really taxed your ankle joints -
So exercises were a 'must' -
Excruciating though they were
No single day could we defer
The limbering up, the 'stretches' all,
Feet in 'positions' 'gainst the wall
Along the barr and 'stand up *tall!*'

Then, Fred and Ginger came on screen
And off we went to try to glean
The *gorgeous* steps of each routine;
Oh, what a glimpse of grand romance
When we were taught the art of dance -
Miss Pilkington, Miss Pilkington.

Dorothy Thompson

Pondering Parables Of Jesus

Parables of vital learning for our path
Offered in motivation of support and saving care
Not just handing us truths upon a plate
Investing stories of wisdom that invite us
Showing us we have our own fulfilling part to play
Blessings of glory an active faith can build so freely
Nudging us with hyperboles of unexpected exaggeration
Enabling us to perceive with compelling objective clarity
Absorbing us creatively, challenging us to respond
To best harvest from His hallowed, inspiring words.

We the soil in which He scattered quality seed
Germinating potential to live the righteous life
In loving purposes and enhancing moral values
So aware then of Creator's designs He knew were fruitful
Aware too of just how much we mattered to Him
From the outcrop of relevant and stimulating thought
His love and ours meet in beauty of sacred purpose
To be lifted to divine journeys of growth and flourishing
Joyfully come together in God's planned Kingdom of Heaven
Linked on Earth to dwell in hearts of love.

Don Harris

Yesteryears

Attune your mind to pre-war days ere Hitler rose to power
Our goal worldwide depression to defeat
Such frugal times with jobless figures rising by the hour
A constant struggle just to make ends meet.

Despite those hardships, decency and truth were common in those days
Whilst many misdemeanours carried shame
And stigma which for sure these days an eyebrow would not raise
Police knew likely petty crooks by name.

My old headmaster's vision for his boys was plain to see
Obedience and kindness his main themes
Team spirit, fairness and of course unswerving loyalty
Our old school motto crystallised his dreams.

'Do stand aside and show respect for elders,' he would say
Politeness and good manners his concern
Are his old values lost in changing attitudes today?
An oldie now still waiting for my turn.

Alf Parry

Memories . . . (A Mixed Bag)

I could do without memories.
So many that one can find,
oft causing such inner mayhem
foolish acts recalled to mind.

Those so childish japes, avoiding
more serious work at hand.
Playfully dodging those things that
many wise teachers had planned.

So much lack of concentration,
though able to read and write,
thus evading explanations
of what's wrong and what is right.

Nothing serious in my mind
though naught that was very wrong,
I'd much prefer a feeble joke
or maybe a silly song.

Rescued, at last, by change of school
to one of technology.
Dabbling with brick, concrete and drains -
Building methodology!

Emerging as from a chrysalis
giving wings to mind and heart,
thus moving on to higher things -
Architecture, Queen of Arts!

Planning future development
to build for a better day.
Looking back is not so bad
in the light of hindsight's ray.

Jo Allen

My Mum

(In loving memory of Alice - my mum)

The memories of you will always be there
There are many and are very strong,
I will cherish them all and no doubt will share,
They will never fade away, no matter how long.

Five weeks ago I lost you Mum, the world
Crumbled and dark blocked out the sun,
Why were you taken, it was so unfair,
It was so unjust, you were my mum!

Each day seems so long because I can't
Speak to you on the phone,
How are we all going to get through this?
We are so alone.

We knew this dreadful time that has come upon us
Would eventually come,
But not now, not this time,
Not my mum!

The world is quiet as we mourn for you, no sounds
Of others, or traffic coming through,
I suppose as this cloud lifts and we get further on,
The will to survive and who is left behind
Will finally come.

Part of my existence was to look after you,
Now you have gone, what am I to do?
My life feels so pointless anymore -
What keeps me going is my little boy,
He is only nine, how strong he is,
He has been so brave through all of this.

Peace now Mum, you have now joined my dad,
For this I shouldn't be woeful and sad,
You are finally together and this means joy,
I've even explained this to my little boy,
Goodnight, God bless, we all love you Mum,
Memories will stay, even when the
Cloud clears away from the sun.

Jill K Gilbert

Dear Friend Of Mine

Dear friend of mine
Of sleepless nights and bitter wine
Through all the endless nights you shine
So sublime, so divine:
Dear friend of mine
As gods now watch your spirits climb
They know that in yon fiery tempest breast
A seed of soft compassion gently rests
So sublime, so divine:
Dear friend of mine
With healing hands and heart of mystic powers
Within thy breast that seed will grow until it flowers
So sublime, so divine:
Dear friend of mine
It is indeed a pleasure to know you
Alack! Alas! Our years are but so few
So always be gentle to the others
The ones you know, the ones you knew
But most of all; stay gentle to you yourself
I dearly and truly love you!

Leslie de la Haye

Mother's Day

Mother dear, we think of you every single day
Of all the things you used to do and all you used to say
When we were small you wiped away the tears we often shed
And listened while we said our prayers before we climbed into bed
When school was over and friends departed,
You were always there at the door
To take and hang our coats up, never ever to be left on the floor.
When we were ill you hovered, your brow creased in a worried frown
When we were well, your smile reached up to your twinkling eyes of brown.
As we got older, in our teens, with all childish things put away
You were always there to guide us, with your gentle loving ways
As one by one we left the 'nest', you were proud of all we'd achieved
And we were proud of our wonderful mother
And the pattern in our lives you had weaved
Now Mother's Day is dawning and these flowers we're sending to you
To thank you for all those wonderful years
We will cherish our whole lives through.

Iris Forster

Engagement

Do you remember that day in June,
The day you said you would be mine?
A brilliant scorching afternoon,
That day you said you would be mine.
We walked together, hand in hand
Wandering through the woodland shade,
We laughed, we sang, we talked, we planned,
Such happiness in Heaven was made!

And as we roamed the little wood
Filled with the scent of sundrenched pine,
Life was joyful, life was good,
That day you said you would be mine.
We strolled where yew and larch tree grew,
Black lace against a summer sky,
A cloudless sky of purest blue,
And we were happy, you and I.

Do you recall the path we took
Where celandine and speedwell grew?
The wooden bridge that spanned the brook;
Nettles, foxgloves, feverfew?
The air was still, no creature stirred,
To us the hot, calm air was wine,
Our happiness was all we heard
That day you said you would be mine.

The years have gone, the children grown,
So many years of love and strife,
And now, again, we're left alone,
Nearing the end of mortal life.
The trees are taller, we are slow
But still we walk 'neath larch and pine,
Hand in hand, where wild flowers grow -
Content you said you would be mine!

Bee Kenchington

Memories Of Grandad

As I lie here alone in the dark of the night
Wishing you onward in your heavenward flight,
My mind wanders back over the decades of time
And memories of you flash into my mind.

As a small girl it was my early morning treat
To watch you milk the cows on your three-legged seat,
As the stream of frothy milk hit the metal pail
Stray cats around your feet kept up a hungry wail.

Then donning your hat, off to work you would go
Your bait in a bag and at your side old Carlo,
To supervise the pickers, to prune and to spray
Before coming home tired at the end of the day.

To be first down the stairs was your morning routine
To stoke up the Rayburn and brew up the tea,
I liked watching you shave at the sink in your vest
With the Brylcreem slapped on you'd pass any test!

On Sundays off to church we would go at half nine
Parking the car as the bells began to chime,
Giving out the hymn books as the people drifted in
And standing beside you, we'd all begin to sing.

Feeling so proud as you followed me up the aisle
Greeting all your friends with a nod and a smile,
Your big hands took the bread as we knelt reverently
Whilst the crimson-clad choir sang hymns quietly.

Often when I came, down the garden you'd be found
Planting bulbs and seeds and digging in the ground,
Picking ripe tomatoes in the greenhouse for tea
The riot of colour was quite a sight to see!

So farewell gentle Grandad, I bid you goodbye
May angels escort you as heavenwards you fly;
As you shake off this world's shackles and rise above
Our memories of you will be coloured with love.

Katrina Cracknell

Camber Sands, 1939

Wooden chalet hidden deep,
Midst the sand hills, smooth and steep,
Summer sun through curtains calling,
Had the eager children falling -
Out of bed and swiftly dressed,
Chasing o'er the sand warmness,
Up the crest and down the side,
To the sand smoothed by the tide,
Where the little rivulets flow
There the naked child-feet go.

Cross sandy plain and dipped rock pools
To where the sea's soft wavelets swirl,
Laughing, shouting in the sun,
Joyful holidays begun.
Till a voice will call them back -
To the summer wooden shack.
Breakfast done, again they go
Happy in the sun's kind glow,
Golden hours played away
In the sand and cool sea spray.

Lunch al fresco on the beach,
Sea and sand still in reach,
Crisps and rolls, with sand, they eat,
Ice cream given for a treat.
Castles built and seashell-decked
Till by sea waves they are wrecked.
Home again to wooden house,
Each one quiet as a mouse.
Tired and happy, set for tea,
Then to bed, they all agree.

Peggy Sinclair

My Mum

The 25th August is very dear to me,
It's the day my mother died, at the age of 43.
My memories are very clear, the way she wore her hair.
The way she dressed, the way she smiled, she had quite a flair.

Her brown eyes always smiling, she had dainty little feet.
A lady like my mum, I have yet to meet.
Fifty-seven years have passed, where has the time all gone?
My memories are like pure gold, will not tarnish or grow old
Of my mum.

Marion Elizabeth Joyce

My Son Paul

Before I know it, he will be grown
Before I know it, he'll be a man
Before I know it, he will leave home
To find a new life of his own.

Where have the years gone, I just don't know
The weeks and months just come and go
It seems a little while since he was small
He's quickly growing so very tall, my son Paul.

It seems only yesterday when he was born
Tomorrow will come too soon, the years have flown
Time won't stand still, I know it's true
He'll be a young man in a year or two.

I want to treasure these happy years
He brings me pleasure and a few little tears
He'll be a man in a few years time
My dedication to him is this rhyme.

Before I know it, he'll meet his wife
Before I know it, a change of life
Before I know it, he'll have a home
Maybe a family of his own.

Julie Taylor

Angel From Heaven

Her love was so warm and tender
Her love was so soft but strong
Her love was that of an angel
I will always love
My whole life long
But that angel from Heaven has gone
And I'm now all alone
On this world of pain and sorrow
And I know I'll have
No more happy tomorrows
Without that angel from Heaven
Walking by my side
But on this war-torn world of ours
There will never be another
Because that loving angel from Heaven
Was my tender loving mother.

Donald John Tye

Peter Pan World
(Nostalgia's Last Stand)

Coming over all wistful
once again
through rose-tinted glasses
looking back to then . . .

Ponytails and bobby socks
giggling girls
like starling flocks.

Cycling miles
in wind and rain
in the angst and hope
of youth's short dream.

Going all together
soft in the head
wincing over
words once said . . .

The café and the sledging hill
the old school tie
worn loosely still.

Year book photograph
slow walks with a girl
straw-haired days
in a Peter Pan world.

Mike Monaghan

On Ari Atoll

On Ari Atoll at the close of day
small flares on sticks the scene embrace
to offer Valentine our annual grace.

Ten couples at their watery tables sit
and with them glowing on her seat
my lovely Valentine has soft wet feet.

The turquoise Indian sea beneath is lit
by flickering flames that ghostly mark
the lazy passage of a black-tipped shark.

And shallow ripples softly pass along
Maldivian hems of her sarong
and cool her coral-sanded, soft, wet feet.

Godfrey Ackers

On Becoming A Grandfather

So this is what the old 'uns meant!
Time irreversibly
Turns circle finally
And all the memories of thirty years ago
Canoe life's rapids and its pools to flow
Clear, bright, sharp as the Christmas thorn.
Not just the images of what we used to do -
Of up all night and morning's dawn well worn -
But smells and sounds evoke the signal clue
To needs age-old of every soul newborn.
The habits of our twenties we renew -
Cradle the grandson in the same crook arm,
Speak softly so as not to cause alarm,
Interpret every movement of his eye
And, with cracked voice, sing gentle lullaby.

So this is why my mother shed her tears!
The world's a dreadful place
Bereft of innocence and grace
Those times the Devil strips away love's shell
And looses every demon out of Hell.
But here is hope, potential, future strong,
The needful that's required to raise the man,
The love to help him sing love's song
And so achieve the age-old Master plan.
My legs no longer run, my teeth grow long,
And sands of time forever quickly ran:
My new friend Death, who draws old friends away,
Can never be gainsaid his calling day,
But Mother's, Father's blood will still run bright
In this small, precious bundle of delight.

Raymond Holley

Aspect On A Fine Night

The daylight gone,
My eyes can see the stars
Rough-hewn against the velvet,
Blackened sky.
The rain has ceased and mother moon,
Benevolence her gift,
Looks down upon the Earth,
The expression that she wears upon her face
Is wry!

Carole Mary Smith

A Poignant Memory

The thirteenth on a Friday brings to me
A poignant memory of yesteryear.
When, in November nineteenfiftythree,
I got the news I'd waited long to hear.
I was a British soldier in Korea,
My pregnant wife in England all alone;
Communication was, at best, severe.
A cable took four days, there was no phone
And so it was I got the waited news
I'd been a dad already for four days.
'Twas time to celebrate, perhaps to muse,
And to a loving wife, and God, give praise.
Another year would pass before I see
My Caroline, born ninth November fiftythree.

Christopher Head

My Husband's Memories

My husband I lost
A few months ago
The memories and love
We shared in the past
Will help me along
My lonely way.

He was so joyful
Full of fun
He loved good music
Song and dance
It really was a true romance.

I often look at his photo
And see him smiling at me
That gives me strength
To carry on.

With this in mind
I shall get stronger
Day by day
Then he will look down
And smile at me
Until we meet again one day.

Catherine Wigglesworth

Fish For Tea

A very special memory for me
Visiting the fishing boats
As they returned from sea
Where we were given two live crabs
To take home for our tea
A slightly hairy moment
Discovering pincer movements
On the back seat of the car
Arriving home in triumph
We gave our spoils to Mum
To deal with expertly
This she firmly vetoed
With no such inhibitions
Father and I took charge
Boiled our crabs in a bucket
Then cleaned and dressed them too
After all this trauma
Tea finally was set
The moment of success
Now but a fading memory
Just cannot remember how they tasted
Only exhaustion remained.

B Williams

Flying Reindeer

It seems such a long, long while ago
When everywhere was deep in snow
I looked up at the starry sky
Waiting for Santa to pass by.

I really should have been fast asleep
But thought it wouldn't hurt to take a peep
And see the sleigh guided through the sky
By the reindeer who were going to fly.

I waited and waited to see that sight
And sat up I'm sure, half of the night
But at last was overcome by sleep
And then was awakened by the radio bleep.

All of the toys were on the bed
Again I had missed that man in red
And the reindeer in the sky
I really did want to see them fly.

Violetta Ferguson

Papa

Well then Dad, you of 'kitchen football' fame,
Who broke the clock and never took the blame,
And bought me planks of wood for my eighth birthday,
Promising a go-kart would be on the way,
But then on its first run down the hill nearby,
The wheels fell off and I went for a fly!

Or when we walked to school, those were nice days,
(We walked backwards to confuse the aeroplanes!)
And moved pretty sharpish when we saw that frog,
By the 'Cuckoo Steps' on top of that log.

And sometimes on a Thursday after football,
You'd buy me the *Beano* on the way home,
And remember when you drove me to that hockey trial?
So cold that we had to defrost for a while.
Before we were warm enough to travel back,
Talk about frosty, my dad Jack!

You helped me paint my room, it's 'feature' filled,
From the ceiling to the window sills,
And when you tripped over the carpet, I couldn't breathe for laughter,
Because you kept on talking, even after
You were on the floor and had disappeared from view,
It still makes me laugh, thinking of you!
Like at car boot sales when you called our junk 'stock'
Or rode my bike through the woods, so easy to mock!

I get my music from you, just my luck, is
That neither of us can carry a tune in a bucket!
But that doesn't stop us, we don't care a jot,
For we still sing loudly and sing a lot!

And in a world of uncertainty, to bank on one thing, I can
That you will always run for the ice cream van!

Ruth Morris

A Dream Gratefully Remembered

She took white shoes off. Who am I
to understand or tell you why?
Along a cinder path she stole
some fragments clinging to her sole
but she walked on. I bade her stand.
I knelt beside her. With my hand
(that painful blisters might not form)
brushed off those fragments. Smooth and warm
her feet. As at a private joke
she smiled. I smiled.
                              And I awoke.

Martin Summers

Always My Home

Meg and I are on the beach
Summer has begun
The cliffs seem steep and out of reach
But to climb them could be fun

Seaweed is strewn in strands
The crabs run in the rocks
School is out, bring on the band!
Come on take off those socks!

After a paddle, the ice cream parlour
Some boys give us a glance
'Let's go to the pavilion,' Meg says
'It's only tuppence a dance'

We danced well together
From waltz, tango to the twist
But the local lads are missing
So we cross it off our list

Those days seemed so full of fun
No cares for a twelve-year-old
All day playing in the sun
Never rainy or cold

Singing in a children's choir
Me with a solo song
A silver medal to my name
When did that go wrong?

Years go by, the love affairs
That never seem to last
Then I met the one and only
So the die was cast

It never did happen
That great love affair
All ended when the war came
So our lives we did not share

But the memories remain
Although most friends have passed away
I will smile and shed a tear
On my eighty-ninth birthday!

Alice Porteous

Schooldays

We didn't have computers
When I attended school
And never used such fancy words
As brill or ace or cool.

The playgrounds all had shelters
In case there was a raid
We'd hear the siren, then all clear
Sometimes we were afraid.

We didn't need our parents
To take us to the park
We'd climb and swing and use the slide
And play till almost dark.

We'd listen to the radio
There wasn't any telly
And love our birthday parties
With ice cream, cake and jelly.

I did enjoy my schooldays
And I think it's true to say
We behaved a whole lot better
Than the children of today.

Beryl Upshall

Our Home

A little thatched cabin that was once our home.
Now stands out there in the wilderness
Deserted and on its own.
No light on the window, no welcome at the door.
No smoke from its chimney, weeds now cover the floor.
Where our momma once sat in mourning. Time for her
Stood still since our papa went asleep
At the other side of the hill a dark
Cloud now hangs over the little homestead
It dims the day's light. If they should awake tomorrow
Again there would be light.
The home was not a castle we never did pretend.
We had peace and happiness we thought
Would never end.

Richard Mahoney

Fond Memories

Blackpool is my home town,
We go there every year
To meet our friends and family
And walk along the pier.
Like children, up and down we go
Aboard the carousel,
Why do I finish at the top
When the driver rings his bell?

The lift goes up and down the tower,
We walk from pier to pier,
To see the sand and donkeys
And enjoy a glass of beer.
On to the sandy beach we stroll
To splash along the shore
And wish that we could live there,
Like we did in days of yore.

A stick of rock, some candyfloss
Or maybe fish and chips,
A Mr Whippy cornet
Will make us lick our lips.
We'll see a show or cabaret,
Or have a game of bingo
And to find out what's in store for us
See Gypsy Petulengro.

A week is really not enough
For all Blackpool's delights,
The Aquarium, the Wavepool,
The Pleasure Beach, the Lights,
The Ice Show and Eclipse,
Surprises by the sackful,
A week is really not enough
To enjoy the best of Blackpool.

Kathleen Day

101

When We Were Young

Down our little country lane, the 'great' steamroller came,
And the smell of boiling tar, it filled the air,
But, it heralded bad news, as it stuck fast to our shoes
And our poor hard-working mums, they all went spare!

A white-coated gentleman used to drive the Co-op van,
It was the only shop for miles around.
A silver sixpence bought you sweets, toffee sticks and rosebud treats,
You could get a lot of groceries for a pound.

In the fields we used to play, whilst the sun shone, all the day,
We'd pick mushrooms, blackberries and bitter sloe.
Then inside the hessian sacks we'd bag the crusty old cowpats,
And it didn't half make our roses grow.

We cycled miles on our bikes, as traffic then was light,
To the river, for a picnic and a swim.
Wild garlic, sweet primrose and scented violets lined the road,
Then we'd wend our way back home as light got dim.

Now there's hardly any green, just houses where it's been,
And the traffic queues get bigger day by day.
We've computers, mobile phones, all *mod cons* in our homes,
But inside I'll keep my *dreams of yesterday!*

Heather Overfield

Schooldays

At school we stood in one long row
For Nitty Nora to poke about in our hair
We all looked neat and tidy
Till old Nora rummaged there
On the index finger of her right hand
Was the most disgusting plaster seen
I looked at her and rudely said,
'Don't put that near my head
I don't know where it's been.'
A few days later she'd be back
This time to probe our mouth
Thank goodness in this day and age
She's surely get the sack
For on her index finger
Still wrapped around it there
Was the self-same filthy plaster
That had rummaged through our hair.

Daphne Fryer

My Bike

When I was a boy (and not just a boy)
I'd spend all day on my bike,
I'd be away for most of the day
And sometimes part of the night!

In spring and summer when the days were long,
Pushing the pedals hard and strong,
Puffing up hills like an old steam train,
Legs flying like wings, coming down again!

What joys I knew of the open road
Like a king in his carriage with flowing robe,
Looked over hedges, fences and trees,
Wind whispered through arms, I felt so free!

Rushing past village church and spire,
Pushing down hard as the hill grew higher,
Coming to rest on the summit of hill,
Looking o'er landscape gave me a thrill!

Down into valley racing again,
Trying to keep pace with passing train,
Scattering ducks, geese and hens,
Drunk on fresh air, skimming the bends!

Brakes on hard at the crossing gates locked,
Forced by the railway to come to a stop,
Waved to the driver with cheery, 'Hello,'
'Boys will be boys' his look to me showed!

Pushing on through as road is unblocked
Gypsies straddled the road, forced me to stop,
'Nice new bike,' they shouted to me,
But I'm off like the wind, whistling free!

Encountered a tramp with a large heavy load
In a pack on his back like a drunk man he strode,
I was getting quite thirsty and hungry too,
Found a quiet field with a very good view.

I lay on my back and looked at the sky,
Heard a farmer's tractor nearby,
'This is the life,' I said to myself,
Nodding like sage to the wind,
But all that is past and we know cannot last,
Though boyhood is always in spring!

Graham K A Walker

The Well Of Memory

I remember walks I had
At night with our pet dog and Dad,
The three of us together strode
In harmony along the road
Where street lamps cast their ghastly light
And made our faces greenish-white.

So many years ago it seems
That memories are more like dreams,
And yet so vivid is the scene
Just yesterday it might have been;
And how I wish the years to be
All still to come for them and me!

But when in life our joys are past -
Those lovely times that cannot last -
We dip into that deep recess,
That store of joy and yet sadness,
And live again in imagery
Those times from the well of memory.

Betty McIlroy

Hills And Plains

As I walk around the hills and plains
Will anything be the same
For I have lost my nice young wife
To some white men who stole her life.

As I walk around the hills and plains
In search of the nation's Shamen
Who can point me onto the right track
To get my nice young wife back.

As I walk around the hills and plains
I am now a warrior who understands the game
For on my side now is the god of life
For with a new horse and warpaint I have won the right
And once again beside me is my nice young wife.

Keith L Powell

Memories

In the depths of the night I begin my fight
With the demons of memory until first light
I wrestle and keep my thoughts at bay
But I cannot push the memories away.
Reliving the day, the journey in a haze
Confronting reality in the longest of days.
Music playing to soothe the way and avoid power of thought
Simply increased the emotions, tears welling from nought.

It all comes back in the dead of night
To haunt and upset, never far out of sight.

I think of Dad alone without Mam, so lost
Nearly sixty years, the loss is not without cost.
Suddenly to lose your loved one so dear
Unexpectedly, without warning, no time for words of cheer.
How will he cope with family dispersed?
But neighbours are stars, seeing him well nursed.
Writing words helps to undertake grieving
When inwardly the wrench is all against leaving.

It all comes back in the dead of the night
To haunt and upset, never far out of sight.

No time to go back and omit the mistakes of the past.
There's no opportunity to remedy the fate that's been cast.
We each love each other in our own special way
Mam knew that, I am sure, no need to say.
And as each day passes, we remember the moments
Of love and of joy mixed with more negative actions.
But the latter we consign to the dustbin of time
Preferring to recall the best of those times.

It all comes back in the dead of the night
To haunt and upset, never far out of sight.

Trevor Huntington

I Remember

I remember, I remember when I was in my teens
Dancing round the bandstand in the park so green.
White wedge shoes, pleated skirt, painted legs of brown,
Nylons weren't invented then, clothing coupons were around.
It didn't seem to worry us, the lack of many things,
We found our joys in simple ways, my love was always dancing.
Three pennies up the swimming baths we hurried for the pleasure
To meet our friends and take a swim, enjoying hours of leisure.
The old church hall on Saturday nights where we would hold our dance,
A shilling piece was all it cost, hoping for romance.
Sundays at the cinema, one shilling and three pence,
The boys got in for nothing - coming through the gents.
Five Woodbine cigs we all shared out to prove that we were grown,
Something we didn't dare to do once we were back at home.
Sitting on a neighbour's wall, singing in the rain,
Until a window opened up, the owner to complain.
Riding on the underground for tuppence all the way,
A favourite pastime with us all, on cold and rainy days.
Sitting in the 'Pie and Mash' was a special treat -
A gorgeous smell of baking, sawdust at our feet.
Our days were full - the nights were grand - will never come again,
I'm sorry for the kids today, their fun is not the same.
They have the lot - money is spent on everything that's going,
There is no thrill of making do, boredom's always showing.
We are to blame, the mums and dads, we gave too much too soon,
They've only got the tinsel, we had the stars and moon.
The fun of little jokes and laughs, of making do, inventing
Things to do, the lack of cash never once preventing,
I sit here as memory wings back along the years,
Joy beyond all measure,
I'm glad I had my teen years then, my cup was full of pleasure
I had the best with little cost and oh those golden days
Of happiness, my teenage years, my youthful salad days.

Sylvia Reynolds

In Love

We met in the army
Pals from the start,
Sent to North Africa
It was there we had to part.
Reunited, four years had passed
'Will you come to my wedding?' he asked.
I went to the wedding
Seems a long time ago,
Travelled with my ex-army pal
To where hops and apples grow.
Met the bride's sister Dorothy
I said, 'My name is Fred,'
Should have gone home Sunday
But left on the Monday instead.
We married the following Easter,
Settled to a very good life.
That's why I've always liked weddings
Because that's where I met my wife.
Dorothy had been in the forces
And what came out of the blue
Took a penfriend letter home to her sister
Which happened to be my army pal too.
Now, Dorothy has gone
My love for her lingers on,
Those days together slipped into the past
Pity they were not meant to last.
And as I wipe a tear from my cheek
Memories of my love for her I keep.

Frederick Coles

Anaesthesia

Our current living is like an anaesthesia towards time,
We no longer feel time anymore,
I remember days lasting longer than weeks now,
Years dragging for decades,
When we had all the time in the world,
It feels like I've lived through three thousand summers
When I've only lived thirty,
And the thought of only having forty more is intimidating,
Lying in the garden with cool drinks during the warm weather,
Only another thirty-nine times
As another one has passed,
Best make the most of it,
At least.

Anthony Ward

Thoughts

When I lie awake in my lonely bed
So many thoughts go round in my head.
I think of the days when I was young
When really my life had just begun.
I think of the pleasure when I first read a book
When I turned every page and had a good look
At the words written there, beckoning to me
About life in the world I'd yet to see.
The love of music when I first learnt to play
Religiously practised for hours each day.
Going to school and making new friends
More things to learn, the list never ends.
So many 'firsts' came along in my life
Dancing and working then being a wife.
The pleasure I had when my children were born
And passing on knowledge to them in their turn.
All these thoughts are there, going round in my head
As I lie awake in my lonely bed
The pleasures they bring fill my heart with cheer
To dream on again when night-time draws near.

Joyce Woods

Nostalgia

There it stands, the house where I was born
Its white-washed walls now darkened from neglect
The curtains at the window drab and torn
The windows now too clouded to reflect.
Where once was joy and laughter I recall
We children playing games so merrily.
The sparkle of the ancient waterfall:
The blossom on the winter cherry tree.
The summerhouse where once we used to play:
The broken swing, now stilled by rotted rope.
Such fun we had when in the holidays
We had no time to hang around and mope.
I look again and now sad thoughts recede:
I see bright poppies blooming through the weeds.

Frances Heckler

Childhood

Dear Mother when from bed we rose
And went downstairs to warm our toes
By the fire which you had made
And found the breakfast table laid

When we'd had our porridge oats
We'd wash our hands and don our coats
Then slowly off to school we'd go
To learn of things we didn't know

At Valentine's our dear old dad
Played tricks on us and drove us mad
When we answered that rat-a-tat-tat
We'd find a herring on the mat

When summer holidays came around
There on the beach we would be found
Building sandcastles, playing cricket
Using driftwood for a wicket

A bag of sweets, not too many
An ice cream cornet for a penny
That's the way it used to be
Around nineteen hundred and thirty-three.

Ivy Nichols

December Decorations

Just one week before Christmas
My dad said to Mother and me,
'I'm going to take young Arthur
And buy our Christmas tree.'
Our mam went quite pale
All the world could see,
She said, 'I always buy the tree.'
Dad said, 'Leave it to me.'
So while they'd gone
Mam got the box of trimmings
For the tree,
Baubles, tinsel and paperchains,
What a sight to see.
We dressed up that little tree
Our mam and Arthur and me.
And after Christmas was over
Our dad took our little tree
Into the garden and set it.
And he turned to Arthur and me,
'You watch that little tree growing
Next year it'll be six-foot three.'

Hazel J Palmer

Autumn

The trees are shedding their multicoloured leaves
For autumn once more is here
And it's with a heavy heart I watch them fall
And I recall memories of yesteryear

For like those leaves that flitter to the ground
My memories of past times also fall
Past loved ones pictured, though faces now dim
Old words of love are harder to recall

The dead leaves rustle and crunch underfoot
As I walk down my lonely road
They have no tree now to give them life
And I have no one to share my load

In the winter the trees will stand, stark and proud
And eagerly await next year's spring
For me there will be no joy in the year ahead
For I've lost my world, my everything

In nature for every tree or plant that is lost
Another new one takes its vacated space
Why then am I doomed to wander this world
Ever searching for her love to replace?

Don Woods

The Same Vicious Circumstances

Coping with savage memories since I was a small child
A mother - an alcoholic, a father so violent and so wild

My brothers and sisters sought me for their protection
Behind our closed doors, cruelty - a daily subjection

Always so hungry and grubby, dirty clothes set us all aside
Taunted, even tormented daily, how could we show any self pride?

We clung to each other, as we grew closely side by side
As children, knew true love between us, that was never denied

Now we all are grown adults, have sweet families of our own
We pray those tragic relentless memories would leave us all alone

Strength lies in numbers, my own brothers and sisters qualify this
In sadness, those cuddles together, our only moments of family bliss.

Maureen Westwood O'Hara

From A Distance

I watched from a distance,
Not knowing your name.
You walked up to me and said the same.
Two perfect strangers,
Meeting by chance.
You held my hand and asked for a dance.

We danced all night,
We danced all day.
To be like this forever we prayed.
I looked in your eyes,
You looked into mine.
Then I looked at our fingers entwined.

I'd watched from a distance,
Wanting to know your name.
You'd walked into my life and said the same.
Two perfect strangers,
Meeting by chance.
You'd held my hand and asked for a dance.

But you are married
No, it's not the same.
You promised to love only one on your wedding day.
So I will leave now.

Ann Williamson

On Reflection

On days like today we can remember,
When we walked in the sun 'neath the blue sky,
And wishing the day would never end,
As we stood by the stream near the old oak,
Our reflections distorted by the breeze,
And the minnows darted from reed to reed,
Whilst the ducks landed with hardly a splash,
We picked the flowers that grew in the wood,
To decorate the kitchen window sill,
Placed in a jam jar till they faded,
Then home to tea and Mum's, 'Had a nice day?'
As we tucked into strawberries and cream,
And so to bed with a kiss and, 'Sleep tight,
See you tomorrow,' Mum put out the light.

Jim Dolbear

Time Changes

I was sitting here and thinking
Of days that are now long-gone
Life was lived at a slower pace
And fewer things got me down.
Now I find everything is a rush
Little time to stop and pause
Demands made from all directions
I'm told, in a very good cause.
With all this new technology
I find it hard to understand
How I coped with job and home
And children, who were planned.
We never had a brand new car
Or managed holidays abroad
We always felt our life was good
No debts, just what we could afford.
Today, folk have become selfish
They're not satisfied with their life
Never being happy with their lot
Will only cause a lot more strife.
I wonder where it all will end
One day, perhaps the answer I'll find
To the one question we need to ask
'Where can we find peace of mind?'

Judith Watts

Memories

Soft visions of happiness of days gone by,
Bring warmth and closeness to the inner eye.
Present day troubles and cares melt away,
The darkness of doubt merges to a bright day.
A soft caress, a laugh, and a kiss,
Are treasured memories you find that you miss.
But your heart is wise, for it does know
That happiness can come, but will always go.
The past is like a burnt out flame.
Do not bring it back, it is not the same.
But do not forget it, just store it away.
And use it to help pull through a grey day.

John D Robertson

Memories Are Made Of This

A Child's Magic Hour

Friendly warmth of burning coals, flicker from the fire
Throwing dancing patterns across the old stone walls
Heavy swaying drapes edged with golden braids
Thick oak door creaks welcome to anyone who calls

Sparkling, polished, copper kettle whispering to itself
Competing with the stately stick of silver wedding clock
Cosy handmade rugs that hide a child's small toes
Treasure-packed, old window seat guarded with a lock

Pictures, now dark brown, of mums and dads when they were small
Freshly picked flowers squeezed in vases of fine cut crystal glass
Embroidered fluffy cushion that wraps around the human form
Tiny little windows to greet the neighbours as they pass

Waxed walnut carefully protected by lacy table mats
Small cold pantry filled to bursting with fruity home-made jams
Sharp sage aroma falls from drying ceiling hung sprays
Black, unused smoothing iron secures the door that slams

My mum and dad have purchased an ultra-modern house
The trendy stylish things have replaced all the old
Thermal blocks and double-glazing all the way around
But even with the heating on, it still seems very cold

Plastic tables harshly lit with long fluorescent tubes
Kitchen lined with the unused tools that modern life demands
Hard nylon carpets form a base for ugly chipboard frames
That's why for just one hour a week I like to visit Gran's.

Stephen John Whitehouse

The Beauty Of Nature

A wonderful picture in my mind inspires words to treasure
Creating a universe where beauty is appreciated
Nature itself inspires poets and artists alike
To celebrate the creation of images enfolding since life began.

Blossoms bursting into bloom as spring makes it debut
Continues to bring growth in abundance to the garden
As creatures come out of hibernation and scurry about
Making each day a start for their comings and goings.

Lambs gambol in the spring sunshine
And birdsong wakes us up at early dawn
As nature prepares us for its natural beauty
We celebrate just what the world has to offer.

Marjory Price

Departure

All the rooms in our house
Are empty now. The drapes hang
Dusty at the windows, reflecting
The desert within.
Even the clocks need winding.

I wander in and out the now closed doors.
I pick up photographs neat in their frames,
And run my fingers across
The familiar smiles,
Tracing their miles with my love.

I open, at random, a drawer,
And gaze, and gaze at its contents
Without seeing them at all.
Standing, solitary, in the
Middle of the soft pile carpet.

I hear the shrieks and laughter,
Across a score of years.
Perching on the edge of the
Bare mattress - I feel the texture
Of grief of their departure.

The dog belly-flops, nose pointing expectantly
At the outside edge of bedroom doors - waiting
Then, snorting, pads softly downstairs,
Tail between legs, disconsolately,
Uncomprehending, to curl into his basket.

I peer, blindly out of the picture window.
No pulse. No heartbeat. Vision departed.
I ask - questioning, 'Where are our children gone?'
Our life's work. All the rooms in our house
Are empty now.

Aleene Hatchard

114

Bodmin Road 1958

I remember travelling down
Through woods and trees near Doublebois
A whistling train - towards the end
Of epic journey going west.

That afternoon - so long ago
We changed for slower pace of life
Adjacent in the branch line bay
Prairie gently blowing steam.

Thus off we went by Camel banks
Past Grogley Halt with no one there
Wadebridge next where tracks divide
Meandering to Waterloo.

Our destination - Padstow's charms
Few caravans in windswept fields
True Cornwall and her unspoilt coves
Like Mother Ivey's bracing sands.

A fortnight of such carefree days
Then back once more - slow lengthy crawl
To Reading General - cream and brown
Lost Mecca for those 'Castle' names.

Alas, all gone - now railway books
With pictures of a vanished Age
The world's moved on - but mine has stopped
Preserved in time at Bodmin Road.

Steve Glason

Amongst The Trees

A feeling has come over me
Of complete and utter ease
It surrounded me just today
As I walked amongst the trees

The path it took me deeper
Winding on and on
Spotting wildlife here and there
And hearing birds in song

I know why I am comforted
And so very much at ease
It's because I'm not troubled
When I walk amongst the trees.

Gail Goree

Going Back

Back I have been to my playground
To walk the old streets up and down
Privet that once grew green and trim
Replaced by driveways out and in

Pathways once played hopscotch on
Replaced by tarmac the slabs are gone
The kids still skip but without a rope
From school they skip, they've no hope

The green where cricket once was played
Now a car park with tickets to be displayed
Trees on which I used to climb and swing
Gone to make way for an electric thing

Streets that once were empty and bare
Now have cars bumper to bumper there
Doorsteps are no longer cardinal reds
Now they are all white plastic instead.

Swallows muddy nest are no more seen
Replaced by satellite dishes for telly screens
That's why I see no kids at play
They're watching telly day after day

Me, I can see how things have changed
How time has moved on to rearrange
Kids today will grow up blind
They'll have no memories to seek and find.

James E Friday

My Best Friend Memory Lane

My best friend has passed
I am so very sad
She was the best gal that you could ever had
Our friendship started when I sat in with her son
So she could go out with her dear loved one
We played games together until it was time for his bed
Then I would read until his parents returned from their treat
She treated me like a daughter, she called me her second mum
Nothing was too much trouble if you needed any help
When I was not well, she was here all the time
She was so kind, she had a heart of gold
I will always remember her, she will be on my mind
I will always have fond memories of my wonderful friend
God bless you.

Eileen Finlinson

I Remember Grandma

I remember Grandma, the day the telegram came
After that day, things would never be the same
That was the day my life was changed
And everything had to be rearranged
No more laughter - no more fun
My childhood gone, adulthood begun
Her other children came to comfort her and made a commotion
They sent for the doctor who administered a sleeping potion
It was the War Office telegram that she had dreamed of with dread
It said that her son was missing in action and now presumed dead
Then another communication to say her son was a prisoner of war
How Grandma fretted and worried for the son she had bore
Now that the worst of her fears had been realised
One of the worst of human acts that Man had devised
During the long lonely years that her son was locked away
Grandma spent that time on her knees for to pray
When at last the good news came that her son would get his release
Grandma sighed deeply and went to her eternal rest in peace.

Elizabeth Farrelly

Nostalgia Perhaps!

I love to remember the charming ways of the past
And just forget everything when they were not going to last
Summers were hot 'it's the canicule' said my mother
Winters were cold 'time to stay at home' said my father.

After the second war, people appreciated the value of liberty
No one was bored like some young persons; it's a pity
People weren't spoiled with television and techno
But they loved to sit down and listen to the radio.

We were eating organic meals with the greens
No additives, no fast food, just meals for our needs
Mums were at home looking after the children
And all the kids were growing up even.

We didn't have a telephone, now we have five
The life was not so competitive, but fairly alive
No pressure from the media, for dieting and fashion
Everything was subject at a subtle discretion.

Yes, I have some nostalgia of the good old days
Bit in my comfortable home, I love to have my own ways
And if, you ask me to choose between past or present for the best
Give up my appliances, my car. No, I'm afraid there's no contest.

Victorine Lejeune Stubbs

A Requiem

Walking sadly by the silent water
Our boots bruising grass still wet from the storm.
Feeling the wind's breath stealing through the trees
As tears of rain from every bough and twig
Drop, leaf by leaf, upon the sad damp earth.

Somewhere, within the woods a lone thrush calls
Not with the vibrant voice of waking spring,
But soft plaintive songs of passing summer
When swifts and swallows begin to gather
To plot their journey southwards to the sun.

Young coots sail line astern across the lake
Until the wind-borne ripples crease the water
To ride the ducklings on rocking-horse waves,
Then dancing on to kiss the pebbled shore
But, like us, the knowing stones find no joy.

A ring of grey and solemn herons stand
Silent as mourners by the water's edge
Waiting, hunch-backed, for careless fish.
Disturbed, they rise again on leaden wings
And flap away to less troubled waters.

Above the lake, the church stands on its hill
Steepled in a thousand years of history.
Its precarious gravestones leaning over,
Heavy with names and legends of the past
Now lost in weeds and long grass of neglect.

We see the village green below, circled
With dim white figures, silent as herons
Waiting for the careless shot from the crease
But now the light has gone, the game has done.
Soon the restless bulldozers will be here.

John Eccles

The Greengrocer's Shop

Supermarkets spring up all over the place
The death knell of small shops we knew,
Of course it's our fault, we forget times past
And follow new trends that is true.
But just here and there old shops can be found
Where old-fashioned courtesy holds sway
How quaint we say, almost tears in our eyes
The merrily go on our way.

I've heard of one shop in a village quite small
With which superstores cannot compete
An old style greengrocers where everyone goes
With a smile as they walk down the street.
The displays are fantastic in green, red and yellow
Courgettes and peppers and melons so mellow.
Cabbages, cauliflowers, beans and potatoes,
Lettuce and radish and lovely tomatoes.

Behind all the fruit and veg is a riot of flowers
This shop is known to be open all hours.
And once you've met Howard and his wonderful wife
You'll shop there again for the rest of your life.
Supermarkets, who cares, they take all the fun
Out of shopping, as in the old days 'twas done
If you see this shop with bright coloured array
Don't walk past, just call in as you go on your way.

Barbara Dunning

The Past

The past is gone and won't return
But the past remains inside my mind
And inside my heart I can't help but yearn
Searching for something I cannot find
The past is somewhere where I was young
It is a place where I used to dream
Of all the places where I was going
Now it's all the places I have been
The past is ghosts that will not rest
And bridges that will not burn
People I loved and cared for as the best
And of all the things that I still yearn
Because there are still some bridges that will not burn.

Alan Dennis

Southern Magic

I love the south, I love its ambience
Of distant days and well-remembered dreams,
Its genteel air of old-world elegance
Where all is just as lovely as it seems.

I saw it at its best in early spring
When nature wore its fresh resplendent crown.
New life was flowing into everything
And sunny skies had melted winter's frown.

Magnificent magnolias were in flower
Where pink touched white to tinge with roseate hue.
Light winds blew blossoms in a creamy shower
To land on grass bejewelled with the dew.

And night was just as beautiful to me
When darkness veiled the light with soothing hand,
Casting its shades and setting creatures free
To wander where they willed throughout the land.

Like sequins on a velvet canopy
The twinkling stars lit up the midnight sky.
The silvered clouds like sailing ships at sea
Floated athwart the Heaven's nocturnal eye.

The River Walk in San Antonio,
The Cajun village near Lafayette,
And sunset on the Gulf of Mexico;
These are the vistas I cannot forget.

The sound of carriages at Jackson Square,
The mighty Mississippi rolling by,
And noisy revels at the Easter Fair
Joined the cathedral carillon on high.

These vibrant scenes, though rich beyond compare,
Were equalled by the southern welcoming.
The friendliness that I encountered there
Revives sweet memories of that glorious spring.

Celia G Thomas

120

The Secret

We were friends for years,
Shared laughter and tears,
Happily talked for hours and hours,
Took long walks in sunshine and showers;
They said we made a perfect pair,
Yet nothing more than friendship did we share;
You sought my advice when Cupid's arrow hit you,
When love fell apart, I did my best to comfort you;
You teased me playfully about my crushes
And when things went wrong tried to spare my blushes;
The day we had to part, I waved goodbye,
Hiding from you the tear in my eye;
Because the one thing you never knew
Was that secretly I always loved you.

Annabelle Tipper

The Late Eighties

That was the era of the yuppies
That strode into the world
With gadgets all anew
When all was the latest gadget
In every form
When all the conversations
Were of the latest sound system
And how the house price had risen
And how many shares could be bought
For how little money
And how much could be done
Oh Lord, how much.

We could all be millionaires
If we put our minds to it
And how we all thought of that and what was to come
And how it all would go on and on
Us partaking of the bonanza
With our filofaxes
And our new computers
Yet we did not know the Internet
And mobile phones were a thing of the future
But how much money there seemed to be then
Before it all went pear-shaped
And vast currents of potential disappeared
Again in the full-blown recession
Of the early nineties.

Alasdair Sclater

A Sandwich Between Friends

It seems like only yesterday
When we lived between two friends
Numbers 9 and 5 and we were 7
Where Catrina Avenue wends.
Now Allen was a master
Of fishing, if you please,
You should have seen his freezer -
It even attracted bees.
Later we went our fishing
In a dear little motorboat
We'd follow the seagulls swooping
Throwing lines over with a float.
The sky was blue above us,
The air was salty and sweet,
We could hardly cope with the number
Of fish! What a treat!
Our memories also extend
To Katrina and Robin, her friend
Who with Allen and Jennifer, the eldest
Made a wonderful threesome blend.
We owe all this to the Skudders
In whose home we were lucky to stay
While they were in Malaysia
Their kindness won the day.
I haven't yet mentioned Beverley,
The spokeswoman for the three
Who with Jason and Mary her mother
Made us welcome as welcome could be.
We thank you so much for your kindness
And we wish Allen, at our behest
To hope for a gradual recovery
Our love and good wishes - *the best!*

Valma Streatfield

The Opening Of A Field Of Corn

(For the binder - Circa: 47)

Wi' slight stooping torso and a-bending of knees
And much swinging of arms wi' a pendulum's ease,
The swishing of the razor-sharp blade runs so sweet,
As he's shuffling forward wi' piston-like feet.

To the right and to the left across him deft sweeping -
Cutting and gathering, the ears all a-leaping,
In lines neatly lay'n' there by a man wi' a scythe -
With granite-faced features, so relentlessly lithe.

The effort with which his monotonous motion,
Be like any wave that rolls o'er any ocean,
Seems to the observer so natur'lly gifted -
The way of the rewing o'corn that he's shifted.

And around and around of the field twice over,
Revealing the budding young vetches and clover,
A swain there be after, fain bunching and tying -
As fast as he's cutting, be sheaves there a-lying.

The headland be opened, the binder be reaping
And the sheaves there be stooked in rows for the keeping.
The scythe be a-whetted and the rabbit and hare -
Be running for cover a-most everywhere.

Derek Haskett-Jones

Love's Sweet Memories

When only nineteen
we walked
lover's path
beneath an avenue of trees
engulfed in one another's talk.
Lover's sweet innocent dreams,
we took one another's hearts.
Promised only in death, ever to part.
What fun we, hummed the songs,
of those days
sixty years on from then,
still humming old songs,
which were new then.
Forever lingers on,
genuine love forever lives on.
Sweet memories of them.

Bryan George Clarke

Getting Locked Out

I can amuse myself
Laugh and cry
Having understood the reason
How and why
What a misery to get
Locked out of your door
This happened to me
Times four
A split second of forgetfulness
Could cause immense worry and
It's the culprit I suppose who makes
The fool out of me in a hurry

Now I have a concept
Of a foolproof remedy
Both ends of a piece of string tied to
My handbag and the keys
Hopefully this is the simple
Solution to this malady

Ha, ha, ha, friends
I am a winner with this remedy
No more of falling
Into this misery
Much better than
Undergoing therapy.

Kamala Perera

Memories

Memories of winter days waiting for the train to arrive
Bringing Mum and Dad on their way to see me
I remember the big hug, the twinkle in his eyes,
The love in his smile and Mum warm in her loving smile.

We did a spot of shopping, for it was Christmas time
And tea and scones in the Grand Hotel, was so divine
Then a taxi took us to my home, a nice drink after tea
Music played and smiles.

Sadly, all that is gone forever, for Dad passed away
But I will always have that special memory
To keep in my heart, forever.

Gillian Robson

Echoes In The Park

When I walk through the Park,
I remember the time,
When I was a child
I skipped to a rhyme.

All my friends would join in
We would sing with one voice,
Many rhymes we could chant
For we had plenty of choice.

Day and night, trains would shunt
Up and down the track,
Carrying goods from the docks
To the factory and back.

Once in the Park
There stood a great Hall,
Now there stands a mighty Palace
Just for the game of football.

The streets are now silent
But the houses have gone,
For its residents and children
Have all moved on.

In my heart, happy memories
Have left their mark,
When I was young
And lived in *Trafford Park*.

Jean-Ruth

Apple Charlotte Days

Remembering the apple Charlotte days
In the autumn of my youth brings much joy.
Collecting fallen walnuts with sunrays
Forming shafts between the branches. The toy
Left in the grass to rust and rot away.
The morning mist so cooling, yet greeting
To the dawn. The rustic leaves swirl and sway
Until they drop to rot and feed, meeting
Mother Earth once more to blend and enrich;
Then sleeping for a while, just resting first
Quiet in slumber, to form the new pitch
So rich in colour, crisp, fresh, newest thirst

For spring in all its splendour, joyful song . . .
To cast its royal carpet, nature's throng.

Pearl M Burdock

Cathy

Yesterday I was sixteen again, for a while
Or so it seemed, until my world stood still, when we parted.
It started with a smile, then your sparkling eyes shone as stars
Into my lonely sky, lighting up my empty soul
Filling the barren waste of my lost yearning, searching, hoping heart,
So wanting love that's true, but too scared to give it away
And feel that lovely pain, then loosing again.
Saving lost hope of finding such a gem again are few. I pray.
Then my dreams come true - for when we met that day
All my senses came alive.
But I fell, let go the rope of reason
For fences facing had fallen away
And for a day or two more than I could ever hope, came true
Thank you, Cathy
Please stay my friend
Not someone I once knew.

Yesterday I was sixteen again, or so it seemed
But now I am old with the pain of young lost years
For only love can break your heart
Forgotten Hell when lovers part
Long gone but found again at last
I didn't seek it, but I did jump over the cliff for real
Old scars never really heal and those who took part of your heart
With them are special, yet we seek them still.
The new ones hurt as before and bleed when lost love tears
At the crying heart
For when lovers part, it's sad, especially when it's been so long ago
That I felt this way before have passed
For when you showed me the door, in case I tasted that love
You hold for him.
Respect for those before, made me love you even more
Than at the start.
We shouldn't part, my old heart can't take anymore lost love
Salty tears are all that's left - for memories are past
And today is tomorrow's dreams.

Terry Davy

Hymns To Yesteryear

Suddenly, when certain songs return,
They are caressing me anew,
When the fires of youth, inherent, burn;
Once more my dance dress, powder blue,
Evokes delight, satin, sashed and fine.
Sentiment, not sickly sweet, but pure
Commandeers that static heart of mine;
Memories, through music, breed allure.
My reveries redirect idea,
Reborn, ballads honey what was home,
Bringing half-forgotten moments near;
Annals of experience I comb,
Lust and love, desire and splintered dreams
Now recede, at lilt of violin
I thrill to familiar colour schemes.
Are they really gone, my kith and kin?
Should they haunt how gentle are their ways,
The silent folk wafting through a score
Of sound, legacy of former days.
Subtle hint brings forth what went before.
Now nostalgic nuances provide
Peep behind the curtain of despair;
A house evolves with Pa and Ma inside
And always a part of me is there.

Ruth Daviat

The Magic Of Remembering

In the magic of our childhood
There are dreams on which to feast
We are always looking forward
To the most and not the least
Thought we lack the worldly treasures
We can always stand and stare
At the shining lamp that pleasures
For the magic's always there
As we go deep into age
Some still hear the sound of lute
And with joy, turn every page
To dimming light, sound almost mute.

Roland Seager

Snow Day!

The first flakes of snow falling,
Like a flurry of pixie dust.
The excitement is growing,
Layer upon layer,
Like the snow.

Stillness settles outside,
Traffic halted, schools closed.
But inside every child,
A quiet buzz is growing.

Pulling on Wellingtons and gloves,
The stillness is broken by childish shouts.
Coldness seems forgotten,
As the snowballs begin to fly.

The street is filled with laughter,
A flurry of activity once more.
Teamwork flourishing,
To build and shovel and throw!

As day turns to evening,
The snow to grey sludge,
Weary children trudge home.
Gloves soaked through
And noses pink,
But with memories that will never melt.

Naomi Cumberland

Memories Of Mother

Safe and secure, the feeling
When the large hand clasped in mine
A smiling face looked down at me
Then everything was fine
No responsibility, just playing in the field
Gathering wild flowers, as by the pond I kneeled
Here you are, dear Mother, as I handed her the blooms
Soon she would put them in a vase to brighten up the rooms
Happy childhood memories
When I was very small
And parents seemed like giants
When they really weren't at all

J M Chaffer

Thursday's Child

We met again from over the years
And talked as siblings do
Of memories long past -
Things which made us laugh or smile.

Yet, your fortunes of late
Were of a bitter brew of remembrance,
Lying in a pool between the years.
But you were Thursday's Child
And as foretold, your path would be long
(Sometimes thorny!)

See, now it is time for you to join your kin -
Those who have loved you in years gone by
And together we will share our past times;
There lies a golden treasure from our yesteryears.
You know I am a child of the Sabbath,
You witnessed my collision into the world -
It was written that such a child, would be
'Blithe, bonny, good and gay',
I doubt I have been,
Yet our stories can entwine;
A chequered pathway to a glorious sunset.

Dorothy Brookes

I Remember It Well

I was just a little girl
Aged eight years old and happy
When suddenly,
My world was quickly turned upside down.
Along came Adolph Hitler
Living in a German town
He planned to destroy our lovely isle with force!
However, with help from other countries
Alongside our British troops
We gained our homeland back again
And they told him
To take his blooming hook!

Joyce Hargreaves

Lunch With Nancy, Lady Astor

A scholarship kid
In the 1940s,
Home, two up, two down,
Outside loo and
One parent family
There was much to prove.

The 'paid for' kids
Looked down on us,
But hard work paid off,
A sixth form honour
Came my way and
I became Head Girl.

One task of mine,
On the school speech day,
Was the vote of thanks
To the visiting luminary;
None other than Lady Astor
From famous Clivedon nearby.

I practised on a soap box
In our steamy kitchen and
When the great night came,
I knew the speech by heart,
It somehow pleased Her Ladyship
Who enquired of my chosen career.

To teach, was my burning desire,
But we were undeniably poor.
College fees were out of reach.
Miracles! A whole week later,
Came the wonderful news
That Lady A would fund my fees!
Wow!

And I had a date for lunch
With her at the Clivedon Manor,
What a day it was!
Two buses and a long mile walk
Gymslip swinging, pigtails bobbing,
I arrived at the huge gates.

The lodge keeper checked,
And I was on my way
Up the drive of the enormous house.
The bell pull was tricky, but
Soon the butler ushered me in,
To the book-stacked library.

Lady A swept in and confirmed
My college place was safe!
With that, in to lunch.

Memories Are Made Of This

The doors opened to reveal
A gigantic hall and long tables
Set for dozens and dozens!

Then, a far door opened and
In they came; Canadian military
Housed in the grounds, pips galore!
They filled the vacant places.
Pips to the right, pips to the left,
Plus Lady A and rookie me! (17)

With a canteen of cutlery
Beside the set places,
It was a challenge, but beady eyes
Followed the done thing, till
The arrival of a half-moon plate
To be filled with? Yes - salad.

All was well, then condiments
Came my way, the salt, small heap,
But the pepper - I shook hard -
As I did in our steamy kitchen -
Oh no! It cascaded over lettuce
Like sand on the seashore!

I had no option, I had to eat.
Each mouthful was a choker
But I kept my cool, with
False smiles of satisfaction.
I can't recall what else we ate,
I don't remember saying goodbye,

But I *do* remember pepper!

Jean McPherson

A Brief Delight

I heard the clear, crisp sound of hooves on hard ground,
With their rhythmically tuneful style.

Then they came into view and delighted my eye,
With their colours of chestnut, dapple and brown.

So mighty they looked and so majestic,
Like beautiful moving sculptures.

My hand wanted to reach over
And stroke their silky-smooth bodies,
But they were past me so swiftly, too swiftly.
These horses of noble breed.

And I watched them trot away, their bushy tails swaying,
An enchanting moment in a wonderful day.

Garry Mitchell

Blitz - Avonmouth 1940

'Come on boys! Get up twins! The guns are all firing!
Oh, come on now! Wake up! There's bombers above!
Come on now! Come on! Can't you hear the bombs falling?
Put on your wellies, your coats and your gloves . . .'

I slid out of bed, but my knees were of jelly,
My brain still slept . . . of senses bereft.
My coat fought with me, I couldn't find my wellies,
And when I did, my right foot was my left.
We stumbled downstairs, not daring a light,
Out thro' the kitchen. Out to the backdoor.
And stood staring out at the blackness of night
And 'twas then that I caught my first sight of war . . .

Searchlights were waltzing to the tune of the gunfire
And shrapnel was raining, *ping-panging* around,
The shells were a-bursting, like bright stars a-twinkling
In a mad pandemonium of sight and of sound.
And flares there were, dripping white fire from the sky,
Flames dribbled, a scene most macabre,
'Gainst black of the sky and ten thousand stars,
And the flares hanging there, like huge candelabra . . .
And the noise! Oh, the noise! A chaos of sound,
As down the long path we ran, all helter-skelter,
Guns banging, bells clanging, bombs bursting around,
As we ran down the path to our air raid shelter.

And two thousand seagulls flew about in the dark
All shrieking and calling, in a sound oh, so sad,
As they all flew around, staring down at the flames,
And asking each other, are all humans mad . . . ?

John Whittock

Silent Moments

Memories are like cobwebs . . .
floating, intangible, ethereal strands
totally unseen
but there
to float into our minds when vulnerable
. . . the plate clean . . .
with room for delicious cold shivering
thoughts of delight,
of moments gone by
never to return.

Margaret Kaye

Springtime In The Garden As A Child

I remember so well
The yellow carpet of the daffodils
And blue of the bluebells
And the delicate flower of the primrose
Were all signs of spring.
As trees revealed their green
And buds appeared, we knew
That spring wasn't far away.
We thanked the Lord that winter was passing
And spring and summer were on the way.
Sometimes the rain was heavy
And sometimes it was very light.
Rain was sent to keep the flowers
And us their beauty in spring.

Jean Martin-Doyle

Childhood Memories

It's nice to walk down memory lane.
Recall childhood long ago.
I often sit and ponder now
in the firelight's afterglow.

We made our own amusement.
Days spent in harmless fun.
Hide-and-seek and hopscotch,
then home when day is done.

Sometimes we could be naughty,
but Mum nipped it in the bud,
'You won't go out again,' she'd say,
'Till you learn how to be good.'

We learned a lot from discipline,
knew just how far to stray,
but our friendly village policeman
would always guide us on our way.

No television in those days,
nor the latest computer game.
We didn't have a 'Nanny State'
saying parents were to blame!

Spare the rod and spoil the child
the adage of the day!
But a parent's undivided love
will always be the way!

Greta Gaskin

133

Spirit Of Love

Today's today
You sit and dream.
Yesterday was yesterday
Is where you long to be,
Living with your memories
That's treasured by the score,
Thinking thoughts of the love they brought
To last you evermore.

The tears you shed
A heartache revealed,
Others see just how you really feel.
Sadness turns to happiness
Which outweighs your hopes and dreams,
Lifting your heart
For the world to see,
What memories you have given me.

I did not sit weeping
We never said goodbye.
I yelled! I love you - shouting to the sky,
Taking my heart with you
As I held you close to me.
No time for my heart
To go to pieces,
As I knew you still needed me.

No time for heartache
No time for tears,
No bonds broken
In years and years.
Releasing your hands
As they take you away.
Now it's time
For heartache and pain.

Forever in my heart you'll be
That is a treasured memory.
Dreams remaining
Of bygone days,
But most of all
Love hasn't changed.
Here I sit with a heavenly sigh
My angel on high - you did not die.

Margaret J Franklin

Recalling

'Bring the butter when you come in,'
From kitchen to dining room
I forgot
Ask me who I sat next to at school
I know straight away
And yet
So long ago and far away it seems
Cherished memories flow
Like dreams
Picking cowslips in the fields in spring
Blackberries from the autumn hedge
Remembering
Coal fires burning in the winter stove
We huddled round the wireless set
Hearing Uncle Mac
White socks on at Easter time
Wool stockings packed away
Sunshine every day
Of those I knew remain but few
Chance meetings can recall
Reminiscence for all.

Betty Gilman

The Old Photograph

A boy lay laughing in the sun
In summertime, in summertime,
A boy for whom all life was fun,
For whom the best had just begun
In summertime, sweet summertime.

And as the years went rolling past,
In autumn time, in autumn time,
The boy became a man, at last
And life was earnest, life was fast,
In autumn time, brave autumn time.

And now his seasons were but few
In wintertime, in wintertime;
The man in age and wisdom grew
And found content in all he knew
In wintertime, kind wintertime.

But, through the years, my picture shows
In summertime, in summertime,
A happy youngster in repose,
Within whose face the laughter glows,
In summertime, sweet summertime.

Pleione Tooley

One Hundred And Twenty Roast Dinners And Counting

I was born in 1931,
No computers or mobile phones for company,
Just the love of my mother,
A memory of a winter's coal fire,
A kiss on my cheek at night,
A warm smile to start the day,
What a safe life.

Time passed, I did this, I did that,
I learned this, I lost that!
Sometimes tears filled my eyes.

I met my first girlfriend, Vera, when I was twenty-three,
She worked in the bakery,
The best-looking girl I ever saw,
At that moment, I felt free.
In time, she fell for another,
This was life, a hurting time.
Love returned again, Rose, my wife for fifty years,
A good talker, a good thinker, a good everything
As our seven children showed!

At the age of seventy-six
What's left to do or fix?
How many roast dinners are left to eat?
One hundred and twenty and counting,
Maybe more, maybe less.

Andrew Ryan

Chelmsford

Orange brick steaming
Shimmering metal abstracted
Arched viaduct above my turning roundabout
So much grass
Mixed with slabs of crisp cornet
White vanilla ice cream
Of my childhood memory dream
Melting in the shafts of sunlight.

Graham Peter Metson

Hedgehog Brush

Being nosy, wanting to explore
Climbing the forbidden stairs
Spotting someone coming
Then rolling downstairs, to the floor.

Calling out to Mummy
'You've left your brush outside'
Her reply, 'I brought it inside'
And finding it was really a hedgehog!

Knelt on the chair
Gazing through the window
Looking up at the sky
Dreaming, imagining another world
Then moving and finding my knees
Wedged in the seat slats.

Playing in the garden
Desperately trying to do a cartwheel
And landing flat on my back.
Walking down the road
Not looking where I was going,
Bumping into a tree and
Sitting in the corner with
Butter on the bump!

Mary Stevens

Lost Places

It's the place I hold so dear
Church bells, sunshine and cricket here
The very place I hold with affection
Friends, kind people with fond recollection

Now you step outside into the street
Where are the neighbours you never meet?
Litter on the pavements, on that you can depend
In towns, cars line the streets, end to end

Dogs' mess on the carpet, gum on your shoes
Spray paint everywhere, vandalised loos
Where is my town? It's no longer here
Where is the place my memory holds dear?

Suzanne Tucker

Memories Are Made Of This

Amid Ox And Ass And Other Animals

Never deep or crisp or even, the 'White Christmas' promise
faded as dawn-drawn curtains revealed another dull day.
Though Danny Kaye smiled, he lied through his
snowflake glistening teeth, as Bing and his saccharine crew
sing sleigh bell baloney in the Hollywood false, flat backdrop -
as they did every Christmas.
The only snow was sprayed on the tree;
artifice compensating reality again - as always.
No herald angels carolled, though 'Songs of Praise'
would raise the roof fund high as Christmas Day clean faces
shone and thundered wondrously for the TV cameras.
No celestial choirs. Only a discord of collecting Cubs croaking
cut-price carols asthmatically on the doorstep.
The heavenly host was Round Tablers, jingle-belling tins
with Santa ho-ho-ho on a lorry tricked out in lights
with piped music and a crappy crib, a wonky-legged donkey
and a tottering ox. No adoring shepherds to complete the scene.
They must have been still watching their flocks, or 'Hawaii Five-O'.
Good will to all men, meant armistice with sisters
until presents forced from unwilling piggy banks were exchanged
and hostilities could resume. The spoils of war
were guarded jealously, except for the usual gaudy tie
from dotty Aunt Dotty (who wasn't a real aunt). That item
that gave the lie about the thought that counts, I would slip
in the rubbish bin, under greasy chicken bones and
ripped wrapping paper. What malfunction of the adult heart
thought 'Teach Yourself Mathematics' right for a
ten-years rip-roaring cowboy who coveted that annual
with more lust than was suitable for the sacred season? For all I
know, Roy Rogers lies still in the newsagents, unrescued under
the scalping knife. But amid the pile of intricate, expensive gifts,
The greatest joy, my star of wonder and light, was a little
Indian canoe that shot from a cracker, Sioux arrow straight into
my Davy Crocket heart.
Gunmetal-grey, an inch long - no more - it was as sweet as a nut
cracked whole from its shell. All that invalid, rump-picked winter,
when not even plumptious Barbara daily jabbing me full of penicillin,
nor the artful blandishments of Enid Blyton, could outshine that
little peace on Earth that rode the rapids of my bedridden blankets
and Niagara-ed my knees, I learnt the joy of little things, the pleasure
of small treasures and knew in my cynical heart of hearts
the sham of gaudy expense. And that if the shepherds saw anything
that night, they calmly turned aside and continued washing their socks.

Keith Linley

The Pedlar

Remember the pedlar who came calling at your door
Carrying in his suitcase, many things in store
Plenty were the goods, for the lady and the gent
Shaving soap, bath salts or perhaps a drop of scent

He had clothes brush, nail brush, brushes for the hair
Shoe brush and floor brush and laces by the pair
Hand cream and hair cream, cream to put on shoes
Face cream and Brylcreem and cream to clean the loos

He had shirts and he had ties
Dressed and working socks
Stockings for the ladies
And hankies in a box
He had scarves and head squares
Silk and linen too
Jerseys and pullovers
Both polo neck and crew

He had safety pins and needles
Drawing pins and tacks
Polish for the brown shoes
Aye and polish for the black
He had zips and buttons
Darning wool and thread
Covers for the cushions and pillowcases for the bed

He had hairgrips, hairpins, pins for the hat
Cufflinks, collar studs, both for front and back
Gloves for the hands, slippers for the feet
Corkscrew and shoehorn
And a bairn's dummy teat

He had leather belts and cloth belts
Brollies for the rain
Under vest and underpants, bras to take the strain
Aye, many were the items, he carried in his case
But now the man has vanished
Lost without a trace.

Peter P Gear

Treasured Memories

It seems like only yesterday
When a little girl was born,
The year was nineteen-forty
With war, the country torn.
Now as I sit and reminisce
Precious memories I do recall,
Thankful of parent's love and care
When young, innocent and small.

The summer days were long and warm
And winters deep in snow,
No television, what did we do?
Played games, outside did go.
Then off to school, so blithe and gay
Proud pupil and scholar to be,
Respecting our teachers and elders too
Joyous days were all trouble free.

I was a one and only child
Who found it very lonely,
My home was in the country wild
It was very nice, if only,
I'd had a friend to play with me
On Saturday and Sunday,
I found it such a bore, you see
I always longed for Monday.

On leaving school, I started work
Fifty years I was employed,
A rapport with friends and public
Every minute of that enjoyed.
My wedded bliss was thirty years
Then my soulmate passed away,
Leaving my life with such a void
And I wish he was here today.

With a loving son we were blest
Who made our life complete,
Remembering well our blissful times
Then our destiny we had to meet.
My loyal family and trusty pets
Helped me to face a new day,
Abundant memories, so happy and warm
Forever with me, will stay.

Rosalind A Sim

Childhood Memories

I was born in 1931 in Portsmouth
We were very poor, but life was fun
It was safe to play outside
We made a bat out of a banana box
With a rag wrapped around, to avoid splinters
Girls and boys played together
Whatever the weather.

We had a tin bath out on the garden wall
And it was brought in on bath night
So cosy in front of the fire,
Other days, we slid down the coal chute
From the pavement, on an old sack
Into the basement, then ran up the stairs
To begin again, covered in coal dust.

A gas mantle gave erratic shadows
On the wall at bedtime
Mum put a brick in the oven to get hot
Then wrapped it in an old blanket
And put it in the bed
And although we were poor, we were well fed
Suet puddings, apple pies, stew and dumplings
In great supply.

I sat on the mat by the fire
With a slice of bread on a toasting fork
No Big Macs, no French fries,
Only smoke in my eyes
I now have modern things
And remember with fond thoughts
My childhood days
When we had freedom to roam and play.

J M Waller

A Kiss

Two hearts
Beating in one place,
Yours and mine
In cold and wet snow.

Pleasure is all yours and mine.

Barry Welburn

Christmas 1926

It was a very cold December morn
And snow lay thick upon the ground,
One felt such magic all around,
It was just ten days before Christmas,
Frost glistened in the morning light
Nipping at my feet and hands
But quite unnoticed as I was warmed
By thoughts of the errand I was on.
My mission was to an Aladdin's cave:
A little shop which had everything
From rocking horses, to whip and tops
Dolls of all sizes and little toy shops
Nativity sets and some one could make
Bright coloured balls, pencils and paints,
Red trykes, play bricks and little green barrows,
Colouring books, annuals, toy trowels and rakes,
Coloured paper, bright baubles, tinsel galore,
To make fancy dresses, or decking the tree,
Oh yes! I almost forgot about me!
Mechanical toys, lots of models to make,
From this wondrous collection, I was to take
My family's presents for Christmas.
At just eight months past eleven
To be on such a mission was, to me, Heaven
And for me it could have been quite a thrill
Were it not for the fact that Mother was ill,
But having arrived with my box of 'surprises',
To see Mum's smile and appreciative tear
Was quite my best present for Christmas that year.

Ethel M Lang

Flying Our Kites

I lived in London as a child
No garden to play in, or TV to see.
I listened to radio's Children's Hour
With my brothers, whilst having our tea.

Bad things did happen in those days
So no playing out in the street,
But flying a kite on Parliament Hill
Now that was a real good treat.

Just little kites, but oh! what fun!
To run down the hill holding the string
And see our kite flying way up aloft
And wish we could do the same thing.

Elsie Whipp

Rainbow's End

Green hills once, not far away
Where children cycled up and down
Grass covered slopes, avoiding bumps
And where wild rabbits used to play
In shade small shy faces found in bloom
Secret camps, hidden trails
Tracking chalked arrows woodland pathways
Imaginary pastimes not, remembered outdoor fun
Childhood carefree yesterdays.

Those green hills now flattened
Beneath concrete manmade motorways
Woods, lush fields and meadows replaced
By monotonous drone, power-driven wheels
Gone forever once upon a time simple pleasure
Global fashion today demands extravagant
In many ways more costly leisure.

Luggage runway stacked yet more runways planned
Mainly tourism need, go now pay later spree
Flight paths multiply overhead peace shattering noise
Day by day ongoing peak disruption
Traveller and travel agent joy pin numbers
'Rainbow's End' modern-day pocket gold corruption.

Observant nature-loving people stunned
Trees wilt, shrubs wildlife suffers too
As this island green, visible signs non-survival
Excess luxury travellers seemingly care not
Diesel petrol fumes, spiral spewed pollution
Waste ecology ages late, recycled flotsam salvage
Ash beyond challenge, the legacy before children of evolution.

Mildred F Barney

Strange Memories

As a child I remember,
A strange thing happened to me,
As I was walking up the stairs,
Because I saw a man who wasn't there.
Looking again in the morning,
I saw he was still there.
I tried to look away,
But he was still there,
I wished that man would go away . . .

Andrew Pratt

The Orchard

Remembering my childhood days when I would wake
And in the orchard, hear the hens, the sound they'd make
A soft and pleasant sound as they would strut and scratch
In the brown earth they'd make a powdery patch
And sometimes sit in soft brown feathery mounds
And rest contented, hearing country sounds
Or suddenly squawk and fight over some seeds
They'd rush to peck up 'midst the scrubby weeds.

'Come on, arise and shine,' my mum would call
'Get up, get dressed, a lovely day, no school at all.'
And with my friends, I'd run, climb trees and play
Or pick wild flowers to make a small bouquet
To give my mum who'd find a jar to fill
And place this treasured gift upon the window sill
Then after lunch we'd soon be off once more
Continuing the game we'd left before.

Sometimes in the orchard, we would stay
Be near my house when skies turned dull and grey
And if it rained we'd colour, draw or paint
Some trees, a garden, a cottage, old and quaint
Kids think old-fashioned were those days, it seems
We had such simple pleasures, but we had our dreams
So if sometimes I'm lost in thought and sigh
I'm wandering through those days in my mind's eye.

A Heathershaw

My Grandad

Lonely through war, you took my hand
And showed me delights as we walked on the sand,
I loved to brush your thick white hair.

Lonely in peacetime and growing up fast
You taught me to write and win at draughts
Your thick white hair got thinner on top.

Careless in teens of the love that you gave
Draughts was a bore and discos the rave
I stopped stroking your thick white hair.

Lonely in age, I take your hand in mine
Let you win at draughts and say you are fine
Your thick white hair fading to yellow.

Lonely through loss, missing your dear love
And memories only aren't nearly enough
Never again to touch your thick white hair.

Judith Palser

The Abusive Father

I tried to avoid hurt,
Perhaps I sounded curt,
Your age and unchanging dialogue,
Bears no impact, this I log . . .
I articulated how I felt,
Still . . . verbal blow you dealt,
With no comprehension of my life,
You bear malice like a twisting knife . . .
Dictating here, dictating there,
Opinionated with empathy rare,
Always ready to inflict,
Emotional trauma with resulting conflict . . .
Never there as I had hoped,
God knows how I have coped,
Couldn't walk me down the aisle,
Others thought . . . oh, how vile . . . !
Didn't speak for one year,
I had not complied, had I my dear!
Becoming a parent altered things,
With the tenderness it brings,
You spoke to me and eased some pain,
However, trusting you can never be again . . .
Because no matter how I feel,
Your verbal blows are always the deal . . .

Liz Edmonds

Memories Are Made Of This

I remember the days as a little child,
The warmth of the sun and the air so mild,
When life was full of hope and joy,
A skipping rope, my favourite toy,
Then, as the days and years flew by,
Time had gone, as a blink of the eye,
Friendships were made that lasted for years,
With fun and laughter, joy and tears,
A newborn babe to hug and kiss,
Fond memories are made of this.

Barbara Rowley-Blake

The Learning Curve

We formed the crew in Jerusalem in deepest Palestine
Six of us, including Tom who thought he had served his time.
For Tom had done two tours of Ops and fancied taking leave
Starting a third with a crew of sprogs he felt somewhat aggrieved.

His rank was Flying Officer so he wore a thin blue band
We used to call him Skipper in the way of Coastal Command.
The rest of the crew were NCOs, Co-pilot Nav and three Wops
The Skipper's task was to team us up, then fly us all on Ops.

In the second's seat sat Paddy, who sported an Irish brogue,
Bubbles the Nav, a Mersey lad and quite a likeable rogue.
Then three of us as Wop/A/g's Eric, me and Skelly
Destined to fly that fine machine we all knew as the Welly.

Our posting to an OTU was delayed by adverse weather.
Surrounded now by orange groves, at last we reached Ein Shemer.
The Coastal role required the Wops with ASV to wrestle
An early radar system used to detect a surface vessel.

The Welly that we flew in was called the Stickleback
Spiked with aerials nose to fin, the enemy's subs to track.
With these arrays for Search and Home we soon learnt the drill
When the closing blip was central, you were lined up for the kill.

Our training now intensified as we quartered the Eastern Med
We practised flying searches square and creep-in-line ahead.
And homed on tiny fishing boats that gave a good return
Occasionally doing a shoot-up run to give us all a burn.

We'd never flown at night before and wondered how we'd fare,
Our Skipper said, 'Don't worry lads, I know a special prayer.'
The Wops took turns at the radar, a change from *dah, dah, ditting*.
First watch for me was the radar searching the Med for shipping.

I saw some blips on the radar scope still some distance away
Selecting the aerials to Homing, I switched on the Yagi array.
The blips now straddled the centre at thirty-five miles dead ahead
I passed on this gen to the Skipper, 'Roger, keep looking,' he said.

In the rear turret was Skelly, who asked permission to change
We passed in the dark on the catwalk the ships now into range
'The ships are below us,' said Skelly, updating the radar report
Seated now behind the guns, there's not much to look at, I thought.

But flashing past came tracers, arcing through the night
Not mentioned at our briefing, this gave me quite a fright.
Switching the mic on quickly, 'I think we're being shot at,' I said
The Skipper responded with, 'Roger, I think I'm allergic to lead.'

Memories Are Made Of This

'Swing your turret around,' said the Skipper, 'have a shufti about.'
'You're seeing sparks from an engine, if not, then give me a shout.'
I did as the Skipper requested and had to agree, he was right
It's quite unknown for an engine to shoot down an aircraft at night.

Landing, I braced for the ribbing, the jokes I thought I deserved
Just put it down to experience, a part of the steep learning curve.
I was saved by the bell in the morning, our OTU training complete
The very next day we were posted to join 221 Squadron in Greece.

Ron Houghton

The Life Of A Farmer

Oh, to be a farmer
Now that harvest time has come
I used to follow the binder
When the corn has been ripened by the sun

We used to stack the sheaves in stocks
As the binder turned them out
Sometimes the binder twine got clogged
And the sheaves would not come out

Of course, it's different now
It's combine harvesters today
And multi-furrowed plough
It's much easier and looks like child's play

But some things never change
The sun still ripens the corn
The farmer still surveys his range
And still rises with the dawn

They sow the seed in the soil
And watch it spring into life
In the field all day they toil
Then go home to the wife

The farmers do not get the credit
They so richly deserve
They provide us with the food we eat
We, the public, that they serve

So the next time you sit at the table
Spare a thought for the farmer
And be glad that he was able
To drive that tractor and the binder.

William G Evans

Echoes

There are so many memories we all keep in store,
Some people like to listen, to others, you're just a bore.
But to us, these memories are special, we keep them very close
And when we're feeling sad or blue, we just take a dose.
We reminisce on childhood, those happy, carefree days,
The games we played, we all enjoyed, in many different ways.
Time to us then was endless, it just went on and on,
We'd be tired, but happy, when the day was done.
I remember the first steps my grandson took, tottering towards me,
A great big smile upon his face, as pleased as he could be.
Remembering walks in the countryside, trailing behind my dad
And him telling me about 'those days' when he was just a lad.
Ah! Those unforgettable moments walking barefoot by the sea,
Hand in hand with my man, who only had eyes for me.
And now the golden days of autumn are knocking at my door,
I look back on those memories much more than before.
Memories are but echoes of a past life, now gone,
But if we listen carefully, we can hear every one.
They stay with us forever, to hug close or to share,
Our little piece of Heaven we know is always there.

Iris Taylor

The Love Of My Life

Sometimes I daydream - I'm back in '53,
This lovely person takes my hand and smiles at me.
I wasn't to know then, he'd be the love of my life,
Or that someday, much later, I'd become his wife.

I was in a daze on our wedding day,
We were _so_ happy, though skies were grey.
The years that followed were wonderful too
And our love for each other just grew and grew.

Suddenly, this lovely person was taken from me!
He was loving and kind, so why should this be?
At such a young age he shouldn't have died,
I was in shock, and _so_ angry - oh! how I cried!

He's in my thoughts every day, I miss him so much,
What I would give, just to feel his touch.
The days seem longer, and at night I'm alone,
I _wish_ I could chat with him - on the phone!

Jeannette Kelly

Shipton Hill

As I wandered upon the brow of the hill
Our tiny village seems hushed and still
The spring flowers are now in bloom
Chasing away winter's cold and gloom
The little snowdrops were the first to appear
But now the beautiful primrose is here
Daffodils like golden trumpets herald the spring
And the promises of the forest, bluebells cling
In amongst the trees on the hill
I love this pretty place and always will

I'm gazing down from this heavenly place
The breeze like an angel's kiss touched my face
Warm sunshine flows all around
But showery raindrops come falling down
Blue River Bourne like a ribbon threaded through
You sparkle in the sun, all glittering and new
I will be sad when you disappear
When summer sunshine blazes hot down here
Little birds building nests in the hedges
For little chicks listen now to their parents' pledges

But now, as I wander towards the old track
My thoughts and memories come flooding back
To days gone by so long ago
When we were children, I want to go
Back to those days when we played here
In the old house on the croft so dear
We used to pick cherries down by the gate
Run up the old steps to the top and wait
We played up here all summer long
It makes me sad to know that these days are gone.

Josie Smith

An Engaging Saturday

You saw the jewellery display and
Pointed to the rings
With a hint, a sigh and
That glint in your eye,
For you knew I'd return to
Buy one of those sparkly things.

John Edward McBride

What We Had

What we had together
Was so special
A love that grew
That blossomed
With time
You never
Wanted things
A gentleness
A strength within
Your ways so kind
So precious
Did I find
Like a solid rock
You were there
Your wants few
And brought
Us together
From teenage years
To older years be
A man, a family
You loved so well
There through good
And sad times
Deep within
What you did
I wore your ring
Placed upon my finger
A band of gold
You were there
We laughed and cried
But still
By my side
The years, the miles
Children, grandchildren
And great-grandchildren
Each one
A special place
Within my heart
These are memories
So rich, deep within
The heart.

Maureen Thornton

Memories Are Made Of This

Oliver

The still proud head
Grizzled by the tears of age
Eyes dimmed with the cast of years
Reminders of the passage of time

All were forgotten when we walked
My companion of many years
Sought out the still warm scents
As he scurried along the darkened street

The familiar intransigence
On finding that 'special spot'
The inevitable battle when I walked on
Strong, despite his size, he reluctantly acceded

For those few moments, young again
Passing all too quickly as we returned home
The agued bones taking their toll
Stiffened his gait as he prepared for sleep

I remember those long summers
When he ran tirelessly seeking his quarry
Bounding lost through grass and nettles
Reappearing successful, again ready for the off

He slept much more towards the end
Ever raucous in response to noise
His grimace gap-toothed still threatened
Perhaps he too recalled our yesterdays.

Martin Blakemore Davis

Seaside Memories

I remember, I remember
Look back through the years
Lots of love and joy and a few tears
One summer, with my sisters
Mum thought Ramsgate was good
So we went there for our holiday
And to get us in the mood
There were donkeys to ride
Sandcastles to build
The fair with all its fun
Or just sitting by the sea
Relaxing in the sun.
Seventy years have come and gone
But this lovely memory lingers on.

Leila McLeish

A Londoner In Wales

One day, in old Carmarthen Town
A small evacuee
Met a gang of Welsh boys
And they adopted me

Bryn was the leader
We all looked up to Bryn
Saunders was a redhead
Who lived each day to win
Johnny was the joker
His antics kept us high
And Gwylem was my first pure love
And I'll love him till I die

The summer break was endless
We all met up the Koot
Raced around the tinworks
Through the stingers and the soot

The boys set a commando course
Completing it was hell
Greasy poles to swing across
Mud ditches if you fell

One hazy, humid, drizzly eve
As I played all alone
Voices growing louder, threatened
'Londoner! Go home!'
I cupped my hands
Bent the thumbs
Gave our distress call
The Gang appeared from nowhere
And the bullies jumped the wall

We played walking stick hockey
Using a tennis ball
And no one thought of 'packing in'
Till night began to fall

We climbed steep slopes
Swung on bars
Then headed home
Our torch, the stars

Some say your schooldays are the best
For some that well may be
But my best times
Were at Park Hynes
In nineteen forty-three.

Joan Croft Todd

Memories

A mop of curls,
A cute little face,
A cheeky smile,
A dress of lace.

But not for long,
In jeans she's dressed.
Hair cropped short,
I'm not impressed.

But what is this?
An old organ plays,
The jeans have gone,
A minister prays.

My child a bride,
How can that be?
Only yesterday
She sat on my knee.

Now she is gone,
Across the seas,
Dwelling in my heart
And in my memories.

Josephine Herron

Changes In Life

I'm on the inside looking out,
'How did those changes come about?'
Hair, once resembling golden corn,
Looks more like snow on a winter's morn.
The eyes have faded a paler blue,
'I think those are laughter lines - don't you?'
They can't be wrinkles creeping in,
Around the brow, neck and chin.
The ears too, are wearing out,
As people around me have to shout.
But the heart is still strong.
Weary limbs creak with the strain,
The brain is quite active, so I mustn't complain.
So, when I take note of the last seventy years,
The joy and laughter, silent-shed tears.
I'll keep taking the tablets and saying my prayers
Till the good Lord calls me to go up those stairs.

Pauline Vinters

Sweet Memories

Sweets in big glass jars
High up on the shelf
Penny and two penny chocolate bars
A bargain tray from which to help yourself.
Your toffees were weighed
Then put in a bag
And you hurried off home to savour your swag.

Sherbet bombs and liquorice roots
Twisted barley sugar sticks
Boiled sweets and acid drops
Sugar mice and jelly fruits
And lovely coloured lollipops.

Those were the days when
With your Saturday penny
You went to the sweet shop
With a laugh and a skip and a hop.
But that was back then
Are there still sweet shops?
If so, not so many.

Now, it's off to the supermarket
I think it's a shame
Whatever your wealth
Pre-packed plastic packets
Can't thrill quite the same
As sweets in big glass jars
High up on the shelf.

Barbara Sleath

The Cauldron Of My Love

In the recesses of unvoiced delight,
Deep down, in the vast deepness of my heart,
Down where the passions form, expand, unite,
Where love is born, where loving feelings start;
Where longings linger, pulsating with desire,
That's where you are, ensconced in effervescent fire.

Robert McIlveen

Precious

Three years ago we lost our Mum
We lost our Dad last year.
Precious people in our lives,
Memories held so dear.

We packaged up those happy times,
When our childhood home was sold.
Fun and laughter into 'boxes',
Those stories to be retold.

Our thoughts are filled with happiness,
Of a childhood full of love.
Mum and Dad looking after us,
Which they still do, from above.

We are left with all those memories,
To treasure, to preserve, to revive.
We can recall all those precious times,
To keep Mum's and Dad's 'spirit' alive.

C J Duxbury

Down Memory Lane

Sometimes I wander down memory lane,
Retracing life's footsteps once again,
Back to the happy, carefree childhood days,
Feeling safe, protected and loved, always.

Recalling the precious teenage years,
Wartime restrictions, blood, sweat and tears;
Growing, maturing, preparing for life,
When peace returned after years of strife.

Falling in love, marriage and motherhood,
Years of fulfilment, life was so good,
Vowing our love would last forever,
Nothing, not even death, could sever.

Blest with children, family and friends,
Faith in God's love that never ends,
Two more generations have followed on,
One wonders where all the time has gone.

Changes come as the years come and go,
Carried along in life's swift ebb and flow,
Meetings and partings, celebrations,
Sad and happy special occasions.

All the loving, caring and giving,
Simple pleasures, the joy of living,
A gentle touch, a smile, a tender kiss,
Life and memories are made of all this.

Edith Stell

Memories Are Made Of These . . .

Pale sun and showers
Tiny buds on trees
Skipping in the street
Hot cross buns for tea
Easter.

Summer sun and heat
Butterflies and bees
Making daisy chains
Swimming in the sea
Holidays.

Autumn mist and fog
Leaves tumbling down
Sparklers in my hand
Conkers on the ground
Hallowe'en.

Winter frost and snow
Holly on the door
Tree to decorate
Paper chains galore
Christmas.

Time passes swiftly
But why should we mourn
All through our lifetime
Memory lingers on.

Audrey Parks

If Only

Memories always take the stage, the nights you cannot sleep,
You open up Pandora's Box, instead of counting sheep,
Then the faces and the voices of people you have met,
Come gliding past and most of them, you wish you could forget.
We've all got something tucked away, no one is as white as snow
And the midnight memory dwells on bits, you hope nobody knows,
The few things we are proud of, somehow get pushed behind,
You can't stand up and say, 'Look folks, I'm me
A great guy and so kind,'
Some memories get you tearful, that things turned out this way,
But nobody can alter things that happened yesterday,
The moving finger having writ, we know, of course, moves on
And leaves us with the pieces, to try and build upon,
Again this starts that train of thought, if only you'd thought twice,
If only you had said, 'I can't,' or better still, 'No thanks.'
Memories aren't the stuff of dreams, someone played a part,
When they went back on a promise, that almost broke your heart,
A face appears like magic and you hear again the voice,
That years ago was all it took, to make your heart rejoice,
If only you had not gone out, or gone some other way,
Alternatives still haunting, like they did for many a day,
You can't do much about it now, too long ago for that
And memories, unfortunately,
Are all made up of fact.

Charles Boyett

The Final Result

If memory should serve me well, there'd be plenty I could tell
Of incidents and what I did in early years - and me a kid.
There was so much to do
And all of it, brand spanking new.

It's my belief that what you did defined the way you grew
And if nature were the driving force
There could not be a better course, to shape and mould,
Right through life, until you're old.

Those were the days when creatures' ways
Were better known to me.
I could ramble, amble; scramble,
Through hazel bush and bramble.
I'd suffer as my legs were scratched
When checking if some eggs were hatched.

Go through gathered cows at milking time
To nearby fields; their horns an inch away;
Go making hay on such a working day,
While they gave their yields.
A country lad - and somewhat wild,
But now, I'm like good ale: I'm old and mild.

Eric Chapman

Memory Of A Bunch Of Roses

Such a lovely bunch of roses, my darling son
When your life begun
A tiny teardrop in each heart,
Sweet in its simplicity
Little rosebuds nestling there,
A bunch of glorious hue
Lovers hold them to their hearts,
Some moist with a tear or two
A lovely bunch of roses red,
When I think of you, now dead, my son
A lovely bunch of roses
And thoughts of you
As the years slip by
The roses blossom still in hearts,
But memories of you will never die,
David.

J Patrickson

Participant Memory Research

Think of a Tuesday morning
some years ago
when you brushed your teeth
really well.

Think of a spring dawn
bright and early in 1989
and the sound, nearby,
of that chirpy birdsong.

Think of getting up
on your sixth birthday
and the feel of the handkerchief
when you blew your nose.

Think of the hot Sunday afternoon
last summer
and how that second drink
helped to quench your thirst.

Think of whether
your left foot has moved
since you began reading
this poem.

It's a funny business, memory.

Geoff Lowe

The Old Railway Bridge

The bridge
Where we used to wave at steam trains.
Nobody waves at diesels!
Smoke-blackened bricks rebuilt with virgin sandstone
The tunnel where the daring would enter
Hiding in niches
Lungs filling
With smoke
Steam
And soot
As the world shuddered
With the power of a Stanier Black 5
Late out of Euston.

Paul Wilkins

Snapshots

Me, skirt tucked into knickers, splashing in the sea;
Dad, with hankie on his head and his eye on me;
Mum, in a deckchair with the usual flask of tea;
I look at childhood snapshots and this is what I see.

Me, riding bareback, on a huge Clydesdale horse;
Dad walks beside me, his eye on me, of course;
Mum, with the camera, takes the snap, because
She hates her picture taken and she's the driving force.

Me with lots of cousins, all swinging on a gate;
Anne, Kathleen, Sheila, Barry, with Ivy, Ann and Kate.
I'm the eldest present, the others all came late.
All of us are under six and so the fun is great.

In the summer holidays, to Grandpa's we were sent
To visit him and Aunty, where we on pleasure bent,
Were snapped in Grandpa's garden, making a play tent,
My cousins all beside me; many happy days we spent.

And other snaps of childhood days too numerous to tell
Remind me now of days gone by, what stories they can tell.
I look at them and often say, 'Now that one rings a bell!'
And I bless the box Brownie which served my family well.

Liz Rae

Memories

My first memories - soft as it sound
Is how my mum's love knew no bounds
Long summer days when tans were gained
Sun always shone . . . it seldom rained
Great childhood friends were there with me
Of which now I think, but seldom see
As years went by some grew uncouth
With the wild exuberance of youth
In '83 when Aberdeen Football was on the up
Culminating in the European Cup Winners Cup
Next thing along my road of life
Was getting married, my dearest wife
Then the best we've ever done
Was first our girl and then our son
There were wonderful times whatever their age
And we were there, loving every single stage
You remember the good, rather than the bad
As it's better being happy than being sad
You can't bring back things from your past
But your memories will forever last.

Chris Leith

War Baby

When I had reached the age of two
And my brother, three months old,
The news that said the world's at war
Was starting to unfold.

Although so young, the memories
Remain so clear and strong
Some created by the trauma
All around us for so long.

I recall the siren's warning sound -
Take shelter, danger near
Then the noise of planes, the fires
And all in constant fear.

This was followed by another noise,
A welcome sound this time;
The all-clear called, it's safe,
Perhaps today will turn out fine.

Of all the tales I could relate
About my early years,
There's one that always makes me smile
From memories still so clear.

The month of May, year - '45
Noise woke me from my sleep;
And shouting loudest, my friend, John
Ran up and down the street.

He was still in his pyjamas
Calling us to join the fun
And everyone was celebrating
VE Day, the war was won.

Mary Hoy

Our Gift For Spring

Welcome beloved babe, our harbinger of spring,
As certain love surrounds you from heraldic
Continents - Africa, where your dear family
Sired your mother, who bore and nursed you
With God's ample blessing.
And Europe where your father's lineage
Of princes from North Wales look kindly
On his care and love of you and of
Your mother through all of the time you
Waited in her womb.
Welcome dear Gareth - as you bring God's blessing on us all.

Kathleen Lloyd Morris

I Remember

I remember, I remember, the days of long ago,
The summers drenched in sunshine; the winters deep in snow
And paths among the fields and woods which only children know.

I remember every detail of home and work and play
Much clearer than the recent things which happened yesterday.

The calves which sucked one's fingers, lambs thawing by the fire,
Milk pinging in the bucket as the cows stood in the byre,
The place the robin built her nest; all things small boys desire.

The thought of summer holidays to make spirits soar
But now I can't remember if I've even locked the door!

Woodpeckers on the anthills and doves that cooed all day,
Red squirrels darting up the trees, many splendoured jay
The river singing over stones, the pools where still trout lay.

The summer days seemed endless and life an endless game
But now it's coming to a close - a candle's guttering flame.

I remember, I remember, more things than can be told,
Memories on memories, more precious now than gold,
All minted in that coinage that is not bought or sold.

And as I limp along the way where once I blithely strode
They are summer's rays in winter to light a darkening road.

David Griffiths

The Echoing Surf

Just as I roamed the garden alone
As a child and made discoveries,
When by the sea I combed the tide line
For shells and pebbles which caught my eye.
At night my dreams were of glistening
Strands of seaweed, the feel of warm sand
On the soles of my feet and always
The sound of waves breaking on the shore.
Their steady rhythm had the power
To soothe or disturb, to change a mood
From silky calm to unleashed anger,
From wavelets to flying foam and spray
And from azure to menacing grey.
When walking in the woods I still hear
The wind-surf echoing through the trees
And childhood once so far away seems
Near and I can capture again that
Time of receptiveness when I fell
Under the spell of a clear rock pool
And could shrink to the size of a shell.

Rosina Winiarski

A Country Childhood

There were fields at the top of our garden,
Where cows did so peacefully graze,
But sometimes they'd wander through fencing
And through kitchen windows would gaze!
Now cows and my mother did *not* mix!
She did not take kindly to them,
Especially when over her Weetabix,
She'd be gazed at by this bovine femme!

There were woods at the top of our road
Where primrose and bluebell did grow,
And sometimes we'd gather a load
To take home to Mum for a show;
With old farmer Farnham about
When we wandered home from our school,
'Hello boys!' he would loudly shout,
That we were girls did not matter at all!

He would drive his old horse and manure cart,
A real village character was he!
Whilst Claris, his daughter, drove milk cart,
More like a man, she seemed to me;
Then when they built new houses
Where our bluebell woods used to be,
We'd play in those buildings for hours
When the workmen went home for their tea!

I know that it's dangerous today
And it's something kids must not do,
But we'd have such fun there at play
And our parents - they never knew!
I have so much more I could tell you
Of Guide camps, Crusaders and school,
Of holidays I'll not forget too,
Yes, I think my childhood was 'cool'!

Irene Hart

Childhood Memories

(Dedicated to my parents, Beatrice and Ernest Callison)

My thoughts go back over seventy years ago
the very first film I saw was Cinderella
oh, what a show!
Mum, Dad and I went every Saturday
with a very large bag of sweets.
On the way home we bought a coconut
that was my special treat.
Then came that horrible war in 1939
the men went away in the forces,
some went down the mine,
my dad couldn't join the army, he had a faulty heart
so he joined the fire brigade,
that way he played his part.
Our house was bombed,
so we lived with an aunt the last year of the war.
I had much further to go to school,
so with gas mask on my back,
off down the road I tore.
The air raid siren wailing, I pedalled as fast
as fast as I could, faster and faster,
at last I was almost there.
Into the shelter, everyone dashed,
we sang songs until we heard the all-clear.
Everyone helped each other,
no muggings or attacks in the streets.
We had ration books for food and clothes
and coupons to buy a few sweets.
It was good living at Auntie's,
Uncle fried chips every day,
he also made a dolls' house and furniture
so my younger cousin and I found much play.
One of the best times of my life
was when I became a Girl Guide,
on church parades we all scrubbed up.
I carried the flag with pride.
our captain was very active,
rather short and twice as wide.
Camping was a big event, with lots of girls to be fed.
We cooked on an open fire,
picking out grass from the eggy bread.
We learned the Morse code and compass,
studied maps and collected leaves
to press into an album when we got back.
it was great, but oh, those poor old knees!
Where, oh where, has that time gone,
as I look back over the years?
There has been lots of happiness
with a sprinkling of tears.

Memories Are Made Of This

The memories of my parents
who gave me everything they were able.
they taught me how to be tolerant, patient
and polite, to make my life feel stable.
Through the trauma of Dad fighting fires
amongst the debris and the harm,
Mum made me feel so safe during the air raids
at night she was brave and oh, so calm.
All the happy times we had,
also the occasional strife,
please God keep them in your tender care,
I'll pray for them for the rest of my life.

June Jefferson

Someone Special

You knew me, before I knew you,
And before I knew you were there.
You knew me, before I knew you,
And before I knew who you were.

Later, I knew who you were,
When you would pick me up and hold me up so high.
I must have been at that age, I just knew if I wished,
You would even help me touch the clouds in the sky.

Most evenings, you would take me into 'Stella's Shop',
And always there, a treat.
But when grown up, I heard you had lost a few girlfriends,
As you didn't always arrive, at the arranged time to meet.

And there were the family weekends and holidays,
Usually by the sea and the beach.
And I don't need the photographs to remind me,
That you were rarely out of reach.

Then you were away from home,
For what seemed to me, such a very long time.
But when you wrote your letters home,
There was always a page, that was mine.

So many things to mention,
But would take too many pages to fill.
But I know, you knew you were special to many of us,
Before, and when you became so ill.

I hope there is a special place,
Where good memories linger on.
And I hope they make you smile,
Even though, from here, you're gone.

Roberta Davies

Loving Memories Of Little Tess

Little Tess was a standard Yorkshire terrier
Born on the 15th of May, 1991.
A birthday present to my wife, Marjorie
From me and Michael, our youngest son.
The equivalent to potty training took some time,
But eventually, she was fine.
Pinching socks was her delight
She hoped we would chase her
She would run with all her might.
In her younger days she loved to lay
On top of the bottom of our bed,
Later years, she lay on my side
In her bed on the floor and oh boy! could she snore!
Resting her little head and dreaming dreams by the score.
About 7am or thereabouts,
Two little paws would land on the edge of the bed
As I looked down, Tessie's sleepy head
Was staring at me, telling me
That she wanted to go out into our garden and have a wee
Followed shortly after, with her favourite biscuit
And a saucer of tea.
Whenever post or papers came through the door
Tess would spring into action and run down the corridor,
She would jump up and grab the mail,
Shaking it as if it were a rat with a tail.
Tess loved all our grandchildren when they were young,
Grandson David on Sundays, took Tess for a run
And they had some fun.
Ten-year-old Connor, a family friend,
Gave Tess Christmas and birthday presents
And Tess returned his kindness
With presents right to the end.
Our next-door neighbour, Edna Crewe, loved little Tess
And invited Tess into her house for biscuits and tea,
Little Tess looked forward to those treats
Wagging her little tail with glee.
In December 1999, when little Tess started panting in a studio,
While sitting on my knee
She lost the opportunity to appear
In a British Telecom commercial on TV.
We shall always cherish the memory
Of our darling little Tess
She will always be remember with love and affection
And have a place in our hearts,
Tess was one of the best, oh yes.

Peter Guy Towner

Treasures In The Sand

One of my pleasant memories as a child,
Was in St Monance, out in the wild,
Playing with other children around.
Treasures in the sandpit to be found.
I would get a lift so high,
Treasures to be found nearby.
I looked upon it as my treasure store,
I would dream of going just there, more and more.

Nearby, was a large chute,
Went from the caravan site.
Off you go, with a push so light,
Down, down, to the beach below.
Shout to the Lord, as we onward go,
Onward Christian Soldiers ride,
Sliding forward on the victory side,
With our swords in our hand.
Join the happy band.

I began speaking of treasures, gay.
However, that was just child's play.
Now I have found a real treasure and sword,
Found only in Jesus Christ, my Lord.

Gordon Cameron

A Special Day

I was married in 1978
After nine years of waiting in 1986
I was lucky to have a baby boy
With him came so much joy.
Fifteen years earlier, I had two names ready
Stuart for a boy, Ann-Marie for a girl.
The years have flown by in a whirl.
We've had our fair share of ups and downs
The family nearly lost me to heart failure
By having a new heart valve,
I have a new life
That was ten years ago.
Now my not-so-little boy
Has grown to be an adult now
Twenty-one years old on September 18th, 2007.
I remember the day as if only yesterday
I still get excited when birthdays come
Cards appear through the letter box
I feel very proud to be his mum.

Marian Clark

At Christmas Time

When I was young at Christmas time
The world seemed calm and cheerful,
I'd go out Christmas singing
And when I began to sing, they really got an earful!
I'd sing at least two carols
And then recite this poem:
'Christmas is coming, the geese are getting fat,
Please put a penny in the old man's hat.
If you haven't got a penny, a halfpenny will do,
If you haven't got a halfpenny, God bless you'.

Lots of kids were cheeky when they went out to sing,
If they didn't get any coppers, this ditty they would shout:
'I hope you have a turkey hanging on a string,
I hope the bogger chokes you, for letting us sing'.

I miss the family parties we always used to have
All the games and singsongs around the Christmas tree.
The blazing fires, the Christmas treats,
Whilst outside, the snow would glisten.

I remember on one Christmas Eve, my mother sent me shopping,
On my way back, I got a shock, my knees were really knocking.
Santa Claus was on our street, I thought he'd pass me by
And wouldn't fill my stocking.

I wonder how many people feel like I do today,
I know there must be progress, but, just for one great day,
Why can't we have a good old-fashioned Christmas,
On this my special day,
You see, I feel very honoured, as I was born on . . .
Christmas Day.
C Cook

My Friend

The loss of my friend was a very say day,
I said goodbye in my own special way,
Please don't think badly of me, that I couldn't be there,
With thoughts of my friend, doesn't mean I didn't care.
Your mum knew my thoughts on religion,
But her friendship was always true,
I hope you will all forgive me
And feel the same way too.
Your mum and dad are together again
And travelling that eternal place,
But I bet, like me, if you shut your eyes
You can still see her face.
They are free of the suffering,
Free from the pain
And waiting there for you,
Until you all meet again.
Just believe she's right there with you,
If you really try hard, you can see,
She wouldn't want you sad any longer,
It's not how she would want you to be.
A very special lady, who was honest, kind and true,
You only have to believe it,
And she will always be there with you.

Lin Hodson

Helping Hands

Other hands will tend to our flowers
After we have left and gone
Into another house to live
Time passes on, changes come
Other hands will till our garden
Sow the seeds and watch them grow
Look after the weak ones, do the weeding
Where the breezes play and flow
Circumstances alter cases
We cannot live our lives alone
We have to depend on one another
And we reap what we have sown
There are different ways of doing things
We are always learning so be a blessing to someone today.

George Camp

My Childhood Memories

Sailing from old Ireland
Just a child of five
Landing here in Liverpool
How I cried and cried.

My mom and dad
They told me off
Said don't be such a pain
We're here to start a new life
Then I cried and cried again.

I missed my friends and relatives
I did not want to leave
But Mom and Dad needed money
And a decent place to live.

A little cottage here we found
Right by a flowing stream
My mind, it used to wander
And there, I'd often dream.

Now time has passed
I'm all grown-up
Married, with children of my own
The memories of my childhood
Remain locked in my heart alone.

Emma Hardwick

Mother Love

Making dinners and dolls' clothes
And delightful days,
Filling my childhood with love and laughter
Lots of 'happy ever afters'.

Then I became a woman . . .
You and I still giggled like children!
No wonder when you died, I cried
'Whatever will I do?'

But memories are living things
Six years since you left this earth
You're still making your presence known,
Helping me to cope with tragedy and pain,
Still nurturing me, giving strength
And the joyful reassurance
That hope and love and souls remain.

Jeanne Hutton

The Day I Won The Bard

'The Complete Works of Shakespeare'
From bulging shelves I take
And when I see the volume
Old memories awake.

I'm at my school's prize-giving
And when I get the call,
I know my legs are shaking
And fear that I will fall.

I still remember clearly
That it was rather hard,
To climb steps to the platform
The day I won the Bard.

A civic worthy met me
And uttered words of praise -
These words have now escaped me
I was in such a daze.

And when I was descending
'Don't look!' I wished to say,
With navy pants appearing
As down I made my way.

I will remember always
How great it was, but hard,
To make my debut on the stage
The day I won the Bard.

Marguerite Pratt

The Miracle Of Life

A baby into your life has come,
A real joy, for the dad and mum.
A baby to care for and to share their love,
This miracle from God up above.

To love and to guide, through life's ups and downs,
To see baby smile and the comical frown.
To teach the ways, to live life to the full,
Each day with respect and love one and all.

The first smile a pleasure, will fetch tears to your eyes,
The first words will come, with some surprise.
Into the first milestone of life, there to take first steps,
A future unknown, a secret well kept.

May God bless you and guide you, in all that you do,
To protect your new baby, its whole life through.
For into your life, this miracle was placed,
This miracle of life, into the whole human race.

V M Foulger

Summer's Passing

Oh, where have they gone - the days of our youth?
The days when love held sway
When summer was just beginning
And autumn far away.

My love and I walked in the sun
And dreamed away the hours.
We kissed and laughed while the grass grew tall
And the world was filled with flowers.

The swallows dipped above our heads,
Bees hummed on the wing.
This time must surely last forever -
Autumn seemed a far-off thing.

The dreaming hours stretched into years,
We watched our young ones grow.
The days were filled with hope and gladness
And summer's passing slow.

But now the summer's gone, my love,
The swallows flown away
And with them went the days of our youth -
They could no longer stay.

Elaine Hutchings

Lucy

Lucy was my first love
We met at seventeen
A bit rough around the edges
And hardly the prom queen
Seven years together
We went on loads of dates
And really were inseparable
Truly the best of mates
Then finally it happened
Good things come to an end
We became bored of each other
So would she stay my friend?
She's been around the clock twice
And done too many miles
Our last trip to the knacker's yard
Brought more tears than smiles
Lucy was my first love
No female I've met finer
I will always love you, Lucy
My yellow Morris Minor.

Coxy

172

Peace 1945

This land of ours may well rejoice
Upon this glorious day of days,
For war and strife at last has ceased,
Nation with nation is at peace.
In every corner of the land
The cry of peace is gladly heard.
And here on England's tiny isle,
We see the tears and happy smiles
Of people, glad the battle o'er
And none shall invade our shores.

The streets and buildings are made gay,
To celebrate this splendid day.
The Union Jack stands out supreme
Acknowledged emblem, freedom's queen,
Red, white and blue emblazoned there,
Proudly, she billows in mid-air.

Into the early hours of morn,
The people do their joy express,
Singing and dancing down the street,
Six years of cramped-ness are released.
Great thankfulness lies in our hearts,
Those from whom we had to part
Will soon, we hope, be back once more
And we shall open wide our doors
To those brave men who fought for peace
On land and sea and in the air.

But never let our hearts forget
Those who died that we might yet
Make this world a lovely place,
To live in peace with every race.
So may be cherish peace forever,
Keep it safe and lose it never.

Edith Mary Hardman

Norfolk? Where's That?

Norfolk is where the pine trees
Surge forward over the dunes,
And whisper to one another,
Soughing their age-old tunes.

Norfolk's where streamlets, wide and slow,
Meander amid their reeds -
Home for the willow warblers,
Where the barn owl flits and feeds.

Norfolk is minds at peace with the world,
People with kindly ways,
And wise in the old, old country style,
That means just what it says.

Norfolk is where the butterflies,
Fly up from the rambling briar,
Flaunting and flittering in the sun,
Colours blazing with brightness afire.

Norfolk is where the skies are wide
As wide as the skies Above,
A feeling of space, of life, of hope -
A place I slowly grew to love.

They're not so keen on strangers,
On 'people from away',
Who think themselves superior
And can't understand what they say.

Best to come quietly to Norfolk,
And try slowly to understand,
How people whose lives were once so hard,
Gained their wisdom from the land.

Rosemary Harvey

A Simple Life

Wonders of childhood, brimming with joy,
Nothing to harm us, girl or boy.
Fragrance of meadows, silvery streams
Dens in the dark wood, fuelling our dreams.

Perpetual sunshine, endless days,
Warmth in the closeness of nature's ways.
Grass-perfumed haystacks, dragonflies' wings -
Life was a web of magical things.

Now gone is the magic, for all we tried -
We live in a land where childhood died.

Lilian Perriman

Summer Floods

Cobalt-blue sky with fluffy white clouds,
Fades to dark indigo.
Then total blue-blackness overhead, left and right.
Lost in a barrel mixture of pitted black olives marinating in squid ink.

Then distant rumblings become punctuated by vivid flashing gashes,
Quickly followed by spears of stair rods,
Piercing the already sodden surface.
Water rises but nowhere to go.
Will it ever stop raining?

Rats dash in synchronised flight
Ahead of rising levels.
A tree slowly crashes over
As the soil is washed away from its anchorage.

A cow bellows as it is forced to swim to higher ground,
The wind whistles then howls round the pylons,
But still the water rises,
Will it ever stop?
Swirls and eddies round every obstruction.

Swans paddle up the high street,
Ricocheting off bits of flotsam.
Brave elderly couple supporting each other, arm in arm.
Wonder if the baker's shop will open today?
Dead West Country sheep upends and dies,
As it floats past with feet in the air.

Fence posts vanish below the rising meniscus.
A flock of Canada geese land in what was once Market Street,
Creating surging wake to bounce off house walls
Abandoned cars with water up to window levels
Multiply like rabbits in a warren,
Car parks become mini lakes.

Elderly widow wrings hands in despair,
Tears burning deep creases down her cheeks
No husband to comfort her,

But still the water level rises,
Will it ever stop?
Her taps ran dry days ago,
What is she to do but hope and pray?
Will it ever stop?

She prays that passing soldiers in rubber boat
Will stop at her door with food and water,
Or someone will find her dead on the floor
In the mud with her dog,
When the floodwaters abate.
Will it ever stop raining?

Barry Kendall

Memories Are Made Of This

Memories Of Troublesome Grandchildren

Emma and James are playing with their games,
For drawing and painting are a little too tame.
Sternly, Emma tells her dolls to sit still in the car,
James has toy soldiers fiercely fighting a war.
The soldiers explode a thermonuclear device,
Emma complains, 'That noise wakened my dolls twice.'
James replies, 'Atomic bombs are not that cheap,
So smack your dolls till they go back to sleep.'
Emma opens her sweet shop, but rather too late,
Grandma and James must be patient and wait.
James demands an ultra-large, green lollipop,
But Emma has eaten the only one in her shop.
Says James, 'My troops must know what you've got,
If it's nothing, then I will have all of you shot.
Or I might just decide to execute Grandad instead,
At my bedtime, anyway, I will chop off his head.'
Now James is a policeman, Emma, detective,
They both ignore Daddy's bath time directive.
If he reminds them, 'It's nearly bedtime.'
Caution, then handcuff him, for a mythical crime,
Warn him, 'Mind your step and carefully tread,
Lest like Uncle Grandad, you are minus your head.'

Anne Omnibus

True Friendship!

I value my friendship with Philip,
In winter,
True friendship keeps me warm!
I value my friendship with Philip,
In springtime,
True friendship again reborn!
I value my friendship with Philip,
In summer,
True friendship feels the heat!
I value my friendship with Philip,
In autumn,
Oh, for true friendship,
How I know I've fallen!
True friendship helps life to be complete!

Graham Mitchell

176

Memories Are Made Of This
They Are Closer When You Think!

Memories are kept in a part of the brain
from where they're recovered without any strain,
through touch, taste or odour, hearing or sight,
you can call them whenever, daytime or night.
Use the cry of the newborn, the peace of the moors,
the sounds of the city, inside or outdoors!

The smell of the hayrick, standing close by
is drenched by the overlaid stench of the sty!
The clean milky scent of a babe at the breast
is exceeded for lovers, nevertheless,
by the ravishing odour of a body adored
with a deep constancy, at home and abroad.

The sight of the flight of a bird in the sky,
the hues of the rainbow as rain falls nearby;
the halo surrounding a crisp icy moon
the sky-fire of evening at the set of the sun.
The countless bright stars that last until morn,
when they're banished once more, heralding dawn!

The bouquet of wine that bursts on your tongue,
the flavour of cheese causes taste buds to long
while the tang of the bramble and the rose-hip
are dwarfed into nothing by merely a sip
of the nectar you'll taste on your lover's mouth
like the touch of the sun in the tropical south?

Though valued, these catalysts bring just a smile
like that first touch of fingers, teenager-style,
while friends and your lovers may glow every day
when caresses are shared or given away.
These five senses create your memories in part
but the sixth is found only in an instinctive heart!

Ian T Colley

Reminiscing

When you get old and eyes grow dim you think of all things past,
The good times and bad times and love that still does last.
You look around your room at photos in their frames,
The faces that all greet you have long-forgotten names.
You think about your first love and try to see his face,
And how when you had grown a bit, how another took his place.
Your memories come flooding back, all sorts of wondrous ones,
The day that you were at the church to christen all your sons.
But one thing no one can take away is the love that's in your heart
For all your loving family, whether near or far apart.

Ann Morgan

Some Childhood Cameos

We went out into the fields as children,
Strolling along country lanes and cart tracks,
Inspecting things of nature on the way.
When we arrived at our destination,
Girls played tag, did gymnastics, just gossiped.
A few boys showed off whilst climbing up trees.
Most favoured was cowboys and Indians.
We were safe then without supervision.

My parents took me on a steam train trip
To stay with cousins for a holiday.
When it was fine, we sauntered to the park,
Played on swings, splashed and paddled in the pool.
On wet days, we played indoor games, read
Or used a local cinema to watch films.

Mother, our dog and I, walked to and from
Our next village to purchase home-grown fruit.
There were farms with orchards and cottages,
Mostly occupied by farm labourers.
The buildings now have commuter owners
Farm properties are altered, orchards gone.

Twice on Sundays when young, later three times,
We hurried to and from chapel on foot.
I went with friends along the village street
From its beginning, nearly to its end.
Parents said I must attend, so I did.
In teen years, I joined the chapel youth club
And choirs, took scripture exams, worshipped there.
I would not have dreamt of going elsewhere.

Parents and older folk were respected.
I cannot recall ever being bored.

E Joan Knight

A Tender View

Clear water ripples through a sunlit stream
to join a bubbling waterfall.
Small fish dart,
a green frog stretches
and apples hang on shadowy trees
all those many years ago.

Frank W Pittman

Moving House

In everyone's time of life, it's true,
There are beginnings and ends of all that we do.
One moment we're drifting along with the wind,
Counting our blessings and loving all things.
Then along comes a day when things start to change,
The time to move on and be rearranged.
Houses to empty and others to view,
Things to sort out and so much to do.
Will I be certain that this time is right?
Will I stay calm or put up a fight?
That time has now come to move out of our zone,
Changes are coming and this won't be our home.
The times we have shared, the good and the bad,
The tears and the laughter, the fun we have had,
Memories are special, but some we let go,
So when the time comes, we shall surely know,
That we have a great shepherd who sees all our needs,
He leads us and guides us to where we should be.
The day is so close and the move is in view,
He speaks so clearly and He has the clue
To the place He's prepared, with our interests in mind,
You will soon find the answer to all He will find.
So keep on searching and you will soon see,
The place is soon coming, where you're meant to be.
Just look to your Maker and you will then find,
That the memories you hold will be left behind.
Some we recall with fear and regret,
But the sweetest memories we will not forget.
So open your heart and greet the new way,
Only memories you cherish will forever stay.

Jackie Allingham

Through The Years

So many years now passed and gone
But memories still linger on
The difficulties of childhood, adolescence, teens
Growing up quite quickly, before our time it seems
Never to be forgotten, looming threats of war
Dark days, fearful days, never known before
Families torn, loved ones gone
How did we manage to carry on
Survive we did, start afresh
Rebuild our lives, share happiness
We shared life together, we spent happy years
Just memories are left and hearts full of tears.

Ethel M Harrison

Memories Of Our Life

Do not grieve me when I am gone, for I am not far away
I will live forever in your heart and in your memories I shall stay
Remember the first time that we met
Of course you don't, but I do and yet
When I remind you of that night
When you strayed into my sight
You say you don't remember that first meeting
I was with your ex when she came a-greeting.

I thought, *I'll marry him one day*
And then we both walked away
A year passed until we met again
At the village hall dance, down a country lane
It was my birthday and you asked me to dance
You said, 'I would buy you a gift, if I had the chance.'
You followed me home and came in that night
Then we met again and it just seemed right.

The day we married, it poured with rain
The traffic was bad and I was late again
The wedding car was five minutes from the church
Another five more you said and you would have left me in the lurch.

Over forty years we have now been wed
It will never last, they are too young, they said
But our memories will linger on
Many years after we have gone
Two children and three grandchildren too
Fond ones we hope, of me and you.

Sheila Margaret Storr

Diana
Princess Of Wales 1961-1997

In memory's garden
She will always flourish
As our English rose
Whose protocol stretched
Beyond the realms of ceremony,
Out-foxing the status quo . . .
Let, therefore, history's pen
Endow this Lady Knight
With graciousness, chivalry
And sweet repose, as she herself
Was blest with love and care,
Diana, our English rose.

Terrence St John

Eccentric Of Cherry Hill

Priscilla the lady in the trees,
Her home enclosed by trees and shrubs.
Nearing a century, she was there, before
Grandfather, who lived to be ninety-seven.

A rich, long, fruitful life she lived,
Never an angry word did she ever yell.
Her grey-black hair in a dainty bun,
A smile as welcoming as the morning sun.

Every morning, on the way to school,
By the tree-lined gateway, she stood.
She wished the neighbourhood children,
The best of everything for the day.

This advice she freely gave,
Be studious, polite and kind.
Your blessings will be great,
She would wave and walk away.

Early, every Sunday morning,
Dressed in a black, flowered dress.
Bible tucked under her arm,
To the chapel she went to pray.

Old eccentric Nathan of Cherry Hill,
Lived mainly for himself.
A kind and generous life he lived,
Sat silently and watched the passing world.

Never did he have very much to say,
His life was ordained that way.
Behind his house, was a vibrant orchard,
Mangos, cherries, apples, plums and oranges.

The produce he freely gave
Take enough to satisfy your needs.
Take not for your father and mother
Neither for your sisters and brothers.

Burgess Jay Barrow

Fond Memories

No television, but we made our own fun,
Card games, Monopoly, learning to knit,
Sewing lessons at school,
Baggy garments that didn't fit!

Holidays at Granny's were such a delight,
Good, wholesome food, freshly made jam,
Punnets of strawberries were soon bubbling
In the berry pan.

Running errands, learning to ride a bike,
Simple pleasures all filled with delight,
Occasionally, a visit to Auntie's,
A rare ride in a car,
I felt like a princess!
Although we didn't go far.

We appreciated things in those days,
School sports days were happy events,
Sometimes camping in the back garden,
Oh, the joys of a tent!

However, time marches on and changes abound,
Only black and white photographs then,
Digital cameras were not around!
Singsongs around the piano, bedtime stories too,
It's been good to reminisce and share
Fond memories with you.

J C Igesund

The Bells

I heard the joyous bells sounding from afar,
And I thought of the distant days of yore,
Of the days I thought I'd forgotten, as of now,
But they wound themselves to my heart's warm core.

The hours of happy friendship, the times of joyful love,
Came gladly ringing through my mind, as swiftly as a dove:
Sounds of precious laughter, holidays by the sea
And all the places I declare so wonderful to be.

Ring joyfully, dear bells, ring gladly through my heart:
Pleasant are the sounds you make, from when to ring you start:
You speak of grand occasions, of every family friend,
Of Christmas time, of Easter time and the joys that they extend.

I heard the joyful bells, a-ringing nearer now
And I thought of recent times and how
At many times happiness I've known,
And into contentment great I have grown.

John Ellis

Some Of My Memories

When I'm all alone with just my memories
I sit and think of what might have been
If only you had asked me to be your wife
I would have been so happy to have shared your life
Memories of when everything was fine
And I still had dreams one day you would be mine
Then memories of you just passing me by
And memories of wiping the tears from my eyes
Sometimes I wonder where are you
And if you live near or have travelled far
But I doubt you have any memories of me
As I was just someone you didn't seem to see
Memories of seeing you by the old school gate
Wishing I could see you again before it is too late
But my memories have helped me get through
And although I loved you, you never knew
I have so many memories of all the years gone by
And I can see you so clearly when I close my eyes
Some memories are happy and some are sad
And in my mind I still think and see you as a lad
Yes, all these memories have helped to make my life
But I'll always wish I could have been your wife.

Eileen Kyte

Eighty-Two Years Ago

He was only five-years-old
When he gazed in awe
At the older boys and girls
As they rode their bicycles
Down a very steep hill

I can do that, he thought
He strolled up the steep hill
With his three-wheel bicycle
And descended at great speed
Halfway down, he lost control

He hobbled home in tears
His knees were covered in blood
And tarmac from the road embodied
His mother said, 'You silly boy!'
I still have the tarmac on my knee.

A W Holden

Memory In Focus

Momentous occasions one cannot forget,
Love at first sight and the moment we met,
Proposal of marriage, sealed with a kiss,
Life's fondest memories, truly yield bliss.

Brief 'mind's eye' snapshots,
Country walks, beauty spots,
The very best held in store,
To be brought on to the fore.

Present, instantly is gone,
Life continuously moves on,
Each second fades to second hand,
Yet we always understand.

Many past times can be listed,
Sometimes we doubt how they existed,
Though details may be confused,
Discussing the past keeps us amused.

Clive Robson

Do You Remember?

Do you remember when we were young,
How we played, wasn't it fun.
When you were sad, it made me too,
When you felt bad, I'd be with you.

As the years went by and were getting older,
You went off and became a soldier,
But you said we would never part,
And there was always a special place in your heart.

You told me that you would come back,
The coat you left, still on the rack,
The war is over and where is thee,
Do you remember the promise made to me.

On the day you left me, I looked deep into your eyes,
I never told you how I felt, I just now realised,
All the time we spent together,
The chances I had, seem to be gone forever.

But you now have done what was promised,
For you now are back with me,
The doctors said your memory's gone . . .
But may have to wait and see.

So, I'll be here, right by your side,
Just as we did when young,
Do you remember how we played?
Wasn't it just fun . . .

Dominica Kelly

Holiday Snapshots

Just a week we had.
This was the cottage,
quite pretty, but,
raining at first, you see.
Next day, still raining,
we all had lunch at the pub.
Waitress took that one.
Sunday - down to the beach,
the kids were that keen.
I'm behind the windbreak.
Monday it was so windy,
we went inland,
tramped round a castle,
it's on the back, some Welsh name.
Tuesday it was nice all day,
that's our two, on the donkeys
and some kid they played with.
This is our picnic,
in the country park.
You needed sunglasses, that day.
Thursday they have a market,
that's me, buying bananas.
Friday it was scorching,
he shouldn't really wear shorts,
always gets burnt like that.
Didn't leave till midday,
it was so nice, sorry to go.
I took that one when we stopped,
at the services, all with ice creams.
It's nice to have mementoes,
happy holidays.

Pat McLean

The Old Wooden Bench

The old wooden bench at the end of the garden,
set against the fence,
made of oak, I think
once rested outside the family cottage.

My father often sat there.
He had more time than he knew what to do with.
I, too, sit here with time on my hands,
connected.

Judith Garrett

Carefree Days

Oh, what it was like
To be young!
The world was fresh and exciting
A playground waiting
To be explored.

Fishing for tadpoles
In a local pond.
Nets at the ready
Jars waiting to be filled.

Going for walks
Across the fields,
Cycling along quiet
Country lanes.
Without cars rushing
Here and there.

Evenings huddled together
Around the fire.
Flames crackling
Giving out a warm glow.
The radio gently playing
In the background,
As we read our books.
No TV to dominate
The evenings!

Christmas get-togethers
Where there was fun.
A real tree stood in the corner
Dropping its pines.
Nobody minded
After all, it was Christmas!

Yes, those were the days
When the world was a better place
To live.

Julie Smith

Memories Are Made Of This

Summer In Perthshire

Organic strawberries home-grown
Fresh cream, sugar and chilled white wine,
Served by our host on his front lawn.
Summer has arrived in this most inviting, memorable
Historic setting of Highland Perthshire.
A feast both of taste and of the eye.
This sharing between friends.
Who could fail to marvel at the splendour of the day?
A house of several centuries
Set in a magnificent mature garden,
An artist's paradise
With inspirational contour and character in abundance.
A further gift is given -
Two roses:
I hold now in my hand, flowers of ancient plantings,
One, a soft pink bud,
The Sutherland;
The other of palest lemon, rare and delicate,
The Menzies;
A timely, priceless reminder of a former lady
Of this beautiful home of homes.
This glorious place where time does not stand still,
High on a hill,
Above a world of constant movement, yet peaceful;
People in a hurry below,
Do not even know, we are here
Enjoying what they cannot see;
Far beyond the moving traffic
Is an entire panorama of nature's fields, hills
And the quiet meandering of the river.
This day of enrichment,
A Sunday never to be forgotten.

Wilma Paton

LNER Line

In late afternoon it frames the sun,
It carried the London-Leicester run.
From springs to key complete the span,
Laid in blue bricks with angled seam,
On wooden template suitably made;
By Victorian artisans perched on
Poles held tightly by rope of braid.

Now ecological railway laying waste,
Artefacts strewn and left to rot,
LNER written on telephone pot.
The might of our engineering past,
More revered where we have lost.
Closing this line and other tracks;
To encourage cars off the factory line.

Regrets over increased carbon gasses
As motorways eat up the grasses.
Now a bridge, but only in shape
Parapet and its coping gone.
Man's inability to plan the future,
Because of political short-term gain.
In early evening it framed the sun, it had
Carried the London to Leicester run.

John L Wigley

Summer Days

Many summer days, now long gone,
When we were together, together as one.
We walked and we swam, we didn't have a care,
It didn't really matter, as long as you were there.

Into your hand my hand would fit,
We'd find a place, where we could sit.
We planned the future, so many summer days,
All of which were shrouded, in a summer haze.

In our summer dreams, imaginary children ran along the beach,
Laughing and dancing, for things out of reach.
Picnics and sandcastles in our imaginary world,
Summer would be our canvas, as our lives unfurled.

We had our summer days, too short, too few,
We had our children, just the two.
Then our lovely summers ran out for you,
And I am left with wonderful memories of summer days,
And you.

Anne Roberts

Memories Of Elvis On The 30th Anniversary Of His Death

Elvis Presley, the man with Valentino eyes,
A perfect face and warm, shy smile,
Hiding the torment in his soul.
Did no one know? Did no one care?
Did no one hear his silent prayer,
For peace of body and of mind?

There were those people who loved this gentle man,
His family, some real, true friends
And then there were the others,
Grasping, greedy, using him,
They took and took, but never gave
And pretended that they cared.

This beautiful man just died alone,
With no one there to comfort him,
To hold him and to weep,
No one but God, who took his soul
And took away his pain.

The real and genuine tears were shed,
By millions of his fans,
The candles, love and flowers,
I know he saw them all,
He knows how much we love him
And that we always will.

Sheila Giles

Memory Snapshot

Sound of Lancasters' flypast triggers instant recall
Of school days; bright, white pages of feint ruled foolscap,
Then a memory, exchanged for exercise books
Of woodchip-like paper;
Pencil points newly sharpened, pens with
Untrustworthy metal nibs
Dipping into inkwells filled with DIY ink powder
Mixed with water
Scratchy crossed nibs dipping into sunken pots,
Hooking shreds of soggy, once-pink blotting paper and now
Heavy with navy blue sludge, spluttering against splinters
On the page and making a blot.
'Fifty lines please, before next week's lesson,'
Intones the Mrs, whose time has come
Whilst Miss and Sir are serving as soldiers somewhere.

J Greenall

The Gatecrasher

We invited these people for dinner
They duly arrived with a hound
We were upset
They'd brought their pet
But politely did not make a sound

He came to us all for a titbit
A habit I simply deplore
We coped, somehow
But I made a vow
Not to ask them anymore

When the time came to go
I nudged Fido
Asleep with his head between paws
I said, 'Please don't forget
To take your pet'
They said, *'He's not ours -*

Isn't he yours?'

Olive Cason

Fisherman's Cove

The farmhouse stood within lush fields
High on the cliffs above the cove
Warm sun breaks on the August day
Wispy clouds drift over azure skies
Seagull calls echo on the still air
Excited children with golden tans
Race over mushroom fields
Through the small wooden gate
And down the steep winding path
To the cove, at last
A safe haven, a magical place
Rock pools bursting with life
A bay where bathing was safe
Beautiful shells to collect
Smooth washed pebbles, large and small
Soft sand beneath the feet
Huge square rocks on which to lie
Fishermen return from their fishing trip
So generous with their mackerel catch
Happy carefree days of summer sun
Wonderful days of childhood, long gone
But those memories linger on.

Sheila A Waterhouse

My Blessings

I've had so many blessings in my life
I first was a daughter and then became a wife
Four children came along for me
I've cherished every minute
Of every joy from all of them
And everything that was in it.

I now have grandchildren too
And what a thrill that's been
To watch them grow and wonder
At things they've done and seen.

I'm getting older now
But wouldn't change a thing
My life has been so wonderfully blessed
With all these treasured things.

I hope they will remember
All the things I've said
I've loved them all so very much
But now it's time for bed.

P Elvins

Walney Isle

As I stand on the shore and gaze out to sea
My childhood memories come back to me,
Walney had the baths and the pavilion too,
The summers were long and the skies were blue.

We would pack up the sandwiches and off we would go,
What time we would get back, we did not know,
We would spend hours paddling in the sea,
Then go to the pavilion for a cup of tea.

There were ice cream stalls and lots to do,
Everywhere you went there would be a queue,
In those days, Walney was the place to be,
Amid the sun, the sand and the Irish Sea.

Now, sadly the baths and pavilion are no more
And nowhere to go along the shore,
Times have now changed and Walney too,
Even the summer skies are not as blue.

But I still have my memories of what used to be,
Of Walney Island by the sea.

Robert Beach

Cameras

Taking photos is easy,
Wherever you are,
You can take a picture,
You don't have to travel far.

You just click the button
And you're done,
It's so quick and easy,
It's not that fun.

Yet; as years pass
And we get older,
We look at our memories,
Stored in a folder.

They may not seem special,
At the time they're taken,
But as we look at them,
The memories waken.

The happiness and laughter,
Come flooding back,
That photos can't capture,
But our memories keep track.

So, wherever you are,
However old you may be,
These photos become memories,
I know they do for me.

Gemma Musgrove

Time Apart

It breaks my heart to see you go
Though I'll see you soon
I pray for days to end
And gladly welcome out the moon

The time we are apart
I'm always thinking of you
Missing you like mad
Wishing you could take me too

Your face goes round in my head
As I lay awake at night
Wishing you were next to me
Holding me so tight

When you're not around
It feels like forever
I wish I could fast forward time
So we could be together.

Natalie Louise West

Mystical Garden

Her garden, my mother's garden, was once a battlefield,
Not one of carnage or real blood, but imaginary,
A soldier she had unearthed, a toy soldier with a gun,
Perished along with the memories, a sigh, lain to rest.

Countless children converged upon that garden,
With a deft movement of her garden fork, much was re-ignited,
Some of the persons who studiously placed that soldier 'midst the mud,
Are now themselves 'neath the earth, but not lost, nor forgotten.

We laughed as we drank our tea, a marble was tilled,
Don't put them in your mouth and swallow, Grandma would say,
A dozen children in a circle lay, tongues protruding in concentration,
Different colours inside, unbreakable or so we thought, but fun.

With all the verve of an amateur archaeologist she hoed,
Metal upon metal, all wheels intact, lay unearthed before us,
Racetrack and dirt roads long since reclaimed by nature,
So very many tiny hands steered that car, so much pleasure had.

Normally a leg might constitute a shocking and grisly discovery,
Squeals of joy and laughter, softie girls and embarrassed boys,
It is not uncommon at number 75 for body parts to be exhumed,
Action Men and Barbie Dolls regularly fought upon the sacred turf.

My mother's back garden is not a playground for the rich and famous,
More a playground for the waifs and strays of the neighbourhood,
Some can sit and gaze upon that mystical plot of land in wonder,
Many more can look down upon us, silent voices, eternal memories.

Michael Hartshorne

Ways To Kielder Village School

We marched to school the road way -
past waiting black spiders in hedges,
webs seemingly innocently sparkling,
once a coiled roadside adder,
skirted fearfully.

We meandered home the wood way -
searching for wild blackberries,
sweet summer strawberries,
tiny newts captured in jam jars,
a deer in the forest;

we followed the river,
deep, tree-tangled,
jumped across from stone to stone,
in winter
slid out over the ice -

It always took us longer to walk home.

Carole Luke

A Memorable Party

That evening, when the party began,
Will be etched on my memory forever,
Watching groups on the lawn, dressed according to plan,
In 'Twenties' attire, so witty and clever.

We drifted about to the wind-up gramophone
Playing 'Twenties' music, enjoying the scene,
In the heat of the sun, setting the tone,
Reliving the glamour, feeling smart and serene.

Years away in time, we indulged in the dream
Of days gone by, a drink in hand,
No rush or panic, no need to scheme,
To make decisions, organise or command.

We were there to relax and celebrate
Eighty-five years of life's ups and downs,
To sip from a glass and eat off a plate,
To absorb the scene, its colours and sounds.

The views of trees, distant hills and blue sky
Erased town noises, pollution and stress,
There was time to talk and let thoughts fly,
To escape the present, into the past, no more, no less.

S J Dodwell

Past Christmases

Childhood Christmases, fond memories have I
My mum, she worked very hard,
A widow she became, since I was three,
The youngest of five children, you see.

In two rooms we managed well,
All happy, Mum doing her best,
Decorations, a tree as well,
Mum having a well-earned rest.

An orange, apple, nuts in our stocking,
Also a gift stuck on top,
A small bar of chocolate the small ones had,
My dolly, was called Flip-Flop.

The smell of market stalls aglow,
Hot chestnuts cooking, well done,
Fruit and veg, all piled very high,
Carol singers, carols all are sung.

Now that's all gone, Mum as well,
Three of us have died too,
Christmas is now just memories,
Because now it makes me blue.

Jacqueline Farrell

194

Looking Back

I love Lincolnshire
Where I was born and bred
In a big old farmhouse
Where I was clothed and fed

In the lazy days of summer
We played the hours away
Often at the beck fishing
As happy as larks in May

Mother knitted some yellow cosies
So we could paddle in the pond
When wet they sagged down to our knees
And sometimes way beyond

Down to the meadow we'd run
Looking for wild flowers
Kingcups, harebells and trembling grass
We'd be away for hours

A cuckoo would sing in a tree
Rabbits would play in the sun
Mother would call us to come in
So we'd set off for home with a run

Some days we'd play in the trees
Pretending to be Robin Hood
We made Lincoln-green outfits
Bows and arrows were made of wood

Childhood days are long since gone
I'm married with a family of four
Living in the wolds of Lincolnshire
A place I really adore

The years have come and gone
But there's still beauty everywhere
Spring, summer, autumn, winter
Lincolnshire is for us to share.

Joan M Littleworth

Seven Brooks

One of the seven brooks that cross our quaint old town
Runs from the great lake, cascading down the falls
Onto the rocks below.
It passes the old Pretoria mine, where 344 men and boys
Lost their lives.
The brook seems to swell as it meanders on by,
Some folk say with tears in their eyes.
Trapped down below all those years ago.

The brook runs alongside a forgotten footpath,
Before exploding into my secret garden.
Once inside, it feels as though you have stepped back in time
With rhyme 'n' reason,
Your thoughts take you through every season.

Sitting alone in my garden in spring,
Listening to the early songbird sing.
Hidden from view of prying eyes,
Apple blossom trees blot out the bright sunlit sky.

Summer's now here, the brook looks divine,
Fishing for sticklebacks in the warm sunshine.
In the cool mountain stream, I paddle my feet,
Rabbits at play within easy reach.

The autumn leaves of golden brown,
Fall gently to the ground.
The hedgehogs and squirrels hurry to fill up their larder,
In winter they would find life much harder.

Winter comes along and my garden's now bare,
The brook's now a raging torrent, but it won't notice me
As it sweeps out to sea.
A robin now flies onto my holly tree, there are a few berries left
For a friend oh, so true,
But I can't understand why he stays
To see winter through?

I'll be back early next year,
For it's my time well spent,
In my secret garden,
On the edge of dear old Chowbent.

Ken Pendlebury

The Faraway Lake

The sparkling waters of the lake
Were invitation irresistible
On that day of sultry heat
Out there in a foreign land.

Confident and strong in youth
Armando climbed a rocky height
His tanned skin glistened in the sudden sun
Burst free from concealing cloud.

Proud, he stood a moment, poised
Knowing her eyes were watching every move
He let his body fall in perfect dive
Slicing the waiting waters of the lake.

No sign of him, as minutes crawled like hours
And fear screamed through the air;
She saw his head appear - he looked confused
His arms were flailing as he disappeared again.

Now panic rose and Seela ran, half-clothed
Plunged into unfamiliar waters
Frantically, she swam.
She caught his upraised hand and with a lunge
Clamped it to the rock he'd hit.

The touch of something solid
Seemed to wake him with a shock
He shook the water from his eyes and smiled
But could not hide
The fear and the relief that Seela saw
And shared.

Oonagh Twomey

Just Memories

Memories can be hurtful when you are five
Locked in a cupboard, not knowing the time.
Memories never fade away when you are five.
Happy days now, but the memory still remains
Locked in a cupboard when you were five.
Happy days now.
Memories come and go, but you *never* forget
Locked in a cupboard when you were five.

Roland Edgar Torn

I Remember

I remember the village where I was born
And the old terrace house in the street:
The garden with apple trees grown by my gran,
The Solomon's Seal and the lilac so sweet.

I remember the river and its two sandy beaches
At the foot of the bridge where we paddled and played
And Mill Hill and The Glen, where we picnicked in summer
Under the trees in its deep, mossy shade.

I remember the farm boys sideways on their horses,
Pulling the carts full of beet,
To the barges that lay await on the river
And the throb of the tugs in my sleep.

I remember the day when, a small, lonely child,
I set off with my bear in his pram,
To the house of another alone little girl
And a lifetime of friendship began.

I remember so much of a world that has gone,
Of a village, its byways and lanes;
The busy High Street and the people we knew:
Now only the memory remains.

Daphne Foreman

Thank God For The Memories:

I sit and gaze through the firelight gleam,
Recalling memories from long long ago.
Memories of when there were two of us
Enjoying the peace of the firelight glow.
I thank God for these memories, for how else would I pass
These lonely evenings sat here on my own?
For now there seems nothing to break the silence
As one sits through the wintry nights all alone.
The memories bring back our lives from the past
When, for comfort, we each had the other,
But now it is hard to be brave to the end
Without the true love and help from another.
Please God, help us know we are still not alone
Although you've taken one half of the pair,
Let us know they are with us, helping us along the way
For, as we follow on, we know they are there.

Jean C Pease

Friends

(In memory of Michael Keogh)

Friends, they come,
Friends, they go,
When their time's up,
You'll never know,
One day they're here,
The next, they're gone,
But no matter what happens,
Their memory lives on,
Now and forever,
In all of our hearts,
No one forgets,
The times they shared,
No one forgets,
They were always there,
All you can do now,
Is sit and pray,
Knowing they're resting,
In a better place.

Daniel Barry

Some Summer Memories

Whenever I start to reminisce
It's the summer memories I choose
To recall, the first boy's tender kiss,
Summer-brown legs, black patent shoes,
Swirling white pleated tennis shorts;
A myriad blooms of every hue.
Learning all the summer sports,
Discovering the sea is green, not blue.
Resting on the feathery waves, listening
To the happy voices on the shore.
Watching sailing boats go by, glistening.
The shiny lino on the floor
A sticky paper bag, humbugs within,
Scratchy straw hats with cotton flowers
And tight elastic that chafed my chin;
The storm that lasted for hours and hours.
These memories are so clear and dear
I know that they'll never fade away
(As will the photographs of yesteryear)
They're mine until my dying day.

Sylvia Moulds

A Tale Of Yesterday

I was born in Runcorn Town,
of which I'm proud.
When I was small, so long ago,
the world was full of war and woe.
Ration books were the rule,
so I with many, were sent to a town not far away.
Blackpool by the sea, you know
this was the place that I had to go
where along the beach
one day did learn to swim the proper way.

But home was where my heart lay
so I wrote to Mum I could not stay
so home once more during bombing raids
down the cellar we would go
till all at once, the all clear rang out.

But days were warm and sunny then
lots of fun and games to play up by the lake
we made our boats to see whose paper boat would float
then off back home in time for tea
to sit by the fire, toast muffins to eat.

Whit walks with bands and all the town
marched to the park
then sat around eating ice cream and riding on the fair
go on the big dipper, if you dare.

We sat in the winter nights
making rugs by candlelight
listening to the radio run on batteries
to music and Dick Barton
then cocoa, toast
for soon it's time for bed for us children all around.

Mum and Dad were great to us
who gave us lots of love and lots of trust,
laughter too
I had a happy childhood.
We always had brown sandwiches and jelly
for tea on Sunday.
More memories that can be told
now that I'm growing old.

To cross the River Mersey
we walk the railway bridge,
it cost one penny to come back home again
then on the transporter bridge
so merry this too cost a penny,
but it took cars and bikes as well
over the water and sand it rattled and shook,
but stood the time, till new ways of crossing could be found -
a bridge now spans that famous place
I could go on, but that's my lot.
Elizabeth Wilkinson

Memories Are Made Of This

Scamp – Nov 1992–Aug 2007

On 22nd August 2007, it was time to say goodbye
You knew of my sadness and saw the tears I cried
I couldn't let you carry on being so very poorly
So I sent you to Heaven where you can now rest for me.

I know you'll be happier and will not be in pain again
My pain will still continue, every day will feel the same
You are my dearest friend, the one by my side, in good times and bad
My heart is completely broken and I feel so empty and sad.

Where do I go from here? Who do I talk to now?
When I get lonely and fill up with tears, I always had you around
To comfort me and lay by my side, giving me unconditional love
You've now gone to a happier place and my days ahead are going to be tough.

You were put to sleep as you lay in my arms - closeness I won't ever forget
I took the pain away from you and that's something I won't ever regret
Your picture sits beside a candle that I light in memory of you
I know in time my pain will heal and your spirit will see me through.

On 25th August 2007, I released a balloon for you up in the sky
I felt some of the pain lift away from me, a release of the tears I cry
I now have your ashes and I will plant a rose where you sleep
No matter where I go, you will never be too far from me.

I miss you so much and it's a feeling I cannot describe
The emptiness that followed when it was time for me to say goodbye
I thought I was prepared, 'Be strong' I kept telling myself
You had to go to a better place, where you would no longer be in ill health.

I will never forget you - I won't ever replace you for another
This is it for me, now your precious life is over
I will forever keep our special moments locked inside my heart
I have so many happy memories of you so we will never be apart.

Louise Allen

Memories Of Tomorrow

On the lip-smacking tip
Of my dreams, I taste
A love, dark as Bourneville
And a rosy Worcester Permain
Windfall of uncomfortable deeds
Long-hoped forgotten
Shufflefoots through my
Armstrong-Siddeley Sapphire
Running-board back bedroom carpet
Of the Dinky toy past,
Where I am brave
As Hiawatha again;
Free in the forests
Of Feeling-no-Pain;
Asleep in the romantic
Bow-tied saxophoned Mecca
Of my quick-stepping youth,
Where ginghamed girls creaked
In petticoats stiff
As a grandmother's morality
And the last bus home
Was never delayed
But always came too soon
Behind the lipstick promises
And a vinegar greaseproof
Sixpenny-mix fumbling
Memory ache in
The indigestible dark.
Tonight
I'll sleep forever safe
In my painless dreaming,
Never wake to the breathless
Turmoil of a morning's
Pill counting and
Blackpool will win the cup
On a bright day in May
When yesterday's smile
Hugs me alive
And my mum has ironed
Creases in my shorts again.
I'll sweeten
The glass-alli rolling day
In spo and crab-apple mush sauce;
Dig air nuts from south wind
Blow-dried hillside verges;
Eat my tea playing backyard
Hopscotch, baggsy-not-me;
Listen to Grandad's hymn
To the sweat-streaked moulding-hole

Memories Are Made Of This

Bronchitic graveyard of his happy days
And at nine-o'clock news
I'll swim into the heedless sheets
Chasing warm teacake balmy-glowed
Swaddling-embered memories of tomorrow
And I will never die.

Jim Rogerson

The Old Soldier

''Twer never like this when I were a lad,'
The old soldier used to say.
'Had to do what I were told
No nonsense in my childhood day.'
Of his service days he never spoke
A portion of his life that was kept
Deep within, only reappearing in
Dreadful dreams, whilst he slept.

He dreamt of his home so far away,
Of his loving wife and son.
He dreamt of noise and blood and gore
Of when this war was done.
As a youth he fought for God and King
And something he could never understand;
How he came to lose his precious wife and son
Whilst he fought in foreign lands.

So now he lives by manners and rules of old
And tells how things were then.
But you won't be told how bad it was,
How war took boys and made them men.
He keeps the memories of his wife and son,
Of comrades who beside him fell.
And perhaps he listens to other
Souls who have sad tales to tell.

''Twer not like this when I were a lad,'
Is how *his* story goes.
He doesn't say his life was sad,
He thinks nobody knows.
His rheumy eyes may look back on life
But no words are ever said.
Because he can never speak
Of the type of youth he led.

Mary Howcroft

203

First Kiss By The River

The river in shallows, murmured and chattered.
In deep pools, sighing, swishing and swirling.
The sun blazing down on great patches of gold,
The gorse bushes popping, their seed pods exploding;
While the broom gently swayed, wafting its perfume
On the delicate touch of the breeze from the river.

Nature itself could not have been kinder
That day, as we walked in its splendour
We shyly held hands - it was our first meeting.
Then, we sat on the grass in quiet conversation.
Long pauses, deep sighs, then trickles of words,
Nervous laughs, like the sounds of the river
As it flowed past our feet.

We turned to each other with lips slightly pouting,
Both of us nervous of that very first kiss.
Our lips barely touched, like a butterfly flutter,
Or was it a puff from the wind on the river?
Your sweet tiny face seemed mounted in gold,
Eyes open wide and kingfisher blue.

New love, young love, needs time to mature,
But we drifted apart, then found love once again.
True love, mature love, but not with each other.
Yet still the broom, its perfume heart stopping
And the golden gorse goes on pleasing
Down by the river, for other loves walking,
Just as it did when we were so young.

A R (David) Lewis

Twilights

Carefree days full of love and laughter,
I was a child when we walked country tracks
Relished the glorious golden rays of sunset
Gleaming on velvet fields that we passed.

Honeysuckle's distinctive fragrance
Danced around us from hedgerows nearby,
A million buttercups peppered the ground
Intermingled with delicate daisies open-eyed.

The fragile fleeting beauty of wild roses
Exuberantly bloomed enduring charm,
Bleating sheep sporadically broke the silence
Impetuous blackbirds sometimes clattered alarms.

As gentle as a rosebud, my little mother,
She loved these simple pleasures and more,
Skylarks that warbled and bluebell woods,
Triumphant daffodils that opened spring's door.

Many years we walked contentedly together,
Embracing the passing shadows of time,
Admiring atmospheric landscapes
Savouring nature's splendour so sublime.

Rest now, little mother, twilight again approaches
Precious memories your legacy, my inspiration
Soon you will rejoice in unparalleled serenity
Witness startling sunsets beyond imagination.

Celia Auld

Memories

Memories are like dewdrops in the garden of your mind
Sparkling like diamonds - of days you've left behind
Childhood days of jumping high until you touched the sky
Adolescent teenager - so often wondering, 'Why'
Falling in and out of love and back in love again
The meeting of magnetic minds with boys and then of men
Until one day, 'the one' appears who stands out in the crowd
Your spirit soars, your heart beats, oh, so very loud
Romance turns into wedded bliss
There's laughter, love and tears
Then homes and work and babies to fill the passing years
Before you know they're reared and grown
And you are left behind
But memories are like dewdrops in the garden of your mind.

Margaret Rogan

I Hide Inside Myself

I count my blessings, one and two,
Three and four, there must be more!
I hide inside myself and look.

The first must be my birth
Into the love and care of a happy home.
Next, a childhood glowing with
Fun and learning in equal measure.
I hide inside myself and look.

What comes next? You ask,
No need to search, it's there.
In memories of love and kisses
Stolen; freely given; heart-caught
New-knowledge for my youth.
I hide inside myself and look.

And yes, a major blessing looms,
Taking my life and filling it with joy.
Marriage, children, anxious days,
Broken nights and sheer blessed bliss
With loved ones; hugs and kisses . . .
I hide inside myself and look . . .

It's great!
Patricia M Smith

A Long Time Ago

Now that I am eighty-four
I remember more and more of
Many years when I was young
Good and bad times come alive
I was eight, my sister five.

There was a garden, very small
Dad made for children there to play.
A hut, a sandpit, or the swing
In rain or cold friends all came in.

In the hut small chairs and table
There we played at games or drew.
Now all are gone, but this I know
How good it was, and even now
In my old age
I clearly see all that
Dad then gave to me.

M M Sleeboom-Derbyshire

206

Time Was

Father and son, fishing by the stream
Lovers strolling in the park with their heads full of dreams
These were the days of yesteryears
When it was safe to roam
Before TV sets took over most of our homes.

Some very good programmes, I don't doubt
But what a lot of rubbish we can all do without,
Where there used to be Mam and Dad waiting at home,
Children now reach out for the remote control.
They learn so much from the box in the corner,
Oh, bring back the days of Little Jack Horner.

For the lessons, then learnt at their mother's knees
Were of far more value to children, than these
So come on you men in the TV game,
Bring back some stories with morals
That worked in the past.
Let's see more people playing the game, so to speak,
Showing kindness and love when dealing with others,
Help children realise we are all sisters and brothers.
Then a better world will start to take shape
Once again our streets will be safe to roam
Through parks, woodlands and mountain tops
Even playing in the street with whip and top
With the knowledge they are never alone
With a good family life and a secure home.

Kathleen Lockwood

Selective Recall

Unsummoned they come like snowdrops in spring,
Bring light to the eyes and joy to the heart;
These are sweet memories that leap and dart
Into our remembrance and make us sing.
More bitter are those memories which cling
Like burrs to remind us of sorrow's part
In lives that from the moment when they start
Must learn how rapture is a fleeting thing.
Let go the pangs of your remembered grief;
You have survived, in spite of all you live.
Cling to the recall of your happy years;
Heed not the words of those whose sad belief
Bids us hoard all moments that life may give.
Choose memories that nurture hope, not tears.

C Wolstenholme

Looking Back

It is too quiet now at times.
Often it is too nondescript.
There's peace, of course, that rhymes
Almost with dullness - it is not chipped
With quick, deft words that dart like birds
Or shared laughter or a teasing, gentle hint -
All of which served to create impressionslike stars in herds
Scintillating in a blue midnight sky or sparks from flint.

I remember it as it was.
Nothing seems to alter or to change.
It wasn't always laughter-gilded because
That isn't what real life is like - the range
In feelings inevitably touched us all.
But oh! how warm it was - how full of life!
And did I know that it would last beyond the first sad call
Until the last - that it would outlast the strife

Of parting, illness, worry, the passage of time,
New friends, old enemies and the dilution of my prime?

I knew it not, then -
But I have learned it well - now!

And - I dwell not in memory only when
All seemed warm and bright - *I live now!*
S V Batten

The Times I Will Never Forget

Home-cooked chips and treacle pudding, pancakes tossed so high
A coal fire burning and music playing as snow fell from the sky
Family gatherings with sparklers and cartwheels, a bonfire we built with a guy
A snowman at Christmas with large carrot nose and pieces of coal for his eyes
Decorations at Christmas we made out of paper, a castle a Nativity set
We sang carols on doorsteps, left Santa a sherry, it's times that you never forget
Two laughing parents, a brother, a sister, a terrier dog as a pet
With rabbits and fish, a budgie, canary, we were constantly calling the vet
We went swimming and fishing, had picnics galore, wore minis
and Kaftans that draped on the floor
We picked snowdrops and daffodils, primroses too
Made blackberry jelly, had trips to the zoo
Went to parties and dances, cinema shows
With interesting hair and imaginative clothes
Those were the days with little regrets
Those were the times I will never forget.
Amanda Bosson

Memories Are Made Of This

I Remember Now

I remember bright golden days of childhood,
Summers seemed to last for all time,
What fun we had watching the Punch and Judy shows,
I remember all the different games we played,
We would climb down the cliffs, go swimming in the sea,
I would sit in the middle of the field for hours with my friend
Making buttercups or daisy chains,
Mum would take us for long walks,
We would gather blackberries during September
So that Mum could make a blackberry pie,
When out on our own, we would go scrumping
So that made it even better,
A blackberry and apple pie, scrumptious!
My two brothers, Tony and Ray, would go through the fields
Early morning gathering mushrooms,
They would also go into the fields to try and catch a rabbit,
I will always remember Ray saying,
'I nearly caught a rabbit today, Mum!'
But he never succeeded,
The rabbits could move much quicker than Ray.
If we wanted to go to the cinema,
We would gather empty jam jars or lemonade bottles
Take them into the shop
Where we would be given a half-pence for each jar or bottle we had,
I was a child through the Second World War years
And there was no money for toys, so different to what they are today.
I remember clearly what fun we had,
I also remember the pure happiness of being a child.

Phyllis Laidlaw

Remembering

Memories are made of this
Like a photo that you miss
You just have to call to mind
And there you will eventually find
A picture of what happened then
And you can do this - where or when

So if there's something that you miss
You can summon it up just like this
Like a magician - cast your spell
And in a moment, time will tell
Just like a video that you rewind
You will be back there in that time.

Barbara Coward

Old Geordie Land

My mother was a Scottish lass.
Her soft voice had a lilt.
A very clever tailoress,
She could even make a kilt.
There was mass unemployment.
Those times were rather hard,
How oft' the dreaded news came out,
'They've closed another yard.'
To keep the family going,
My mam was always willing.
She treadled that old Singer,
Just to earn an extra shilling.
The children entertained themselves
And played all sorts of games.
We had tops, whips and marbles
And called each other names.
Christmas was a special time,
When everyone was jolly.
The house was hung with paper chains
And mistletoe and holly.
Stockings hung by the fire,
A constant source of joy,
An apple, orange, sweets and nuts,
With luck, a special toy.
The kitchen had a fragrance,
That no one could mistake.
That gorgeous, spicy, fruity smell
Of a baking Christmas cake.
The smell of roasting chicken,
In those days, quite a treat.
A Christmas 'pud' with brandy sauce,
A very wholesome sweet.
The next week was the New Year,
Which my Mam called Hogmanay.
We were allowed to stay up late
To 'see in' New Year's Day.
The solemn rites of 'First Foot'
We all thought it was fine.
We ate our Scottish shortbread
And had homemade ginger wine.
Holidays over, back to school,
One hurried through the gate.
We knew that we would 'get the strap'
If we should turn up late.
By now my dad was back at work
But the day that I minded most
We packed 'all wor stuff' on the coalman's lorry
And 'shifted' to the coast.
I quickly lost my city pallor and had a ruddy tan.

Memories Are Made Of This

I was so delighted that I didn't walk, I ran.
We played 'Foreign Legion',
A gallant bunch of chaps.
With our little wooden rifles
And hankies stuffed in caps.
Sadly this all ended with the voice of Chamberlain,
As he informed the nation, 'We are at war again.'
Now food was strictly rationed,
But scraps were never wasted,
They all went into lovely broth,
That 'posh' folks never tasted.
Now I am old and do not work,
My life is not too bad and I still recall
The fun I had, when I was just a lad.

James M Davies

Mum – Centre Of My Life

Mum, warm, wise, caring and always full of love
As long as she was in my life, Heaven was above
In the mornings she woke me with a cup of tea
Bustling in and urging me on, a welcome face to see

Down in the warm farmhouse kitchen, was breakfast
Before jumping on my cycle and peddling so fast
To catch the train to school and later, work
Never allowed to stay in bed and duties shirk

Coming home in the evening, there she was again
If she was there to greet me, life was right as rain
Home, caring for us all, was where she wanted to be
Life, for her, was all about, caring for her family

Then, one dark, wet evening as she walked back
From visiting her mother, hit by a car, she lay like a sack
Broken body, near to death and wracked with pain
It was many, many months before she was home again

We were so glad to have her back, in her rightful place
And to see her wonderful, kind and caring face
Now she needed care and love, we were happy to repay
Her with a love for her that was deeper than words can say

For all her life she was everything, the centre of my life
To come into her warm presence soothed away all strife
If she was there, then everything was right in my world again
She made the outside world fade away with all its pain

I hope that she knew how important she was to me
And that how much I adored her, she could see
I hope that I have been half as good a Mum as she
If I have inspired such love, how happy I would be.

Margaret Meagher

When You Were Three

What made you cry?
A graze on the knee
Daddy late home for tea.
Soap in your eye
Pet rabbit might die.
Favourite toy being lost
Fingers frozen by frost.
Time for bed
A bang on the head.
A lost sock or shoe
Just not much to do.
A squashed snail
A black thumbnail.
Bare feet on sand
A splinter in your hand.
Tea not ready yet
A promise not met.
Painting gone wrong
Forgotten words of a song.
A scratch from the cat
Nest of ants where you sat.
Brother's cross word
And 'Sorry' not heard.
A pain in the tummy
A frown from Mummy.

But what made you laugh?
A butterfly in flight
A kiss and goodnight.
The cat's soft fur
And to hear her purr.
Brother home from school
An ice lolly so cool.
A walk in the park
Hide-and-seek in the dark.
A daisy so small
A game of football.
To paddle in the sea
Or sit on my knee.
Bubbles in the bath
A spider on the path.
The scent of a rose
A tickle on the nose.
Going high on a swing
And hearing birds sing.
Your Grandma's cuddles
To splash in puddles.
Hear a church clock strike
Or a revving motorbike.
Just living each day
In your own special way.

Margaret Rowe

Do You Remember . . .

Do you remember Spangles?
Such a lovely fruity sweet.
With many different flavours,
And so really nice to eat.

Do you remember Jackie?
With those posters for the wall.
Bowie, Essex and Bolan,
There were pictures of them all.

Do you remember Magpie?
Blue Peter wasn't so cool.
With Tony, Mick and Susan,
We all watched it after school.

Do you remember tank tops?
I was never such a fan.
With all their stripy colours,
They were knitted by your nan!

Do you remember childhood?
When things seemed so much better.
The sun was always hotter,
And rain was so much wetter!

Kaz

Wartime Memories

A siren moans, a frightening sound
I'm caught in a raid, was homeward-bound.
Run to a shelter, not far from here,
Then waiting, hoping for the all-clear.

Looking out from the shelter, shrapnel flying about,
It's dark now, somehow I must go out.
Running, then, the drone of enemy plane,
I turn up a side road, lie by a wall in the rain.

As I lie in the dark praying, you see,
The ground starts to rock around me.
German plane drops a landmine, such a thud!
Less than a mile, as I lie in the mud.

Now all is quiet, running, I see an unlit bus,
Fortunately it waits for me, what a rush.
Leaving the bus, I see on a nearby seat
A dog, lying unconscious, it looks asleep.

In my arms I carry it, close to another wall,
Praying, please God, give me strength not to fall.
Into our garden shelter, I stagger, I'm home,
The dog survived, we found the owner, no more to roam.

A Pincombe

Memories Of A Visit To Friends

Days sped by that were so full
So much to see and never dull.
The body quickened to the pace
Of filling time and in our haste,
You filled the moments with delight
Our eyes beholding many a sight
Of that fair land now far away
But memories hold it safe to stay.

We arrived in sunshine bright
To glimpse your face, a wondrous sight,
In time to see your daughter wed
Then on our travels we were sped.
Through mountain high and valley deep
With goat, deer, fish, opossum, sheep.
Seeing the sights of yesteryear
With joyful singing in the ear.

Water around us everywhere,
River, stream and fountain fair.
Falls that pound from great height
Or gush in flurries dazzling white.
The sea's about, not far away,
With shore and beaches for our play.
A cliff to climb and bush to roam
Feet on sand, rock, wood and loam.

Mid the shades of nature's green
Travelling on through changing scene
By car, bus, cable, sky lift, train,
Viewed shore and isles via boat and plane.
Museum, mission, house and church
Preserved, restored that in our search
To see and know more of this land,
The way of life to understand.

From dawn to dusk we shared each day
A precious gift, light-hearted, gay
With people met, old friends to see
That meant so much, so much to me.
For being blest each day that passed
With memories, treasures that last
Of time spent in your land enthralled
Where for short season, home we called.

H G Wainwright

A Walk In The Dales

(Junior School Trip - 1950s)

It was a long way for small legs,
up from the grey-stone village quaint
in its steady regularity of life,
its air of possessing age-old truths
lost to us town kids.

Over dry stone walls,
across fields speckled with sheep droppings,
tripping over boulders that for centuries
had unfooted the unwary,
moving breathlessly upwards,
breasting one rise,
only to find another rearing ahead;
our limbs, used only to playground skipping
or rounders, heavy from the strenuous climb.

Then a yell of triumph - a boy had reached the top.

Inspired, we cracked on, heedless now
of grazed knees and ankles,
badges of our struggles,
sinking onto sheep-cropped grass,
gulping the fresh air,
the small bottles of orange juice.

Did we then find inspiring
the grandeur of the sight laid out for us?
The grey-green slopes below,
the expanse of blue sky unclouded by factory smoke,
sun and shadow chasing each other across the landscape,
humankind living and working cheek by jowl with nature,
each shaping the other.

Or did we, child-like, demolish crisps and chocolate,
run around scattering sheep, before racing one another
down to the next village?

Marion Porter

Last Card – 14th August 1997

Still in my sight, those bright blue irises are,
Blooming lovely on its front.
Their showy heads of three large
Petals and leaves as long as reeds, could imply
That in the sizzling summertime it was best for her
To leave hot London behind in search of paradise,
With cool waters around:

To breathe fresh breeze, to get things off her chest,
To gather strength and laugh her troubles away
In the company of a protective, powerful guy,
To have a whale of a time! At night
I wanted her to dance and charm
All in a chic, floral design ballgown.

To celebrate achievements to date,
As a roving ambassador, in humanity's defence!
To back up my message, the face of Margot Fonteyn,
The most accomplished ballerina of our days,
Was on the stamp attached. Not once

Did it flash my mind that her life was under threat
Of any kind! Unlike the Queen Mum,
Nearing a hundred fast, she was in her prime.
I still rationalise. Never had it felt that
I was saying goodbye, or, God forbid, in my hand
Not just my last card to her I held, but her fate.

I wish I'd had powers to see future facts!
About a trip to France, I would have advised
The Queen of Hearts to think twice. A fortnight
Was enough for things to reorganise, to avert
The worst tragedy on Earth, to alter not only a bad plan,
To alter, but the history of the UK and the world!

Lucy Carrington

Sundays Past

Where are the children this Sabbath day
A lie-in in bed or out to play?
How different things were when I was young
Toys and riches, there were none

We went to Chapel three times a day
Morning, afternoon and night
Wearing pretty dresses
Shoes that were always white

The ladies, they wore fancy hats
With bows, feathers and flowers
The preacher used to shout *so* loud
He seemed to go on for hours

Because Chapel was so far away
Down my nan's I would stay
For my dinner, then my tea
Night-time Nan came to Chapel with me

On Sundays, my nan was very strict
No knitting or sewing to be unpicked
Daren't mention going down the shop
For a bag of sweets or a bottle of pop

The Whitsun turnout was a treat
Walked for miles, aching feet
Sandwiches, seed cake, oh, what fun
Then a game of rounders, we always won

I'm sure if we had these times again
There would be no more drugs, violence and pain
More happiness and peace in the world there would be
If children had a childhood, like me.

Jill Williams

The Excursion

(Jesus said, 'I am the Bread of Life': John 6:35)

A daytrip to the seaside
Where my pal hadn't been
Money was scarce in those days
The sea, she'd never seen!
As the train got closer
To Portrush, by the sea
Her face lit up in wonder
She clapped her hands with glee
'Oh this is all such fun
Let's have a great *big splash!*'
Off came her clothes for her swimsuit
Into those wave did dash!
Then a string of donkeys
Came trotting o'er the Strand
So we paid our money over
That ride, made us feel grand
We queued up for ice cream
With 'swooshy' gel on top
Then in a hall we all had food
We were a hungry lot!
With our lunchtime over
To 'Barry's' we did go
Where we rode upon 'the ghost train'
And screamed and yelled out so!
To 'the hall of mirrors'
Which made us fat or thin
Or with big, long, nosey faces
Then a wide, ugly grin
My pal rode 'the bumpers'
I, on the big wheel seat
Ate candyfloss and sticks of rock
That was *our* seaside treat!
Time goes by so swiftly
When we were having fun
Sweet memories of yesteryear
When she and I were young.

Beth Stewart

Landscape Of Dreams

When the winter is hard outside
and the world of waking is cruel
I dream of the paths I used to walk.

bluebells on the slopes,
carpets round the roots of trees
in shadow and quietness.

my dreamscape is seasonless.
snowdrop and dog rose bloom
next to each other.

meadows of buttercup
clover and thistle
stretch in my dreaming

to the mountains of heather
where nobody ventured
except me and my dog.

down a long disused lane
of willowherb and daffodil
to an old ruined cottage.

a hedge bright with fuchsia,
walls draped with honeysuckle
where crocuses smile.

I dream of the perfumes
of blossoms of levity.
they planted their seeds

in my brain, so that now
that the landscape is weeded
and usefully tended

they bloom in my dreaming
disarranged, out of season,
those long carefree walks
in the sunshine of childhood.
into one panorama
of flowers and hope,
despite the coldcity
and long lonely nights.

Fred Brown

Firstborn

(The Sweetest Thing)

Apple-dumpling fingers,
jelly-baby toes,
roly-poly tummy,
chocolate button nose;

Barley sugar dimples,
pink marshmallow chin,
cotton-candy tresses,
honeysuckle skin;

Babycham complexion,
bubbles through and through,
heart of gold shines brightly,
even when she's blue;

Lemon sherbet kisses,
cherry blossom cheeks,
satin when she whispers,
velvet when she speaks;

Tiny diamond teardrops,
sparkling emerald eyes,
sunshine when she's smiling,
rainbows when she cries;

Sugar, spice and honey,
sweet as sweet can be;
precious little angel,
our lovely fleur-de-lys.

D Hague

Memories Never Die

Oh what colourful tapestry to life's memories
Does the richness of love weave upon our hearts
Those of our parents that secured our background
Which built firm and dependable family ties
Their devotion of love was our upbringing
Our character is what we reaped from their labour
As they coaxed us to venture forth in life
Their guidelines were the sinews that helped us grow strong
At the time we were too young and naïve to understand
But when we look back into our memories
We can clearly see how much we are indebted to them
I am so thankful to God for my parents
That I had a mum and dad who loved and appreciated me.

Stephen Wyles

Memories Of Tibby

Tibby was our cat,
A family member he,
Striped like a tiger,
As anyone could see.

Our breakfast was ready,
On porridge we fed,
From the big iron pan,
Cooked on the fire red.

'Please bring Tibby's plate,'
Our mother she said,
Of all the family,
He was first to be fed.

Over the fields,
To school we would pass,
Where Father had scythed
A way through the grass.

Tibby, he followed,
Part of the way;
To wait our return
At the end of the day.

Warming, our Sunday roast
On the steel fender stood,
Tibby *never* sniffed it,
Though it smelled so good -
　　Because -
'Please bring Tibby's plate,'
Our mother she said,
Of all our family,
First slice to *him* was fed.

B B Brown

Christmas Gift

Some 96 years ago it was
My cousins came to stay
It was to be a jolly time
For it took in Christmas Day.

They hung up many paper chains
We drew and coloured cards
And helped to make the pastry
By rubbing in the lard.

We went into my aunty's bedroom
Singing 'Good Day It's Christmas Eve Morn'
And a sweet little baby girl was there
A gift, that had just been born.

'What will you call her?' we wanted to know
'She will be Marianne Eve for this day'
And I was to look after her, being the eldest
It made me feel very important that way.

My cousins went home the very next week
After little Marianne Eve had been named
And I looked after that new little baby
Whom Marianne had been named.

Georgina Ivison

Memories To Me

The excitement of the engagement
The beautiful wedding day
The birth of my only child
The first words he would say
The initial step into freedom
The day he started school
The achievement of passing the right exam
The entry to grammar school
The passing of the driving test
The owning of the very first car
The attainment of the right grades
The 18th birthday so bizarre
The time for further education
The acceptance into university
The struggle with the studies
The elation of gaining the degree
The triumph of graduation
The 21st birthday so special to me
The milestones and events in my life
These recollections are 'memories to me'.

Nigel Lloyd Maltby

Fairy Heart Splashes Memorised

(Dedicated to Robert Fagg and Emma Fagg)

True brew memories are made of
all loving happenings and passions which
delight the sways and rainbow sprays
upon our spiritual happiness trees. All
our brain marbles gather upon the magic
carpets to take flys around our body
souls to feel the greets and meets to
all organ warriors who adore all
memory patterns to our cornfield heartland
warriors. Who never do deals upon the
forgets as they know all the memorised
and natured wildlife tours while living
their spirits within upon these natured
finest evergreen lands. The highlighted
mountains are their favourite destinations
as when reaching the tops all gentle
fairy heart gangs are under these crystal
clear water fountains. As all souls
love to feel the unders with the fairy
heart wings making the perfect and
delicate splashes upon our love dove
clubs so we will never explore the forgets.

Steven Pearson

As It Was In The Beginning

I live on the edge of a precipice.
Many years I have spent up here,
waiting and cocking a listening ear.

Time has moved on, but still I stay.
'That is stupid,' I hear them say,
'why not pack and go away?'

The answer is simple,
if you care to hear:
I have grown used
to the beckoning height;
used to the morning
and evening light
that brightens my failing,
now desperate, sight.

I came with the foothold of youth
with its search for knowledge and truth,
with my head in the gathering clouds,
till time took hold and held me fast,
till every inch of future turned to past.

Mary Nugent

Blue Anchor

Slamming doors, steam clouds, heavy cases deposited
on a white edged platform.
A call, 'Blue Anchor',
We have arrived!
The winding lane heads inland
With room for only one car.
In the distance the castle at Dunster stands proud.
A sunny day's outing through the orchards awaits,
Twenty minutes on Western National to the magic village.
The market cross, olde world bottled glass-windowed shops
And the overshadowing dark mysterious Exmoor.
'We'll do that on Monday.'

Right now, never mind unpacking,
'Let's go to the beach!'
Its rock pools and shell-strewn shore,
All I needed was one single bucket and spade.
The small rejected broken union flag we found
To top our own castle created carefully and craftfully,
But, alas, washed right away at high tide.
These ingredients, simple and uncomplicated
Are the lasting building blocks of a five-year-old's holiday.

Six days later, the rain splashes endlessly
And dark drear doldrums clouds herald the week to its end.
The station platform is freshly soaked and puddled,
Its flower beds well anointed and the tell-tale willowherb given a boost.
In the distance, a plume of steam and smoke
Announces the approaching end of the chapter.
The rapid rattle and judder of the level crossing,
In the signalbox, busy levers crash and bells ring rapidly.
Just a few more minutes and then it's over for another year.
Soon we'll be aboard with comfy seats to whisk us away.
The time has come,
'Let's go to the beach!'
Michael Withey

Memories Are Made Of This

Playing hopscotch in the street
With chalked numbers one to twelve
Holding a pebble, ready, aim, throw
Hop, jump, there and back you go.
Then up to the woods with trees to climb
Reaching up as high as you can
To view the scene far below
Making sure that your knickers don't show,
Then laughter as you slide down
Trying not to fall your greatest wish
And memories are made of this.

Childhood's fun but you grow up
Leave school, start work, lots to do,
New things to learn, new friends to meet
No more playing in the street.
Boyfriends come with other things in mind
Ooh remember that first kiss?
What sweetness that tender touch.
Is love in the air? Oh, what a rush
Of feelings that make no sense
But you feel good so on a star wish
Because memories are made of this.

Holding my new baby son,
So much joy watching him grow.
Along comes a brother, now there's two
Much laughter but tears are few.
Then strangers meet and life turns around
They're drawn together by fate.
When their eyes meet all else goes
What the future holds nobody knows
But this is a love too strong
To turn your back - life is now a whizz
And memories are made of this.

The years roll along life's road
There's happy times, sad ones too
A roller coaster of ups and downs
And as you get older you frown -
You can't remember yesterday's date,
You're so full of aches and pains
But you can look way, way back
And you see clear as a bell
All that has happened and so it is
That memories are made like this.

Joan Earle Broad

Remembering

Growing up in a country village
Life centred around the local shop and post office
I remember years ago, waiting at the shop counter
While villagers discussed the latest news, amidst much laughter.

The village church and chapel were strong in the community
No games played or shops open then on a Sunday,
Fond memories of dancing lessons held in the church hall,
Old tyme and ballroom dancing was the theme, and thoroughly enjoyed by all.

Special memories of summer fêtes held in the vicarage grounds
With stalls of homemade products and vegetables home-grown,
I remember Cornish cream teas being served on the vicarage lawn
The pure white tablecloths, cutlery sparkling in the sun.

I used to help on the jumble stall, which was always busy
Everyone wanted a bargain, some items sold for a penny.
Wonderful memories of the Sunday school trips,
A day on the beach, exploring rock pools below towering cliffs.

Remembering the good times at the village school
With many friends, they were happy days, but teachers ruled,
School holidays, mostly spent outdoors, were full of adventure
Friends gathered at the village park, happy together.

We played on the downs, walked across the moors,
Gathered bluebells from woods, caught tadpoles in jars,
Went blackberry picking, for Mum to make a pie,
Arrived home with stained faces, but welcomed with a smile.

I remember when schooldays came to an end, childhood days were over,
Nervously, I started work, no friends at my shoulder.
As the years pass, with all the trials life brings,
       I often look back - remembering.

Lorna June Burdon

Leg-Work Tour Memories

A lot of my youth was involved with walking here, there
and everywhere,
And it was not because of what I may be charged on a 'bus, coach,
or any transport vehicle fare.

I chose to exercise my legs, and swing my arms
while I observed the scene,
Returning home, I stored in my brain the amazing images
of where I had been.

As a woman, I recall fondly, the innocent safety of my girlhood days
that had to cease,
Now, if a solitary female takes a stroll, she needs protection
from the police.

Every particle of my pity goes to those of you
who have not explored by Shanks's pony,
Your lives are as empty as the people whose eyes
only beauty, skin-deep see.

I'm truly grateful I have travelled by ramble, trek and hike,
before my knees buckle and my chest starts to wheeze,
So that when my pace slows and stride shortens,
I can look back on picturesque and enchanting sweet memories.

Joy R Gunstone

A Childhood Memory

As a child I wandered the fields
I never felt threatened.
One day as I drifted in nature
A strange sombre buzzing assailed my ears.
It came closer and louder and louder
Then a huge dark shape came into sight.

I'd never seen anything like this
A moving great sausage
Humming its Zeppelin tune.
Yes! The R100
Homing in to Cardington.

Years later I passed by its home,
Cardington, where it spent time resting
Moored to a great wondersome structure
Resting or quietly slumbering
Oh, the blessings of memory.

Joan R Gilmour

Once Upon A Time

As I strolled through our village of yesteryear,
I couldn't camouflage, or stop a tear,
A tear which cradled, a long time past,
A village, taken for granted, recognised to last,

I felt for a moment, time had just returned,
To an era of village life, quietly confirmed.
A time when shops exchanged the personal touch,
One to one service, a customer meant so much.

It was Mr or Mrs, or Christian name terms,
A friendly welcome, with genuine concern,
Enquiring of the family when illness had occurred,
A gift of six eggs would now seem absurd.

Views were extensive, across the forest's plain,
The wildness, the openness, revealing sandy lanes,
A contentment enveloped the spirit's driving will,
When wandering o'er the forest, experiencing its magical thrill,

The quietness of the village, a noticeable return,
Vehicles weren't many, a cyclist's wheels caused no concern,
All add to this fond memory, sadly now has gone to rest,
Progression of time has surfaced,
We now experience the modern quest.

Lorna Tippett

Memories Of Days Gone By

Memories of my younger years,
Lots of laughter and a few tears,
Out until it was nearly dark,
As we came home from the swings in the park.

There were happy times at the fair,
The music, lights and swinging chair.
Stalls and games you would try to win,
A goldfish if you were lucky, that brought a grin.

Once my dad went to the fair,
He was very lucky while he was there,
Couldn't get home quick enough to show us his prize -
A scooter he had won. What a lovely surprise!

I shed a few tears the very next day,
Coming off my scooter as I was at play.
Writing this has brought it all back,
The carefree days we seem to lack.

Evelyn M Harding

To A Dear Friend

Recurring memories
of a child's dream
to be together

He so tall, and she scarce reaching his knee;
Following and falling;
Falling and following;
Fearful lest aught should separate;
Jealous of the short time spent together;
Proud of the roughness of his uniform,
of the warm clasp of his hand,
Praying each day, a child's prayer
that God would not take him;
That the big plane in which he flew
would come back.

Would return, as so many days without him
saddened the child's heart;
For no one could understand
the love betwixt them both.
There was much joy in his company
much laughter in their play together
in the gentle understanding
of one for the other.

A child's dream
to be together
where death cannot separate,
in the field where so many poppies grow.

Ann R Bailey

Brightness

Some memories of mine will be
Sandcastles by a blue, blue sea,
A tender mother's sweet caress
Patent shoes and a pretty dress.

Feeding guinea pigs in a hutch
With squeaks and fur; I loved them much.
Jumping in pools and sparkling springs
Swimming costumes and rubber rings.

Climbing up a grassy slope
With all the joy and all the hope.
Balmy days all sunny and bright
Bathed a childhood of delight.

Christine Jacobs

The Pipe Band

(A childhood memory)

Away in the distance we just hear the drum
The crowd stirs and jostles to the sound of *brum-brum,*
A flash of bright tartan - their ribbons a-flutter
'They're coming, they're coming,' hear the crowd mutter.

The skirl o' the pipes now we can hear
The excitement grows as we know they are near
It's time for me to be swung up on high
A pair of broad shoulders - my seat in the sky.

Union Street is long and straight
I can see right down to Castlegate.
He's head and shoulders above the rest
He's the one that I love best
The leopardskin man with the great big drum
And his two long sticks beating out *brum-brum.*

How handsome, how striking, they look in their kilts
They're swinging and swaying in time to the lilt
Even as a child the sight moves you to tears
It's something that stays with you all down the years.

The pipers - they're blawing for all they are worth
Their cheeks pink and shiny look fit to burst
They reach a crescendo, as by us they pass
Overwhelming us all, every laddie and lass.

The precise wee drummers with their staccato beat
I was always intrigued with their white puttied feet
The tiny wee buttons up the outside
What did they cover, what did they hide?

Playing tunes of old Scotland we all know so well
Of mountains and glens, and where heroes fell
On the back of my neck up goes the hair
There it is! It's my favourite, they're playing 'Black Bear'!

The sense of loss as they pass me by
The sun seemed to dip and die in the sky
But if I get my father to run real fast
We'll just be in time for another march past!

Phyllis Henderson

The Lemon Tree

As the wind of change is blowing
Through the mists of time I see
That life is bright and bitter
Like the fruit of the lemon tree

Of years I am now older
As the seasons slip away
I think of friends and places
That have passed along my way

My days of early childhood
I dwell on more and more
But they are left forever
Like shells upon the shore

Those years were hard but happy
Filled with summer sun
Now to secret caves and woods
My thoughts so often run

The years were days of learning
As in life you always will
But of those friends and places
Are they remaining still?

Now with my children's children
I once again return
Though older, am I wiser
Or am I like them to learn?

Life is just a circle
Filled with thoughts and memory
My past becomes the future
Through the seeds of the lemon tree.

Terry White

The Perfect Day

Breakfast on the balcony
Fresh smell of morning air
Yoghurt, fruit and honey
Loose clad, without a care

Late morning stroll to the sea
A walk along the beach
You sitting close to me
Grapevine just out of reach

Return for your siesta's due
I read while you sleep
Then showered and dressed on cue
We share an aperitif

We meander talking, laughing
You choose a taverna with knack
Watch the young men dancing
Horse and carriage ride back

Our day ends as it began
Upon our balcony
One contented woman and man
The moon to make it three

It really was a perfect day
Alas the last of many
The years have failed to take away
A bittersweet memory.

Elaine Rowlands

Untitled

Yesterday is just a memory
Today is becoming past tense
Your words are resounding between the two
Should I stop and believe you
Your hesitance is due to memories
And fears of future yet to come
But dance today with me
And replace the bag of misery
That holds you to yesterday
Strike forth and greet today
Yesterday's memories are gone
Today is your new memories
So come and dance today with me
And be glad of today's memories.

Dawn Young

232

Knockholt 1937

A hill where ancient times there stood
The leafy groves of oaken wood,
A mighty forest long forgot
To yield a cherished beauty spot -
A fitting place upon that knoll
To take a gentle family stroll.
Dad led the way, big brother Will,
And I, scarce more than toddler still.
But sudden gust came there all swirling,
Snatched at me in its twisting, twirling,
A demon force to work me harms,
Saved by my dad's protecting arms.

How often since near danger's snare
Have I kept safe with loving care,
Yet hardly recognised that hour
Our Heavenly Father's mighty power?
But still 'Our Father' day by day
Fulfils with meaning as I pray,
When gold-clad memory I know
That day at Knockholt long ago.

Barrie Williams

Life's Gems

Memories are gems we treasure
More and more as time goes by.
Childhood moments filled with pleasure,
Darker times when tears are nigh.
Exciting smells of old steam trains
As we set off for the coast again;
Swimming, playing on the sand,
Mother's crab sandwiches - best in the land!
Cycle tours when fit and able
With yarns exchanged at the evening table.
Setting sun and rising moon
Reflect on Derwent Water.
The joy and pride when we first saw
Our precious new granddaughter.
The wonder of the Cullins
On the magic Isle of Skye,
And happy times enjoyed with friends
On that great holiday.
Yes, memories are gems we treasure
More and more as time goes by.
They cheer us in our autumn years
And brighten up our winter sky.

Margaret Simmons

233

Post-War Baby

Who is this man full six feet tall
With balding head, moustache and all
And booming shout that rends the air
And joints that creak more than his chair?
He mists the air with his cigar
But glimpses through to days afar . . .

Who is that boy with grubby knees
Who swears and spits and hides in trees
And watches black and white TV
And cries, 'Fatty, come and catch me!'
He will not eat his meat or greens,
He shuns nice slacks for drainpipe jeans.

And yet, when all is said and done,
That man and boy are merely one.
A needy soul who wades through time,
He begs for reason, yearns for rhyme,
And gazes back to days long past
When time moved slow but legs ran fast.

Where are those tall and endless fields,
Those rutted lanes, those steaming meals
Beside the fire, those shining cheeks
Of kids in snow, and hide-and-seek
And childish loves and freezing hands
In soaking gloves and foreign lands
In atlas bright to feed the dreamer
Through the night?

The tall man knows the fields are gone
So he will pause - then journey on.

David J Ayres

A Mother Writes To Miscarriage

Cupboardised, sweet child, core and after, to date,
Cherries have communed amongst the tired
Windfalls: each a kind awoken before
Their abrupt stalks have lightened to survival.

Demands are rosaries in them, who,
Had they sought religion, would only have heard
The huge between here and eternity
Squeezing tightly beneath their knees.

As prayers for monsoons in Mongolia,
We answer this Earth with turgid sanctity;
Restless to grin and spread a marshland,
Outward, idiot, aborted.

How we think of *them* does not slow
Man's immensity; and Man shall descend
In every single weather; slack with aching jaws,
Slack with the dwelt contemplations of youth.

For a few, life is not sensed;
But most live in life, and most sing the few
To lift and lighten as a life; so writing
That you *are* shall not betray a Decalogue
Nor any woman's libel in a common law of man.

The rival of Christ is the proof of endless birth;
So too, the raft of life shall come to doom's eyes;
And as much as Man has need, so too zealous seed
Will sting with swings and maturity's martyr.

James Bellamy

Images Of The Past

If I were only young once more
Oh, how my heart would sing
To open up without a doubt
Those happy, carefree days like spring.

Fields to play, no restrictions anywhere
Friends you loved and were always there
Next-door neighbours and communities
Helping each other without saying please.

Church on Sunday, dressed in your best
Singing in the choir, vocals full of zest
Home to Mum's roast dinner, delicious to taste
Nothing ready cooked, nothing done in haste.

Monday was wash day and off we were packed
With a halfpenny fare, on a tram to Wanstead Flats
A jar, a net on a stick, to go and catch fish
Tiddlers they were, but we often wished
That they could be goldfish that we could keep in a dish.

Phyllis Wright

Firstborn

As I gathered you into my arms
And held you close to my heart
We made the physical bond
Which was started nine months ago.
You quietly searched my face
And I marvelled at the wonder in your eyes.
'Can he really see me?' I asked.
'No, but he knows you're his mum.'

As you were the firstborn child
It was a voyage of discovery for us both.
The miracle which brought you to me
Unfolded the miracle of the world
As I saw it each day through your eyes
And felt the joy of rebirth.
My world had opened to yours
And I lived and I learnt like a child.

Angela Bernardi

236

Seasons Of Childhood

When I was a child my world was brand new
And I would play under skies of bright blue
Cowslips, buttercups and a sweet daisy chain
The end of a rainbow to search for in vain

Spring in her mantle so colourful and gay
Garlands and dancing on the first day of May
The soft fleece of a lamb in this season of birth
The planting of seeds in this bountiful Earth

With lazy summer days and warm sultry nights
Meadowsweet flowers for a honeybee's delight
Then a flash of lightning and thunder rolled
And I, from my window, watched the storm unfold

Blackberries on hedgerows and crops on the land
A choice of fare from Mother Nature's fair hand
Harvest Festival with fruit and gold, rippling corn
A spider's web spangled with dewdrops at dawn

Sparkling Jack Frost and snow, soft and white
A blazing log fire to warm me at night
Holly and mistletoe, a Christmas tree tall
Impatiently waiting for Santa to call

Christmas carols, the Nativity, a child's simple faith
Wide-eyed with innocence and daydreams to chase
The seasons of my childhood, the circle of life
A world full of wonder, a world without strife.

Sylvia Partridge

The May Queen

She sat upon a throne of gold,
She wore a flower-decked crown.
Her hair was like the sunlight's gleam,
Her skin looked soft as down.

She'd walked ahead of the parade,
With a long cloak, velvet red
And the sun shone on her flaxen curls,
Piled high upon her head.

The Morris dancers followed her,
Their dresses white and blue,
Before she crossed the meadow,
Where the grass was wet with dew.

Then she sat down to be crowned,
From Mum's arms I could see her
And oh, but more than anything,
I wanted so to be her.

Frankie Shepherd

Yesteryear

The rain trickles down the windowpane
Reminding me of a house 'Sunny Bank' where
The scent of crab apples smelling sweetly in the summer rain
I surveyed all the leaves shimmering in the morning dew
Everything looked pure and new.
How I ache for those past years again
The days of my childhood bright and clean
The rows of cabbages in Mr Evans' allotment
Broccoli too, which we ate raw, with glee:
'Bryn Hyfryd' it certainly was
Recall playing marbles, most of them clay
With his daughter Joan and her cousin Mary
Doing my homework with Mary whilst her mother the table lay.
Her father smoking his pipe by the fire
Their own unmistakable odour around them, their attire
How strange we recall our childhood with a sense of smell
The scent of the briar rose so heavenly, which I remember
Distinctly in Mr Manners' field.
Going in the early hours of the morn - September
Picking mushrooms with my younger sister
How lovely it all was, now I am past sixty.
The thought disturbs me, how short is our lifespan
So we must make the best of it whilst we can.

Gwyneth E Scott

The Day I Became A Christian

40 years ago, something good happened to me
I was at the Youth Fellowship and oh, what a glee.
Do you know what they said - I have not forgotten
If I gave my heart to Jesus - salvation begotten.

Wait, I could not, till He'd take me forever
I prayed - forgive my sins and leave me never.

He sees me through trouble, and even when I laugh,
Jesus, the best friend there is, on my behalf.
Everything He is, so precious and lowly,
I sing hallelujah, Almighty, Loving, Holy.

Anne Black

A Memory Of Devon

A memory of Devon sleeps in my mind
And wakes to be remembered once more
Remembering a time and a journey by train
Through childhood eyes filled with awe

I still see the coastlines embracing the sea
Shimmering 'neath unblemished blue skies
Seeing the English Riviera baked by the sun
And waiting for the next cultural surprise

We travelled to Paignton then Goodrington sands
To a residence not far from the beach
To a humble abode in a caravan park
Which was to be home for the week

An interesting week where I could run wild
Where the adventures were mine to command
The soft summer breeze became a temporary friend
As I walked upon that soft golden sand

The sea was warm like a Sunday night bath
Changing magically from blues into greens
And I battled its waves on fine afternoons
Until my parents interrupted my dreams

I visited villages whose names I forget
Sampled the delights of Devon's cream teas
And ate Cornish pasties to my heart's content
And languished in the West Country breeze

The harbour of Brixham was a memorable sight
A splendour that still raises a smile
With its coastal walks and views of Torbay
All its beauty was mine for a while

These memories of Devon are memories I prize
That I see through twelve-year-old eyes.

David Bridgewater

One Small Gift

Phone call from Dad on Saturday morn,
telling us little Freya was born.
A new life had arrived today,
two young brothers were on their way.
Quickly put into the car,
happy not going very far.
Mum with daughter pleased to see,
Jack and Ben glad as can be.
Cuddles from family are a lot,
cards, also presents, never forgot.
Having good times around again,
things we cherish always remain.

Sue Jordan

Fireside Recollections In 2007

As I lie in the firelight gloaming
My thoughts forever roaming,
I look back on my childhood days
When life was different in many ways.

There were no mobile phones to use
Everything was coal and steam
With just a little electricity,
Hay carts were pulled by Drysdales
And life was full of simplicity.

Children's parties were full of fun
Crackers, jugglers, paper hats and clowns.
No National Health and not so much wealth,
Not nearly so much crime,
But life was easier for me and mine
As my thoughts wander back to 1939.

Then there came a change and a war broke out
How terrible life became then.
People joined the Forces, children went to the country
Where homes were found for each evacuee.

After six years of strife on land, air and sea
Folk started to wend their way back to Blighty,
Once more to settle to reality.
This was in 1945,
When normality once more began to thrive.
Oh, how lucky we are to be safe and to be alive!

Blanche C Rice

Memories Day By Day

A family of seven,
Two boys and five girls,
Four of us with straight hair
And the other three with curls.

We lived in a village,
With two up and two down,
A lovely little cottage,
Just four miles from town.

A friendly community,
Hard-working and good,
We did not go hungry,
But only just sufficient food.

Our parents sent us to chapel,
Each Sunday a.m.
I loved it so much
And went also p.m.

We learnt about Jesus,
He became real in my life,
Sadly not widespread,
No, not over rife.

I am now over eighty years,
And He has been wonderful to me,
I pray much for the world,
This will ever be my plea.

M L Smith

Cause And Effect

Bombed 1940
Bang - darkness - silence.
My mother's comforting arm
Encircles me in reassurance.
Dust, broken glass, smell of soot,
The crunch of plaster underfoot.
Outside the room, Dad is alive -
Mum, my brothers and I survive,
The blast of bombs dropped all around,
Nearby houses razed to the ground.
We live, unlike our neighbours, when sudden death
Fell from the skies and stilled their breath.

> Usually happy,
> Sometimes sad,
> Occasionally frightening
> And really bad.
> Memories imprinted
> From times afar,
> Some only beautiful,
> Some only scar.

Wedding photos 1970
Through flurries of snow
Posed photos were shot,
Small groups, big groups,
The happy couple - the lot.

Almost forty years on - what do I see?
I see faces now older,
Faces now dead,
Children now adults,
But it has to be said
The bride and the groom
Though maturer today
Still share their love
That those photos portray.

> Deeply buried memories, photos remind
> Us of events, people, places which gently try
> To revive something forgotten, something to find
> Of a past now fading as time goes by.

Gerard Chamberlain

Golden Memories

(As recalled by the woman I married)

Sweet memories are made of this,
That moonlight walk, his goodnight kiss,
His proposal down on bended knee,
When he said, 'Will you marry me?'

Oh joy of joys, my heart stood still,
As through my tears I said, 'I will.'
The church was booked, the date was set,
That day I never will forget.

The limo ride to the church in town,
Resplendent in my bridal gown,
Beside me, Dad, all 'prim and proper',
In his Moss Bros suit and smart grey topper.

I wore Nan's old tiara, though the veil it was brand new,
My silk gloves had been borrowed and my garter was deep blue,
Like a princess I waved to the world from the car,
And I swear that some of the men shouted hurrah.

And as Dad walked me down the aisle,
'Neath her picture hat I saw Mum smile,
As we stood at the altar, my husband and I,
My mother and my bridesmaids started to cry.

We vowed we would stay faithful to each other for life,
The vicar then blessed us, saying, *'You are now man and wife'*
And so it has been to this very day,
Like Derby and Joan with hair turning grey.

I've not worn that dress since the day we were wed,
The veil and tiara have not touched my head.
They hang there in my wardrobe, still white as snow,
Reminding me of our perfect day, fifty years ago.

Bill Dovey

Reminiscing

Summer scents drifting on the breeze
Sounds of humming from the bumblebees
Remind me of when I was a child

Butterflies emerging from their safe cocoons
Are things I cherish during the month of June

Sweet-smelling roses surrounding the terrace
Swaying of the lilies on stems so precarious

The fragrance of jasmine in the still morning air
Sweet peas and pinks, their aroma so rare
Remind me of when I was a child.

Christine Hardemon

Memories Of A Special Hymn

(Love Divine)

This well-known hymn means much to me,
It holds a precious memory.
Though years ago, still crystal clear,
A picture of my father dear.
For it was on my wedding day,
He didn't give the bride away,
Instead, within a small church hall
With blushing bride and bridegroom tall,
As minister he joined us two,
In holy matrimony true.

Vows were exchanged and then the ring,
At length the hymn so many sing
Upon that most momentous day,
Before the final time to pray.
Now, when I hear this hymn, I see
So clearly in my memory,
The features of my father dear,
As he stood facing me, so near.
His voice in fancy I still hear,
With tenor notes both true and clear.

A loyal servant of the Lord,
True to his calling and God's word.
His faithful ministry now done,
For him the earthly race is won.
Fulfilled, those hymn words have come true,
May this be so for me and you,
When earthly things are left behind
And immortality we find,
In Heaven to also take our place,
'Lost in Wonder, Love and Praise'.

E Phillis

Days To Remember

Those days we had in the countryside,
We'd run in the fields and pretend to hide,
We'd take out the car and drive around,
Enjoying the scenery and peaceful sounds!

Primrose picking was my favourite thing,
We'd put them in bunches, tied up with string,
We jumped over ditches, we had such fun,
It was a fantastic day for everyone!

We drove out for miles, for flowers to pick,
The day always seemed to pass by so quick,
I'll always remember those special days,
You can't do it now, but the memories will stay!

My childhood days were simply the best,
There were plenty of laughs, fun and all the rest,
If only those times would come back for good,
I'd go back to those days, if only I could!

Patricia Daly

One Winter's Day

Overnight it had snowed, which delighted us children,
As with tea trays we played on the farmer's steep field.
Round our heads were wrapped warm woolly scarves,
From the searing cold our young throats to shield.

Our friends from the street all have the same thought;
Homemade sledges, a snow-clad scene of genuine joy.
Squeals of delight and now and then a small whimper
While proud parents toboggan with their girl or boy.

Excited we hold onto our tray. Our dad pushes us.
Down the steep slope we slide, but head for the ditch.
Nearing the bottom, the tray's corner catches a clod.
Up in the air we fly. Into a snowdrift we pitch.

Father, laughing aloud runs down the slope to help,
Mother, hand to mouth, anxiously stands rock-still
As if she's suddenly turned into a woman of ice,
Viewing the upturned tray from the top of the hill.

All's well as it turns out; we have had a great time.
Our faces from the cold snow are glowing bright red.
Safely holding us on broad shoulders and strong arms,
Up the slope, in the tea tray furrow, Dad's feet tread.

Time passes. We mature and become more refined.
Adjusting our behaviour patterns, steadily we grow
Into fine men and women and tell our own children
Stories of tea trays sliding down slopes in the snow.

Wendy A Nottingham

My Childhood Days In Port Sudan

I wish I could convey to you,
The wonder of my childhood days -
Flamingo Bay, the stinging rays,
Those Red Sea sails and skies of cloudless blue.

My brother left for boarding school
And dreaming on, I spent my days
Absorbed in all my little ways
'Til black night fell and backed each sparkling jewel.

Huge melons warm, soft bearded corn,
My dog to love and ducks to feed -
I tended to their every need,
Then lay each night beneath the stars 'til dawn.

Each tranquil moment there, I'd pray
For a baby brother to hold.
He came, I went - hot climes, to cold,
But brothers and parents will always stay,
Close to our hearts.

Susan Bradbury

Diana

Dearest Diana, it still hurts that you have gone
People now know you were treated very wrong
Looking back though, we must not be sad
You achieved so much and made so many glad
Taken from us, we were robbed overnight
A void no one can fill as you are out of sight
We must be thankful for all the love and hope you gave
In return, millions give their respect at your island grave
Your sons are growing into fine respectable young men
Who know their minds and amaze again and again
Be so proud of the lives you created
Your association with Charles was definitely fated
You tried to go on and build a new life
Sadly, the media caused you trouble and strife
You know who set out to do you wrong
The truth will be out before not too long
We can't bring you back, so we remember you with love
Take care Diana, in that paradise up above.

Anne Sackey

Memories

I have many lovely memories
Some happy and some sad,
A wonderful memory I recall,
Is a day out with my dad.

I was only eight years old
And now I am eighty-one,
He took me to the shops
And that's where it began

In this lovely shop
High up on a shelf,
Sat this lovely dolly,
I thought I'd like her for myself.

My dad looked to me and said,
'Would you love her like your brother
And care for her and treat her
Just like you do your mother?'

So my dad bought me that lovely dolly,
I treasure her like gold,
She sits beside my bedside
And does as she is told.

My dolly has sat just like that
For seventy-three long years,
The memory of that lovely day
Has lived with me through happiness and tears.

I had to say goodbye to Dad
When I was only ten,
But my dolly has shared my life with me
And this memory will be there until the very end.

Maureen Rosina Batchelor

Darling Nan

My earliest memory of you, Nan
Is in the prefab up the Mayfair
I used to go up and play with Rex
Summers spent without a care

In the morning we would go
To buy something for our tea
A lovely piece of fish for you
And Spam and chips for me

Before we left you made me wrap up warm
In my new mittens, hat and scarf
You had knitted them since getting up
As well as stuffing a toy giraffe

On the way we'd always go
To see my Uncle John
He would be in his shop laughing
We may even get a song

'Here comes the old witch,' he would say, where have you parked your broom?'
You would reply, 'You cheeky beggar' and issue a swift clout
I don't think it hurt him all that much
But boy didn't he half shout

We would always pop out the back
For a cup of tea and chat to Aunty Mary
I didn't like that storage room
It was dark and a little scary

When we left you would always get me
An apple or banana
Then it's off to play with Rob and Meme
And see my Aunty Ena

Some of my fondest memories
Are when it was just the two of us
I loved to spend time around your flat
Playing cards like Snap and Stop the Bus

We would laugh and play for hours
Until it was time for bed
Then you would tuck me in
And kiss me gently on the head

When it came to go, next day
I didn't want to leave
So you'd wipe away all my tears
With that hankie up your sleeve

I never will forget you
And the love you gave to me
I know you're in a better place
With my grandad finally

Memories Are Made Of This

Now you're strolling with your soul mate
Smiling, hand in hand
You have waited so long to be with him
As you walk along the sand

God bless you, Nan, you will be greatly missed
By both friends and family
But most of all I hope you know
How much you'll be missed by me.

Brian

My Special Man

You may think this is a sad song
And in some ways you are right
For I had a loving father
But only for a short part of my life.
My dad was a dad in a million
So loving, true and kind -
But he was taken from me
And life was never the same.
He loved his little family
And he also loved his bike
I used to ride on pillion
And that was the thrill of my life.
My mother rode in the sidecar
With my sister on her knee.
One day as we were driving
My mother's hat blew off
And whilst the bike still driving
I got off to rescue that hat.
I still feel the pain from that transit
But I won't tell you where it hurt.
This is just one of the memories
I treasure after all these years
But most I treasure his teaching
Of how to live a good life.
As he's watched from his star up in Heaven
I hope he's been pleased with my life
For he was the best - a real treasure
The most special man in my life.

J Mary Kirkland

Daydreaming

Perhaps I'll sit and dream a while
Maybe I'll nod off too.
I'll go back to my youthful days
When I was young like you.
And in my dreams I'll run and play,
Have fun upon a swing.
I'll climb up to the hilltops
And my heart will really sing.
My legs are old and feeble
And my eyes are short on sight,
But in my dreams I'm strong and fit
And live with all my might.
Am dreaming still - I've reached the stars
And stand at heaven's gate,
I knock and knock, but no one's there
Alas, I am too late.
I'm back to Earth and hear a voice calling urgently,
'Grannie, Grannie, come at once
I've made your cup of tea.'

Pat Adams

Memories Of Village Childhood

The first sharp days of spring,
Tempting wintry sunshine, bring,
Country walks, the woods to browse,
Shy violets, bluebells, primrose, house.
Wild garlic and rich earth smelling of must.
Pendant catkins sprinkling their fairy dust.
The wood, a magical place, forbidden,
So many unexplored wonders stay hidden.
I can almost feel the biting cold, so cold,
On the bare chapped legs, exposed, bold.
The house is so warm, fire banked high.
Intoxicating, scrumptious smells, vie
For favour. Succulent Sunday roast,
Yorkshire puddings and gravy, host
Roasties, sauces and vegetables galore.
Family gathered together, why want more?
Memories are treasures, ours to keep,
Sometimes in dreams they appear in our sleep,
Visions of village life looms large in my past,
Kinship and friendship are things sure to last.

Mary Parker

250

Moving Out

Sixty odd years I've been sitting here,
They are moving me today.
If you come tomorrow you'll have to stand,
They are taking me away.
I've seen some things in all that time,
Moments I wouldn't swap,
It's the end of an era for me you see,
The old bench near the bus stop.
I was brand new and polished in thirty-nine,
The 'bombed out' slept right here,
An air raid warden died in my arms,
Just after that night's 'all clear'.
I nursed a young pilot, who'd lost all his mates
And a Yank, who proposed to his honey,
She said yes and he took her back to the States.
He's a judge now with plenty of money.
The fifties and sixties, the rock and roll years,
The teddy boys combing DAs,
They all sat with me while they wait for the bus,
You're right mate, I've seen better days.
Late for their dates, or early for church,
The initials on me are the best,
The young ones going to dances,
Or the old ones who came for a rest.
So now we've arrived at the disposable age,
A wooden bench is a great waste of space,
You'll sit on green plastic which tips up your shopping,
Splashes water onto your face.
I am moving into the churchyard
For a rest and a nice bit of peace,
Just me and the starlings, but don't shed a tear,
For me it's a happy release.

Irene Ison

Childhood Memories

Black crust of newly baked bread that lingers between teeth and tongue, plus butter and stinky feet cheese. Sliced without a thought of calorie intake or cholesterol count. Always waiting on a slab of marble to feed that after school hunger.

He's home, familiar sounds of hammer on last a weekly chore. Segs between teeth as I wait his instructions 'Aye lass, that's the right size.' Leather from assorted packs bought from Woolworths with the wooden floor. Always on the right spot, hammer never missing, I watch as he paints the edges, blending the new with the old and a smell of leather and paint evade.

The comfort of always being there, she would wrap you up in hot camphorated oil, socks and flannelette nightdress, when winter colds prevailed. Receptacles of cold white fat, remnants of yesterday's dinner, hiding brown essence, adorned crusty white bread, always the best bit. Cold clean sheets every night a welcoming experience, as worn hands tuck down tight a cocoon of hot comfort, often awakening as when you first entered sleep.

The unity of growing up within a large family that enjoyed the simple things. The pre-ordained existence, of traditional values within the church. Star cards and an annual treat of the latest literature and the pleasure that came from that initial read.

Singing at Christmas in front of grown-ups. Carol singing and snow never failing to provide the Xmas scene. Hot summers as play dominated, hot hay fields. Sunday school and flower shows, dancing round the maypole, building houses out of stacks of hay. Saturday morning cinema and bags of 1p fish crackle, a golden treat, washed down with lemonade. Scrambling round the coal tips, remains of man's toil, immune to dirt and dust. Skipping in the road, seeking houses for your treasured two tennis balls, invading people's privacy as the sound echoed, ball on brick.
Gardening for sixpence a week and tuppence for a matchbox of caterpillars picked off of cabbages. Hiding in the garden shed, a source of comfort when the world around me became daunting. My father's old chair providing a makeshift bed as the smell of his hair oil provided that necessary reassurance.

Time has made changes as my life has progressed. I close my eyes and recall the things I miss the most.
Mai Clarke-Edden

Autumn Leaves

Autumn leaves remind me
Of my birthday in October
And of yours in November
They remind me of you
And they make me remember
You and that you passed away
In November - on Remembrance Day
A fitting day for an old soldier
To end his life and fade away
On that gloomy wet November day.

Outside no doubt the trees
Were russet-coloured and most days
There was an autumnal glow
A crisp bite in the air
But not that day!
That day was drear and wet and cold
That day the leaves weren't red or gold
They were wet and they just hung
In a soggy, sorry mess
Limply from the trees.

They echoed my mood of sadness
And when I see them now
My mind goes back to that
Remembrance Day and I have made a vow
That now that twenty years have passed
I will plant a tree to remember
You and give thanks for your life
I will plant a little conifer tree
To stand with those you planted
Long ago in our garden.

Marjorie R Simpson

Looking Back

On looking back
At what I have had
I think to myself
Life hasn't been bad

The glory of youth
As I turn back the pages
The starting of work
My very first wages

From love's young dream
When a kiss was first tasted
Led me through a life
That has never been wasted

And as maturity came in later years
The sound of life's music
Was sweet to my ears

But now I am old
All's gone before me
I've time to look back
On a past filled with glory

There has been happiness
Mingled with strife
But I think to myself
What a wonderful life.

Albert Fox

My Dear Old Dog, Sally

The music from within
The soul turns
Just like the wind
The silence of life
Brings out all within.
The understanding silence
Holds the heart by its strings
The depth of life
Having no time
Bringing peace into the world.
Nature lets it flow
The inner depth of feelings
The mystery of life beyond
To treat each day so special
To show love to you each day
I love you, my dear Sally
In every kind of way.

Tracey Dixon

When I Was Young

Playing marbles, hopscotch or football in the street
Everyone was friendly, even the policeman on the beat
There was Lifebuoys, Boy Scouts, Brownies and Girl Guides too
So all the young people had plenty of things to do
Not many people had motorcars or TV sets at home
Most of us could afford the cinema, so we were never alone
A lot of parents were strict, but also very fair
Got plenty of freedom, complete with loving care
Picnics were all the rage during the summertime
Us children went off to the meadow, leaving our parents behind
During the harvest season we spent two weeks on a farm
Gathering potatoes mostly, earning money and doing no harm
We had no drink or drugs problem when we were young
Did not even smoke, just played records and sung
Fifty families were living on the estate
Can't recall any of them spreading any hate
It's not nice, to see the world has changed so bad
Children are not so friendly, and their lives seem so sad
Money and power, and a thing called 'street cred'
Every day now, some young person is found dead
Being young in my time, it was good to be alive
Dancing to rock 'n' roll music and learning to jive.

Robert Henry

Memories Are Made Of This

I wish I could go back
To when I was young
Life was a wonder
And just begun
Going to school
Playing with friends
Having some fun
But the day had to end
Helping with chores
You did't want to do
Chapel on Sunday
Singing a song or two
Going to Nan's
Every other week
Hoping the toilet roof wouldn't leak
Waiting for the holidays to come
Staying in a caravan was great fun
How the weeks seemed to drag on
Now you only turn around and they're gone
Those lovely days have gone forever
Sadly missed, forgotten never.

J Smith

Christmas Eve 1940

As I lay in my bed - top tier of a double bunk,
Fully clothed with one blanket, on a straw mattress,
I would glance over my head up to the frosty window.
Outside, the night was cold, clear and serene.
A full moon beamed down upon me, seeming to say:
'Fear not, you are safe here, with the 60 other internees.'

Yes, we were all British civilians, captured in occupied territories,
At the shouts of 'lights out', the room was plunged in darkness.
Any other night, this was the time for jokes, banter, repartee.
Tonight, however, was special, everyone chose to be quiet,
The mood betrayed thoughts about the war and loved ones at home.

And yet, I could just perceive, at some distance,
The melodious strains of 'Silent Night'
Was I having auditory hallucinations
After weeks at Liege, on a starvation diet?
Thank God, I wasn't hallucinating; after a pause,
The melody was heard again, a little louder this time.

A few more pauses and the carol was played nearer,
Then the door of our room was opened quite gently.
I could just make out our camp musicians,
A quartet of violin, guitar, bass and accordion.
They played sweetly and solemnly for us as they had done
For all the rooms along the long corridor of the asylum.

With the last chord ebbing away, and the door closing slowly,
The musicians wished us a merry Christmas.
The moment was heavenly, the silence and stillness
Disturbed only by the sound of muffled sobs here and there.

Andrew Cox

Old Time Summers - In Par Beach Huts

Look at those lonely beach huts
Standing all forlorn,
When caravans over the pathway
Are used from night to morn,
Lit up by steaming clay-dry
At the harbour-side
As though for America Leaving
Upon the rising tide.

Once, they were filled with people,
Bunks with blankets laid,
And awnings flapped over the step-ways
As supper there was made.
Oil lanterns sang and sputtered,
Primus flames danced round
Each kettle until it would whistle
With dead-awak'ning sound.

Deckchairs were carried over,
When the stars appeared,
To show-times in theatre dug-out,
From top to bottom tiered.
There, by the lake in moonlight,
Sang Miss Gibbs her song:
With her 'California, here I
Come', all would sing along.

So through those lazy summers,
Whitsun to the Fall,
The regulars came on the steam train
Their friendships to recall.
Even the war and barbed wire
Only changed the tunes:
The huts were dismantled and stored, then
Rebuilt upon the dunes.

Yet, by the nineteen-sixties,
They were deemed unfit:
Facilities were not provided,
So night-birds had to quit.
Now, in their dreams, they hover -
Wafted from afar
On wings of the past - to remember
The good time huts at Par.

Pat Munn

Tea At Irvine's

Oh, those Saturday teas at Irvine's -
Lovely afternoons!
China plates and pastry forks, and
Little silver spoons:
Linen traycloths hand-embroidered,
Dainty napkins, too;
Kipling cakes and chocolate fingers -
Always something new.
Irvine, elegant as always -
Ageing? No, not she!
Velvet trousers, satin tunic,
Earrings swinging free.
'China tea or best Darjeeling?'
'Best Darjeeling, please.'
So we settle down to gossip,
Plates upon our knees.
Mutual friends and office colleagues
Wittily recalled;
Happy memories, sadder moments,
Things that once appalled.
Many a laugh, a few soft tears,
Happy, carefree days!
Memory keeps them fresh, despite
The parting of our ways,
For friendships linger in our hearts,
So easy to recall.
Who can forget good times, good friends,
The very best of all?

Patricia Fallace

Christmas Memories

Advent - Christmas almost here,
Make some puddings, add some beer,
Have a stir with a wooden spoon
Wishing, eyes closed, 'make it soon.'

That long white beard, and coat so red,
My stocking hanging on the bed.
Whispering behind closed doors -
Oh, I believed in Santa Claus.

Trying to be good as gold,
Or my stocking nought would hold.
Reindeer, sleighs and sacks galore -
Will he stop at my front door?

Church bells, candles, sweet mulled wine,
Angels, holly, fresh mince pies,
Breathless wonder at the thought
Of what dear Santa Claus has brought.

Carol singers, sweet and low,
Marzipan, icing, mistletoe.
The Christmas tree! Oh, pure delight,
Tinsel, fairy, flashing lights.

But through all this we did remember
That one dark and cold December,
God sent a babe, to save us all,
Though He was cradled in a stall.

Shepherds, cattle and great kings
Came with love and precious things,
And through all the pomp and glory
Shines the wondrous Christmas story.

Tricia Dyer

Nanny State

My tired eyes wandered the nursery
Over cornice and wash basin stand
Even sick to my tummy
I wouldn't call Mummy
She didn't, like you, understand.

Lilac laced, you whispered endearments
Softly breathing and rocking me slow
A click of the handle
The light from the candle
Your face in the coppery glow.

My alacrity's taken a beating
In this college as ancient as Hell
Where the dominant lesson
Includes a digression
To stand up to punishment well.

There are times after lights out and biscuits
And the coughing subsides in the dorm
When I've opened my letter
Unparcelled my sweater
I wish that I'd never been born.

Dad's in futures commuting to Paris
Mummy's pad is in Bloomsbury Square
I'm a fag-ridden minor
To a third year diviner
Who resorts to occasional prayer.

Pater phoned saying he couldn't make it
He and Mummy are living apart
And to top it all, Porter
Bowled me out with a snorter
When I'd made such a reasonable start

Yesterday and today were disasters
We were beaten, but put up a fight
Oh, the cup has been lost
And my bridges are crossed
Nanny, Nanny, be with me tonight.

Clive W Macdonald

An Echo Of The Mind

Memories are like a melody
They fade, but never die
And now and then return to mind
Then leave with just a sigh.

Remember your love and how you met,
The sweetness of her being,
The instant love between you two,
That first kiss you'll never forget.

Did it linger a while,
Did it make you smile,
Did you think you were on the moon,
Or was it over too soon?

Memories of your children's birth,
The happiness that they brought,
The peace and content you often sought,
That made you the happiest on Earth.

Memories are sometimes cruel,
But so often sweet and tender.
The cruel you try to forget and sometimes can,
But the good you will always remember.

W E Clements

Memories

Wistful eyes of a three-year-old
Look way down to the scene below,
Little urchins sat on the kerbstone,
Outside the pub across the road.

Long, unwashed hair frames grubby faces,
Worn out shoes with undone laces,
Dirty dresses, tattered and torn,
Boys wearing trousers their brothers had worn.

How I longed to be out there to play,
But my mum was disgusted and dragged me away,
Lest I should witness the shocking display
As their parents came out at the end of the day,
Swearing and cursing, 'cause they'd spent all their pay.

Laura Harris

The Photograph

Is it not a marvellous thing
That to our eyes and hearts can bring
A frozen tear or smile or laugh
Held within the photograph?
Encapsulated in a frame
Precious moments, wild or tame,
Once-remembered views and times,
The happiest ones or the worst of crimes.
All these things forever kept
As they were, yet we accept
That we must change, the pictures can't -
Is that why they still enchant?
Neither can they tell us much
About our feelings or the touch
And warmth and smell of our love,
The one who is just like a dove.
Yet the photographs remain -
The memories may give us pain
But frequently the joy shines through
In retrospective déjà-vu.
The photographs are fragments too
Of our lives, both old and new
Recording things we might forget
Or wish to - still, a treasure yet.

R T Kiel

Di, Queen Of Hearts

Your life touched so many,
From beggars to the crown.
For us the world a sadder place,
Now you're no longer around.

The gift of touch given, to the chosen few,
With hope sent on rainbows, blown on the wind by you.
Your smile in our memories, for the rest of our days.
We'll remember you, in so many ways.

A shining light, like the brightest star,
You pulled at our heartstrings, both near and far.
Showing all nations a better way,
To live in harmony every day.

Our Queen of Hearts you'll always be,
Born of a spirit that's wild and free.
But now Mother Teresa can hold your hand,
Together again, in the Promised Land.

Janice Thorogood

It Will Never Change

It was where I first, found my feet
Way back then, it could not be beat
It was where my mind, began to expand
Only those born there, can understand.

A sense of purpose, a sense of pride
Every step I took, was a giant stride
The tower blocks, the local estates
The entry name, on all the park gates.

The local markets, the old town hall
Those places where, I went to school
Over the park, police on horseback
Over the garden wall, the railway track.

The small library, the local church
Giant oaks, and trees of birch
The common and, the local pubs
The garden where Dad, planted shrubs.

Where we lived, that little place
Still plants a smile, upon my face
Under the bridge, the local shops
The deference paid, to local cops.

The tiny kitchen, bread pudding from Mum
Glasses of brandy, glasses of rum
The sustenance gained from well cooked meals
The local fairs, giving so many thrills.

The family parties, which meant so much
Some who attended, still keep in touch
The daily route, I took to school
A lifetime's friendship, with my mate, Paul.

The rowing lake, the athletics track
Heavy sacks upon the coalman's back
Though now it is completely strange
The Hackney I loved will never change.

B W Ballard

Summer 2006

June, July and August were very sad months for me
An operation, a love lost and then to follow, redundancy
The day and time seemed to drag but the weather though was very hot
So time and recuperation was spent in the garden
Thinking over just what had I got?

I pondered many hours and one day from out of the sky
A lovely white feather floated by me and brought a tear to my eye
It was the first of many and everywhere I trod, I would see a lovely white feather
Could this be sent from God?
Just a little reminder from time to time for me
To tell me I am being looked after and cared for even though I may not see

Then there was the female blackbird that flew down by my side
She seemed to look up at me and see the sadness in my eyes
She fed daily from my garden and performed so many a flight
And whenever I was feeling down, she always came into sight.
Soon I was to recover and although now feeding from my hand
She must have had some other works to do and knew I would understand
Off she flew with no goodbye, she had been a friend to me
And always when I saw her, I would smile contentedly

It's been a strange time for me, the summer of two thousand and six
My pattern of life and security all broken into bits.
I managed to come through it, with help from family and friends
Also the magic and mystery of nature was there, on that I could depend

I had to keep in sight of something as I went from day to day
To help me through a bad patch and often I would say
A great big thank you for my life here on Planet Earth
For friends, family and nature, right from my very birth.

June Slater

The Memory Of John

I remember all about him, as his wife for many years,
Bereavement honed my memory, after all the tears.
There were good times, and the bad, much happiness, then the sad,
His mannerisms I recall, his character the best of all,
Kind, good, generous and brave, honest and truthful to his grave.
Six feet and one inch, brown eyes, black hair, large hands, cleft chin with a dimple there.
Well built, no scars except right shin, climbing rocks at Ladram Bay, tide was coming in.
I knew him at fourteen years old, even then he was brave and bold,
Which stood him in good stead, when cancer took a hold.
From diagnosis to death it was eight years long, operations and treatment, then he was strong,
Proving to me what a great man I had, fighting the odds, we thought he was mad.
Now he has gone, I am left all alone with memories of a wonderful husband, God called home.

Patricia Evans

Everlasting Love

Precious thoughts that grow with love
Will last for evermore.
Some may be sad . . . some not so bad:
All hidden in the store.
So savour every memory
And relive its brilliant hue,
To lift the spirits high again
When feeling low and blue.
    Memories are so powerful
    They come when least expected;
    And like the tiny poppy seed,
    Bloom quite unexpected!
Memories tell of now and then
And are simply made of feelings
That wake and flood the heart again
To set the senses reeling!
    Live again, through mists of time
    And pause to reminisce;
    Hold tight each dearest hope once more;
    And feel each precious kiss;

        For everlasting memories
        Are surely made like this . . .

Patricia E Woodley

Yesteryear

In this rushed and busy world,
I dream of yesteryear,
When we could walk the streets at night,
Walking without fear.
Children could wander alone to play,
Catch tiddlers in a jar;
Picnic in the meadows -
They didn't need a car.
Wander through the bluebell wood,
Seek birds' nests in the hedges;
Sliding down the hills in snow
On homemade wooden sledges.
Buy fresh bread every day,
Not have to pay for parking;
Play conkers in the village street,
No noise except dogs barking.
We'd leave the front door on the latch -
We didn't need a key;
No stealing, greed or violence,
It's yesteryear for me.

Pat Knowles

Golden Days

I thought about those bygone days
And of the joys I knew,
For golden days were happy days,
Yet they seemed so few.
I picture my mother's smile
As she waved us off to school,
School was then a part of God
And was the golden rule.
Church bells ringing on a Sunday morn,
Calling us to pray and this
Was part of Lancashire.

And my golden days.
I can see my father's coal face
As he came back from the mill,
After stoking boilers all day,
Our bellies for to fill.
Mills depended on men like him,
He had to build up steam to drive the mighty engine
Which ran the spinning machines,
For Lancashire's fame came from skill and crafts,
From yarns spun on mules
Which were made to last.

At sixteen years I joined the tread
And followed the footsteps
Of my friends onto those
Famous factory floors,
My family had trod many years ago.
Kind folk in the cotton mills
Taught me all there was to know.
Most of them became my friends,
None became my foe,
I soon learned how to piece up ends
And pull off a rimband when it broke
And lace a driving strap.

The lasses in those cotton mills
Were the finest of them all,
They looked so smart in cotton dresses
And wearing clogs and shawls.
When they chose the cotton queen,
They really went to town,
It was just like the Coronation
As they handed her the crown.
The lads they were the greatest,
Always full of fun,
For the few hearts that were broken,
Many a true fond heart was won.
Cotton mills are just a memory,
Their buildings stand as monuments
Of days that used to be.

Memories Are Made Of This

Famous names like Broadstone
With its gleaming copper domes,
Reminds me of so many friends,
My family and my home.
Other mills like Welkin, Vine and Delta,
Too help to shape the memories
Of the Lancashire I knew.
Today I picture her in many different ways,
For like the many friends I knew,
She made my golden days.

Sylvia Quayle

The Standard

I'm proud to be a Legionnaire,
Have been since '53,
I've held each office in the branch,
All have enriched me.

In '54 I carried the Standard,
And still do to this day (2007),
The highlight of these wonderful years,
Is what I have to say.

In 2007 we went to Ypres,
To visit a sad war grave,
We laid our wreath to honour this lad,
Whose life he willingly gave.

On Saturday night at the Menin Gate,
My proudest moment came,
I carried our Standard, held it high
In our branch's name.

My eyes were moist that Saturday night,
As were many others,
But the moment that those bugles played,
We thought of all our brothers.

That was my proudest moment,
Nothing will change that . . . yet,
I'll remember the night I carried the flag,
A memory I'll never forget.

Joyce Hammond

A Labour Of Love

Each evening at home after his work
My dad toiled with those pieces of wood.
With chisel and saw crafting a form
To be near as accurate a shape as he could.

Being small, I never then understood
All that labour he spent was for me;
Nor watching him carefully sand each part
A model aeroplane could I see.

In one hole where a wing would be glued,
Just for fun a little man he drew.
So simple, yet part of his love
In those times when presents were few.

Finally the great day arrived
When, simply painted all over pale blue,
A Mosquito fighter I held in my hand
And away on those wings my dreams flew.

Much later, scarred and battered
It disappeared - I know not how,
That aeroplane once lovingly made for me
 - But how I wish I could hold it now!

Ken Single

Friendship

The gift of friendship freely given
Is the greatest gift in life,
As loyalty, love and mutual affection
Can have no purchase price.

Friendship is helping someone
Without a second thought,
Knowing that there is no fee
For friendship can't be bought.

Friends can be confided in
Whenever there is a need,
Remember how the saying goes
'You are a friend indeed'.

If you find a special person
Who truly is a friend,
Plant that seed in life's garden
For true friendship has no end.

J m G

The Summer Of '76

If I could keep time in a bubble,
There are memories I'd always keep
To take out and look at and dream on
In the night when I just couldn't sleep.

Like the packet of fags on the table
'Just in case we run out' you explained,
Summer days when we lazed in the garden,
The night when it thundered and rained.

I'll remember that day on the river
In search of the great crested grebe,
And the fun and the laughs and the shiver
And that rope that you had to retrieve!

Oh, if I could keep time in a bubble,
I'd relive all those kisses we shared
Now *they* are all worth the remembering
As I suddenly realised I cared.

There were times I don't want to remember,
But so much that we've shared and enjoyed
All those days in the hottest of summers
When we could have been better employed!

Yes, if I could keep time in a bubble,
Like the herbs that we planted and grew
All the happiness shared and the laughter
I would know that I owed all to you.

Mary Thomas

Cornish Delights

Sunny beaches, rock pools,
Sand, surf and sea,
Fish 'n' chips, mushy peas,
Butter, jam and scones for tea.

Bales of hay,
Cattle grazing peacefully
On the green, green grass
Of this beautiful county.

Ancient history,
Coastal footpaths,
Fresh air and stunning scenery,
Will remain close to my heart -
As a lasting memory.

Cathy Mearman

Life's Candles

My eyes barely see, my ears faintly hear, my
Mind searches deep inside,
Some of it escapes somewhere else away from me
And hides in darkness and lies,
Other voices and thoughts pervade, they too confuse,
Alighting in yesterday's muse,
They mingle and jingle, some wave goodbye, most
Never to return in tune,
My eyes see despairingly, with vision blurred in tears
Among retreating words,
Sound replacing moving pictures, yet afar, of tomorrow,
Yesterday, today is so absurd,
Flitter and fade, touch lightly then move on, there on
The cusp of understanding,
My faculties escape, they cannot wait but awhile, blowing
Upon my life's candles,
Too many lit, by smiles and tears, with rain inside, broken
Is my heart, all jingles and jangles,
Sleep repays, replacing with silence the words I search for,
Sliding through that opening door,
Memory flits back of joyous years, 'exit' it says upon it,
There will be no more encores.

George Carrick

No More Cricket

It was a summer's day
Cricket played a lot
Start on time at eleven
Play then till ten o'clock
Stop we would for lunch
Then again for tea
You'd have a record score line
But retire at 1,000,000 runs
Now it's dark by nine
So you've no more fun
Plus we have computer games
This played on mobile
The only consequence one has
Is that of wry smile.

Michael D Bedford

This Little Life

(Dedicated to my son, Barry)

Many years ago, I was carrying this little life
Things went badly wrong, rushed to hospital, surgeon's knife
They said the baby stood no chance, abortion was the only way
I heard the little one's heart beat, I said no, and began to pray
Two months of hospital routine, but I was not about to give in
As long as my child was fighting, I was too, I had to win
Born very weak, taken away, I could only sit and look
I read many stories from his nursery rhyme book
Three weeks on they let me home and slowly he gained weight
Sleepless nights and many tears, we did not know his fate
After many months he gained strength, Cubs, Scouts, he did the lot
After school he got a job, at night he was always out
Now after so much concern I am truly proud to say
My son is getting married, now he is on his way
How glad I am I didn't listen, how glad I am I prayed
To see him now a grown up man, the right decision I made
Sadly his dad is no longer here, but I know when the day comes along
He will be around us, for he's the one that kept us strong
So proud he would be as my son walks up the aisle
One more thing to say, he has his dad's exact style.

Sue Starling

Love Letters And Notes

(With such a strength of feeling)

They're difficult to read,
But they all express a need -
Those times we were apart,
It nearly broke his heart!

And now, again I learn -
How he longed for my return.
So many years ago -
But memories still glow!

If only he were here -
Could be awkward, yet so dear!
We'd hug each other, then
Our lives would start again!

Jo Brookes

Memories Of Gillian

I will love you for all eternity,
And that's a long, long time.
Sweet Gillian, I have not seen you,
For three long years.
You are my wife, my woman,
My delight.
You are my immortal beloved,
You can twist me round
Your little finger,
Like Walter could my late mother.

Your dog can look at you,
But I cannot -
Why kid, why?

I know you are epileptic.
Dear Jesus, please cure Gillian
And may she come to this house,
As my wife. You married us
In a secret marriage at St Joseph's
That Easter. We can have a child
And be blissfully happy
All our lives, both writers.
You are the Holy Spirit,
My queen and my god.
You are tall and slim,
With pale lips, green eyes,
And long dark brown hair.
You like to wear long gowns.

You are my ever compassionate one.
Sweet Gillian, please let me see you.

R O'Shaughnessy

Thank You Mother

There's many a slip
'Twixt the cup and the lip,
Just some of the words of advice
Our mother gave to her seven children,
And always 'twixt, not just between.
This barely school-educated
But highly literate, wise woman
Gave us the urge to learn.
If you hear or just read, you forget,
If you *do,* you remember, she'd say.
We worked our childish ways
Through what she had to offer,
We learned, we questioned, we always questioned;
Learning is a deep, very deep well,
But you do not learn by paddling your toes,
You have to drink in order to learn;
She led us all to the well,
Explained, and left the rest to us.
First we sipped, then we tasted more,
Then we drank deep, we *did,*
And, learning, we learned how to learn.
Much of what we learned
Would be deemed inconsequential,
Old music hall songs, silly jokes,
Ribald and deeply funny,
Sayings as old as civilisation,
Words of wisdom from life experience,
The mutual usefulness of friendship,
The true value of money, and the dangers,
The need and the chance to read, read, read,
Comics and picture books, the classics,
A deep love of poetry, art and nature,
And respect for all life, and death.

Bill Fletcher

Memories Are Made Of This

Memories Are . . .

Saturday afternoon spent wi' Gran'pa,
watchin' th' football or cricket;
Wi' nothin' as good as a Boro'ome win,
or Everton Weekes at th' wicket.

Trips t' th' coast wi' me parents,
to Southport or even Blackpool;
Sittin' in t' back of 'Owd Bertha' (Dad's car):
To me this were proper cool.

My first day at school an' standin' i' line;
O' the years spent in t' Lakes as a boarder;
O' climbin' th' fells an' skirtin' th' tarns:
It couldn't o' been any 'arder.

O' goin' th' flicks on a Sat'day,
t' watch my favourite show;
O' walkin' round town wi' two bob i' me 'and:
(I thought I were 'it' don't y' know?)

O' Black Jacks, Fruit Salad an' liquorice wood,
Sports mixture, Love Hearts an' Lips;
Of owd English Spangles an' spearmint chews,
of milk chews an' sweet sherbet dips.

Of loved ones now sadly departed,
of past friends who now have gone
away, but don't be downhearted:
In our memories they will live on.

Ian Briant

Summertime

Through the long winter months each year,
Thoughts of spring and summer raise a cheer,
Oh, for the long days of sun that are here,
Always worth waiting for and glad when so near.

So many things fit into the summer pattern,
Rain and sun have their part to let it happen,
With gardens, estates and hilltop locations,
Joining in from all parts of countrysides.

Children from far and wide take it in their stride,
Long days and holidays adding to a great divide,
Freedom to travel far afield no doubt,
With sightseeing being sought and bought.

Even workers leave daily jobs for breaks,
Cotton mills, industrial giants, close gates,
Industry takes a rest from daily chores,
Even factories and plants close doors.

Bill Burkitt

51 Podmore Street

A long time ago,
Dad was working in our backyard,
He called to us,
Sisters - Mona, Vilma, brother Frank and me,
'Come over here, let's make a memory.'

The cement was soft,
He pressed our hands down hard,
Then below each print, plain for all to see,
'M' for Mona, 'V' for Vilma, 'F' for Frank,
And a 'B' for me.

Then he drew a square around the prints,
And as an afterthought, he wrote 51 Podmore Street,
Below the square.
It was as if he knew our old house,
Someday wouldn't be there.

Time went by and we moved away,
But I remember it,
Just like yesterday.

I was working close to our old house,
The demolition men had stopped for tea,
So I looked to see where our old house would be.

The path was smashed,
But I saw a piece of cement.
Handprints - four,
But 51 Podmore Street was no more.

Now if you visit my house,
Four little handprints plain to see,
'M' for Mona, 'V' for Vilma, 'F' for Frank
And 'B' for me.

Brian L Bateman

Schoolday Memories Of The Thirties

Walking to school in the wintertime,
Short trousers, chapped knees and hands;
Handing out pencils and rulers,
With books and maps of foreign lands.
Milk bottles bubbling in the hearth.
Monday's practise with the fire bell;
A young lad fainting from hunger,
A cut on his head where he fell.
One small girl with irons on her legs,
That squeaked and rattled as she walked;
Tears running down her tiny face,
As the other kids giggled and talked.
A lone sick boy in the corner,
Struggling to breathe as he wheezed;
Teacher's own special favourite,
Doing whatsoever she pleased.
Charging around in the playground,
Cigarette card games and conkers;
Black eyes - cut lips from the bully,
Cos someone said he was bonkers.
Dancing the maypole for the girls,
Football and cricket for the boys,
Tatty old clothes and holes in shoes,
No pennies left over for toys.
Dental nurse - 'Those three must come out';
Head inspection for 'crawlie things',
Misbehaving - 'Come out here boy';
Whack! Try not to cry as it stings.
Hoping the pain will go away
And dreading to go back next day.

David T Wicking

The Luxuriance Of The 'Bournemouth Belle'

When I was an affable young boy
My only pleasure was watching
The wheels of steam power
It did more for me
Than any given toy
It was a splendid sight to see
And I always smile in wonder
The sleek brown and white
Posh carriages with their lit up
Sperging tables swaying slightly
As the train blowing
Out its full steam hissing mightily
And curving along the Victorian viaduct
Hastily to get on the main line
The crowded smartly dressed dignitaries
At Bournemouth climbed aboard in line
In the true tradition
Until the passengers reached Waterloo
And quickly dispersed through
The gates in all directions.

Sammy Michael Davis

Who Walked A Lane

Where wild flowers grew and airborne seeds fell on rocks and grew,
Fell on banks and grew taller, fell everywhere and grew
made the borders of our hedgerow glow.
Colour of the crimson, amber, yellow, copper, greens of any shade
to lime, grass and fair who walked the lanes and drank it in.
Foxgloves in their plenty, stately, princely in the purple,
highly powerful in their growth.
The ferns curled and sheltered them, fair grasses soften them,
all around stood stalwart flocks, as tiny stars of Bethlehem
swarmed in.
Oaks, briars, nettles, many beeches copper and the greens come
creeping in.
Mark marching on, just strolling along drinking it all in,
a peaceful lane in west Wales.
How easily sits the cross of foxgloves on the ferns
by the resting place, of the one who walks no more.

Margaret Gleeson Spanos

Memories Are Made Of This

Patricia

My sister was a pickle, into everything was she,
She loved getting grubby, and made
mud pies with glee.
She was very clever too and started
school at four,
She lined up all our dollies and 'taught'
them sums galore.
She really loved our little cat and dressed
him up with care,
She put him in the dolly's pram and he
would stay in there.
She had dark hair and big brown eyes
and a really cheeky grin,
But she had a temper too, frustration then set in.
She'd stamp her foot and scream out loud
and soon made Daddy cross,
But such endearing charm she had, we all
knew who was boss.
Then Trish became a teacher, the dollies
then were girls,
She met and married Eric and put him in a whirl.
One score year and seven, soul mates were the pair,
She handled drills and hammers, but baked
a cake with care.
Around the world they travelled, Trish enjoyed life to the full,
Then one day the angels came and then
the world grew dull.

My dearest baby sister, who was my little pal,
We'll meet again in Heaven, along
God's Golden Mall.

Anne Baker

Treasure Trove Of Memories

This house is such a treasure trove
Just look around, you'll see
The trinkets, the pictures on the walls
They mean so much to me.

Of happy years that have passed by
But which I treasure still
These walls could tell of wondrous things
Just ask them, and they will.

A lovely place to sit and dream
Of happy times gone by
The Christmas-tides, the laughter
The children full of joy.

It's now I sit and ponder
As the years upon me creep
It's oft a tear runs down my cheek
When lonely nights I keep.

The good times, the sad times
In spirit all are here
A treasure trove of memories
All of which I hold so dear.

My family roots are planted well
I have no desire to roam
Don't look on it as just a house
It's much better
It's my home.

John Ellson

Sunshine Maureen

I heard the shattering news today
About Maureen from Homecare
Full of smiles and laughter
Frowns I saw not one
She was sunshine Maureen
Not a cloud nor shower did e'er once
Show its lousy power
Many colleagues and friends and clients too
Will miss her very much
But whatever cloud can try to block the glowing sun?
Maureen is the sunshine which makes us go on
Our memories are a thing no storm can take away
Those things will be with each and every day.

P Edwards

Memories

How oft do we, when sat alone,
With silence and the firelight's glow,
Recall in sentimental tone
The memories of long ago?

That day when Mother scolded you
When you cam home with feet all wet.
The puddles you had trampled through
To see how dirty you could get.

The birthday bike when you were ten,
The one you'd dreamed of night and day,
And how you showed it proudly when
Your friends called in for you to play.

Those happy times on Bonfire Night,
With coloured stars and crackers gay.
The Christmas tree with fairy lights
And gifts for all on Christmas Day.

The rambles through the countryside
In spring and sunny summertime.
The tadpole pond and, close beside,
An old oak tree you used to climb.

Your first day's work - do you recall
The morning when you went to start?
How strange you felt - so shy and small,
With lump in throat and quickening heart.

And then there was your wedding day,
And your first baby daughter too.
All these things seem but yesterday.
The memories ring so clear and true.

And yet they happened long ago
Along the journey up life's lane,
And, though the years roll by, you know
These pleasant memories will remain.

And, when you're by your fireside,
Alone and, maybe, feeling blue,
They'll come to comfort and provide
The smiles to keep you smiling through.

Alan Edmundson

Not Beaten Yet?

It takes quite a time in the morning
Unfolding myself from my bed
Into the bathroom I crawl very slowly
Whilst holding my hands to my head.

For today's a life-changing dilemma
I can no longer go kidding myself
I need all the help I can get now
From those lotions sat there on the shelf.

I look in the mirror and I am startled
Who the heck was that staring at me
I think I need one of those thingies
That airbrushes what you don't want to see!

I should also get one of those 'Trainers'
And would - if I had lots of wealth
So I pull on my tracksuit, cursing the doctor
Who said, 'Exercise was *good* for the health'.

For I am trying my best to look younger
But this has become quite a feat
For my body overnight has exploded
And I appear now quite wide at the seat.

No clubbing or pubbing or eating
Just water and vitamin pills
Detoxing, kick-boxing and swimming
Will sort out all kinds of my ills.

Well - I've been up for an hour and I'm ready
For my Horlicks and a quick power nap
This keeping fit is OK for the youngsters
You can keep it and music called 'rap'.

So as I sink back into my old sofa
With wrinkles and greying long hair
I'll start the diet and fitness programme - tomorrow
For today I'm 'chilling out' baby - so there!

Anne E Roberts

Close Your Eyes For Just A While

Close your eyes for just a while
And think of times gone by,
When you were very young and fancy free.
Think not of any bad things
But just about the good,
And a glance down memory lane, is what you'll see.

That street or road where you could play,
With friends you can recall,
The names of games that once you played
With rope or bat and ball.

Policemen, they seemed everywhere
You heard of little crime,
Perhaps a scuffle, or two, arose
When the publicans had called 'time'.

Every day, seemed like a summer's day
The sun shone all around,
And when the winter months arrived
Snow lay upon the ground.

The future was too far ahead
The past was way behind,
You lived for the day
To do nothing, but play,
With just happiness in your mind.

So, if, when you look around today
You see trouble, stress and toil,
Find a quiet corner, and
Close your eyes for just a while.

Leslie Frank Checkley

Memories

How quick the span of life does pass
    An aged parent, from a little lass.
Looking back over the years,
    Happy memories outnumber the tears.

A child at school, oh, how free
    Summer holidays by the sea.
Before I reached twenty came the war
    Blackened out windows, shelters galore.

I joined the girls in Airforce Blue
    My bit for England I did do.
I met my man, became a bride
    Once more in England peace did abide.

A little house, a garden plot
    Then arrived our first little tot.
Then a brother and sister three
    Such happy days ahead of me.

Fishing, camping, laughter, tears,
    Bedtime stories, ghostly fears.
School behind them, they try their skill
    Each one struggling up the hill.

They travelled far, and travelled wide
    And took what came within their stride.
Now all gone their separate ways
    I live with memories,
        Of the golden days.

E M Rose

Memories Last Forever

On that long and winding road
Those loving aunties so kind and dear
That lovely village of Bishopthorpe
How could one ever forget?
So down south I come
And mother too, married to a southern man.
Illegitimate child was not easy you see.
So life was not pleasant any more,
Those serious things were not so good.
The war begins, so I'm on my way.
So one walks down that road
No looking back, and no goodbyes
I am so happy I'm getting away
Thank God I made it through till the end.
My loving wife and children
Were waiting for me too
God bless them all.

F Crawford

Motherly Love

There is nobody quite like your mother
Someone who's always there
You can't quite put your finger
On that special bond you share

Maybe it stems from your birth
And the lifeline she gave to you
Only a mother will know
Exactly what she went through

For nine months you snuggled inside her
She felt your every move
She gave you the gift of life
Something she'll never lose

She takes you in her arms
And there you feel safe
She'll try and guide you through your life
And learn from her mistakes

A mother's love is special
No one can take her place
That special love you still feel
Is etched upon her face

It's a closeness you'll always share
Something that's always there
No matter how young or old you are
You know she'll always care.

Andrea Lynne Taylor

Boots

'Why were you absent yesterday?' the teacher asked of me,
She looked quite cross, I was only six, I trembled miserably.
'Daddy had to mend my boots,' I nervously replied,
'They had some holes, my feet got wet.' She stared at me wide-eyed.

'You could have worn another pair,' she tapped me on the hand.
What did she mean, another pair, I didn't understand.
'I haven't got another pair,' the tears rolled down my face,
Was to only have one pair of boots a terrible disgrace?

She seemed quite shocked, she looked around, all faces turned her way,
She stood in silence for a while, then uttered with dismay,
'How many of you children have no other boots to wear?'
I heard her gasp to see how many hands shot in the air.

All eyes went down to teacher's feet, it created quite a stir,
For she wore shoes - not ugly boots, oh! how we envied her!
She'd clearly never worked before with children such as we,
Who knew no other kind of life than abject poverty.

She seemed more patient after that,
Much kinder too, I thought,
Perhaps, in teaching us - she too,
A lesson had been taught!

D Morgan

Future Memories

Memories are not to be forgotten:
Memories are made of time and place
Hours and scenes gone past,
Have registered their pleasures or their pains upon the mind.
Once noticed at the time, the camera can often be produced
To aid the memory at a future date,
Perhaps years hence -
Impressions call to mind thoughts that may be
Remembered best with glowing happiness and pride.
Young people then and now have grown and aged.
Sunrise and sunset and much between
In spring or autumn show the colours of the flowers
In villages and towns and fields.
Places where stability is known
Retain their force long hence,
And after winter, spring will always come
To recall fine days gone by,
And bring the more for recollection later on.
Memories are not to be forgotten.

Gwilym Beechey

Our Lady's Shrine

My son drove me to Nazareth
the vision of Our Lady
    tranquil day with Glenn:

O Walsingham, O Walsingham
listen to the angels chorusing
    I knew God nearby.

In this town
spent peaceful hours -
and yet I see
    bright evening star
her spirit on my mind
whose divine zeal
    once lit our world
one day may return
    perhaps not far away.

Herbert Wilson

The Seaside

I went away to the seaside where the salt stays on your lips.
Had my fill of real ice cream and luscious fish and chips.
The fishing boats coming home, seagulls flying overhead,
Bringing fish to the quayside in boats of blue and red.
It's so nice at the seaside; the air is fresh and clean
And the grass is kept real short, a lovely emerald green.
The folk are nice at the seaside, they've got time to stop and talk.
You invariably meet a friendly face whenever you go for a walk.
It's always the same at the seaside; you get that seaside smell,
Real ice cream and toffee apples, candyfloss as well.
Mussels, cockles and winkles, they supply you with a pin,
Always lots of vinegar, for you to soak them in.
When it's dark you all go down for a walk along the pier,
Children with a bag of chips, dads with a bottle of beer.
In the morning sun comes up, everyone ready to go,
Buckets and spades at the ready, wait for the sea to flow.
Children waiting eagerly to build castles in the sand.
Mums in deckchairs with flasks of tea and towels ready to hand.
Dad with a knotted handkerchief stuck on the top of his head,
Seagulls hovering round real close, hoping to be fed.
Where would we be without seasides? It's the British thing to do.
You can stay there in a boarding house or go for a day trip too.
Whichever seaside you prefer, be it east or south or west,
There's always something to see and do, something of interest.
So try our wonderful seasides, they are the best on Earth.
I'm sure you will enjoy yourselves and get your money's worth.

Dorothy Fuller

The Baker's Cart

Granpa was a baker,
A master of his art,
He'd deliver all his goodies
From his shiny baker's cart.

With a chestnut cob called Ginger
And Granpa at the reins
They'd travel lanes and byways
To 'there and back again'.

The cart was gleaming green and gold
And all the folk would see
When Granpa jogged along their road
There'd be cakes and buns for tea!

But days and years pass quickly
That time is now long gone
The shiny cart now stands forlorn
Deliveries all done.

But a little girl climbs to the seat
Where Granpa used to be
And the baker's cart will live again
Scenes only she can see.

That green and gold and shiny cart
Is now a wagon train
And Ginger is a cowboy horse
Galloping 'cross the plain.

And sometimes it's a spaceship
Or a golden coach and four
Or a sailing ship which carries her
To many a distant shore.

The cart now holds so many dreams
And secrets whispered low
Of teenage romance, teenage tears
Only granddaughters know.

So Granpa's cart's a memory
The baker's round all done
But somehow, somewhere in my heart
The magic still lives on.

C Aitken

The Magic Age!

I liked to travel by tramcar,
Especially on the top,
And one day on Princes Street,
That is where I was.
As the tram swung along
By the Waverley Steps,
The wind became a gale!
The elastic snapped,
And my Panama hat
Flew up -
And over the rail.

Jessica Boak

SS Canberra

Back in 1984 we went to join our ship
SS Canberra was its name, we had to get adrift
She weighed 44,000 ton and wide across her girth
The cruise it cost a lot, the money it was well worth,
Built in Belfast - was well known for its fame
And now it's gone, what an awful shame!

We sailed off, throwing out our streamers
The ship it was big and white and gleaming,
Royal Marines played us off, we sang 'We Are Sailing'
Out into the unknown for us
My! It was different from a bus.

It held 18 hundred people
I'd say it was higher than a steeple,
You needed a map to get around
It's the best holiday I have found,
There was always something going on
Dancing, pictures, talks, shows, lots of fun.

Each day saw a different place
You lived each day at a slower pace
You saw such beautiful scenery
I've never seen so much greenery
The sea, I could watch for hours and hours
It changed so much, waves like towers.

A sight to be seen - ships with sails
And if you happened to be in a gale
It would make you feel quite, quite pale
I wish that ship could still be here
When I was on it, I felt no fear.

Sheila Moore

An Old-Fashioned Plate

Give me an old-fashioned plate
With carrots and dumplings and stew.
Roast beef on a Sunday
A pie every Monday
Steak and kidney to name but a few.

Cooked breakfast to start off the day
A-sizzling away in the pan,
Crisp bacon and slice
Of fried bread, very nice
Topped up with an egg if you can.
We all had a break at eleven
With a biscuit to soak up our brew
The coffee was perked
And nobody shirked
When it came to 'just one lump or two?'

Midday was the time for our dinner,
We weren't very posh in our day,
It was 'afters' not 'sweet'
But our meal was complete
To keep the diseases at bay.
Our tea time was fit for a queen
Fresh bread cut thick spread with jam,
It was marg, and not butter
And no one dare mutter
When Father was fed with fresh ham.

At the end of the day we had supper
Bread and cheese and a cup of hot todd
Spring onions and pickle
Our palates did tickle
Then off quick to the sweet land of Nod.

Helen E Langstone

1931 Remembered

Timeless were those village days,
Where infant fantasy held sway;
I learned to toddle and to function,
Truly as an individual,
Exploring hedgerows, meadows, thickets,
Watching water-boatmen skate on ponds.

I scrambled over a five-barred gate,
To thwart the fast approaching bull,
Whose aim in life, or so it seemed,
To skewer my frame with its sharp horns.

Those first few days at infant school,
So occupied a permanent place,
In my receptive, dizzy head.
Tip and run, five-stones, and coloured marbles,
Turned a walled-in playground,
Into a joyous three-ring circus.

May Day celebrations came,
Found me dancing around the maypole,
Proudly clutching scarlet ribbon;
Then chosen for the role of page boy,
To the pretty teen-age May Queen,
Whose crown I carried on a cushion,
In the parade, to much applause.

That night, from cottage bedroom window,
I watched a full moon wink at me,
As clouds passed quickly across its face.
I winked right back, and had the feeling,
That all was right with this strange world.

Raymond W Seaton

Ships In The Bath

Pains of childhood forgotten in an old tin bath.
The Atlantic,
Vicious waves and whirlpools,
At the flourish of a hand,
Swamp the Armada of white-sailed ships,
Wood-hulled, penknife hewn.
A fleet, glorious,
Launched in splendour
From the dockyard on the kitchen floor.

Glenys M E Davies

Memories Of My Youth

The sweet memories you store in your mind
Help when times become tough you will find
Memories of loved ones and times together
Keep you strong in your heart in the future

The time we went to tap dancing lessons
And then they were no more
It was found out
We were going through the floor

Christmas, Dad and daughters
Making the decorations
Mum making a lovely dinner
We were still on rations

A stocking each with orange and apple
Our Christmas presents and a pencil sharpener
A book and a new dress
And love from our parents.

Dad cut the local farmer's hair
He did it in our kitchen
All our living room chairs
We carried through for them to sit on

In the living room we sat on the carpet
And looked through the window at the farmers in the kitchen
They always had a jolly time
We then went on playing

The trip to the cinema in Lanark when I was ten
To see Walt Disney's film
'Snow White And The Seven Dwarfs'
Hi-ho, hi-ho, it's off to work we go
Magical for me and my two younger sisters

The farmer who had the only TV nearby
Invited everyone to watch the Coronation in his living room
What a celebration that was
All sitting on forms admiring our beautiful young Queen.

Rachel Ritchie

Childhood

Once in a lifetime
When untarnished memories are prime,
Across the meadows green,
Cattle calmly chewing cud serene.

With schools closed in recess,
Forget all swotting and the tests.
Enjoy long hot summer days,
With snow at Christmas.

Chiming church bells ring,
Chorusing doorstep carollers sing.
Roasting chestnuts in a row,
Beside an homely fireside glow.

Living in a fascinating world,
Where even the old appeared new.
Toasting the new year in,
Singing the old year out.

Debt to society to be redeemed,
We were so young, so fey,
Ripe old age it seemed
Was an eternity away.

Birthdays subliminal footprints,
Declining down the years.
Forever leaving visceral imprints,
Midst laughter and the tears.

R Reddy

Noel

He stood upon the altar
Platform to another land
A gift from God around me
I know was picked by hand

A smile to light the darkest night
A hand outstretched in love
He shines and casts the brightest light
Channelled from above.

A friend (perhaps if He allows)
A memory's glance in time
A hero - if He accepts He is
I know that He is mine.

Lesley Glendinning

Memories

Tell me my friend, please tell me
    Is the summer sun in the sky
Does the gentle breeze move the summer trees
    Does the sun shine in Diakos' eyes

    Does he still look out over the island
Are his eyes filled with sorrow and pride
    As the sound of the sea whispers gently
Men's names who once fought by his side

    How is Mandraki this morning
Do the yachts still pull on their lines
    Are the brown-faced men selling sponges
    Did the Symi boats leave right on time

Have you brought me back here to Zephyros
    To the place of the sun-warmed stones
Where young men who died are remembered with pride
    As they lay here a long way from home

    Is this the road to Sianna
    To Monolithos then on to the sea
Through the groves of ripening olives
To the place where the wind blows free

    Are we here now at Prassonissi
Where the ocean reclaims the land
Where gods and men walk together
    Leaving no prints in the sand

Thank you my friend for the memories
    For taking me back through my time
For these last days of Rodos sunshine
    For a last taste of summer wine.

Howard Atkinson

Childhood

Memories: ah yes, divine and of such pure innocence
they embrace my soul.
Misled: oh no, my innermost mind knew that such love
was indelibly whole.
Love: heartfelt, and gentle hands caressed
my worldly childhood perception.
Happiness: a three-up-three-down,
with a glowing fire for a warm reception.

Grandfather: twinkling eyes, strong arms raised me
to the ceiling or the sky.
Silvery hair: bristly stubble, comfortingly kind
until his body said bye-bye.
Grandmother: small, bright and beaming of smile
that betrayed a lost mind.
Deception: never, my love for that lady was
always sincere and never blind.

Great auntie: a fount of fun, so vital and generous
with a most genial laugh.
Spinster: yes, a love lost in war kept her single and
as steady as an oak staff.
Uncle: country trips, the whistle of steam trains
and cool sparkling streams.
Auntie: understanding, flower fragrances and cuddles
are within my dreams.

Mother: very precious, doting and radiant
as the very first rays of sunshine.
Bond: unbreakable, unable to repay mother's love
within decades of time.
Support: rock-like, nurtured by spiritual warmth
and expressive eyes of blue.
Mother: singing soprano, wearing light floral frocks
and elegant dresses too.

Father: fairly tall, hardworking so we'd have
a key to our own front door.
Father: and grandfather, off for a few brews
and to buy some for their store.
Family: laughter, sitting around a fire to
tell of stories of times long passed.
Happy: oh yes, just being in their company was
all that I could have asked.

Possessions: a few, but wealthy regarding
individual hopes and expectations.
Sister: wee Mo, many magical times playing together
and sharing situations.
Christmas: family circle, fireside aromas of
roasts and custard on currant pud.
Presents: excitable times, we lived a simple life
in a world that seemed good.

Michael Kendrick

Thoughts And Memories

Sometimes we need to collect our thoughts,
Yet we think nothing of it. But sitting here at
This moment in time, I've started to think about it.
First I thought about my age, and my seventy-
Five years gone by. Then I wondered about the
Memories that we keep stored inside.
The mind is such a wonderful thing, it reminds
Me of a book, but we don't have to turn the
Pages, all we need to do is think and our
Thoughts go to the memories and we quickly
Find the link. So thanks be to God for this
Wonderful gift, that all of us are given
And just be sure it's filled with thoughts
Of the lifetime you are living.

Ellen Walt

We Miss You

We all still miss you
My head, my heart and I
In our dreams you are there
And we all start to cry

It's many years since we've seen you
But you still haunt our dreams
You're still as we remember you
Beautiful as ever it seems

We try to hold the moment
But the dream quickly fades away
So we're not over you
We love you to this day

It seems you will always be with us
My head, my heart and I
We will never hold you
But love you till we die

We accept, all we can do is dream
And cry when we awake
But wish someone above
Would give us a break

We all still love you
My head, my heart and I
And to get over you
We will try, my head, my heart and I.

B Page

The Question Was . . .

What will I grow up to be?
A big question this, you will agree.
This question has now found the answer,
Being now 75, no never a dancer.
Being a child I've had to grow,
I've learned to swim, to drive you know.
National Service, I've stayed alive and survived,
I don't think I've ever been a child,
Working every hour I could, memories filed,
Labouring on farms, picking fruits, hops and spuds,
Cherries from trees, blackcurrant from shrubs,
Picking up potatoes, swedes, carrots too.
This earned me money, bringing food to chew.
Working hard I've always done,
Yes, born in 1931, the war was to come.
Mom gave birth to four daughters and four sons,
Times were hard, winters so cold,
Hot summers, cricket and football I played.
British summertime came to stay.
A voice to sing on many a stage, yes a tenor range,
Many times I've sung, 'Hughie Greene' did engage.
I've written lyrics for 34 songs,
Ballads, songs I've written, just sing along.
I'm always wanting to burst out in song.
Now I'm old, poetry I love to compose,
Living my life has been a water hose.
I've answered the question what will I be,
My mind now full, my mind can see.
The question now is when will I die,
The question won't be answered, I sigh.

Derrick C A Bright

Remember?

Dus'tha remember Cliff's first hit,
Juke Box an' Bobby sox?
Coffee bars. Bum freezer suits an' Chelsea boots?
W'en a walk through t'park wer considered a date,
An' a snogging session wer' a kiss, stood at front gate.
An' thi' dad behind curtains lying in wait.

Dus'tha remember Bill Hayley?
Rock an' Roll and jive?
Wen sex wer' a number that followed five.

Dus'tha remember, mini skirts, kiss curls, stiletto-heeled shoes?
Sunday dinners. Thi' dad fast asleep smellin' a booze.
Monday, wash day, bubble an' squeak.
Granny's special treat, a bob or two on't football sweep?
Sat'dy tuppenny matinee, Mother Riley, Rin Tin Tin, Errol Flynn
An' for' thi' tea, salmon arta a tin.

A bet tha remembers wen tha did summet bad
Tha'd get a clout from t' bobby and another from thi' dad
An' tha' really did feel sad.
Dus'tha remember Whit walks int' rain?
Wen tha cud still afford to catch a train
Children's Hour, Dick Barton, Mrs Dale,
Teachers that really wielded cane
Can tha remember t'Coronation
Suez Canal, telegrams
Liberty bodices
Kaolin, poultice, electric trams,
Black Market petrol coupons.
Cars wi' running boards.
An' AA men who saluted.

A can remember wen folk knew who tha' wer'
An' thi' mam and thi' dad. An' thi' gran'father
Wen tha' met 'em th' alus sed
Ow a thi'? an ment it.
People who shared a backyard
Friends who cem when times were hard
For a chat an' a cup a tea an' summet that wife 'ad baked
'just for thee'
Well lad 'ad be last to say tha' shud live int' past
An' a dun't no how long memories shud last
Though I often suspect
That life seems rosier in retrospect.

R T Vickerson

The Picnic

(A photograph, 1937)

Down from the Talbot, in chosen bosky glade,
With the silver sand, and the attendant waterfall
Glassing its mossy steps; there; ready-made;
The tea in Thermos flasks, unloaded all,
The teacloth spread, the hamper's all outlaid.
In the still magic that the gossamers made,
The gnats danced mazy; and they talked of things
To do with summer, and familiar themes,
While the child in the centre, idly played,
Her face glazed by the wood's pellucid dreams.
More real than real, this dream caught, rapt in time
That cannot move from this enchanted spot
They chose for picnicking, and so they gaze
Into the camera, and the instant's shot
Lies here before me forty years away -
Miss Mills, Miss Thickbroom, ladies we took out,
Old friends, extinguished by large hats, one stout
As her squat name, beams like a genial toad,
While Miss Mills sweetly simpers, there, sun-smote;
Thelma - the gauche girl whom they had to stay
(I much admired her name: her thick, bobbed hair
Gave her a certain quality). All are there.
The camera has marooned that afternoon,
As out of time; we; only half aware
Are ghosts before our funerals, undismayed,
That anyone from later time, may stare,
And laugh at us so vulnerably displayed.
The car's extinct now, and the ladies died.
I, still the child, though half a world away,
More there than here (there I am unafraid),
Faded, yet still the sun smites fiercely
As I sit there entranced with faeried hair -
Look out at me. Look out. I here, you there!

Elsa Ivor

Memories Of A 60s Community

The terrace is deserted now
No laughter, tears or sorrows
Broken panes, a wellington boot
Gone forever all those tomorrows.

Brambles curse the route
That was once worn smooth
Along the grassy lane.
Now only phantoms push to and fro,
How long do memories remain?

Stones still hold their secrets,
Pieces of pottery plate decorate empty rooms.
Lost lives in discarded mail
Mildewed silk cards, remembered regrets
Cradled as babes in Welsh wombs
How quickly a generation forgets!

Silence veils this trail
To a community destroyed by neglect
Scattered to concrete estates;
Ashes tossed in a gale.

Dai Davies, his metal milk pail
Clanging against the stone wall.
Ceiwen, her hearty hail
Shouting, 'The postman's late.'
As she feeds stock
Snorting at the bottom gate.

Rouged Rhana, curlers in tact,
Beating a rag rug to ribbon
In a daily destructive act,
Her husband never forgiven
For squashing her best Sunday hat.

Jones the feet of 'Banchi Bach'
Dapper, dyed hair, feminine ways,
Peered into cat places after dark
In the hope of rescuing strays.

Black Bob, black-eyed, unshaven
Had tales to tell whilst he dreamt
Of a seafarer's haven.

I hear their voices still
They whisper and sound like the sea
The terrace is deserted now
But its memories still haunt me.

Jean Charlotte Houghland

Nine Happy Children

Easter was very special,
When I was a child.
A nice new straw bonnet -
With broad ribbons on it.
A visit to Granny,
With all my brothers,
There were lots of boiled eggs,
So beautifully coloured.
We met with our cousins,
Then off to the park.
Joyfully rolling our eggs -
And feeding the ducks was a lark.
Treasured memories,
On a sacred day.
Only three of us left.
What more can I say?

Fay Fleck

Memory . . .

She was my mentor, role model, dearest friend:
Her life came to an untimely end.
The fragile shell of Kathleen lay
In hospital a month and a day
No longer recognising those who visited.
They left feeling quite dispirited.
At six am the phone began to ring;
What joker could do this thing
To me, telling that Kathleen had shed this world.
I could neither believe nor understand the word.
The shock remains with me still,
Her loss even now, a bitter pill.
She loved her God, her faith was very deep,
I was the one left to weep and weep.
When I saw her in the chapel of rest
And placed a rose upon her chest,
She smiled at me, she was at ease,
I knew then, she really was at peace.

Patricia Kennett

A Walk In The Sun

How many people can honestly say
I've been to Hell and came away
To walk alone a foreign land
There was no soil just sun-bleached sand
A desert mirage in the glare
Knowing the truth but still you stare

Mile after mile to be marched
Sun-cracked lips, throat so parched
Water scarce and dense heat
A fiery furnace blistering feet
Making sure there was no shade
This was the hell the Devil made

Finding relief with fading light
A cool desert breeze came at night
It was the dawn you started to dread
The morning sun would soon be red
Though your legs are tired and sore
Finding the strength to walk some more

The will to live and to survive
Sharpens your instincts to stay alive
Proving your efforts were not in vain
When from that desert, free again
So how many people can honestly say
I've been to Hell and walked away?

Dennis N Davies

Childhood Playground

My brother and I once lived in a house,
With a field at the back to play in.
We climbed through a window on fine summer days,
To play games till the cows drove us in.

Alongside the field at the back of the house,
Stood a blacksmith and timber yards too.
There were wood piles a-plenty to create a den,
And an ambulance painted blue.

With a choice of playgrounds we had such fun,
Between ourselves and playmates too.
It was never to last, as time moves on,
Far away to pastures new.

On a recent visit I am sad to say,
The workshops are no longer there.
A row of fine houses now stand in their place;
But they can never take memories away.

Diane Pointer

Windows

Mock battles on the slopes of the downs
with rosehip bullets fired by elastic.
I look across to our bungalow perched
on the opposite hill. The white sheet
winks in the dining-room window,

tells me: time to go home,
time to lay down my fork-twigged gun,
leave the sheep-cropped turf,
skylarks and gorse,
and zigzag down the hill,

across the rec, by the swings,
over the soot-soaked railway bridge,
up the steep, chalk-white path
to the snug, safe bungalow -
currant buns, cherry cake and tea.

* * *

Blank, blacked-out window
stares at deserted downs.
Tight, stuffy gas mask,
sirens wailing, tomb shelter
three-quarters underground.

At night I climb the chalk-white path.
Below: shrouded valley, houses invisible.
Above: what a sky! What stars!
The Milky Way shimmers,
a bride's train sewn with diamonds.

'Let me remember this.'
Not the red sky over the downs,
the crunch of guns and bombs.
But walking home up the hill
in this immensity of starlight.

Jackie Hinden

The Good Old Days?

Should history ever weigh the bygone years,
The balance of her scales may well gainsay
The sum of human happiness outweighs
The sum of human misery and tears.
A thin veneer of privilege and wealth
Can scarce conceal the nastiness of want,
The poverty of lives in hovels spent,
The paucity of schools, poor public health,
The quackery, infectious fevers rife,
Communications sparse and travel slow,
The frequency of families brought low
By child-bed deaths and loss of infant life.

In no minds dwell 'The Good Old Days' secure
Save those wherein the memory is poor!

John Beazley

Nature's Magic

While wading in a woodland stream
I looked down and chanced to see
Lots of little coloured stones
Waiting there for me.
So I picked them up and took them home
Just to see
If all those little coloured stones
Could create a picture for me.

So I took them home
And got out my slate
And tried each one to see,
If all these little coloured stones
Would create a magic picture for me.

Then lo and behold
Can you guess what I could see
On the slate in front of me?

There was a beach picture
Created by these stones
Of a sunny beach
With seagulls one, two, three
And on the sand sat one coloured deckchair
Waiting there for me.

Adelaide Marshall

Childhood And Schooldays

Days at school can be such fun
Making friends
Doing new things
Playing rounders in the field
Competitive team games
Keep us fit
Working up an appetite
Lunch is so satisfying
A little lady, Mrs Merry
Cooked such delicious food
How she did it
With just a few ingredients
Was quite incredible
Have nature study
And the walks
Collecting cones and wild flowers
Along the hedgerows
Learning in geography
About different people
How they lived
Did not matter
They were a different colour
Only that all men and women
Were our brothers
Dreams of sitting in a cornfield
Such a simple thing
Chasing butterflies
Letting them go
Catching tadpoles in the brooks
Life was real and it was good
Some of school was not so good
Bullying by pupils and teachers
But others were good to know
They were loyal
And made us glow with joy
Eager to learn
Because they showed
They cared.

E M Moore

Memories

Memories of good times, memories of bad,
Tugging at our heartstrings,
Remembering those so sad,
Thoughts of our childhood, filling us with joys,
Schooldays and all the friends we had,
Playing with our toys in those summers, oh so long.

The haunting tunes and lyrics of a song,
That kept us singing (they still do) all day long,
Our troubles then were few -
The memories of Mum and Dad counting every penny
Bread and jam or toast for tea
Sometimes we had honey!
Making do, darning socks when times were hard
And very little money.

Memories so vivid tugging at your heart,
Longing to relive it all, trying to recall,
Especially the good times, how we loved them all!
Impressions of our lives, recounting every part,
Remembering how good it was,
From the bottom of your heart.

J W Hewing

My Childhood Garden

I often think of my childhood garden
And the things I used to grow
Cos and cabbage lettuce
Parsnips and broad beans
And I see my two bantams
Herbert strutting proudly
Jane pottering behind
A bundle of fawn feathers
As they poke about in the garden
Or enjoy their open run.

I sit now in my armchair
And watch the wind in the trees
But my memories bring me my garden
Which I now enjoy at ease.

Irene Lorch

Memories Are Made Of This

Rebecca

We pulled up outside
Number
Five

And you remarked
How tall
He
Seemed

Against your aged
Frame

I smiled when
You looked in
The
Mirror

To adjust your
Black twin-set
And fiddle with
Your cultured
Pearls

And you said
The familiar
Phrase
'How do I
Look?'

Planting a kiss
On your cheek
I couldn't help
But admire
Your aged poise
And porcelain
Skin

Rebecca.

J Ashford

Bent Wheels And Snotty Sleeves

I was a kid just like any other,
Normal family, one sister, one brother.

Reasonably sane, no problems too scary,
That was until the day I saw Mary.

She was a princess, she was a queen,
Although it wouldn't have mattered what she'd been.

I had a spotty face and greasy hair,
No wonder she didn't stop and stare.

And why would she, she was older,
By 91 days, with hair just below her shoulder.

I had snotty sleeves and a bent bike wheel,
Amazing at my age to have feelings that felt real.

I've got to be careful and not to rush,
Don't want to scare her with my teenage crush.

I had to make a plan that couldn't go wrong,
I'd looked at her the same way for so long.

One day I had a spare apple at lunch,
I wondered if I could give it to her to munch.

Would that be the start of something great,
I'd show up in my best footie scarf on our first date.

But before I could do anything, she was in the room,
I stiffened with fright, felt the impending doom.

It felt like I was the only one in the canteen that day,
And over to me she made her way.

She was looking at me, the sweating started,
What would she do, what would I say before I farted.

She walked straight past me, but said, 'Nice clothes,'
I was shocked, stunned, and then coughed milk out my nose.

Jamie Barnes

Memories Are Made Of This

The Birthday Cake

When I was a young girl, 'blossoming',
as my dad would say into my teenage years,
I had the same hopes and dreams of growing up
and occasionally, a few little fears.
At home, my mum and dad would do their best
to make things as normal as can be,
Both working to bring an extra few pennies in,
to make all our lives better, especially for my brother and me.

I was approaching a special birthday, when Dad announced
one morning, he would make my cake,
We all looked at him in total surprise, but he was really serious,
it showed in his eyes.
We were banished from the kitchen and a 'Do Not Disturb' sign
was placed on the door,
Of course, for someone who doesn't normally cook,
you'd understand why we were pacing the floor . . .

We heard a lot of noises in the kitchen, opening and closing of doors,
cutlery jangling and eggs being broken,
goodness knows how many eggs!
Luckily, the cupboards were always well stocked with flour,
raisins and cake-making bits.
We could hear him reciting from the cookery book
and the occasional word of frustration passed his lips.

Several hours later, Dad opened the door,
the kitchen was remarkably clean,
except for the odd speck of flour on the floor.
Our eyes were drawn to the table, upon which stood the cake,
My cake . . . my birthday cake.
Dad drew me forward and presented it to me;
tears sprang into my eyes,
mostly for the look of wonder and surprise.
On top of the cake was a thick layer of grey-looking icing,
which looked like a slab of lard.
He had used the whole box, because when mixing it,
the icing wouldn't go hard!

On top of the icing stood tiny jelly babies, dolly mixtures,
jelly tots and beans,
they covered every inch of the cake, so no icing could be seen.
Dad had added a secret ingredient, which I'm sure
made it look as if it had an alcoholic glow!

I'm not sure how it tasted . . . but there is one thing of which I'm sure,
the memory of that birthday cake will be in my thoughts
for evermore.

Mary Plumb

To Childhood Days

Take me back, take me back, to the green fields so far away,
Where I roamed, when I was young and now I want to stay,
To my beloved mountains and little hills,
To where I will find contentment and not so many bills.

To watch the early morning sun, creep over the mountain bare,
To where I watch the blue sky, without a worldly care,
To watch again the birds dazzling in the midday sun,
And to remember the children of yesteryear, having such fun.

Now it's all gone, but not forgotten as I stroll across the green plush plain,
To watch again the wild flowers, bushes, briars, humming bees,
Enough to drive you insane.
The memories come flooding back and tears of enjoyment flood my glare,
But those are moments of tranquillity, beauty, all caught up in a snare.

To see again the trout streams, winding through the weeds,
The little fishes diving to and fro as if committing naughty deeds,
They are half-hidden under rocks and green moss banks,
In hiding from the shadows, thrown across their flanks.

I remember it well now, it all comes flooding back,
Walking through the fields of yesterday with my haversack,
All the trials and tears between the years, are now fading away,
I am now again young, young at heart and older in my way.

John Cusack

An Englishman's Elegy

Let me die in England, the country of my birth
And bury me in England, in England's rich brown earth.

For this is the land where my forebears sleep,
Buried in England - safe and deep.

Carry me high and lay me there,
To the ancient words of a Cranmer prayer.
Where the lark soars high and the skies are blue,
And English hearts are stout and true.

Carve my name in English stone,
That men may know where I am gone.
And let me lie in this hallowed ground,
Until the silver trumpets sound.

Janet Cavill

The Walnut Tree

There was a time, so long ago,
when life was just a haze
then, I remember school
at four, my pen a tool
drawing letters, light stroke
up, and heavy one down,
quite out of fashion now.

We had walnut trees in
our garden, green and fine,
sweet nuts cracked proudly
with our teeth (I still have mine)
Rolled hardboiled yellow eggs
down a slope for Easter's Feast
with innocent bliss.

Another time, another country,
sea, blue, clean and cool,
better than any pool,
and I, gloriously free
swam out to sea, watching
small fish, brightly coloured,
no thought of race or apartheid.

I was a happy child, then
carefree days soon ended,
war came, bombs exploded,
nights spent in air raid shelters
children sent to strange
faraway places.

Monica Redhead

Memories Are Our Life

Some say life is like a massive book
There are thousands and thousands of pages
The very first breath is the beginning
And to read it all would take ages
These pages are recorded in our mind
As we live from day to day
There are lots of things we'd rather forget
As life travels on its weary way
But the most important pages
Of our mind we remember best
Are the delightful happy memories
They shine out amongst the rest . . .
When you meet up with an old trusted friend
You haven't seen for years
Just chat about all the good old times
And laughter will bring your eyes to tears . . .
The first time ever you fell in love
Really swept you off your feet
The deep and powerful emotions
That made your heart skip a beat!
The first touch of your firstborn child
Is a very magical moment indeed
You know you created this beautiful life
From a tiny magical seed . . .
We might be listening to the radio
They play an old favourite song
It brings good memories flooding back
Which make you feel great all day long . . .
We all have beautiful memories
We create them every day
And as life travels on its journey
Another page in our mind will stay . . .
So if you're feeling sad and blue
And your heart is sinking low
Just open up the pages in your mind
And let the happiness and laughter flow.

Janet Brook

Pop It In Pocket

Pop it in your pocket - you're sure
to need it - clean white hankie, book -
to read it. Piece of string to measure by -
in case it's cool - you'll need a tie.
Bits of cash, a foreign coin, rubber
bands - odd bits to join.
Dusty mint in case of heartburn -
girlfriend's address your heart to yearn!
Two odd screws (in case of split), three
old stamps to send to Malta. Half a
collar stud, just in case and smallish
scissors to cut the tape when opening
huge, amazing shop, charity-wise where
folks will drop by to see, with oh, great
hope if your pocket's been emptied . . .
because they *need* . . .
half a collar stud, length of string, a couple
of bands and stamps for Malta. Old pair of
scissors (just right size), clean white hankie
when sneeze in surprise! Black 'n' white tie
and a bit of cash and a dusty mint to postpone
heartburn. But, best of all, before a call,
is girlfriend's address on scrap of wallpaper,
so faint you can hardly see, screw up eyes and
pass to me!

Jac Simmons

Memories Are Made Of This

Golden sands, buckets and spades
Ice cream cornets too,
'Let's hold the tide back,'
'Let's build a damn,'
There's lots and lots to do.

Build a sand fort, turrets and all -
One with tunnels right through -
Soldiers come marching,
Tanks behind,
There's still lots more to do.

Home at last - what a lovely day,
Little boy ready for tea -
Then bathed and bed,
With stories read -
And dreams of sand and sea.

Maureen Oglesby

A Country Lane

Just a country lane
Swinging down the slope of Pillow Hill,
Down to the level ground
Then straight,
Straight as an arrow's flight
Towards the water's edge,
A rough cart track
Margins decked with flowers,
Rabbits in the fields,
Wild hedgerows
Festooned with hay
Clutched from the sides
Of horse-drawn carts.
Picnics by the river
Playing in the sun
Sending flat stones skipping
Toward the farther bank,
Splashing in the water,
Catching minnows in a jar,
Pausing every now and then
To watch the pride of LMS
Steam across the viaduct.
Just a country lane,
O, it was more than that
It was holidays,
It was fun.

G R Bell

Revelation

As warfare spreads across the land
Destruction vast, a kidnap band.
No hope, no love, just anger wild,
Disease, abuse, a starving child.
I see the hand of Man.

And then at last I am set free,
I sit beneath an old oak tree.
The valleys deep, the mountains high,
A ripple of water, as birds fly by.
I see the hand of God.

Arts and crafts of wealth untold,
Diamond rings, a bar of gold.
Antiques grand on which to feed,
Bottles of wine to quench his greed.
I see the hand of Man.

So still beneath that old oak tree,
A rose, a lark, a bumblebee.
The setting sun at end of day,
The vast forever of the Milky Way.
I see the hand of God.

Family and friends I must not lose,
No doubt to guess which life I choose.
Soft music fills my heart each day,
Just memories as I wend my way.
A revelation.

Jan Caswell

Mum . . . What Is A Banana?

The discipline of my childhood was the lesson of my life
Nobody could believe that there was to be more strife.
It came about at start of World War number two
As nearer to our home it came, there was such a lot to do.

Blacking out the windows, no lights in streets at all,
Diving for the shelter as the siren wailed its call.
Ration books and coupons were the order of the day,
Starving, cold and miserable if for things you could not pay.

At night the air raid shelter was where we'd often sleep -
Give or take exploding bombs that meant we had to keep
Awake, alert and terrified, no end in sight we'd see,
But at last it was all over, and then came novelty.

No ration books, no coupons, lights in shops and in the streets,
Going to the corner shop and asking for some sweets.
No sirens wailing in the night, a proper bed for rest,
But we were lucky to survive and to have stood the test.

War-weary soldiers coming home but grieving for their friends,
Families mourning loved ones, grief that never ends.
But discipline instilled in kids - we could not disobey,
For safety was the topmost thing each and every day.

As adults we appreciate the things we'd done without
And think that the experience gave us - without a doubt . . .
Order and self-discipline that have stood us in good stead,
But always knowing of the cost, thousands of war dead . . .

Who gave us back our freedom to live life as we choose.
Young people need self-discipline or that freedom they will lose.
And the concrete shelter in my story
Is still standing there - in all its glory.

Aileen A Kelly

Wildlife Muse

Long, long ago when the world began,
There was room for animals, plants and Man,
But Man was allowed to rule and grow,
To kill and destroy the world we know.
The time is coming - not too far away,
When the human race will have had its day,
Then the land will begin to grow and revive,
And we won't have to fight to survive.
The ozone layer will start to renew,
The sky and the sea will become more blue,
And acid rain will no longer fall,
No - we won't miss mankind at all.

Mary Davies

Memories Of The Midsummer Fair

I do recall when I was small when the funfair came to town
Oh, what excitement there would be, for my sister, baby brother and me
Our father saved throughout the year to take us to the fair
Oh my goodness, I remember what fun we all had there
The cherra planes would swing right out into the crowds around
We felt that we were flying, such a long way from the ground
Steam horses painted gold with blue, red and green
Bobbing up and down, all worked by only steam
Coconut shies where the men tried with all their will
To win a coconut and show off their skill
Also roll a penny was there
Where you aimed your penny with a great lot of care
The cakewalk I didn't like, it really gave me such a fright
It pulled my arms so very tight, I had to hold on with all my might
The big wheel going round way up high
It seems to almost touch the sky
The hall of mirrors made us look so funny
With long, thin necks and big, fat tummies
Pony rides were such wonderful fun
To trot up and down or break into a run
Stalls that sold china where the men would shout
'Roll up for your bargains before we run out'
Candyfloss, rock and sweets, toffee apples, such wonderful treats
We would go home happy sleepyheads
Tiggy-backed to our nice warm beds
Next morning remembering our wonderful time there
Looking forward to the next summer fair.

Christine Corby

Spring Song Of The Curlew

Let me but hear that wild sweet song again,
Like angel music, bubbling from the fen.
But whence? 'Twas not the whistling of a man!
It might have been the very Pipes of Pan,
So strangely beautiful it fell just then.

Long years have passed, yet still I seem to hear
The curlews calling, jubilant and clear;
I see the upward wing-beat, sure and strong;
The check - the glide - and then that rippling song
Pours forth the while upon my spirit's ear.

Ghost of the marshes, be thou bird or sprite,
When shall my dreams give place to sound and sight,
And when thy liquid magic be my lure
Across the wild and melancholy moor,
To haunt no more the watches of the night?

Robert Arthur Hardwidge

Old Times

Evening voices footstep
Down narrow studded streets.
Back lane's broken bottled
With coffee-coloured weeds.
Skies, upside down with
Lantern hanging stars,
And men away in nowhere
Fighting nowhere's wars.
Twilight's frost shimmering
On ancient limestone walls
Cat's eyes by firelight
As night-time softly falls.
Shadows at the corner
Flitting to and fro,
Cigarettes at the edge
Of midnight's purple glow.
Women in the kitchen
Neighbours at the door,
Ticking clocks and lamplight
And footsteps on the floor.
Autumn, autumn everywhere
This I remember so,
Once, they lingered somewhere
The people I used to know,
Once, they lingered somewhere,
A long, long time ago.

Michael J Murray

An Ode To The Old Times

There's a grog shop down in Trosnant
Where the Irish navvies go
And at seven o'clock you can't get past the door
For the place it is a-heaving
And the fumes you can't help breathing
As Mike he tries to crawl across the floor.

Through a drift of broken pint pots
He slowly claws his way
Past the feet of men still sober at the bar
If only he could get some air, his brain it seems to say
The doorway doesn't seem so very far.

Across the black and dismal river
Stood the Squire Hanbury's park.
With the deer grazing quiet 'neath the trees
He gazed at them in wonder
All that meat upon the hoof
While all he got was bread, mush and peas.

Digging out the Mon and Brecon
Raised a thirst inside a man
So did rolling red-hot sheets at Lower Mill.
The miners in the valley, cutting out the blacken gold
It was only when you slept that you were still.

It's no wonder that the chapels did a healthy sort of trade
With the righteous singing all their sins away
While Mike was throwing punches
Just to stop from going mad
As he thought about his kids in Galway Bay.

The drovers' dogs were yapping
As the sheep came through the town
Under traps and into shops and who knows where
Past the Tanners and the Brewers
Through the gardens, on they came
To the market pens, and butchers who were there.

What a dreadful press in George Street
As the brakes came down the hill
Packed with girls and boys all roaring to be off
'Twas the trip to Newport Lighthouse
Horses snorting - parents waving
In his clay-stained moleskins Mike was not a toff.

With his flannel shirt-tail flapping
And his hair across his eyes,
Flash from furnace lighting low cloud in the sky.
Drizzle rain had started falling,
Would he get a bed tonight?
Could he find a few odd coppers for a pie?

The nightshift clogged on past him

318

Memories Are Made Of This

Going this way - going that
To twelve hours rolling sheets or cutting coal.
In his stupor this thought cheered him
Because he worked in the day
And in God's air - not deep down like a mole.

Digging out the way for barges
Was his trade, that's all he knew
Puddling bottom, building locks and basins too.
Following the level round the hillsides
From the port down on the coast
With the cut from Ponty' up to Brecon still to do.

So we'll leave our Mike a-digging
With his clay pipe in his jaw
And his 'livener' there beside him in a jar
As the sweat drips from his brow -
The picture fades - we all know now the past is gone
But let's remember while we can.

Rusty sheets are still a-standing
The old smoke stack still rears its head
Broken brickwork in the nettles gives the clue.
But the canal can still be lovely on a summer's afternoon
And we can thank Mike for the job he used to do.

C G Payne

Remember The Sixties

Two bob saw you oh, a grand auld night out
Drinks, fish 'n' chips and change back no doubt
The pictures or coast, cost less than a shilling
To live those days again there? Oh, so many willing

A weekly family shop cost a fiver, change back too
I miss those happy, long gone by days, do you?
The price of a car's insurance the day
Would buy a brand new car, back then I relay

Sweet tobacco and gold dust, lucky bags too
Would make children smile a week long through
Gobstoppers bigger than any old golf ball
Would take kids a week to suck down right small

Black and white telly, three channels was great
Channel eight Tyne Tees, now there was one to debate
When it was radio only, no television to be seen
Families then were something today but a dream

Taking Father's brown ale bottles back for the money
Yet they ore short on glass today, now isn't that funny
Fresh milk on the doorstep, Mother's homemade cooking
Looking at life today, the future it's quite dull-looking.

C R Slater

The River

I went to the river today,
To the beach where I used to play,
Boats bobbed on the glistening water
And sunshine filled the day.

Encased in warmth, my body tingled
As feet again crunched on the shingle.
Listening to the splash of water
I thought of him, and his small granddaughter.

They searched for iridescent shells,
Then delved in mud for cockle shells,
They peeled the seaweed off the rocks
Revealing crabs, too small to shock,
They lifted stones to watch sand hoppers,
And skimmed flat stones across the water.

The years have passed, but nothing's changed,
The river ebbs and flows,
The boats drift past with coloured sails,
And people come and go.

But for the river, time stands still
As it gently laps the shore,
Meandering slowly at its will
It keeps its secrets deep within.

Janet Llewellyn

Toys! Now And Then

On Christmas morn, my granddaughter was sitting on my knee
She asked: 'Were there such things as toys when you were young like me?'
'I am not quite Methuselah,' I said, and felt quite fusty,
The Barbie doll she held was slender, blonde, long-legged and busty.
In my day, dolls were children, so they could not be well-blest,
Then, only Mrs Noah was allowed to have a chest.
I had a dozen dolls and all were dressed quite prettily,
With eyes that closed in china heads stamped 'Made in Germany'.

One doll was made of celluloid and two were double-jointed,
An Ernest the Policeman doll had helmet black and pointed.
Today the parcels 'neath the tree all decked with ribbon bows,
Are DVDs, laptops and Harry Potter videos.
Robots and electronic games are filling the toy shops,
Instead of biff-bats, sorbo bouncers and bright humming tops.
In two thousand and seven these things sound primitive, I know,
But we were just as happy with our toys of long ago.

Grace Cooper

The Abbey

(Cathedral and Abbey Church of St Alban)

Standing tall, beautiful and grand
On a steep hill, amidst green grassland,
Atop the tower flies St George's flag, proud,
Shouting silent praise and glory aloud.

I remember the dark pew where my family sat
Three generations on a seat hard and flat,
My brother a chorister in bright scarlet and white,
Pure-sounding music, the organ strong, soft or light.

Great aunt's funeral - the chapel organ I played.
My father and mother, now at rest, there are laid;
Alongside the wall is placed a marked stone
Covering the still place they together own.

Bridesmaid to my sister and then as a bride
I came to the high altar full of pride.
A baptism followed, way back thirty years,
Our eldest child bringing laughter and tears.

I return for a concert to conduct and play;
Many years before now seem like a day.
The abbey - so large and tall, some say cold,
Holds wonderful warm memories, both new and old.

Phyllis Yeoman

My Father's Wisdom

All the best things in life are free
He said,
Not as a lecture, but almost tenderly.
Don't take things for granted, open your eyes
He said,
To wind, rain, sun, green grass and blue skies.
Then take it, hold it and breathe it in slow
He said,
Watch as you go through life, see it all grow.
Remember, and store all these things in your mind
He said,
For perhaps, when you need them, then you will find.
You will understand one day, all the best things are free
He said,
And that is the way you will always remember me.

Joy Strangward

Bring Them All Back!

Bring back our units,
Let sanity reign -
With the pound and the foot
And the acre again!

Give us our freedom
To measure and weigh,
As we used to before
In a sensible way!

Let us smack naughty children
To teach right from wrong,
And guard them from evil,
Not follow the throng!

Tell them never to steal
Or to covet or kill,
But to honour their parents
Doing good and God's will.

Let's keep sex within marriage
As God has ordained
Being faithful and true
So we cannot be blamed.

This upside-down world
Tells us good things are bad,
Denies God's creation,
Rejects all we had!

Bring back the yard and
The rod, pole or perch -
And much more importantly,
Bring back the birch!

Anthony Manville

A Small Tornado

Fingerprints smeared over doors
squashy peas adorning floors
Objects moved at two foot four
strewn around or laid in drawers

Telling signs that there has been
a quiet tornado never seen
that operates when heads are turned
with smiles serene our questions spurned

Who offers you her licked ice cream
sticky toffees on your knees
Echoes, mimics, Dervish dances
lifts the phone with cheeky glances

Pokes in cupboard, under stairs
tickles cat, backcombs his hair
when he snarls, she's quite surprised
giggles, squeals and even cries

Full of fun to share and play
ring-a-roses is her way
Bouncy, chirpy, come to stay
that's our Annie's holiday.

Rosemary Keith

Summer Holiday

Bags all packed and we're off on the train,
Billowing steam and rattling rail,
A journey of joy designed only to please
To the land of sandcastles and salt sea breeze.

Stalls with refreshments stand by the shore:
'Line up for waffles and ice creams galore!'
Picture-book paradise: stripy deckchair,
Candyfloss days and nights at the fair.

Rows of red cherries - hip hip hooray!
One-armed bandit made us rich for a day!
A round of doughnuts takes all pennies due,
Now let's walk on the cliff and take snaps of the view.

Gathering shells - lingering looks at the sea,
We stroll on the prom so happy and free
On this, the last day of our week-long stay -
Goodbye till next year, Summer Holiday!

Margaret Bernard

Voices From Other Continents

In the searing heat the acacia trees
stand perfectly still, not a hint of a breeze.
Irrigation channels dissect the plain.
The cereal banks are piled high with grain.

Around the new well, giving water that's clean,
repaired homes and latrines have a school in-between.
Life is now good in our village, and yet
many the things that we'll never forget.

The space that we shared with the rats that would roam
along the crumbling walls of our single-roomed home,
the metal sheet roof through which raindrops would seep,
the blanket covering five children on the floor fast asleep.

Walking barefoot twice every day
to collect river water three miles away
The long arid months when the riverbed dried
and the crops in the fields withered and died.

Desperate measures when starvation set in,
when bellies were bloated and skeletons thin.
Crocodiles waiting for something to crunch
in swamps where edible roots would provide us with lunch.

Corn cobs pulverised to sawdust-like flour.
The sting of unripe mangos acidly sour.
Banana roots ground to a porridge-like mash.
Leaves torn from trees, boiled to a hash.

That moistureless day the locust swarms came,
devouring everything that grew on the plain,
ten billion wings displacing the air,
leaving a landscape barren and bare,

People trudging wearily, babies strapped to their backs,
hour after hour along crusted dirt tracks,
remembering fables of lands far away
where people had so much food, they threw it away.

Finding aid trucks on that dusty terrain,
laden with beans, oil, water and grain.
The strangers who said, 'We'll lend a hand,
tell us what you need to restore life to your land.'

Irrigation channels now dissect the plain.
The cereal banks are piled high with grain.
Water has brought new life to our land,
because of the strangers who lent us a hand.

Avril Williams

Is This The Time To Dream?

This is the time of year for looking forward
Or for looking back to coal fires and bulbs
For the spring's bright showing of colour bright,
Catalogues dropping in number through the door
Narrowly missing the cat by a paw.
But as I sit by my fire - electric of course
I think of you, see you again in my dreams
You laughing, taking my hand in yours once more.
Drawing me to you, kissing me on the cheek
Your favourite name for me was 'Bud', why?
Perhaps because you were a gardener,
Tending trees and flowers and all things that grew.
We had a house, housing many pretty things,
In the morning you would sing, in Welsh,
I could not understand a word but liked it,
Then one day you went on holiday - alone
At first you said you met a group of friends
That turned out to be but one alone.
You would disappear for a week or more
To countries abroad or nearer home, I heard.
Then you brought her home to our own house
I knew I must fight or lose everything
My daughter really found out first of all
Don't ask me how, kids know everything that's going.
Oh, the humiliation of it, a heavy load to bear.
Why? I like to think the car was the attraction
Silly me, but its called clutching straws I heard.
And then it ended as it began. A quick flash of anger
Over her endless smoking habit, a smelly cloud
Of dangerous vapour filling the air. He did not.
Then after many years of dodgy health
He left on a last journey, but knowing him
No, he still scolds and tells me when I'm wrong.
Aled and Bryn now sing his favourite songs.

Joyce Williams

Old

I'm not old like you think, I've just lived many years,
the horsepower's not there so I have to change gears,
I doze a bit more but then so would you
if you weren't being chased and told what to do.

I sit and I think, and sometimes just sit,
it's great to do nothing then rest after it;
I go for a walk then rest and walk back,
yes! I have all I want - there is nothing I lack.

I sit with eyes closed and memories recall,
I think back 70 years with no trouble at all,
if you ask who's Exchequer I haven't a clue
but as I'm being questioned - what about you?

I don't drink, I don't smoke, I read and I write,
I don't gamble on horses and try not to fight,
I look at the girlies but cannot think why -
Boy! Am I looking forward to my chicken pie.

I do need some help please, my birthday's next week,
so what shall I do if it's pleasure I seek?
I must celebrate - what on earth can I do,
cos being so perfect, I haven't a clue.

It is so nice to see you to keep me in touch -
I just like to listen, my conversation's not much.
I do still have feelings - it's so hard to explain,
so please don't forget me, please, please, come again.

Jim Pritchard

My Memory

My favourite memory is the day that I got wed
To the love of my life, when he said,
'Will you wait for me, for a year?'
And I said, 'Yes I will, my dear.'

The year passed quickly, the big day draws near,
Church to book, banns to be called, hall for the wedding feast,
Fittings for the wedding dress, and the bridesmaids too,
To look our best for our special day of the year.

Two years later we had our first child,
A daughter, and we were so proud.
Then five years later we had a son,
We both thought it was a job well done.

Mary Crickmore

Do You Remember?

Do you remember days of childhood
Playing football in the park?
Playing hopscotch, tick, and sometimes
Knocking doors just for a lark.
Do you remember, armed with jam jar,
Off to the matinee we did go
With a mass of howling children
Whooping and hollering in the Western show?
Do you remember buying toffees
If your mum the coupons had?
Buying bags of broken biscuits
Never a moment to be sad.
Do you remember, no thought of telly,
Occasional visits to the zoo?
Remember helping in the circus
For a ticket free? I do.
Do you remember during schooldays
A rap with the cane would make us cry?
You do remember? So do I!

James Cooke

Happy Memories

Sheltered Treyarnon cove with rolling
Atlantic waves warmed by Gulf Stream;
Professional beach families of all ages,
Encamping for the day;
Multicoloured windbreaks staking claim
For the family day,
Mixed teams of volleyball and rounders,
Enriched with shrieks of childhood delight,
Children's inquisitive spirit intrigued
By mysterious rock pools
Refreshed by incoming evening tide,
Playful feats of engineered sand
Washed by evening high tide,
High on surrounding green pasture,
White painted houses look down,
They have seen generations of families play,
Returning with next generation to surf,
Play Frisbee;
Home trekking after glorious day of play.

Brian Tallowin

Reminders

Dried flowers, pressed leaves,
sheaves of old folded letters some
crumpled, dog-eared, bound with pale
blue silk ribbon, not just string.

Old snapshots, mostly black and white,
all small, some with worn corners, some
with cracks caused by accidental folds,
yellowed by the passing years within

his old wallet that rested in a jacket
pocket close to and over his now long
dead heart. Some other things, a pocket
diary with just a pencil-stub pushed

into a tubular holder along its spine,
an old key ring with a single Yale,
and just four tiny keys for attaché
cases or the like - and above all

a faint scent, an aroma made of many
essences, including the ghost of sweat,
caused by extreme effort, even fear
perhaps? Who knows, for although he

had survived a war, injury had denied him
a truly normal happy life, though he had
tried and done his best, he left his family
and his wife behind through untimely death.

But still the memory of him remains, the love
they bore him, ever present and refreshed
by these few things - talismans for individual
memories - these things endure, they remind.

Rick Storey

Memory Lane

I took a trip down memory lane
and stayed there for a while
I knew there would be joy and sadness
but I thought it was worth the while

I remember the Busby Babes who perished
in that disastrous winter air crash
and the mining village of Aberfan
when that slag heap crushed every class

and who can forget that wonderful year
when England won the World Cup?
If only the once we've won it
the only way must be up

and can we ever forget that August
in nineteen seventy-seven
when the king of rock and roll died
I was on holiday in Devon

and the day that we lost our princess
in that underpass in France
a nation was in mourning
she was the queen of all our hearts.

The lane of memory is a long one
and with time things may erode
but as long as we live we'll remember
the sum of the memory road.

Esmond Simcock

A Sonnet To Our Memory

Memories - these mental images
And thoughts of days long past -
Buried hopes and feelings
That can forever last
Intangible but strangely fleshed and live.
The substance of our memories
In heart and mind survive.
Some fade perhaps as years roll by
While others staying clearer
Will never really die.
Dementia will an aging mind deplete
But often this cruel murder will not be complete.
In deep recesses there stays an old refrain
And in the failing memory it will revive again.

A Cotter

Memories Of A Lifetime

As I grew through childhood
Learning right from wrong
Memories of families were so strong.
When a toddler getting lost was fun
As home in a police car can be done.
Off to school at the age of four
Then coming home for lunch
Do I have to go back for more?
I thought my time was done!
The years passed too quickly
My teenage years were fun.
Then I married and became a mum
With children of my own to cherish
And the happy times they bring
As growing fast to adult life
Many memories did they furnish
Then I became a nan.
Grandchildren to me,
Great grandchildren to my mum
Who 32 years ago I left behind
To make a life for me and mine.
These years which pass so quickly
As time marches on and on
'Til at last your past comes to rest
And the life you have moves on
Through your children's children
Whose lives and loves
Make more memories.

Gwendoline Woodland

Awakening

Same old situation,
Repetition wins,
Familiar places,
Recognizable faces,
The story now begins.

How can I live a life,
If life will not let me live,
Then an introduction,
And a glimpse of life begins.

Awakening to better days,
With love and brilliant things,
This is the life I want to live,
A life which love can bring.

S Pester

The Blackbird

As I strolled out one morning,
With nature to commune,
I heard a blackbird singing,
How lovely was his tune.
And on that summer's morning,
With the dew still on the ground,
I listened to the blackbird
And marvelled at the sound.
How prodigal I thought him,
With his enchanting melody,
For not once he sang it,
But on repeatedly.
Soon others joined his singing,
It seemed from everywhere,
But of all the birds that sang with him,
His was the sweetest air.
Though fanciful the notion,
The thought occurred to me,
That it was for me alone
That he sang his melody.
But it was just for himself
That he with rapture sang his song,
It was his way of welcoming
The coming of the dawn.

Edward McCartney

On Our Barge

Drifting along at a leisurely pace
No need to rush around or race
Just taking it easy as we go
With or against the water's flow

Taking in the scenery as we pass by
As the sun shines from a cloudless sky
Like fields and meadows full of flowers
Where sheep and cows laze away the hours

Yes it is so peaceful as we chug along
Listening to wild birds' sweet song
Or marveling at the magnificent snow-white swan
So graceful in the current it glides upon

So there is no need to rush, or at hectic pace charge
We live in the slow lane when aboard our barge
Yes we settle for a life so peaceful on the water
Where nothing is hurried, we just leisurely potter

A V Carlin

No Common Clay

Why did I, I wonder still,
From our family effects elect to choose
A dark blue bowl, Art Deco by design,
Shallow, small and undistinguished?
What is its mystery? What memories rise,
Disturbed from their sleep in the subconscious mind?
Matt black within, blue outside.
Dark foliage frames several
Circles of assorted sizes and colours.
Is the foliage waving in wind or water,
The dark night sky, or deep-sea gloom,
Branches wafted by the breeze at nightfall,
Or sea-wrack rolled by the tide?
If the circles are spheres, are they solid or empty;
Planets processing about their parent star,
Or strange sea creatures suspended in the deep,
(Distance denoted by difference of size,
Or size signifying seniority);
Balloons tagged and untethered at the fair,
Or blown for fun at birthdays or Christmas;
Bubbles trembling on the brim of a child's pipe,
Or becalmed in a wash-day bath of blue-bag?
Yellows are the treat I yearned for most,
Slices of bananas, blockaded and blitzed
From my world diminished by warfare's wants,
Or penny moon, peering in at my windowpane.
But best of all brings to mind
The copper dish with cylindrical stamen,
Wound round with wire element,
Electric rose, red and reassuring,
Whose comforting glow guarded my sick-bed.
Its appeal, unprejudiced by pride of intellect,
Or vanity that elevates value above worth,
Eluding explanation, lies secure,
Beyond the range of rhyme or reason.

Roger Newton

The Cycle Of Life

Into her arms they laid her new baby boy
Trembling with emotion her heart filled with joy
Soon he grew into a sturdy wee lad
Trying so hard to be just like his dad

Excelling at school in all he loved best
At times getting up to mischief along with the rest
As a handsome young man he soon found a wife
So happy and content even when dealing with strife

Blessed with a family that he was so rightly proud
He always felt they stood out in a crowd
Tonight reflecting as he sits poking the fire
Mulling over memories now that he has to retire

Thinking of and cherishing his long happy past
Knowing his future is not going to last
Wondering how he will cope on that long lonely road
Hoping he will manage to carry his last heavy load

Will he have the strength to keep to his faith
Praying that mercifully and peacefully he will pass over in death
Where everything is perfect and he will meet his old friends
Sending back a message, 'This place he highly recommends'.

Joyce MacDonald

Memories Are Made Of This

Crumpets by the fireside and honey for our tea,
The lamp casts flickering shadows onto you and me.
In embers from the fireside, pictures I can see,
I will tell a story, just sweet fantasy.
Although there was a war on
We felt safe with country folk,
When the bombers went over, no one ever spoke
Of their fears for their loved ones.
Schooldays were disrupted,
Lives were torn apart,
Many, many tears were shed
And so we all took part
In fighting for our country
And our freedom too,
And so with God, our helper,
We all came winning through.

Mary Staniforth

Memories

Memories, memories, so many to recall
Memories to be remembered by one and all
Memories of childhood and our mother's care
And of our grandma sitting in the old rocking chair

Memories of schooldays when we were learning A, B, C
Literature, geography and history
Memories of the Scriptures, the Bible and the book
The hours we spent in learning and the time it took

Memories of adolescence when we would walk down the street
With a feeling of expectation hoping we would meet
Some girl or boy as we went upon our way
To flirt with and to tease and pass the time of day

Memories of crushes and of our love affairs
The happiness we've found with all the dos and dares
Memories of becoming adults when responsibility began
When I became a woman and you became a man

For some of us our memories will have a richness of their own
While for others not so good as in this life they've grown
But memories still remain whether good or bad
Some are very happy and some are very sad.

Marjorie Tateson

Memory Of A Butterfly Kiss

We danced on a wet and cloudy day,
Then . . .
With our faces less than a breath away,
We opened and closed our eyelids . . .
Then . . .
Our lips . . . touched . . .
And we felt a fluttering . . . sensation,
As our bodies . . . began to sway,
Then . . .
There was nothing we needed to say,
As the music continued to play,
The memory of the Butterfly Kiss,
On that wet and cloudy day,
Will remain in our hearts forever,
And will never fade away.

David Wright

Alston Childhood

They run across the dreaming field
memories lived long ago
soft meadow grass where once we played
and dew had silvered every blade
was ever time so slow?

Racing cloud shadows felltop high
across those Alston hills
in shallow pools beneath the trees
we ventured on a hundred seas
Nattras are you there still?

The shaky bridge above the falls
the cascade's misty light
and in that dappled secret shade
wild strawberries what a feast they made
were ever days so bright?

Beneath the trees of Low Nest Wood
an Amazon was found
imagination's soaring wings
found secret groves and magic springs
it seemed enchanted ground.

The days were long and time so short
a childhood quickly spent
reality comes round at last
the fleeting years so quickly past
and youth is only lent.

Joy Winter

Treasured Ornaments

My treasured ornaments to that I possess,
Have happy memories to caress,
There, on the shelf a dark green and black Scottie canine,
Because my mother gave me, he's a friend of mine,
Around the room sit five more assorted dogs,
When Father died, in his memory
Was given a shire horse, cart and logs,
A pair of candlesticks perch on the shelf,
They were Mother's, she gave me herself,
When I was young, our eggs were kept in a big brown glazed pot,
Now it stands on my window ledge, holding a plant I got,
Last of all, in tribute to my little dogs passed on,
A life-sized West Highland terrier and a Yorkshire on the floor,
sit upon.

Enid Bowerman

Bygone Nelson, Lancashire

Past times, bygone days when I was young and free
Cobbled streets and gas tar to play in
Making mud pies when it rained
Old Lancashire stone flags to play hopscotch on
Weaving mills and the rattle of the looms
The sounds of clogs as the weavers went to work
The sound of the rag and bone man with his horse and cart
The dustbin men, the rattle of the bins, the ash flying about
Going shopping at the old Co-op shop for a bar of soap
Playing in the streets with all the boys and girls
A bath once a week whether I needed it or not
Making an old trolley from an old pram
Making a sledge in the winter to slide down the street
Making a bonfire for the fifth of November
Singing from door to door, bonfire night stars are bright
Singing carols at Christmas
Past times, bygone days, times when I was young and free.

Donald Jay

A Son's Memory Of 'Him'

A great friend and neighbour
A caring grandfather and father
'He' would lend a hand if you asked for a favour

At family gatherings
At the head of the table 'He' would sit
Phone in hand in case anybody rings

Proud to have 'His' family around
Words of wisdom 'He' would preach
Or sit and listen, not making a sound

This memory he'll keep
'His' soul he will remember
In peace 'He' rests forever asleep

He stares at the empty seat
He envisions the face that once sat there
Strong minded and loved by all at 'His' feet

The days feel long and sad
Time will heal but he will never forget
This man he loved, this man he called 'Dad'.

Jane Limani

336

Hands

Those last few days
you couldn't speak
but mouthed, 'Love you,'
when Mum had said,
'We love you so.'

We held your hands,
(limp, not weighty)
and soon recalled
all they had done
in days gone by.

The memories
of babyhood,
your hands clutching ours,
security assured.

And then at school,
learning to write,
conducting the choir -
what joy that brought.

Learning shorthand,
to write more quickly
at home and at uni.
Then business beckoned,
with all its rewards.

Using computers,
editing a journal,
thus helping disabled -
so much appreciated
by people in need.

And now, those fine fingers
we stroked so gently,
though gone forever
in memory remain.

David Oliver

The Memory Box

Memories are our treasures
Stored in a dusty chest,
As years go by the pile grows high,
The oldest are the best.

Those memories of childhood,
Loving parents, happy home,
Picnics, paddling, blackberrying,
The countryside to roam.

The next stage brings back memories
Of fruitful days at school,
Wise head, who earned and taught respect
For people and for rule.

The building's core, old stately house,
Joined on one side, the new.
That upstairs form room, bedroom once,
With lovely garden view.

The gardens were a sheer delight,
Wide lawns, magnolia tree,
The shrubbery with crocus bright,
Lunch hour to wander free.

Some memories are rather grim,
Those troubled years of war,
The blackout and the rationing,
Raid sirens, bombers' roar.

The old grey church holds memories
And these are precious too,
Weddings, plays, shared bread and wine,
Dear faces seen anew.

May memories I leave behind
For those who take my place
Be happy ones to bring a smile
To each rememberer's face.

V E Godfrey

Drunk Driver (Over The Limit)

(To the families who have lost loved ones)

Did you think of me
When you took my life
On that cold and frosty
December night?

Did you think of me
When you sat in the pub,
Another two or three
Won't hurt at all?

Did you think of me
As you drove your car
And crashed into me
On that lonely road?

Did you think of me
As I slowly died
In that twisted wreck
That was my car?

Did you think of me
As you were breathalised?
You failed the test
Quite miserably.

Did you think of me
All cold and still,
All feelings gone
For evermore?

Please think of me,
Don't drink or drive,
You can't undo
What you have done.

Tracey Jane Taylor

Home Fires

Mother lights the fire in the front room on
Sunday, that's today, then we can go in to play,
She carries the hot coals from the back room
Fire to the front, after a while brings in a big lump.

Not long before we get the knock on the wall,
Smoked out is the neighbour's call, the old
Fireplaces are back to back. Flues are worn
And have many cracks.

The damp smell will soon go away, when the
Fire has been burning till midday, we are not
Bothered, we are safely out of Mother's way.

Christmas time the fire was in for a few days
We had parties, played cards, housey housey,
And Mother and Father spoke of yesterdays,
We all like the room, not bothered about the gloom.

All seven of us were born in the same musty
Damp room, all survive, some are doing quite
Well, but sometimes think back to the happy
Days, the damp room with the musty smell.

Anthony Hull

A Few Daffodils

Memories happy, others sad,
Some we would like to forget
Dad saying, 'You have a baby sister.'
Where did she come from?
Being woken up to see the airship
Flying up the Thames.
Climbing trees, fishing in a pond,
Carefree memories but not always.
Mum's tears, no money to buy food,
Dad taking his belt to me.
It hurt, sent to bed with no tea.
The smile on Mum's face, her birthday,
Being given a few daffodils,
The first present from us three.
Happy schooldays, growing up,
Starting work, then a change.
Mum crying when war was declared,
No one knowing what was to come.
War ending, what a joyous day.
Many happy married years, then sadness.
Alone now, what would I do
Without memories to see me through?

Doris Warren

The Spirit Of Christmas

This story was told by my brave Uncle Jim
When on leave in World War I.
He had volunteered at the outbreak of war
And fell ere the fighting was done.

'It happened,' he said, 'on the first Christmas Eve
When, for once, the guns were still.
The stars were bright on that winter's night.
The last thought on our minds was to kill.

Each soldier was thinking of those left at home,
Each Tommy, each Mac, each Pierre,
When suddenly, an incredible sound
Came floating across the still air.

It was singing that came from the German trench
Telling of peace on Earth
And was sung with sweetness and feelings of joy
Because of the Holy birth.

The carol they sang was called 'Stille Nacht'
And on our side we all knew it well
So we joined in the singing of 'Silent Night'
For one moment forgot war was hell.

When the carol was over, we went to our foes
Our hands outstretched in greeting
And the Germans responded and shook our hands
War forgotten in that friendly meeting.

The spirit of Christmas was with us that night
Warming our hearts like a flame.
We knew then the Jerries were just lads like ourselves,
Pawns in a power-mad game.

Christmas over, the war continued apace
Once more the dread carnage began.
The guns roared out their message of death.
Man killing his fellow man.

They certainly killed my brave Uncle Jim
But the words that he spoke will abide.
May the spirit of Christmas those long years ago
Bring peace everlasting worldwide.
Mary Webster

Remember This

When I am gone remember this,
I seal my leaving with a kiss.
I cherish all the things you've done;
You are my moon, my stars, my sun.
For all the love and life we've shared,
For you, my love, my soul is bared.
You made my happiness complete;
Remember this till next we meet.

Sylvia Brice

Memory – The Mind's Computer

Our daily life -
        Ordinary existence
Gets sifted through.
        We have no resistance.

Eyes seeing - bodies feeling
Anger - hatred - friendship - love
Days of misery or joy
Sensing God's love from above.

The computers of mind sift
Memories carefully stored,
Some time past which was hated
People or things once adored.

'Til again emerge scenes of
Our own special bygone years
The tenderness of love plus
Some old tragedies and fears.

What triggers a memory?
A name? A place? Or one look
As we go back to our past
In the opening of life's book?

Perhaps an old letter? Some words?
Photos of eyes - loving - kind?
Other memories quite sad
Jump from 'computers' we find!

Lucky were Adam and Eve
No memories stored as yet
Obsolete all computers -
No list to delve into yet!

What a dull life!
Not like ours!

Daphne Young

As I Was Young

As I was young and carefree
Among my friends and pals
Looking to the future
With open arms.

Time that was young once only
But never to return
Now that I am old and lonely
With all desires burnt.

My only expectation
The end of my misery
In a world full of hatred
And comprehension beyond me.

Love, Charity and Faith
Very difficult to debate
In company with grief
Difficult to please.

Nothing is left to vie for
But the immortality of my soul
Being luckless and lonely
Is my only goal.

Francis Xavier Farrugia

The Girl From Midnight

My eye fell on her moonlit figure, short glances crossed us
in that night, entranced as a moth
drawn to a light.

With inner courage I sidled closer
engulfed by fever blindingly driven, should I dare think
a smile might be given?

Chance plays its part, this part was mine,
gently I spoke that first hello,
my pulse sprinted wildly to where I'll never know.

But I'd struck too far the moment scattered
turned on a heel to the shadows she fled,
humbled in moonlight, cursed vanity ill fed.

Dissolved without reason so it seemed as I turned,
sunk to my pillow, all's lost to overcome, knowing
her shadow breaks the morning sun.

Tom Griffiths

I Am Still Here

Think of me
When gentle
Breezes blow
And footsteps trace
The paths
We used to know
High on the downs
I'll walk again with you
Then stop a while
Enjoy the country view
For I am here and
With you will remain
I am in the sunshine
And the rain
So do not
Cry for me
Do not be sad
Remember all
The happy times
We had

Margaret Thompson

Memories

Sitting outside at the age of six,
The wind blowing through the tree,
I look around watching leaves fall
And feeling happy as can be.

The patter of claws of my best friend, Beau
And barking all around me.
My old cat, Pearl, sat watching a branch,
Pouncing as wood pigeons flee.

The grass of the garden standing tall and crisp,
My dad standing ready to mow,
The chug of the mower as its blades start to spin
And the grass getting cut so low.

Looking around outside the back door,
Children playing skilly and tag,
And walking around to the corner shop
With my big, unfashionable bag.

Rebekah Wheeler (13)

Childhood Memories Of Staying With Grandma

My mind goes back in time to long and happy summer days
Spent in the country, staying with my grandma.
Though sixty years have passed, the memory of those far-off days
Will stay with me forever.

I close my eyes and see the long and winding lane,
Taking 'scraps' to Mr Bernard for his chickens once again,
And see him standing by his hives - with bees all humming round -
A lovely country sound - and taste the honey that I carried back
To Grandma down the lane.

I sit once more upon the little chair, and see the bright rag rugs that Grandma made,
And hear the slow tick-tock of the grandfather clock in the silence.
A doll called Joy and a dog called Bonzo, my only toys,
But oh, the pleasure that they brought!

And such a 'magic garden' Grandma had,
With little winding paths I could explore,
And nooks and crannies - paradise for hide-and-seek!
And fruit trees with their laden boughs, and the fragrant scent
Of lavender and rosemary - I smell them now -
And in my memory am in that garden once more.

Then down to the river - in my mind,
I see the yachts still sailing by, with white and coloured sails
And the houseboats moored. Along the sea wall I see it all,
And smell the seaweed and hear the seagulls cry.

These are my childhood memories - so very dear to me.
Would that I could go back in time and see -
And hear and taste and smell - the things I loved so well.

Brenda King

Childhood Memories

You never will know, my child,
what it was like to be
growing up before the war,
before hostility.

Kentish downs I tramped to seek
shy violets on a bank.
Happy Valley, a favourite haunt,
mysterious, still and dank.
Clumps of yellow primroses,
dark yellow aconites,
skylark singing overhead,
a speck at such a height.

Scars of chalky pits were filled
with blobs of fluffy willow,
gentle breezes blew which caused
yellow clouds to follow.
Dappled woods of scented bluebells,
a glimpse of a chalk-hill blue,
graceful dance of wood anemones
and fields of cowslips grew.

Autumn brought the harvest fruits,
shiny chestnuts lay around,
squirrel-like I gathered them
and blackberries by the pound.
Sloes weighed heavily on the boughs
as tinted leaves were falling,
mushrooms formed in fairy rings
at dawn, on dewy mornings.

You will never know, my child,
what it was like to be
exploring a world, on Kentish downs
alone, quite happily.

Daphne A Baker

Lifetime Memories

Childhood days were always sunny
And in Creation, God was near.
Snowdrops appeared through the snow
Holding their heads up high.
The autumn colours shone so bright,
Christmas would soon be here.

Youthful days were very different
As we stepped out on our own.
Growing up in days of war,
Friendships mattered much more.
The village dances were such fun;
Sundays we could thank God.

Adult days at last were here,
High heels and A-line dresses worn,
Catching the eye of our man
Until his ring we wore.
And in that gown of purest white
We became man and wife.

In old age these memories linger
And golden treasures they become.
Children grown up now help us
And bird songs bring much pleasure.
Little things we can still do
And friendships last forever.

J Stillwell

Little Bit Of Heaven

When I was a teenager my uncle bought me
A brand new racing bike with a yellow frame,
Black mudguards and chrome handle bars and wheels.
The bike also had Sturmy Archer gears and
Water bottles on the handle bars
With plastic straws in them.
I used to ride my bike out into the Welland Valley every Sunday
And sit on the grass watching the trains crossing the viaduct
And the rabbits playing in the fields,
Farmers harvesting their crops.
Sitting there eating my corned beef sandwiches
And drinking a bottle of pop.
All alone in my little bit of heaven.

R Morgan

Daddy

Take my head on your shoulder, Daddy,
Turn your face to the west,
It is just the hour when the sky turns gold,
The hour that Mummy loves best.
The day has been long without you, Daddy,
You've been such a while away,
And now you're as tired of work, Daddy,
As I am tired of my play.
But I've got you and you've got me,
So everything seems right.
I wonder if Mummy is thinking of us,
Because it is my birthday night.
Why do your big tears fall, Daddy?
Mummy's not far away.
I often seem to hear her voice
Falling across my play.
And it sometimes makes me cry, Daddy,
To think none of it's true,
Till I fall asleep to dream, Daddy,
Of home and Mummy and you;
For I've got you and you've got me,
So everything seems right.
We're all the world to each other, Daddy,
For Mummy, dear Mummy, once told me so.
I'm sometimes afraid to think, Daddy,
When I am big like you,
And you are old and grey, Daddy.
What you and I would do,
If when we got to Heaven
And Mummy was waiting there,
She couldn't remember the two she left,
So sad and so lonely here.
But year by year no change
And so will all be right,
We shall always meet her in our dreams,
Daddy, goodnight! Daddy, goodnight!

Dorothy Devlin

My Past Memories

I yearn for days gone by
And feel sorry for the young
The age of innocence is gone
And with it all the fun!

Memories of marbles rolling around
Bombed-out shelters under the ground
Hopscotch, skipping and roller-skates
Hours of playtime with your mates

Stone doorsteps were scrubbed
Mum soaked the laundry in a large *Dolly Tub*
Lines full of washing, a joy to behold
Warming the water with one bag of coal

The wireless crackling announcing our fates
Count up your ration books before it's too late
Rag and bone men yelling their wares
A ride on the tram only tuppence a fare.

Flickering firelight, orange and red
Toasting our supper as Father declared,
'Time for bed!'

Wild flowering gardens each family cherished
Hotpot, dumplings were foods that we relished
The allotments supplied us with veg aplenty
If only we could go back half a century!

Jill Lesley Gilbert

Bliss Bygone

In life is death a part
Times of love and sudden hate
Paradox unlocks confusion
Bewildering search for a bearable solution
Opposites attract but not so often
As they repel fate
Long ago happiness, a gentle late farewell
Safe in the beat of a splintered heart

Still there, the secret certain sort of feeling
You know he could have played rude nude golf
From the chair to the chandelier
Mimed surprise in his twinkling brown eyes
As I flung caution and clothes off
Wrapped my arms around him
Our heartbeats tap-danced up to the ceiling
Yes! Bygone bliss.

Susan Woodbine

A Bitter Experience

I remember a day when I was quite small,
The war had just ended, I seem to recall.
I was playing with friends and climbing a tree
When my brother, who is four years older than me,
Came running across and he held in his hand
A round, yellow, shiny thing, it looked really grand.
I jumped from the tree - I just had to see,
'Watcha got there, can I have a share
Where did you buy it - do you boil it or fry it?'
He said, 'Wait a minute, will your chattering you stop,
I bought it at Dewy's, the greengrocer's shop.'
He said, 'If you want one, you'd better be fast,
People are queuing.'; Then I was downcast.
I suddenly remembered, I hadn't money to spend,
I had bought gobstoppers to share with my friend.
But I was undaunted, I had an idea,
I will buy a yellow thing, never you fear.
I said 'Bye' to my friends and was gone in a flash,
Ran all the way home, slammed the door with a crash.
I emptied my moneybox, there seemed such a lot,
A big pile of farthings with a wren on I'd got.
I gathered them up, to the shop I raced,
Saw them in a box there and with a smile on my face,
Ran up to the counter, stood on tiptoes,
As I poured out my money in one clattering go.
Mr Dewy came over, he was a big happy man.
I said, 'Please, I want one of those things if I can.'
He counted my money then said, 'Sorry m'dear,
They are quite expensive, there's not enough here.'
My smile quickly faded. Oh! What could I do?
Then he saw my face and promptly withdrew
One round, yellow, shiny thing, gave it to me,
Laughed as he said, 'Take it home for your tea.'
I smelt it, and stroked it, gave it a squeeze,
Walked slowly home, my friends to tease.
I smelt it once more, cut it up with a knife,
I'd never felt so lucky before in my life.
I couldn't resist it, I just had to taste it,
In my fingers I placed it, in my mouth I encased it,
I then spat it out, without doubt,
It was horrible, tasted bitter and inedible.
I felt rather sick, glass of water quick.
I felt so let down, my bubble had burst,
It happens to everyone but that was my first
Bitter experience, my disappointment acute,
My beautiful possession was a sour grapefruit.

Barbara Servis

Recycled Love

Hello, my love who used to be
Who's now become my friend -
You left my spirit broken
When you said our love must end.

Oh, how much I missed you
Beyond life's cruellest dreams -
Swallowed by the darkest cloud -
At least that's how it seemed.

And when we held each other close
We'd shut the world away,
I knew the love I felt for you
Was forever here to stay.

Many years have passed now
Our lives went separate ways
But many times I've thought of you
And our love-filled crazy days.

See how this pen moves quickly
As my ode is at an end
And yes, of course I love you still -
But this time - as a friend.

Vanessa Hulme

Memories Are Made Of This

Meeting in wartime
St James' Park - engagement
Atlantic Ocean journeys
Snow, ice-melting heat
Family gatherings and laughter
Achievements of children
Passing of dearest one, friends and family
Sadness, loneliness
The variety of life from birth to death
Such are the memories of life
A kaleidoscope of light and darkness

Esther Greene

Bringing Memories Alive

Sitting by the fire with coals burning red
Candle on a saucer to light your way to bed
The gas mantle so fragile it collapsed at the slightest touch
Whilst the wireless crackled and whistled, sounding like double Dutch
Bathing in the tin bath by the fire gave us a glow
Floors covered in oilcloth so cold to our toes
Wooden table top scrubbed until it came white
And washing day lasted into the night
The air-raid shelter where we would hide
Huddled together side by side
When the all-clear was sounded out we would run
To play hopscotch and marbles, having fun
Hoop-la and skipping ropes came out with the seasons
Singsongs with family and friends started up with no reason
Winters were harsh, we battled the cold
Sitting by the fire whilst stories were told
Summertime was warm and hazy
Making us languid and lazy
I could go on and on with memories from the past
Bringing back the good times or the shadows that life cast
Although it's nice to go back in time and remember the good old days
We must live each day to the full to remember in our own special way

Glenys Hannon

Special Memories

Christmas Days have always been real memories for me,
For many years my sister Anne has treated family,
Dad and Mum, our brother John, Anne's husband Don also,
Along with my sons, Mark and Jon, each year we used to go,
Down to Anne's bungalow and spend a lovely day,
She'd greet us at the door, 'What will you drink?' she'd say,
We'd crowd into the lounge laden with presents for all,
Then pack them all under the tree, so pretty and tall,
We'd all enjoy the chatter asking how have we all been,
Since last Christmas - a year it doesn't seem,
Well before you know it Anne calls 'Dinner, everyone,'
We settle at the table, dinner has begun.
Anne's Don carves the turkey, as the plates begin to fill,
Lots of lovely food, Anne is the best, it really is a thrill,
This year must be possibly ten years since our Anne
Has given Christmas just for us, ever since our mum
Got older so Anne told her, 'Take a rest, it's my turn now,'
And so she's gone on doing it, sometimes I wonder how,
Anne manages to do everything so fine,
She really is one of the best, this sister of mine,
Thank you Anne for giving me lots of lovely memories.

Eileen Southey

One Day When . . .

Of all of the years of remembering when
One always special will be
When I wakened each morning and felt that the world
Was exclusively fashioned for me.

There were tadpoles and tiddlers to catch in the pond,
Old games and new ones to try.
Trees we could climb and birds' nests to find,
Then guard 'til the young ones could fly.

Meadows of wild flowers, apples to scrump,
And then, at the end of the day,
Homeward we'd go full of sunshine and smiles,
So happy and carefree and gay.

This year I returned to where I was born
And thought it would still be the same.
How sad when I found 'most everything changed
The only thing not was the name.

Though tadpoles and tiddlers were still in the pond,
Now a 'No Trespass' board's on the side.
But where were the bluebells, the gorse and the broom,
The elms standing tall in their pride?

Where were the beech trees, the brambles and ferns,
The lane where we stole our first kiss,
And I changed, so it seemed, in the blink of an eye
From a leggy young girl to a 'Miss'?

They're behind the lace curtains and barbeque stands
And gates with a 'Dunroamin' sign.
I know that they needed some place to live,
Bu why did it have to be mine?

So I go in my thoughts to where memories dwell
When the world was exciting and new,
And we were all young and our songs still unsung
And a whole lot of living to do.

Then I sit and remember the days that are gone
And know that forever they'll be
Just as they were when life seemed to begin
In that year that's so special to me.

Marion I Maggs

Moving On

One football boot, amongst a hoard of memories:
I could hear my son now speak, as though a short time, like a week had passed;
'Mum, where's my other boot?' he'd call in high-pitched voice,
From his room along the hall.
Before my answer came, another loud boom would come.
'Got it, Mom.'
I knew I would receive the blame.
Mom had moved it, who else, with the magic vacuum or broom.

I see him now, thundering down the stairs, boots tied around his neck,
'I've found my other boot, where you'd put it, Mom.
I'll be back for dinner, is it OK if I bring Tom?'
I had just been about to ask him, that had been my plan,
But as ever, he had read my thoughts, as one.

I see his room with favourite heroes pinned and bluetacked all over his wall,
A replica trophy cup, an autographed ball, bobbled caps,
Long-fringed scarves with funny faces that made me laugh,

Stickers upon the windows, trophies by the score,
Sometimes so many football magazines piled high behind the door,
That I struggled with vacuum to make a cleaning call.

Strange now to look to street from this empty room,
It seems cold, even though memories have such a hold.
We know that the day usually comes around for us to move forward,
To change our lives, but memories remain and if we love, we have gained.

My wish is his father could have been around to see our son become a man
But that was not to be, that was a heavenly plan.
My memories, how alike they were, as one.

L Hammond Oberansky

It's Your Life

Life, like the sky, is not always blue
Life, just like sailing, can go off course too
Life, like a lift can be elevating
Life, like the lottery, can mean some chance taking
Life, like a jet, can swiftly flash past
Life, is for caring, your loved ones the cast
Life, is a gift, from God up above
Make your life worthwhile
Shroud it in love

Archie Livingstone

Memories

When we were young, joining the Brownies was the thing,
To dance round 'Brown Owl' in a ring,
Jump up and down three times and say, 'Tu-whit, tu-whoo!'
Then sing our own troupe's ditty.
As we were Sprites, it went like this –
    'We are happy little Sprites
    Brave and helpful like the Knights.'
The Elves, Gnomes and Fairies sang their song too
And ended the day with 'Tu-whit, tu-whoo!' Hooray!
Then we'd all go home and polish our badges
And lovely leather belts with brass buckles.
Did it help to shape our lives, I wonder?

Next came Girl Guides, summer camps
And burning sausages over fires we'd built ourselves.
We also did more useful things like
Putting each other's arms in slings
And bandaging fingers, arms and knees
And making splints out of bits of trees.
There was tracking cross-country and reading maps
And watching out for rabbit traps, report them
To the powers that be, it's a cruel thing to do, you see,
And quite upsetting for you and me.
Then country dancing round the maypole,
Queen of the May and scattering rose petals round her way.
New baked bread, applewood bonfires, the smells of summer!
Oh! What bliss!
Some of my memories are made of this.

Beatrice Jones

Looking Back

I'm sixty today,
Not a very great age.
My life as a book I see.
As I turn every page,
Pictures of my girl, my boys,
Just a few tears, lots of joy,
Now all flown the nest,
I'm all alone.
I think was my house a house,
Or was it a home?
I'm sixty today, not a very great age,
But I wish I could turn back
To that very first page.

Parris Perry

I Remember

I remember -
　　Wheels for two, a piano and a song,
　　River walks, cricket on the green,
　　Madelines from the 'Orange Paper' tea shop on a Wednesday afternoon, one each,
　　And cream on our porridge for Sunday breakfast.

I remember -
　　Plates decorated with 'winkle hats', celery and cress,
　　French cream sandwich on a desert painted tea set,
　　Ice from the fishmonger - to suck - when sick
　　Soft roe herrings, bubble and squeak.

I remember -
　　Burning shoes for hurting feet,
　　Steaming trousers under the press,
　　Accumulators, renewed for the football final.
　　'Lobby Lud' and a raggedy dog.

I remember -
　　Washing, flapping wet on the line and baby smells,
　　Linked arms, warm hands and hearts,
　　Sugar shakers, serviettes and sand by the sea,
　　Chick's Own, Film Fun - holiday comics - behind a graveyard wall.

　　　　　　　　　　　　　　　　　　　　　　　I remember.

June Johnson

For Jake - Born Prematurely

Sweet babe, your breath a fading sigh
Is born like gossamer
　　　　　　　　upon a gentle breeze . . .
You are but a hair's breadth away
As you slip peacefully
　　　　　　　　into your final sleep.
Your life is over ere it has begun.
Oh, that I could hold you
　　　　　　　　cuddle you, breathe for you
And will you back to life again!
Your tiny form so perfect
　　　　　　　　will never feel my arms around you
Sweet innocence, a very special boy.
My love wings heavenwards
　　　　　　　　to your bright star in the sky . . .
Sleep my angel, peace my angel,
As I whisper, 'Goodbye ...'
Joanne Burns

Memories Are Made Of This

Lake Windermere Serenade

Relax cruising England's largest Lake Windermere
Ten miles of magical beauty
In Bowness oldest recorded document 1190
First steam-powered 'Lady of the Lake' 1845
The Monks of Furness, given permission
To catch the rare delicacy fish, the 'Char'
Defoe of 'Robinson Crusoe' liked it.

The railway! Lancaster to Carlisle, reached Windermere 1847
Colonel Ridehalgh, 1879, sailed 'Britannia'
Largest boat, 110ft, beam 12ft.

The lake froze in 1895, 1947, 1963, 1982
Thousands of visitors experience skating thrill on ice
The northern tip, known as Waterhead
Ambleside manufacture local wool, paper making

Lancashire cotton mills also bobbing
Sail in swan, teal, tern, cygnet, raven
Experiencing such beauty; Utopia

Nature's wonders, exhilarating.
Craftsmen, boatbuilders appreciated
Enjoy the calm blue waters rippling.

Patricia Turpin

Of The Long Ago

The evening of life now comes my way
As it always does
When past years far outnumber future years to come
And the past, good or bad, lives again
In memory's remembrance.
They come unbidden, uncontrolled.
A long-ago voice will touch your mind,
A long-ago kiss will linger,
A long-ago song will touch your heart
As when he placed his ring on your finger.
And sweet are the sounds of your children at play,
Turn around, they will grow and go their own way,
And so it goes.
Today is my 80th birthday,
We will make some more memories and say,
'We wish you a happy birthday my dear'
And no one can take them away.

Màirie Purcell Herbert

Memory Lane

'Buy some pegs or a pretty flower today?' a gypsy asking,
Then saying, 'Luck will come to stay.'
Household frightened if they don't buy, a curse would come
Their way.
Cardboard placed inside your shoe because the sole had
Worn through.
No money to be had to buy shoes that were new.
Radios, Gert and Daisy, Journey into Space, The Archers
And large gramophone records called 78s.
Snow so high you had to dig your way out from your door.
Watching chestnuts cooking upon a dustpan over an open fire
À la carte,
Remember the rag and bone man with his horse and cart.
Old-fashioned suet puddings, dripping, home-made bread and tripe,
Pig's trotters and Spam, you know this isn't just hype.
Seeing milk churns standing beside a field gate,
The cows pleased to be milked and they hadn't had to wait.
Television's 'Bill and Ben, the Flowerpot Men'.
Your first love, your father showed to the door, telling you soundly,
'You are too young by far.'
The ecstasy you felt at getting good grades in your final exams
At school.
Your first party dress and the one you wore to the school leaving do.
The first pair of six-inch high-heeled shoes you bought,
Wearing them to wobble out of the shoe shop.
The three-wheeler Reliant Robin and the Volkswagen Beetle
Called Herbie.
Teddy-boys you couldn't forget, their style was unique,
Teddy-girls wore black, tight pencil skirts, flat pumps, tight tops
And Vitapoint on the hair.
There was Be-Bop-A-Hula, Mods and Rockers, Rock 'n' Roll,
Flared skirts with organza petticoats, the Twist and of course,
Elvis, the Pelvis, Presley.
Afghan coats, flower power, The Beatles, Buddy Holly, Big Bopper and Bill Haley.
How about beehive hairdos, the urchin cut, the bubble cut, the
Long hair of the seventies and the punk hairdo, platform shoes,
Kitten heels and winkle pickers?
Mini skirts were very popular, you had to be careful when you
Sat down and how you bent down.
Remember television's 'Sesame Street' and the first time you saw
Puppies or kittens being born?
Phew, perhaps now I can take a breather, this reminiscing has
Taken me all night,
But will anybody believe me in the morning that it was reminiscing
That has made me look such a fright?

Heather Dormand

Evensong

How sweet in the evening
When tucked up in bed
The sound of Mam's singing
The night prayers all said
How lovely her voice as the old songs she sang
And far in the distance the church bells rang.

The time came so sadly
So swiftly it came
In hospital bed now
Eyes closed, weak the flame
What can I say to my dear mother now?
Just tell her how much we loved
That sweet evening hour.

Quietly, so quietly she found her lost voice
And a humming so soft
Made her children rejoice
And a young nurse who listened
Joined in with a tear
For she knew in her wisdom
That night-time was near.

Goodbye, gentle mother,
Goodbye, take our love
The love you have given
Take it with you above
We'll always remember the old songs you sang
When far in the distance
The church bells rang.

Hazel Browne

Thinking Back

When we are old and thinking back on life
And remembering the paths, our feet did take,
Pause on all of the small and simple things,
The things from which our memories we make.

Those things that matter only to us two.
The day we met, our first sweet lover's kiss,
Elation at our newborn baby's cry,
The essence of our lives is based on this.

We'll talk of things recalled from long ago,
With hair of grey whilst sitting by the fire,
Memoirs of two lives, joined as one.
To share them all with you is my desire.

Julie Hanstock

Recollections

Memories of Grandad I like to recall,
Of times spent together when I was quite small.
His garden was his pride and joy,
A trade he learnt as a boy,
With rows and rows of plants so neat,
A salad corner, what a treat.
Roses covered the garden wall,
Sunflowers and lupins grew so tall.
Daffodils and snowdrops he grew in the spring,
But tulips and pansies were his favourite thing.
The greenhouse full of plants and pots,
Bunches of onions hung in knots,
Tomatoes and veg he grew by the score,
Often sold them at the door.
On sunny days we liked to be
Sitting under the apple tree.
Grandad taught me his industrious ways,
I love to remember those happy days.

L France

Hard Times On St Helena

Many years ago, when our parents were so poor
They wore clothes made from flour bags
Because they couldn't afford anything more
Our fathers had to work for about two shillings a day
Unlike now, we get a much bigger pay

Out in the flax mills men had to work
This generation today would have gone berserk
With the old rough roads under our feet
Boots, shoes or socks, our wage couldn't meet.

Children had to work before going to school each day
On home arrival work awaiting and no time for play
A strip of Grandpa's felt hat for wick in our oil lamps
Sometimes not a hot bath because the wood was so damp.

Bread and jam then was often our diet
But no one complained, we all took it quiet
To have a lot of meat was all very fine
There were no refrigerators so we had to put it in brine.

Compact radios and tape recorders were then unknown
So Grandpa played the old gramophone
We couldn't afford to paint our homes with pretty paints
But we were not ashamed because we are all saints.

Alison Elizabeth Wade

Memories

I recall with a smile,
Things we did when we were small.
Brothers and sisters on a go-kart,
Hand-made and shared by all,
Boy, did we have a ball.
Climbing trees, making a den,
Life was fun back then.
Cowboys and Indians, bows, arrows,
Imagination running wild,
I was a happy child.
Potato picking, chased by boys with mice,
I could run like the wind,
Getting away in a trice.
Building sites had us building
Our own little nests.
The caretaker chased us
And called us pests.
Hiding in bed and recalling our day,
Sharing with family in our intimate way.

Margaret Mitchell

Memories Are Made Of This

M y mind rolls back across the years
E ncompassing the laughter and the tears
M other and father no longer here
O f treasured memories still held dear
R emembering those wartime years
I n Blitz and bombing they soothed our fears
E very adventure with twin sister shared
S he was my protector when I was scared

A unties spoiling us, always some treats
R ationing I remember, not many sweets
E vacuated quite far away

M issing Mother and Father many a day
A fterwards travel was easier on bus and on train
D istant relatives we'd visit, had holidays again
E specially my grandmother I loved to see

O f her life as a cook she'd often tell me
F or she worked in big houses for people with 'brass'

T here sometimes we'd visit and see 'the upper class'
H ow fast the years vanish and people are gone
I 'm eternally grateful the memories live on
S o perhaps I can share them with others anon.

Brenda Hughes

My Old Posh Frock

I finger your fragile fabric and fleeting memory
teases and ruptures its meniscus of time.
The mirror reflects the soft smile on my face
as I hold you up against me,
your tints sublime washing my eyes in water colours
of gentle green, grey and cerulean blue.
Oh, now I remember,
how I remember, you!

See!
I have found my magical dress,
my so special, sparkling, shimmering dress.
Oh where? Oh where have you been?
What? Deep in this chest full of bloomers and vests,
all set for the skip, the very last trip
to scrub, erase and to clean.
I stroke your soft silk and the memories flare,
my spirits soar and I'm up in the air
a-twirling and spinning and floating on clouds
of delight,
chiffon and glee curling, creaming around
and around and around and around and
I know
My feet do not touch the ground.

Your misty blues, aquas and silvery shimmer
echo my eyes and catch the moon in rare,
crystal glimmers of light.
You were always, always my dress of the night.
Each glorious, glamorous, gregarious night
that you dressed me.

Together we flew to other-world places,
greeted other loves, dreamed with other faces.
Together we danced down the paths of chance,
always and ever embracing romance
by the luminous light of the moon.

Now clasping your folds of aqua and blue,
I still drift in silver and dream with you.
Where have you been, my magical dress,
while I have grown old
and unseeing, I guess?

When was the day I put you away?
Where did all our dreams go?
Padi Vincent

Childhood Days

Childhood days go swiftly by,
On looking back, they seemed to fly,
But thinking now, as in a dream,
Of things we've done and things we've seen.

Of Mum and Dad, they still were there,
And grandma sitting in her chair,
When home from school I loved to see
The table set for having tea.

I loved the day the muffin man
Came calling saying, 'How do, Ma'am?'
His gingham cloth covered basket bright,
When removed, oh, what a sight.

Great big pikelets, muffins too,
All freshly made, the smell was coo;
A bright red fire, with toasting fork,
We all would soon then set to work.

With loads of Danish butter there,
To spread them we would soon prepare,
I think that in these latter years,
I taste them still, moves me to tears.

Oh happy days, those days of yore,
You did not have to lock the door,
We had not got much then to steal,
But helpful neighbours were friends so real.

But now I'm old, my family's gone,
But these wonderful memories still live on.
I thank my God for memory clear,
For wonderful things I hold most dear.

Ivy Griffiths

Yesterdays

A slice of cake upon a plate;
The battered car we played in all that summer,
Our alphabets, our stops, our commas
Pauses to review our games
Of space invaders, cowboys,
Kings and queens and sky gods;
A slice of cherry cake sliced thick
This was our reward
For making ourselves scarce
As the grown-ups entertained.

Years on when we returned
To picnic and recall
We found the battered Mini
A rusting hollow shell
Yet alive with wasps
And feet-high stinging weeds.

We ate our picnic in the kitchen
Where we'd eaten cake before
No grown-ups now except ourselves
The sullen summer heat
The smell of rain.

Katherine Jane Rawlings

The Old Wall Clock

The room was filled with silent pauses
Emphasizing the tock my memory applauses.
A slow, low, rhythmic tock-pause-tock
From my companiable, dependable old wall clock.
'Twas the heartbeat of time itself,
A metronome that calmed myself.
A sound companion, gilding silent moments,
Whilst I contemplated life's involvements.
A monotonous chant, maybe; devoid of any melody.
But the tock, tock, tock was music for my memory,
When engulfed with joy or sorrow whate'er the situation,
I found a peaceful sanctuary providing consolation.
A refuge from the daily clamour,
A diversion from life's panorama.
Within the room of silent pauses,
Sheltered from demanding causes,
I sought the solace of the old wall clock
With its steady regulated tock, tock, tock.

Stan Coombs

Fall Of An Empire
(Battlefield Ballad)

Soldiers, weary and full of defeat,
heads bowed and eyes full of sleep,
thinking of the brutal battle ahead,
of the blood and tears about to be shed,
but they have a duty to go out and fight,
on to that battlefield on a stormy night,
all they see is a dark damned road of fate,
their only light is Heaven's gate.

All stood in a line, they desperately defend,
knowing they are about to face the end.
Then it came, with a clap of thunder,
they looked, some in fright, some in wonder,
at the man poised upon the hill,
his raised hand full of exuberant skill.
His fist embraced the night's air,
then his arm dropped, seemingly without a care.

The soldiers waited and then time froze,
clouds rumbled on the horizon, then a storm arose,
time then awoke, the man's hands upon fire,
an inferno of dreams and desire,
and promises straight from the heart.
Then from that hand falls a spark,
a single ember, the flame is on,
it flickers, dances and then is gone.

Dale Mullock

The Things I Remember

Some things that I remember are just these,
A sky at sunset and a gentle breeze.
Autumn's rustling leaves, a kitten's fur,
The morning song of birds, a cat's low purr.
The crash of breaking waves, a lonely beach,
The shine of sea-washed rocks, now out of reach.
A new-mown lawn with roses all around,
The tumbling shower of a waterfall, a restful sound.
The silver path of moonlight on the sea,
An old steam train that brought you back to me.
An aria from opera, a love duet,
A sentimental song I can't forget.
These things I've always loved, and pray I may
Remember them until my dying day.

Shirley R Thomas

A Memory

When moving out of London as a child of five
To live in a house so we could all thrive
The pavements were unmade, just a lot of clinker
When the workmen came with their tar, what a stinker
We were told the tar smell was good for kids' throats
But it made us cough more and got on our coats
And shoes and hands, well just everywhere!
Mum was at her wits end, for we even seemed to take it to bed
But once it all got dried, there was less to be said.
No room at the school, we had to wait for a space
Easter term came and they crammed us new ones in, then it was a race
Each morning to get a chair or to sit on the floor
Schools at that time must have been very poor,
The teaching must have been good as back in London
Four years later it appeared I was way ahead.
And if it rained playtime, there was no shed
No shelter at all, but we had to go out and got wet.
There was no milk, or drink if you didn't take one and yet
Mostly playtime was fun, tag or skipping, or just running
There was always someone willing to chase, as in a race
And playtime seemed to be over almost before it began.
Then back to the class and out of the sun.
The noise from the scrape of the chairs I'll never forget.
So long ago and yet, it stays in my memory.

Phyllis Wright

Summer Days

I love to think of summer days when I was just a kid,
Remembering the happy hours and all the things we did.
We hadn't got much money but we had a lot of fun,
My little brother, Mum and Dad and me - we loved the sun.

We'd take a bus down to the beach and picnic on the sand,
Then walk along the promenade and listen to the band.
Upon the pier we'd see a show and visit the arcade,
A penny piece was all it cost for each machine we played.

Then later, if the tide was out, we'd go back to the shore,
To play some games, enjoy ourselves - that's what we went there for!
We'd join with other families and kick a ball around,
And oh! The many friends we made - the happiness we found!

In those days, quite unlike today, we'd no time to be bored.
We made the most of every hour and laughter was assured.
Life was much simpler then, and looking back, the Lord I praise
For giving me these memories of golden summer days.

Margaret Altham

Memories Of No 93

'An old house - people gone away,'
That's what some passers-by may say
But inside, there's treasures to find
Amid bits and pieces left behind.
Old photographs and diaries,
Trinkets of childhood, rosaries,
Bees on dresser, peacocks on wall -
Someone who cared had saved them all.
Cups and saucers, dishes and plates
Two clocks still ticking on the grates
Family table, on which to dine
A glass or two for Christmas wine.

Out in the garden, there is still
Wonderful view of distant hill,
Ancient now, but Dad's shed's still there
Wants coat of paint and needs repair.
Golden roses by garden wall
Are spreading beauty over all,
Proud hollyhocks in corner stand
With delicate hues, oh so grand!
One stately foxglove stands alone
And in the spring, bluebells will come.

Years always seem to pass so swiftly by
But the mem'ries will stay, with you and I,
Of those wonderful times that now are gone,
The times of great pleasures with lots of fun.

Betty Gould

Voices From The Past

Gentle voices from times past
Tread the gentle breeze,
Travel down the centuries
Speaking gently into one's ears.

A voice from the past speaks to me.
A voice from the past seeks me.
And is this how I receive thee,
Speaking gently into my ears?

Mary Marriott

Memories Of 'Long' Ago

When I was little, my hair was dark.
A large satin bow was tied at one side.
We played on nearby rough land like a park,
In games with the boys, I was the 'prisoner' with pride.

Roads were for roller-skating, hockey and football
Mibs' was played in the gutter, marbles would get lost.
We played board games and card games, with parents as well.
We gardened and crafted, and wrote letters to post.

Baker, butcher, grocer and milkman delivered our needs.
Milk, full cream, with a jug, from a very large tank
Arrived early each day, on a bike with three wheels.
No fridges or freezers, only 'cool slabs'.

Once my brother was taken by men all in white,
His bedroom was screened, then sanitised clean.
Isolation hospital - scarlet fever the blight.
He recovered, thank goodness, to all our relief.

When eight years of age, nephritis struck me:
A kidney problem, feared much at the time.
Barley water, cornflour custard, warmth and bed rest
Were the cosseting cure over eight weeks of my life.

A large doll, a doll's house and teddy bear,
Were loved, treasured and played with for a very long time.
Parents taught me to read, write and not swear.
Behaviour had rules to obey, or be punished or fined.

Wartime meant that we all had to learn
To manage with little, spin everything out.
We did it, and valued each penny we earned
'No money' told us to all - 'go without'.

Margaret C Cobb

Tastes Of Yesterday

Nothing compares to the toast that was made in front of the coal fire,
On a long, three-prong fork Dad made,
With lashings of Danish butter bought at the market,
A chunk cut from a huge round block
And unceremoniously slapped onto greaseproof paper,
Cheese also was taken from a large slab
And portions cut from it with a wire device,
To start the fire Mum would tie newspaper knots,
Which were intermingled with coal,
And then lit with a match, an acquired trick.

Tasty bread was delivered in a horse-drawn enclosed cart,
And Dad went out with a bucket
To collect any manure deposited for the garden,
On Sundays Grandma came for tea,
And dainty triangular sandwiches were served,
Along with cucumber slices floating in pungent vinegar,
Followed by fruit salad or blancmange and jelly trifle,
Served in green glass bowls along with bread and butter,
Later Mum's delicious home-made cake was cut into wedges,
And liquid chicory, the late fifties' answer to today's coffee,was made.

I remember the chip shop in the lane,
Three pence worth of fish and chips plus a free bag of batter bits,
Cooked to perfection, unlike nowadays,
Pop was delivered by lorry,
It came in large round stone bottles with handles,
And they were filled with ginger beer and dandelion and burdock,
When empty they were used as water bottles,
Wrapped around with an old woolly jumper,
If they fell out of bed in the night they made an almighty crash,
Reminisces of yesterday's tastes.

Ann G Wallace

Don't Forget To Remember

Faces and places, seasons and times,
Children's parties, poetry and rhymes.
That trip abroad, a table with wine,
Flying home to 'Auld Lang Syne'.

Quiet streets on a summer's dawn,
Early mist in a field of corn;
Hoot of an owl on a chill, dark night;
Hallowe'en pranks that gave you a fright.

Fresh-baked bread in the superstore,
A charity walk with your feet so sore.
That talent show that you didn't win;
Your 'never again' when trying to slim!

The gale that blew the dormer down
And devastated half the town.
Summer droughts and hosepipe bans
And loudly wailing ice cream vans.

Remember all the good and bad,
Remember happy and the sad.
Later, you will cherish this
As you recall that teenage kiss.

Sharing, caring, being together,
Having a laugh at the 'funny' weather.
Bonfire night and the fireworks show;
The blazing embers and the afterglow.

There's more to life than what we see,
But that is how it has to be;
So, make the most of every day
And lock your memories all away!

J Unsworth

Times Gone By

Today we had a visit from a family we love,
Sharing precious memories as gentle as a dove,
Time has marked the pages since first it all began.
It was many years ago now that God had a plan,
For the family to move from Bristol with the noise and fears
Of enemy aircraft where they left a trail of tears,
Such devastation all around the city's life,
Homes and churches ruined causing anger and strife,
To the little village of Holcombe with its historic fame,
It was there they settled and heard the story of the name
Of Robert Falcon Scott where his family lived and toiled,
He was remembered from the last South Pole trip that foiled,
His name is carved upon their family stone,
In the old cemetery standing supremely alone.
Now to the family I knew and loved so well,
When in my teens my duties there I would like to tell,
This dear family I cared for throughout their childhood days,
My pay was just by being there and the words of praise,
For some little treat I'd made for their tea,
Often during the day I would take the youngest on my knee,
Damian was the smallest and I loved him best of all,
I loved the others too of course, Elizabeth, Mary and Paul.
For just one pound a week that's what I had,
My days were always full, Paul was quite a lad,
Frogs in the bath was one of the jokes he played,
We laugh about it now as their story is relayed.
Ebeneezer was their dog waiting for me at the crossroads,
Greeting me with a joyful leap, oh how those memories unfold,
Laughter tinged with tears as we recall those precious days,
With their funny childhood ways,
I was young but I responsible must be
To this mischievous loving family
Until their parents returned from the town,
Days when trusting seeds were sown
Once again we are together sharing memories and time,
Their children too are making their family sublime,
A hug from them as we trace days now that are past,
God has enriched us all with the treasures that will last,
He holds the key to our future days, it's safe in His hands,
Each thought, each deed is part of God's plans

Eveline Tucker

Memories

Memories last forever, they are deep down in our hearts,
The ones we really cherish will never, never part,
Of childhood days when we were young,
We played all day, we laughed, had fun,
We made good friends for many years
Then came the partings that brought tears.
We all feel rather sad and blue,
Then I turn around and I find you,
Another friend to see me through,
I bless the day that I met you.

Children coming to and fro,
No one knows just where to go
Another school, some different rules,
We make new friends, we play it cool.
We soon sort out who we like best
And that's another memory to add to the rest.
Hard work, sport, a lot to do,
The years go by, we get older too,
It's time to leave, our schooldays are through,
Again we're feeling sad and blue,
But we have all the memories stored
Of childhood days we had before,
Thankful of tomorrow and what might come,
But all of you are me and - one.

Sandra Hughes

372

This Memory Today

A distant phone call, a sudden funeral,
Meeting relatives today of long ago.
Later chatted, then gazed at black and white photos
Awakening forgotten memories that come and go.

A photo of Auntie Stella was amazing, in her schooldays,
With her three sisters and her only brother,
Dressed as Guides, Brownies and a Cub,
Off to church parade with one another.

Then another photo from tallest to shortest,
In a neat long row they stood,
The five dressed smartly, standing tall and upright,
All smiling cheerfully and looking good.

Then a later family photo group of her brother when married,
With his wife Gwen and their happy family,
Seated on a long settee all together,
Smiling happily with sons, one, two and three.

In amazement we relived many years that had vanished,
Now ten, twenty, thirty years or more,
From schoolchildren, now grown into worldly adults,
We laughed at fashions of years gone before.

We then posed together, capturing today's memory photo,
Promising to continue our renewed acquaintance again.
The three sons in person had now re-met their Auntie Stella,
This memory today will always remain!

Stella M Bush-Payne

Postscript

(To a letter to a daughter who is abroad)

Also that I can see the wren in the hedge from the kitchen window
Also that I hear the telephone ringing, it will stop before I reach it
Also that the caravan next door has not been moved away
Also that the old armchair that you like has been restored
Also that I shall not read all the books I'd like to
Also that I hear Cosmo crowing to tell me his hens are hungry
Also that I am here at home most days and light the fire
Also that our neighbour is under his car poking about
Also that the other neighbour is building a shed against our wall
Also that the water butt is full and an icicle is hanging from the tap
Also when spring comes the duck starts laying her eggs
Also that the rain is pouring down the lane in rivulets
And that I miss you and I want to hold your baby's hand.

Joy Murphy

The Great McAdams, Jock And David

My next-door neighbour died a few days ago, aged 81 years.
As I am reaching up for eighty myself, it realised my fears
That I might not have so long to go in this world myself.
We were neighbours for about 57 years and never a cross word.
It made me think of my life and my schooldays.
I was a very physical boy with a vile temper,
I would have fought with my shadow when provoked.
There was one boy that I never fought in anger,
We had many a wrestle but not in earnest.
Although a bit older than me, he had an unusual feature,
He had been born with only one arm, the other had a stump
Which he used to great effect when wrestling.
He could pin you to the ground with it on your breastbone.
He grew up to be an all-rounder; football, badminton, swimming,
I have never known anyone so able.
I once asked him, 'Is there anything you cannot do?'
He said, 'I can't cut my fingernails.'
We had a young billiard team during the war,
We were invited to play another little village in the area. Jock was playing.
To our astonishment, his opponent had only one arm also.
Wingie, as he was called, had his one right off at the shoulder.
Jock had a tiny turn on his elbow to rest the cue on.
Wingie used the table brush to guide his cue, a game to remember.
About that same time I started playing the drums in his brother's
Dance band, Red McAdam and His Hotcha Boys.
Red (David) had only one leg and the pianist was blind.
Red lost his leg in an accident when young.
Red was self-taught, he played tenor sax, clarinet, piano and drums.
So you see, when I feel down, I remember the McAdams
And what they had to overcome.
Jock died in London working for the Post Office. Red died in his forties.
I will always remember them as the great McAdams.

James Rodger

Not Forgotten

Memories, so precious and so transient,
Of people, places and so many things,
Stored in the deep recesses of our minds
Awaiting recall when and where we please.
Of tastes and sounds and sights,
Emotions and of every other sense,
Brought to the surface to give pleasure,
Or sometimes even pain.
Memories of childhood, so very long ago,
Of endless summers (was there ever rain?)
Of friends at school and holidays,
My loving parents and the happy times
We spent together whilst I was growing up.
The memory of when I fell in love,
Of marriage and my four children's births.
Their childhoods and the fun we had,
Their laughter, love and tears.
Of all the people that I've loved
And lost throughout the years,
My parents and so many friends,
My dearest son who died four years ago,
My memories of him so treasured and so bittersweet.
How bare and cold our lives would be
Without our special memories.

Ann Linney

Fulfillment

I sit and dream in my rocking chair
Of the days that might have been,
Of all the things I hoped to achieve
When I was young and green.
I imagined I'd have the world at my feet,
Be renowned for my beauty or brain,
My outstanding courage, or daring deeds -
No effort would be in vain!

I smile now, recalling that youthful zeal,
Never doubting that God would bless
My every attempt to achieve acclaim
With instant and great success.
Then I rock some more remembering
Not the 'might', but the 'truly has' been
Of smiling eyes and comforting arms
And love, in our house of dreams.

Shoveling coal and chopping sticks
(No central heating there!)
Polishing lino on hands and knees -
I'd energy then, and to spare.
Nappies drying round the fire,
It seems like yesterday,
And then the worldwide terrible war
With my loved one long years away.

And now, I am alone again -
I never did achieve
My hour of fame - my great acclaim
But to hear my grandchildren call my name
Is better by far than these.
- So, I rock and dream (though I'm not a star)
Thanking God for the way things are.

D E Smith

Old Salt Sundays Pre-1953

As quick as you can jump in Dad's van
We're going to Wells next the Sea.
With seaside sandwiches along
Favourite egg and tomato ones,
Plus the Primus for a nice cup of tea.
Sing songs on our way, ahead, a hot summer's day
Passing rhododendrons, heather, bracken and gorse.
Park beneath tall pine trees that swish in the breeze,
We gather our bucket and rake.
Make for the shore to cockle beds galore,
Gather bounty in glorious sun.
Then with ruddy red cheeks, cheery old salt
Rows us safely over fast-running creek,
So tired at the end of the day.
With the best yet to come, Mum says they're done
Amidst steam from pans boiling back home.
We all relish our treat, cockles fresh and so sweet
And our memories forever always.
Now, when there's a murmur of breeze
I remember times like these
Even though I've become old and grey.
Rest easy, old boatman, and thank you.
I'm so grateful for those magical days.

Sheila Margaret Parker

Fires Of Love

The touch of your hand
Sets my heart on fire
That fills my mind
With a burning desire.

A desire to hold you
In my arms once more
Then carry you away
To some far-off shore.

An island of paradise
Where your heart desires
Where only your kisses
Can put out the fires.

Then as the embers
From the fires cool
I think to myself
I'm a lucky fool.

A fool that thought
He would never miss
That wonderful moment
Of a lover's kiss.

John Richard Doughty

Rewind

Moments lost in oblivion
Darkness back in time,
Mind relax, rewind.
Memories revisualised,
To a time that was, and still is,
Frozen, freezes of scenes past
Held in timeless frame
That laugh with you mockingly.

Faces of coloured days long gone
That my mind's eye replays,
Days of youth not always blue
Like Portmarknock by the sea,
Its mile of golden sand dunes
That kissed the waters green,
Those breasts of Mother Dublin
Which lay beautiful in the sea.

I knew them well as a young jackeen
In my youth the summers of fifties and sixties,
They held for me great mysteries
Those islands of my boyhood dreams,
With cupped hands made into goggle
I spied them from sandy shore,
The boats and ships that sailed for pleasure
To me was pirates seeking stolen treasure.

The hot sun that shone its light through fields
Of thinning clouds, made those two rock breasts
Of Lambay Island and Ireland's eye my secret
Treasure chest, they were for me my
Escape from bondage reality, and still to this
Very day, as I rewind fifty years on, they
Are ageless, though the world has moved on.

Philip Anthony McDonnell

Snippets Of Summer

Those idyllic days of summer,
in daisy meadows we would play.
I remember swathes of cornflowers
and the smell of new-mown hay.

Bright jewels of blood-red poppies,
swaying in the summer breeze.
Fluffy seed heads of a dandelion,
that always made me sneeze.

In the River Ouse we'd paddle;
at the shallow end we'd play.
Catching tadpoles in our nets
and take them home that day.

Our mothers didn't go to work,
well, only in the home.
Food was always on the table,
we were never left alone.

We'd play out in the street
or run to the nearby park.
The swings, a slide and roundabout,
kept us occupied till dark.

Then home we'd scamper - ravenous;
to fresh bread and home-made jam.
All these memories remind me
of who I really am.

Ann Potkins

Halcyon Days

On the banks of the river
Stands the little old mill,
With butterflies flitting,
The river never standing still,

Swallows flying and diving,
Lovers kissing, children playing,
This stream carrying the memories
Of days before the war.

The carthorse that plods up and down
With the farmer ploughing the fields,
There will be hard days before us,
Many will die, many will live.

It's sad, gone forever the days of play,
How long can it last? No one can say.
Will it be years? Perhaps just a day,
But gone are the children's days of play,

Parents to lose their sons in conflict,
Daughters grown with no childhood,
Soldiers fighting in the field of battle,
Praying to see another day.

Will we see our loved ones again?
Should we listen to the orders given?
Will we run or be too frightened to move?
I don't know, I am too scared to say.

This day I am thinking so sadly,
But this day is not a dream,
The days I love and remember
Are on the banks of the river; by that stream.

Lennard Clarke

A Special Doggy Friend

Once I had a wee dog called Snoopy
Whose antics were at times quite loopy
He cried like a baby if left alone
But what speed could he chew a bone

A wee black and white spaniel with curls
Always chasing his tail round in whirls
Friendly to everyone young and old
Facing up to bigger dogs acting so bold

His tail wagged from morning until night
Even the morning he gave the postie a fright
Guarding the baby was his delight
Watching and listening, keeping out of sight

Most nights he lay on my lap in my chair
Covering all your clothes with his hair
His companionship was that of a true friend
How I wished our friendship would never end

Alas one day as result of an accident outside
I lost my best friend to the other side
Lost for words and eyes running with tears
I buried my wee friend after all those years.

George Alexander

Memories Kept In Fond Remembrance

During those far-off days of childhood,
When I was but a baby mild,
I was learning how to walk
Before I became a loving child.
My parents would reach out caring hands
And encourage me to walk towards them.
They would hold me up by their hands
Or by my straps, or maybe tug at a hem.
They would praise my every effort,
As each wee faltering step I'd take . . .
But they never got discouraged
Whenever I'd make the odd mistake.
They never did give up
Until I'd first actually learned to walk . . .
And they would also persevere
Until I also learned how to talk.
First I'd learn the ABC
And next I'd learn to count . . .
Then I'd progress to picture books
And then I'd read a fair amount.
I'd pick up bits from what others said,
And I'd be listening to the radio . . .
Then very soon would come the time
As merrily off to school I'd go.
Mummy had taught me all she could
Before I'd even started school . . .
And soon I was enabled
To learn that good old Golden Rule.
Moments kept in fond remembrance,
Some I now just cannot recall . . .
But they are still all the more dear to me
As I look at the scroll upon that wall.

Kevin McCann

I Remember

I remember when I was a child
The golden cornfields on their headlands
Had red poppies growing wild,

And how the lark would shoot up to the sky,
And sing, a dot before the sun
As the horse-drawn binder clattered by,

And how the rabbits and brown hares would run
And jink across the stubble bare
To outwit the farmer with his gun,

And men in collarless tick shirts and trousers navy blue
Would gather up the sheaves to stand in stooks
To let the wind blow through.

And those same men again would come,
Days later, when the grain was ripe and straw was dry
And with long forks, load carts and bring the harvest home,

To where other brown-armed men with strong backs
Would toil and use their skill to forge
The great mass of sheaves into shapely stacks,

Which would be thatched to turn the snow and rain
And at dusk would look like galleons sailing against an autumn sky,
Until months later when the thresher men came.

Then grain and straw went their separate ways
And sweat was lost again, and thirsts were sated
On those noisy, dusty, often bitter, cold days.

E D Bowen

Memories You Never Forget

Memories of a little boy
Who used to some and stay,
And spend such happy times,
For his summer holidays.
Lovely memories of him playing,
Even climbing up the wall,
Going to the seaside,
Paddling in the pools.
Then he grew up from a boy to a man,
Working miles away, carrying life's span.
All of a sudden I get the news,
He is coming to visit, out of the blue.
I was terribly anxious, wondering what to say,
To this man I had not seen for many a day.
But my fears all left me when I opened the door
And saw this handsome man, that was a little boy no more.
We had lots of lovely memories
To hear and talk about,
My memories now are of Terence,
A little boy? No chance.

Hilda Cook

In Beautiful Assisi

Truly spectacular, exquisite, quaint,
Are words attributed to a saint.
A saint who loved both beasts and birds
And gave us prayers with lovely words.

His kindness to the poor we prize
As we enjoy with our own eyes
The inspiration that he gave,
Enriched the lives he came to save.

We journey through the cobbled lanes
And pay respect wherein remains
A powerful, humble, touching story
Mirrored in a sense of glory.

Holy Spirit, gift of God,
To just be here where Francis trod
And see the stunning views as well
Are really more than words can tell.

Norma Anne MacArthur

Spring Yet Again!

Again the chaffinch casts its transient skein of notes, and again,
As if to net the fleeting moment, hold it in,
Then resorts to dint with beak its shiny bit of tin,

Salutes the soft-blown drops of rain
The writhing caterpillar vivid green
The breeding feeding frenzy, the irresistible surge of spring.

Ali Cohen

Nostalgia

Sometimes on hot summer nights
When sleep is an unobtainable yearning
The brain a mass of persistent lights
And the face hot and burning,
Then thoughts surface to far-off days
And become gradually recognizable
Through the semi-conscious haze.

Tonight come dreams of the past
With a pre-war cast,
Each day sublime
The weather always fine,
With a sky bluebell-blue
And your dreams come true.

Those perfect childhood treats,
Ice cream, sea and sand,
Deckchair seats,
Donkey rides affordable
One excursion a year laudable

On with the bathers, Jim,
A quick dip or a swim,
Next the serious task lies
Building sand pies
To be destroyed at a whim.

Later came boiled eggs and Spam,
There's sand in mine,
'You're lucky to have it,' says Mam,
Then pop bottle out, disliked by me,
Never any pop, only cold tea,
This was in the roaring thirties you see.

That's the way we were,
No telly, no cars, no fuss,
Then home on the bus.
Nostalgia is a pleasant vacation
From reality in any location.

Colin O Burnell

Cradle Soliloquy

Today's today and that is all I know;
I've wet myself and I have sucked my toe;
I cried because I had that funny pain.
When will I have my mother's breast again?
What happened yesterday? I'm not too sure;
Today's becoming something of a bore.

I think I'm going to do a little job.
Oh, where's the nipple? Here's my hungry gob!
So, shall I suck my fingers? Yes, that's it
And make believe it's milk and not just spit;
Quite good at first but soon it comes to nought.
Look out! that job was bigger than I thought.

I've had enough. Where's my confounded Ma?
One deep, deep breath, then blast her with my *whaaaaah*.
My *whaaaaah* is super; I'm quite proud of it
And when a chap's all stink or wants the tit
There's not a lot a little bloke can do
'Cept *whaaaaah* through red to purple, then to blue.

I'm now quite comfy in my nether parts
And Mother, after all, is Queen of Hearts.
Her breast is one great blob of sheer delight
But tummy space is getting rather tight.
I gagged just then and had a little cough.
Cor! This is living! Think I'll just drop off.

Frank Sutton

The Cooling Canyon Stream

We shall go a-skinny-dippin'
In the cooling canyon stream,
Just as we used to years ago
And relive our childhood dream;
We'll lie and watch the fireflies
As the gentle blowing breeze
Teases at the branches
Of the over-burdened trees.

We'd take the trap and pony
In those days of yesteryear
And now we'll do it all again
To bring back childhood dear;
We'd splash about and swim awhile,
We'd howl with laughter too,
Carefree innocents lost in ourselves
'Neath those summer skies of blue.

We made that journey to our creek
But we had a shock in store
For now the place was different
From it was in days of yore;
Where once nobody wandered
On that pathway hard to trace,
Our private world had come and gone
And now wore a different face.

The tar-clad path was pounding
With folks coming to and fro,
All out for recreation
Where those gentle waters flow;
And across our childhood meadow,
A freeway now was laid,
To create a stream of traffic
In a non-stop cavalcade.

An iron bridge led to a dam
Where our fallen tree had been
And an ice cream soda parlour
Rounded off our childhood dream.
This hell on wheels was not for us
As the world around us sped,
We silver mops just turned around
And returned to our peaceful spread.

We reflect that life's evolving
And brings changes to such scenes,
That our memories are in the past
And the future holds our dreams,
But we still go a-skinny-dippin'
While we sit at home and dream,
Yet wonder how the world crept up
On our cooling canyon stream.

Ian C Gray

388

In Passing

Come gather round children I'll tell you a story
Of men in black bowlers and days tinged with glory
Of black furled umbrellas, trains running on time
When to chastise a child was not seen as a crime
When mothers stayed home to nurture their child
When youths were termed spirited and beasts described wild
When stray dogs, not children, ran in a pack
When one walked down the street without fear of attack
When children assembled in halls to say prayers
When Easter and Christmas were sacred affairs
When teachers taught reading, writing and math
And administration followed its own path
When school-leavers were all apprenticed in trades
When students attained college because of their grades
When football was played not for money but sport
When care for the elderly could not be bought
When queues at the hospital meant visiting time
When a man reaching fifty was not past his prime
When drugs were dispensed to fight sickness and pain
When acid filled batteries, did not fall like rain
When industry thrived in shipping and steel
In car plants and mines, when real work was *real*
When hedgerows and meadows bloomed everywhere
When everyone breathed unpolluted fresh air
When Europe was Europe and Britain was Britain
When the terms of our betrayal had not yet been written
Now children I've reached the end of my tale
I see that your little cheeks have turned pale
I can't answer your questions, the whos, wheres or whys?
The legacy we've left you is drowning my eyes.

Mary Younger

When The Mountains Are Conquered

What is blessed heaven
When I was a child oh so pure
A toddler with innocent eyes
Nothing permissive would allure.

A baby to loved ones
Even when mature
In my mother's eyes
A million miles away is the future.

The years disperse
And bairns are educated
With swiftly learning knowledge
I prefer my mind blank not frustrated.

Time is alien
The situation is different now
It reminds one of a strange planet
God forbid and stay snow white
It should be allowed.

When giving birth
It is a magnificent rhapsody
What is a higher accolade?
It's worth its weight in gold
There's nothing richer that's no fallacy

When the mountains are conquered
There is no discrepancy
A child is worth priceless paintings
And that my friend makes it ethical.

Straight from birth it's a new ball game
It's like a country being reclaimed
Wee fall and perhaps stumble
And quickly pick up the pieces and never grumble.

John Sneddon

Growing Old Gracefully

When was it that you first looked back
And realised you'd begun to crack,
That you no longer found it easy,
Exertion made you limp and wheezy?

Gone the waking to strident alarm,
When all you wanted was peace and calm,
Gone the rushing and gobbled-down toast,
To make it to work while you still had a post.

When, in your hair, did you notice the grey,
Marking how near is the close of your day?
When did you first see those wrinkles and lines,
That spread round your face like the creeping of vines?

When did you realise you can't rock and roll,
That smooch and slow-foxtrot are nearer your goal?
When did you find that you *are* still alive,
But your pension book says that you've gone sixty-five?

So just accept that you can't beat the clock,
And buy a nice chair that allows you to rock.
Stop chasing those dolly-birds - they'll do you no good,
And learn to relax - well, you *know* that you should.

G K Baker

Saturation Point

(Dedicated to flood victims, summer 2007)

Thoughtfully I watch the river flow fluently by
and I wonder why
it did rage, buffet and enter
my peaceful home nearby.

A wink from waving ripples does tease my eye
and I wonder why
after battering badly
the river can so saucily fault deny.

Floods raid when rudiments rumba feverishly high
and I wonder why
defences did quickly die
leaving devastation to rectify.

An array of repairers' assessors stray
and I wonder why
the damage they survey
looks but an image made of clay.

Memories will one day merge, ebb and surge permitted,
losses remitted
adversity outwitted
and my home will host again unembittered.

P A Findlay

Memories, As Only I Can Tell

High school: always late: attendance, never kept the score!
Arithmetic, useless: English studies good, grammar very poor.

Cricket; the kid that nobody wanted to bat,
Out for a duck! Caught out flat!

Rugby; couldn't run very fast; too fat to run too far,
Cross-country; cheated, thumbed down teacher's car!
(How was I to know?)

Religious studies; appallingly precocious,
Drama; 'very presumptuous!' so said my report;
(Moi? Presumptuous? Never! Reasoned I, with a snort!)

Swimming? Like a brick!
Advise: hold breath for three hours, that should do the trick!
(I'm a Glenwyn, not a penguin!)

Soccer; my ambitious dream,
Come what may each season, try for the football team.

Until at last I finally made it. 'Evans!' yelled the coach. 'Yer in!'
'But this is my final year, Sir, I'm leavin'!'
(I cursed and spat. 'Drat! No matter how hard I try, I never seem to win!')

Glenwyn Peter Evans

Indian Dreams

(Dedicated to Aunt Ida McMichael)

My aunt's friend told us
a story at day's end.
The incense burnt in the room
as we sat in the gloom
and listened intently to what
she had to say.
She told of a wedding day
in India
so far away.
As she described the scene
before our eyes
the sights and sounds of
New Delhi
became real.
I felt I was walking along
those Oriental streets.
The people she described
I could meet.
As the years have passed
I have carried that story
in my heart.
Whenever I browse in a shop
full of Indian things,
a lot of happiness
that memory brings.

Bernadette O'Reilly

Loss

Sweet sixteen. So deep a sleep.
Alas, those left, need to weep.

Sweet sixteen. Just as life should start.
Not the time to still a heart.

Sweet sixteen. No more fun.
Life's last race has just been run.

Sweet sixteen. Blue-eyed and blonde.
Fair of face and justice fond.

Sweet sixteen. Had enjoyed her play.
Riding and Badminton had come her way.

Sweet sixteen. Loving and giving.
No more with us. Among the living.

Zoë Ryle

The Street

The street is bare of children playing now
For cars speed by and parked cars take up space,
Yet I can't help feeling regret somehow
That progress, inhibitions must take place,
For once the streets were free for kids to roam;
Each had his special patch before his home.

I remember the games we used to play . . .
The farmer's in his den, rounders, statues
And all the kids around, day after day
Appeared like debt-collectors chasing dues.
How happily our voices chanted out
Till angry neighbours gave a 'clear off' shout.

I remember the gent's bike I first rode,
Lop-sided, one leg through the high crossbar,
Then wobbling, sped along until the load
At such an angle proved too much by far
And left me thrown down, sore-kneed, but the thrill
Of achievement when riding without spill.

I remember the plays we used to act,
Rehearsing parts on summer days for hours,
Dressed in adult clothes, from rag-bags ransacked,
Then on a stage of paving, decked with flowers,
Our show would run (with parents' kind permission)
And entrance of a halfpenny admission.

I remember my grammar school success,
How jumping up and down triumphantly
Outside my gate so everyone would guess
That I had passed, John Dale rushed up to me
And told me his good news, he'd passed also -
How pleased we were that we were both to go!

I remember that after that, things changed,
For time had played an unfair, unkind trick.
Life suddenly was sober and arranged
With evenings full of dull arithmetic
And so the street lay quiet as time marched on
For all the fun and innocence had gone.

Joy Saunders

Memories Of War

In 1939, on the 3rd September,
A day we shall always remember,
When war was declared with Germany.
Memories there are of ration books,
For sweets we had tokens,
Soap and coal were rationed too,
Gas masks we carried to school.
Bombs fell and cities brought to ruin.
The times were very hard.
We had the ARP and the Home Guard.
Balloons and searchlights filled the sky,
Bombers and fighters to and fro did fly.
Road signs were taken away,
So you didn't know which way to go.

The people shared, and people cared,
Everyone did their best.
Loved ones were lost, families torn apart,
All to great cost.

Armed forces came from miles away,
To aid and help us win the day.
Americans with their chocolate and stockings,
Oh what a treat, some to wear and some to eat.
In 1945, the month of May,
The war ended and some returned home,
Such a glad day, no more to roam.

Memories there are of this awful war,
So many lives lost, it was indeed at great cost.
Times were sad, but not all bad,
For youth will have its way,
And we could laugh and we could play,
Not really understanding, until the day
When we looked back and realised
The horror and the madness.

Grace Maycock

Great Aunt Cilla's Corset

Sunday morning service at the 'Ashton's' cold front room
Waiting for it all to start, in preparatory gloom
I see them now, those high-backed chairs
While sitting in a circle, listening to the prayers
A voice droned on, walking down a righteous path
A glance at Great Aunt Cilla, trying not to laugh
Great Aunt Cilla's corset excruciatingly tight
Couldn't bend her back at all, she had to sit upright
Gasping in the air so fast
As if each breath could be her last
The look of pain upon her face
She tried to sing 'Amazing Grace'
Great Aunt Cilla's corset, she'd bought it just last week
How was she to know the thing would have a rhythmic squeak?
She never wore it any more, don't have to wonder why
Has Great Aunt Cilla's corset gone, to that corsetry in the sky?

Flora Denning

A Happy Day

A photograph, enlarged and framed, hangs upon my wall,
It brings back childhood memories, the wartime I recall,
Theses memories are bittersweet, of perplexity and fear,
A townie in the countryside, away from those held dear,
The picture of a monument, an obelisk so tall,
Standing high upon a hill, seen for miles by all,
The base was thick with blackberries, this day the sun was high,
We picked a basket of beautiful fruit, enough to bake a pie,
We placed a rug upon the ground, we had a picnic tea,
Something I'd never done before, it was a treat for me,
The day this snapshot was taken, I was only seven years old,
A frightened little schoolgirl who wasn't very bold.
Looking back at this picture, it takes away my years,
I'm back enjoying my picnic on a day I forgot my fears.

Jean Burch

50 Years Of Farming

What hard work it was in the hayfield
In the summer of '54,
Eight of us wielding pitchforks
With gossip and blisters galore.

What peace there was in the hayfield
In the summer of '64
Cakes and sandwiches, bottles of tea
A welcome break before milking at four.

What fun it was in the hayfield
In the summer of '74
Young men in the evening loading bales
Banter and teasing and muscles to the fore.

How sad it is in the hayfield
In this millennium
One man in a tractor
With his headphones on.

Vera Banwell

Masha And Joe

anyone there -

echoed in time as
dust particles danced
in light beams sneaking
past closed curtains

the room dwelt on the past
her stick leaning by
grey ashes in a cold hearth;
aid to a broken hip,
a thumbless hand to hold

his image hung on the wall,
young and handsome in a
stripped rugger jersey,
the medal in his hand,
shy pride across his face

the stark emptiness released
stinging tears and memories
of their seventy years together,
joyous almost every minute.

Godfrey Dodds

Christmas

I woke up that morning with a smile on my face,
I ran down the stairs like it was a race.
I waited in the kitchen,
It seemed like forever waiting.

After ten minutes we were able to go in,
There was one really big present,
I hoped it was mine.

After opening most of my presents it came to the big one,
It was mine, I was excited,
Five minutes later I opened it,
It was what I wanted,
It was a motorbike.

I always go on it,
I love zooming around,
I hope I keep it forever,
Even though it makes quite a sound!

Liam Musgrove

Amanda Grace

I'll not forget you, Amanda Grace
As you swung high and laughed with glee
And your daddy laughed too, I know with pride
As he pushed the swing hanging from the pear tree

I'll not forget you, Amanda Grace
Though with time your memories blur at the edge
Of those moments we chatted and chatted
And you called me your 'Friend through the hole in the hedge'

Barbara Robson

God Is The Sun, Our Sammy

'God is the sun, our Sammy,'
Said my old granny, Mary Ellen,
As she bid me say my prayers
Before I climbed into my snug bed,
When some fairy story was read.
One she'd recited time and again.
She told me about a world at war,
Where Grandad Will had been killed,
In a faraway place called 'Belgium'.
They, only a few months married.
Called upon to serve his country.
She sadly recounting the grave event.
A potter who became a soldier boy.
Barely out of his teenage years,
He'd died on those Flanders fields.
Death seemed to me to be so dreadful,
Laid beneath the earth in a final sleep.
Sometimes she wept bitter tears
As she recalled their stolen years.
Measured, never to grow old together.
In her declining 'Seventh Age of Man'
Times remembered when she smiled.
Recalled their courting before the war.
Cycle rides into the local countryside,
Or day excursions made by steam train
To seaside resorts in North Wales.
To Conway Castle and Old Colwyn Bay,
Left love letters and her wedding ring.
Then Mum was born the following spring.
'God shine your light on this child tonight.'

John Pegg

Beautiful Memories

Amongst the many memories I keep locked up in my heart,
Are those so warm and tender from which I'd never part.
And in such thoughts as these which I hold very dear,
Are those to which I often cling and always will, I fear.

A face, a smile a single tear, such moments so sublime -
Remain, as if loathing to accept the passing years of time.
Within the wall of memory nothing can withstand -
Where a world away in time is really close at hand.

The greatest thing we had to learn was to love, and yearn,
And finding out we were being loved in return.
A song, a melody, a prayer or special hymn
Are the memories I conjure up but keep locked away within.

R Oldfield

399

Paper Or Plastic, Sir?

'Paper or plastic, Sir?'
These few simple words can
Take me back to a wondrous place
Timeless, peaceful and safe.

The sun is shining through a bright blue sky
I make my way up Grand View hill
Everything is left behind
Save my few simple things.

The place was miles away
And many years ago
With friends who have now moved on
And haunts that are no longer there.

But all I need hear are these simple words
'Paper or plastic, Sir?'
And in an instant I'm whisked back
As if I never left.

I choose a paper bag
To put my few shopping things in
And beneath a sun through a bright blue sky
I amble home up the hill.

Sharam Gill

My Mother

My mother,
The woman who bore in infantide,
The woman who worked to clothe my hide;
The woman who took me by her side,
The woman for whom I would have died.

The woman by whom I was led,
The woman who slaved to keep me fed;
The woman who always made my bed,
The woman who showed me how to keep my head.

The woman who worked herself to the bone,
The woman who strove to keep me a home;
The woman who taught me never to moan,
The woman who never refused me a loan.

The woman who always was of good cheer,
The woman who taught me never to fear;
The woman who always was so dear,
The woman who stayed with me, when death was near.
My mother.

Douglas J Cleeves

Autumn Leaves

When I was just a tiny child
Walking from school many a day,
Holding tight to Granny's hand,
Through fallen leaves we picked our way.

I always loved the autumn time
For 'twas then that I was born,
Least my grandma told me so
When collecting leaves from oak trees torn.

Of all the trees I watched turn red,
The oak was my favourite tree
And I collected oak leaves fallen
And brought them home for after tea.

Then I would draw round the edge of them,
Colouring in the leaf and veins;
Then, when the fallen ones were dead,
I would still have their picture for my pains.

Now, in the autumn of my life,
I gather in my failing friends
And draw around their work and love;
To keep forever those whom God only lends.

Lorna Moffatt

A Wonderful Friend

Pauline, both sixteen when we met
Up Brighton's Regent Ballroom
Quicksteps, waltzes, foxtrots, rock and roll
We always gave it all our soul

With five children in tow
Austria, great holiday together
Your past holidays wet, ours fine
Up the mountain you went, awful weather

We had stayed back at the hotel
You all arrived like drowned rats
We ached, we laughed so much
You dripped profusely where you sat

We swam, joined the bingo and still danced
We had such fun over the years
You were godmother to Anne-Marie, our youngest
Shared so much, sometimes tears

We all miss you, dear Pauline
You were really unique
A great sense of humour
We all wish there was more

Diana Cramp

Black Faces

(This poem is dedicated to all those men with black faces like my grandfather, James Carlin Hughes (deceased), John Joseph Hughes, Father (deceased), James Halligan (deceased), James Hughes (still alive), also all the other Whitehaven dockers still living and dead)

Eyes that shine behind faces so black
With those upturned smiles that beamed
Buried alive under local black gold
Leveling the cargo in the coal ship's hold
Black worn and tattered clothes soaked in sweat and rain
Kneeling on leather pads to protect their knees from pain
Wagons shunted up and down to drop their heavy loads
Chains ring out and buffers crash as into one and other the wagons slam
The thunder of coal dropping down the chute
Squeaks from the conveyer moving the coal on its path
When the job is complete, it's time for a rest
The men with black faces have done their best
To a dirty black cabin they all retire
It's where they all dry out round a roaring fire
Steam rising above them as their clothes dry out
Because of the noise that they work in they don't talk, they shout
As a child I sat with them amazed and in awe
With all their faces lit up by the fire glow
These memories I hold of a lifestyle now gone
But I will always be proud to be known as a Whitehaven docker's son.

James Carlin Hughes

Future Memories

It could have happened yesterday,
The event not so special,
The company just you and me,
Yet contented as could be.

But it was not play,
You could call it work,
But either way,
It was a memory shared.

It did not happen yesterday,
It happened this very same day,
On our allotment plot,
The flowers in full display.

Those labours create future memories,
To blossom on many a day,
With those blossoms this poem has bloomed,
To add to this grand array.

William Stevens

My Childhood Memories

Left with memories as life goes on,
How often we turn to them to remain strong.
My childhood memories:
Digging up sand eels to go fishing with my dad,
Always great fun as we paddled in the sun,
Using them to fish with amongst the mackerel shoals,
Catching many in the nets, making sure to dodge big holes.
Paddling in the rock pools,
Swimming in the sea,
Picnics by the riverside,
Finding ponds in the woods,
Collecting tadpoles,
Bringing them home in a jar,
Watching them turn into frogs.
Christmas time collecting holly and our special tree
From the nearby wood,
Helping my mum to stir the Christmas pud
While making a wish,
Opening the presents Santa had left
In a sack at the end of the bed,
My mum baking a pasty then
Riding on the back of my dad's motorbike
To bring it to me at school so that I could eat it,
While still hot, during my lunch break.
With such devoted parents and an older, loving sister,
All my childhood memories could not be
Anything else but truly happy ones,
And no doubt being born in Cornwall
Helped these delightful experiences to happen.
Which during my growing-up life,
I am sure has helped me to keep going
And somehow remain strong
When unhappy experiences have come along.

Patricia M Farbrother

Poor Daddy!

One morning when I was four
I woke up early
And thought I'd do
Something new.
I'd give my daddy
A big surprise,
I'd climb on his bed
And prise open his eyes
So he could play
With me,
But when I tried
To prise open his eyes
I heard my mummy say,
'Poor Daddy! Poor Daddy!'
I didn't mean to hurt him
And stopped straight away.
I decided instead
To kiss his eyes better
Then go back to bed.
More than eighty years
Have passed away,
But I still remember
That day, today.

Margaret Nixon

New York, New York

Your twin towers stood out from the rest,
Tall yet strong, they were the best

But life had other plans for you,
That you should fall and spoil the view.

People came from far and near
To look at you, they had no fear

But then one awful autumn day,
Demons came, took you away.

The dust and smoke and shattered glass
Came tumbling down around you,

People cried, many died,
Sadness did surround you.

Farewell, Twin Towers, we'll miss your splendour,
But to this evil we won't surrender

To the people who lost their lives to evil,
We will rise again like the golden eagle.

Anne O'Keeffe

Memories

Memories are thoughts we remember from the past,
Some are so special they really last!
Some people I knew over fifty years ago,
Have been lifelong friends and still remain so!
Sometimes we lose touch for many a year,
But memories we shared I still hold dear.
I met up with an old friend last year from the past.
I was reading the local newspaper one day,
In the family announcements I saw that an old friend's husband had passed away,
He had died suddenly on Christmas Day!
My heart went out to her and I posted a special card.
At this time it must have been especially hard!
I wanted her to know I really cared.
Soon my phone's ringing and her voice was heard!
We are now the best of friends once again,
Love can heal the deepest pain.
She still seems the same friend from years ago,
It is surprising what our memories do!
We share so many things in our lives now,
What a blessing are memories and the people we know!

Joyce Hallifield

Remembering Jim

I've got it all on video
And on a DVD
I watch it when I'm lonely
As it brings him close to me.

I see us at our wedding
With all the family there.
Our hands are clasped together.
Our happiness is clear.

He made me feel so special.
I was his darling wife.
We seemed so right together,
Now that's another life.

I also have the albums
Full of such happy days,
And when I see his photo,
His image with me stays.

I'll always have these memories,
Although he's gone from view.
He often told me 'remember what we had',
And that is what I do.

Margaret C Savage

The Mafia Man

Silver hair impeccably done,
Green eyes that blaze
With knowledge, pain and love.
A craggy, chiselled face
Scarred by old injuries.

Of stocky stature,
Small in height.
The dark suit and immaculate white shirt
The dark tie and gold pin.
The odds against this man
Are YOU cannot win.

His voice is authoritative,
Direct and blunt.
State your needs
And be done.
People shy away in fear,
From this formidable don.

How looks are deceiving,
For inside this man.
Is a joker, a comic,
A comedian, a cad.
The most special thing about him
Is that
He was my dad.

Carol Bradford

Days Of Old

Cowboys, Indians, soldiers, tanks, guns
Daisy chains, bikes, months of sun
Tarzan swings, broken arms, wounds of blood
Fun fighting, writing, innocence, mud

Dennis the Menace, Hardy Boys, woods
Holy communion, confusion, first love
Cathedral towers, April showers, dreams
This life never was nor is what it seems

They say that youth is wasted on the young
But this spirit's alive with many songs unsung

As then is now and now is then
And memories transcend time again
I evoke this childhood place with love
And gaze from river bank in grace, above

To spiritual home where I shall return
To days of old where my soul yearns

For peace
Ian Squire

Wonderful Innocence

Snugly wrapped
in family love,
sleeping soundly
in our Morrison shelter,
a breakfast treat
remembered over sixty years
at least!
A *real* lightly poached egg
on toast!

In our isolated street,
the sight
of a lone man,
ceremoniously dressed
in kilt and sporran,
walking along proudly
playing his bagpipes!

The fun of
taking
my pet rabbits
to the soldiers
on a tank
near our gate

. . . meanwhile
the Kent skies were full of war activity!

Margaret Ann Wheatley

Wonderful Memories

Memories so vivid, they call from afar,
Back to my childhood, loving but poor
Away at fourteen to train as a maid
Who could ask for more?

Wonderful memories of teenage years
Spent in the army with friends
Travelling to places I'll never forget
Learning to trust and not depend.

Heartfelt memories of my wedding day
Yet tinged with a tragic sadness
I lost my dear mother but gained a great husband
I remember them both with gladness.

Never forget your memories
Whether sad or as happy as can be
Memories are something to treasure
They belong to you and me.

Vera Ewers

Memories Are Made Of This

Sam And Tracy

Well here we are!
Two shining stars
Amidst the dark sky,
United together,
The knot to tie.

Words need not be said,
For we can see
Two souls and hearts joined in matrimony.

Smiles and laughter
Say it all,
Don't they look cool
As they stand proud and boldly tall.

A proud parent to my son and daughter-in-law,
Now who could want more.

Sam, the middle of my fine three boys,
Who will now bring joys
To his beloved girl.
'You look beautiful, Tracy, give us a twirl.'

Their life together has just begun,
They are as one,
To brave this world
Wherever, together they may be hurled.

Thousands of blessings,
Tracy and Sam,
You're a special lady and he's a special man.

God bless you both in every way
On this one and only special day.

Cathy Lamb

Vintage Cars

I can remember, as a child,
when at boarding school in Gloucestershire,
going to Staverton airport,
where there was a rally of vintage cars.
Probably even some steamrollers or traction engines -
it was at least 25 years ago!
There was a lot of steam, as you would expect,
coming out of these vehicles.
There have been similar events
at Hengrove, in Bristol, but more of a bus rally.

Wendy Elizabeth Day

Looking Back

The years roll on relentlessly
We cannot bring them back.
Yet always there for us to see
Are memories down the track.
Perhaps we smile or shed a tear
As tender scenes, or acts of strife
Return to mind, so sharp and clear,
For joy and regret are part of life
When remembering.

I think of the past and how long the span
Since the day I stood as a bride.
When a lifetime of marriage spent with one man
Was something we looked on with pride.
The first house we lived in, each item we bought
Was the height of achievement and planning.
Thank God for hire purchase, 'not done' we were taught,
Who knows what trouble you'll land in.

The pathway through life is never smooth,
We feel we could have done better,
It's no use regretting, better to move
To the future and answer that letter.
Although I am old I can still skip and hop
And whirl round the ballroom floor,
I can rush here and there and never stop
Till I open my eyes. Oh what a bore,
I'm only remembering.

Kathleen Holmes

Tender Memories Of A Country Boy

We met when we were seventeen over sixty years ago,
Those precious times stay with me for we loved each other so.
You were a country lad working on the land,
Ploughing, sowing, harvesting the corn, the colour of golden sand.
For hours you were alone in the fields with just the wildlife for company,
This was the life that you sought, the life where you felt free.
We walked the country lanes together, wild flowers grew everywhere,
I still remember those far-off days when we didn't have a care.
I see again the meadows where we strolled under a bright sunny sky,
I never thought that I would lose you, why did you have to die?
When the angels came and took you, part of me went too,
But no one can take my memories away until again I am with you.

Betty Whitcher

Memories Are Made Of This

On the beach, without my glasses,
A lad and his mate happened by,
I chatted quite brightly to these guys
And definitely gave them 'the eye'!
'Come back for a cuppa,' I said,
(We were Ranger Guides camped in a hall),
Then I put in my lenses and had a good look,
The shy one had me enthralled!
A 'date' followed swiftly, and days in the sun -
The holiday soon it was over,
But a kiss by a lake, in a moonlit garden,
Then my love became a 'rover'.
I mourned his loss and did not dance -
'He's really the one, I believe,'
And joy, oh joy, on the Monday next,
When he returned for me!
We were engaged on the day I turned twenty-one
And married two years after,
Then two sons followed, in the next few years
Some tears but also laughter.
We now have two lovely grandchildren
'To perpetuate the seed'
And the times we are with them
Give us joyous memories indeed.
So now we grow older -
With health a larger problem,
But the God who's kept us safe thus far
Teaches the necessary wisdom.
So we face the future, glad we met,
With our memories sometimes fleeting!
And knowing, if we're parted in death,
Up above we'll still be meeting.

Gill Mainwaring

Autumn

Going down the lane tonight
Feeling sprightly and of dance,
I came upon the falling leaves,
Bobbing and dancing in the evening breeze.

My heart took up this fluttering,
My age I then forgot,
As I sprang into a dance
With the leaves in that there spot.

I soon became quite breathless
And found my dignity,
As I settled down to walk
Amongst the rustling, restless leaves.

Beth Spinks

Ode To Making A Memory

I often wonder what makes a memory,
Is it experiences happy and sad?
And what prompts us to remember
These past moments good and bad?
For I remember as a child
Feeling alive and so carefree
When days merged together
With golden memories by the sea.

Those sun-filled days of happiness
Spent discovering the world around.
A maze of faces came and went
Now only memories are to be found.
For I am remembering special images
That filled those innocent days.
I was but a child and yet . . .
These memories remain mine always.

People and places played with
Allowing my spirit to come alive.
As raw emotions began to develop
My heart and mind started to thrive.
Yes, these memories found their niche
They live and now recollection takes place.
Whenever an experience demands
They often stare me in the face.

Today memories come and go
Filling this heart with pure emotion.
I indulge in these silent moments
As my soul learns love and devotion.

Nicky Keel

Memories

Many memories I have,
Good and bad, that's true,
But the good ones are the only ones
That I will give to you.

We had very loving parents,
That is without a doubt,
And though there were a lot of us,
Not one would they do without.

When I met a young man,
He said, 'I'll make you happy if I can,
We'll make a home together
And I'll be your loving man.'

We had many years together
And if we had a tiff,
We'd get ourselves alright again
As we made up with a kiss.

Now many years have gone by
And I am all alone,
But I cheer myself up by thinking
Of the good times I have known.

E Hoy

Thank You, Mum

My favourite recipe is a dream
Concocted by my mother,
A bit of this, a bit of that
And a small bit of the other.
Two spoons of Scotch and one of gin,
A tumbler full of brandy,
To use much less would be a sin
Because it makes me randy.
I've had it now for years and years,
My appetite it pleases,
I find it keeps me in good health
And stops my coughs and sneezes.
If you want to try it out
I can only recommend it.
Give me your name and your address
And gladly I will send it.

R W Meacheam

Caroline's New Bike

Those lovely days -
In a lazy summer haze
I open my window in the morning
Early or late or catch me yawning
In barefoot two-wheeled dream
A little girl - a bike - team.

Dimple-cheeked and deep blue-eyed
Down rosy bordered paths - in loops
Past privet arcs and garden gates
For circling hoops and circling swoops
Forth goes Caroline.

Hers it is and one with her
Which gives her transportation
A mastery of eye and hand and nerve
In delicate co-ordination.

E Love

Timeless Memories

In our tapestry of life we share
Memoried patterns of life's display.
Happy childhood dreams -
Like wind-blown leaves or flakes of snow.

The fun of make-believe. Will dreams come true?
Occasions planned, of family, friends.
Of these events, we wonder still.
Have we left footprints in our timeless view?

Unachievers we, a goal to reach.
What adult pleasures did we seek?
We laugh now at our foolish whims
And wonder what had the future then in store.

Maybe the album of our wedding day,
We looked so young and handsome then.
Oh! Those future plans we made.
Then children came. Our gifts so rare.
Their happiness and mistakes to share.

Sad times too, of sickness, death, despair.
Though time flies by and sorrow heals,
Those memories of our past reveal,
Whilst countless blessings, our hopes renew.

E Saynor

Goodbye, My Dear Old Friend

Goodbye, my dear old friend,
Your friendship was priceless,
Beyond diamonds and rubies.
I must choose my words carefully,
Avoiding being over-sentimental,
Whilst tears well within my eyes,
Though it is not one of sadness,
Rather one of thankful gladness,
For being near to the likes of you
I must refrain from being maudlin,
For your presence was effervescent,
Made the sun shine in wintertime,
The dull grey clouds always dispersed
To expose a most agreeable blue sky.
How we'd chatter on mundane matters,
Still flowers would spring into bloom,
As I watched you make the world anew,
You would tell me of everyday miracles,
Whilst dismissing acts of brutal badness.
Humans behaving like immature children.
Wars deplore as fulminating juveniles.
Famine and pestilence to be conquered,
Then said the deeds of sterling people,
Outnumbered those evil by many score.
How Mother Earth has a way of healing,
Despite the ravages of the human race.
The planet Earth would abide as always,
Long after our species left centre stage.
At your departure I will not say goodbye,
I'll bid you fond adieu, my trusty friend.

Julia Pegg

Summer Long Ago

It was a lovely summer's day,
I was just a boy,
But all the world came out to play
And I was full of joy.

The mice were rustling in the hay,
Rabbits plain to see,
I loved everything that day
And everything loved me.

The sun was golden up above,
Bumbling went the bees,
My heart was bursting with such love
I fell upon my knees.

Then in the blinking of an eye,
Silence fell around,
The world went busy bustling by
And all without a sound.

A voice then rang from everywhere,
Like a mighty bell,
'This is my world that you may share,
All is exceeding well!'

G W Murphy

Saturday Pennies

Inside the village shop I stand,
Pennies clutched tightly in my hand.
Brightly coloured sweets in jars,
Fry's Chocolate Cream in bars.
Liquorice Allsorts, liquorice pipes,
Jelly babies, Turkish delights.
Dolly mixtures, no, not keen,
So much else, a scrumptious scene.
Wine gums, I like the black ones best
But yes, of course, I'll eat the rest.
Toffee slabs to break your jaw,
Sherbet sucked through liquorice straw.
I count my pennies out with care
So I can buy a lot to share
With little ones too young to come.
Then Mrs Ford tots up the sum
And gives me change - one half penny.
Smashing, I didn't think I'd any!

Nancy Wright

Thinking Back

As twilight comes while sat here pondering
Wondering what the next day will bring
Fine weather for us with sunshine burning down,
No need to get dressed up, as we are not going to town.
Thinking back on summers we used to get,
A stroll through the woods with my furry pets.
Watching the children fishing in streams,
Sun's rays coming through trees in light beams.
A day at the races or down on a beach,
Watching yachts go past far out of reach.
Sandcastle competitions down near the pier,
It was lovely the one that won it last year.

Surprising the things children thought to build up,
This year there could be a prize of a cup.
Donkeys nearby ready for young ones to ride,
Someone goes with them, they walk at their side.
Along the beach at the base of the cliffs,
Rock pools are scattered not far from the lifts.
Pulling up stones, looking for crabs and the like,
Sometimes the kiddies used to get into fights.
Walking the beach for sticking up shells,
It's best to find them on the edge of the swell.
The mollusc inside waiting for a meal,
Until they are seen they do not seem real.

Oh! What it would be to do that again,
It's a pity I can't because of these pains.

Ken Copley

Daniel And Emma

There's a baby to be born
Properly in the early morn
The 17th of December they say to me
A girl or boy
We don't know yet
What a surprise
It's going to be
It may be twins
You never know
Whatever the case
A perfect beauty it will be
Because the baby will look like you or me.

Deborah Storey

Allotments At Merryhill, St Elizabeth, Jamaica

A beautiful countryside
Just flashing memories, homesick is not what I am
The heart is full of pride
And remembering also guava jam

Walking in the dewy grass
Earthworms looking healthy
Journeying over the long grass
Clean air and lush vegetation seen as we pass by quickly

Mum and Dad ahead
Olive in Mother's arms most of the way
Some trees seem dead
Dad is collecting rent from those who can pay

Those were far-off days
Visiting allotments at Merryhill
Cultivators working to provide food all day
Before starting evening work at the sugar mill

But God is good
He made memories that haunt our thoughts just fine
He made all things for our good
In yonder thoughts come rain or shine

We pray, come quickly
God of light, provider of the heavenly mansion
Come quickly
Guard us from all unhelpful action

Olive May McIntosh-Stedman

Snapshots

Photographs mean so much to me.
Have you ever forgotten a memory?
For if you click, and snap, or flash at them
And treat photography as a passion
The whole of your life is there to see,
Captured in time, 'a memory'.
I have to make to you a confession,
Photography and I have become an obsession.
Snapping and clicking and flashing's a must,
If the pictures aren't good, you won't see me for dust.

Ellen Spiring

Downside's Old Bell

In the far-off days of my childhood,
While my memory is clear I will tell,
Things I dearly remember,
To the sound of Downside's sweet bell.

I was born in the end cottage of South Street,
No 'mod cons' and water was fetched from the well.
Oil lamps that glowed in the evenings,
In hearing of Downside's sweet bell.

Many happy hours were spent in the long garden.
Over the wall was the farm I knew so well.
Milk was fetched in a jug from the dairy,
Still in hearing of Downside's old bell.

Yellow stone-crop cascaded the farm walls.
Every flower you named was found in the dell:
Wild orchid, foxgloves and bluebell,
We gathered to the sound of that bell.

So come winter and springtime and harvest,
In each season there are joys one can tell,
But always you'll hear in the background,
The donging of Downside's old bell.

But sadly the village is changing,
The village we knew oh so well.
No farm now, sweet shop, or school house remaining,
But forever and always in keeping
Will be the sound of Downside's old bell.

Mary Rose Drury

The Clippie

A jolly-faced bus conductress
used to ride round Pompey town
dispensing tickets left and right
as she sauntered up and down.

Her uniform's trousers (baggy)
matched pocketed jacket (tight)
whose sombre dark grey worsted
sported silver buttons (bright).

A battered cap with crested badge
(The Heavens Light Our Guide)
completed the whole ensemble.
She wore her hat with pride.

But from it bulged a hair net
wherein matted hair grew down;
a grey and grizzled bird's nest,
it was worthy of renown.

With beaming smiles for everyone,
plus jokes for pals she knew,
she'd intersperse a 'Luv' or 'Dear'
and thus her reputation grew . . .

while that mesmerizing hair net
full of tresses long redundant,
with each and every passing year
grew increasingly resplendent.

Penny Smith

Day's End

With a final burst of red across the mirrored Llyn
The sun strikes copper from the glistening organ frieze
Of Glyder Fawr and sets behind Y Garn; old yogin
Lotus-posed, his little lake couched 'twixt his knees:
A begging bowl; where graying locks of old snow
Hang, echoes of Rhaeadr Ogwen far below.

Hands acrid from the inmost, secret, dark recesses
Of the rock face where we late imposed our youthful will,
And throbbing from the answering, stony, harsh caresses
The mountain gave us as we climbed our sated fill,
Vale bent we charge the rising veil of winter night
Rock-hopping through a star-sea of entranced delight.

And, spilling from the summits, every hollow filling
With mist, comes the cold; hardening the patchy snow
Which crackles like a battle's first wicked, chilling
Salvoes; as our tramping, carefree footsteps onward go;
Hushing with frosty breath a million chuckling springs;
And dusting with diamond rime the tussocks' huddled wings.

And, darkling in a nook, bereft all day
Of company, our battered banger, never sold
In cafés in Bethesda, barks its roundelay
And staggers eastward, shying in the cold.
Snake-slippery road, and the rising moon
Dives through the sleeping hilltops like a loon.

So long ago. yet, piercing the decades' mist
Those days of hopeful happiness still shine
Etched into each grey cell, blessed and kissed
By memory, though for want of words' sweet wine
The real, oread magic we knew then
Lies choking with frustration in my pen.

Tony Jennett

The Fifties

Those days of the fifties with our Teddy boy suits
and our Tony Curtis-styled hair.
Slicked up with Brylcreem with sideboards to match
now the top of my head is all bare.
I would spend hours at the mirror
combing my hair into a fashionable DA.
Now I look in the mirror and what do I see?
What is left is totally grey.

I had a jacket with its four-button front,
that almost came down to my knees,
and beer was only a shilling a pint,
so for ten bob I was as drunk as you please.
I had drainpipe trousers and crepe-soled shoes,
and I liked to be where it was at,
in my bright red waistcoat and bootlace tie,
my God I did look a prat . . .

But I felt the business, I was Jack the lad,
when I went out on a Saturday night,
and after having a few beers with my mates,
I was flying as high as a kite.
They invented The Creep, I remember it well,
it was perfect for those that can't dance.
You just held your partner and stared straight ahead,
it looked like you were both in a trance.

We had Elvis the Pelvis, all moody and mean,
oh for those grand times we had.
There was the great Eddie Cochran, Buddy Holly as well,
and Bill Haley who was as old as my dad.
Like the Teddy boy suits that have gone out of fashion,
I too have gone out of style.
But I don't give a damn, we had a good time,
and the world was ours for a while.

David Galvin

Spinsters And Borscht

Traces of the sour smell of borscht
The foggy liquid Miss Elisa used to add
To the soup . . . I would buy it from
The Manole sisters, two spinsters sitting
On the boundary of time who always
Looked old to me; their garden had substance
Indoors, a locked cabinet with treasures
I would politely ask and they would politely allow me
To have a look, sometimes even a touch . . .
The moment would vanish; then I would go
Down the path of their humming garden
With the orchard paving the Negel stream
It was flowing down the slope into other streams
Into other rivers and then into the sea
And the sea into the ocean, a trick with mirrors
I would take the pavements in turns, then
The easy go road past Aaron the grocer,
The easy go road by the paraffin deposit
I would take a sip, only one at a time
From the magical mixture,
From the foggy liquid called borscht
Miss Elisa was waiting in the porch,
On the high steps of the house
With Italian façade and heavy oak door.

Mariana Zavati Gardner

Ringing Place

Along the way of youth's stride
Relive the poodle barking near
School, those rules and uniform
Taken in the shell so making
And fancy dress or new picture
Still broken hearts or tender tip
Flash or gaze, some big blaze
Imagine sweet and apples hung
Tempted yet still so unsung
Harvest of the fields or trees
To go back now never seen
Yet busy bee and open seas
And how it used to be seems
In the melting dream so sees
That happy hunting grounds
Pine the fibre bones no doubt
Even in darkest rainy night.

Malachy Trainor

The End Of A Perfect Childhood Day (About 1932)

The sun slides slowly down behind the trees
And lights a crimson path across the pond.
Then, as it sinks, a soft yet wayward breeze
Is born to stir the rushes' ev'ry frond
Then dance with velvet cat's paws to the edge,
Provoke a sleepy coot to croak her call
And whisper through sibilant reeds and sedge
Then sigh and die as night and darkness fall.

As out from 'neath the tiles of yonder barn
The silken bats take swiftly to the air
Pursuing silent insects 'cross the tarn
With leathern wings their mousey shapes to bear,
So from her tree an owl calls out, 'Be quick!'
Perhaps because her chicks are hungry too,
And as he cruises over scrubland thick
Her mate repeats his query, 'Who, who, whoo?'

The moon now inches higher up in the sky,
Her cold light coats the fields with false white frost.
A dog fox barks his eerie, urgent cry;
His vixen screams, her voice a babe's soul lost.
The hedgerow mice all cower at their call
And seek asylum somewhere underground,
While scurrying Hodge curls up into a ball
And sleepless rabbits tremble at the sound.

G A Baker

Nathan, They Can't Steal Our Memories

They can keep us far apart, but our memories they cannot take
They can say we are not good for each other, but what we feel in our hearts they cannot break
The first time we met, 'til the time we parted will always stay with me
I remember the fun and laughter we shared, I remember your last plea
The memories of our eccentric nights out, and our calmer days I will always treasure
I'll never forget others' influences that ended our friendship under so much pressure
People interfered and thought our friendship was wrong
We did try to forget what they thought, but their criticism was way too strong
All I have since they took you are special memories that I will never forget
The saddest memory of when it was over, and the happiest day of my life of when we first met
I pray you are in deep thought and laughing about our friendship as Ifeel this will keep you strong
Losing a close friend isn't easy but hopefully meeting again will not take too long.

Kirsha Johnson

A Beautiful Place

Love to have Devon as my second home
where when young I used to roam.
Babbacombe was a favourite of mine
the weather was hot and always fine.
The Torquay palms held special appeal
like exotic lands with a foreign feel,
turquoise bays, serene and calm,
sunlit patios full of charm.
Paignton is special because of the zoo
hours were spent in lengthy queues!
An ancestral trace brought much delight
when a relative from Ireland was forced
to take flight.
The destination was Devon, a wonderful base
where children were born, a heavenly place.
Time has concealed much of their fate,
information acquired years too late.

Barbara Jean Harrison

The Mists That Are Memories

We think we will remember, with clarity and truth,
all the things that happened in our past and distant youth.
Yet as the years go by, mists do seem to fall,
and the facts are oft distorted, and harder to recall.
Some though do stand out, as if immortalised in stone,
with everything so clear, the clouds miraculously flown.
Some may be so happy, like the birthdays full of fun.
Others just bring pain, like when grief did overcome.
The smell of freesia flowers reminds me of the time
as a child I suffered illness, of recovery little sign.
Barely four years old, so still . . . so near to death,
so Mother placed the flowers and waited with bated breath.
I was suddenly aware of the fragrance and I woke,
and smiled at my dear mother, in whom tears it did evoke.
Sixty years have passed, and Mother with them too,
but freesia flower perfume, the recollection does renew.
The love mother had for child and the prayers she did implore,
and the faith she had in God earned her Heaven, I am sure.

Cecilia Skudder

In The Things Of Time

Only now do I realise
How much the house meant to me.
It is sold, it is there still,
In the small, peaceful village
I left many years ago.
                              It is there still . . .
La maison où j'ai grandi.

I do not want
To see the house again.

Let me keep it in my mind
As it was, as I loved it.
Only now do I realise
How much . . . how much.
Inside memory,
                    All the time, constantly,
I see . . . my mother, my father.

There is us, living our life.
Idealised and beautiful.

I see the house I grew up in.
Behind it, a field, wild flowers,
Children roaming free, allowed
To walk up to the edge of the forest -
We cooked sausages outside on the fire
                        Using wooden sticks
Sharpened with our pocket knives.

Great . . . freedom, and a lot of joy –
Day after day, every day.

Claire-Lyse Sylvester

Warm Memories

Were there really such days?
Seen through a haze
Of shimmering heat
Smelling of summer sun -
On warm skin, when one
Just soaked up the rays
Of those long hot days
Of summer
The last day of term, couldn't wait
For that date in July
To arrive, felt so alive
A lifetime ahead and no school
To dread.
A week by the sea feeling free
Dad in long shorts and Mum's skirt caught
Up in her knickers, to paddle
Eating ice creams galore
Candyfloss, hot dogs and more
Sandcastles flooded by the incoming tide
Smiles behind hands
As older brother, quite rude
Built a large female nude
In the shifting sands!
Long days, late to bed
Such joy in my head
I slept sound wrapped in pleasure.
These memories I treasure
And can summon at will
Because they can still
Brighten the darkest of days.

Jackie Johnson

426

Reminiscence

When you reach your eighties,
The years that are to be
Are shorter than the ones before,
How precious is memory.

Memories are your very own,
Unique and just for you,
Made up of little things
That life has brought to you.

The days were always sunny,
The winters were severe,
We walked to school and home again
And Mum was always there.

There was no television,
Or computer games to play.
In summer we played ball games,
Dominoes on a winter's day.

The policeman was a big tall man,
The sight of him brought fear,
You didn't get an ASBO,
Just a clip around the ear.

The day I passed the scholarship
And made my parents proud,
Travelling on the service bus
Chanting Latin verbs aloud.

My wedding day, dressed in white,
Was such a happy day.
The day I had my daughter,
Who has brought me much delight.

Now I am a widow,
With parents long since gone,
Memories give me pleasure
About things that I have done.

Lily I Marsh

But The River Runs

Remember days of wild childhood
The deep dark wood.
All those trees, our days of mystery,
Palm, rain, *Arjun,* banyan, *gamari,* and gum.
Days of fission, fish-games, finchy fun.
Green, blue, red, yellow, white, pink, ash
Woodpeckers, cockatoos, swallows, birds in bulrush.
Ah! The sweetness of *hariali* seeping tranquilisers,
The bird nests from the single-legged palms.
A tiny cricket does for the light
A nest in dark alight, our million
Invasions! We the thiasus in the woods
Me, Mohua and Chaiti
Dance like *harial,* the long green road.
Sparkling moods.

River's gone, the forests mushroomed beehive flats,
Zillion of trapezium stairs.
And the crickets? Nothing but dead insects.
No lights or sparks. What happened to the trees?
Ish! Are they all furniture? Tables, cupboards and chairs?
Or are they turned into bricks?
I wonder my heart aches.
But this antic me, deep in my foliate heart
All the global warming, changing weather
Melting of ice, dust and floods.
The triune I, river still runs.

Saleha Chowdhury

A Sonnet - Childhood Memories

Where the winds of fate blow us – no one knows
But memories are to treasure always
Time can heal, but memory . . . it just slows.
Forgotten hours or days ago; stays
Twenty-five years on; yes, those crystal clear
Days of childhood; looking back - but surely
It seems was only yesterday; a tear
Will oft times prick the eye, for so purely
We see those halcyon days, now long gone.
Grazed knees, sticky toffee apples, the fun
Of the fair - good times or bad, the sun shone
It seems, so much brighter then; we could run
Through fields of cornflowers blue - reach up and
Grab the moon . . . and make castles out of sand.

Valerie Hall

Coastal Depression?

Remembering when (I must 'ave been ten)
We sat cross-legged on the prom,
Me dad an' me mam, our Claude an' our Sam,
Aunt Ethel an' poor Uncle Tom.
A day at the coast, in charge of 'mine host'.
Me granny aged sweet eighty-four!
When all in a rush she gave us a push
An' bee-lined for lavatory door.
Half an hour ticked away,
We waited for me gran.
'Best see what she's up to,'
Me aunt said to me mam.
She vanished too, into the loo,
An' tapped at every door
An' peered around until she found
Me granny stretched on t'floor.
She pushed an' shoved at cubicle
But the door wedged on her feet,
Her long johns round her ankles
An' her handbag plonked on t'seat!
Sirens blathered an' crowds quickly gathered
To rescue dear ol' Gran,
Laid out straight, cold an' prostrate,
With her handbag perched on t'pan.
'We'll have t'go over,' said one to the other,
'No way can we shift that door!
Her feet are wedged beneath the edge,
An' she's laid full length on t'floor!'
An ambulance waited patiently
As t'fireman straddled the wall,
He hung by his fingers from t'cistern,
Then gently let himself fall.
'It's OK . . . the old lady's still breathing,'
He hollered from within.
'Is that good?' said Uncle Tom,
(Me dad kicked him on t'shin!)
A strange low moan (an' passing o' wind)
Echoed on the flooring.
'Is she hurt?' me mother wailed . . .
'No,' he replied, 'only snoring!'
Oh I'll never forget that terrible day
When me gran siesta'd in t'loo,
An' the look on the faces of ambulance men
When they had to pull Granny back through!
But Gran? She was no worse fer wear
(Despite her failing ills)
But now we check her 'Sea-legs'
Are *not* her sleeping pills!

Sheila M Birkett

Wartime Youngster

My gas mask was a Mickey Mouse,
(I never had to use it.)
I tried it on though, it smelt weird!
You weren't allowed to lose it.

I kept it in a special box,
The strap hung round my neck.
'If they should use that mustard gas,'
My mum said, 'wear it quick!'

Barrage balloons were quite a sight,
All huge and shiny grey.
They hung, far up above the town
To keep the planes away.

The air-raid sirens warned us all
To get down to the shelter
In your 'jamas and your wellie boots
And coat. Run! Helter skelter!

The shopping, done with ration books,
Did not allow you much.
You had to have your coupons
For your bacon, cheese and such.

Some sugar mixed with cocoa
In a paper bag, to eat.
You wet your finger, dipped it in
And licked it off - a treat!

We'd powdered egg and Spam in tins,
Dried fruit was scarce, *and* fat,
So wedding cakes were cardboard,
You were lucky to get that!

We had apples in the autumn,
And pears and fruit for jam.
(*If* you could get the sugar!)
But bananas? What were them?

Mum dug for victory in our plot,
Grew vegetables from seed.
She kept some chickens too.
They had potato peels for feed.

She sewed my clothes and darned my socks,
Let pieces in, to fit,
And when my sandals got too tight,
She'd cut off the front bit.

I had a siren suit, with hood,
And a knitted pixie hat.
My mum unraveled other things
To get the wool for that.

Memories Are Made Of This

The spivs could get elastic
And, from parachutes, some silk.
You'd make it into knickers, slips
And items of that ilk.

It must have been so hard for Mum,
The bombs, the planes, the tanks.
My memories of the awful bits
Just don't exist. Mum - thanks!

Anne Gardiner

Memories – Past And Present

Oh yes - I have memories of the past,
Some good and some bad we collect,
But mostly I try to forget the bad
Because they do more harm in the end.
I remember the eyes of my babies when born,
The smiles on their faces with joy.
The cuddles they gave me, the words that they spoke,
The pleasure they got from their toys.
I still have my teddy my grandad gave me,
(I think I was five at the time)
I've had it beside me for 82 years,
It's threadbare but it has survived.
I remember the people who came into my life,
Most of them nice to me,
The ones who did me harm at times,
I do not want to see!
But now I'm a carer, and that is all,
I look after a man who can't walk.
We've been together for 55 years,
So we now don't often talk.
But he was a soldier once, you see,
And gave some of his life for me.
We cannot repay them for their loss,
But just help them to keep free.
So memories come and memories go,
We 'make do and mend' when we can.
So I'll carry on caring for as long as it takes
Cos I fear one day soon it will end.
The memories of these last few years
Will not be good, you see,
I'll forget the bad days if I can
And remember I'm still *me*.

Doris E Pullen

Memories Of My Childhood Home

I pulled the curtains back
and disturbed
a lovely red-brown butterfly
gazing exhausted through the glass
to the wind-blown autumn leaves outside.

At once she started up again
her desperate, frantic fluttering
filled with the desire for
the freedom of the open air.

I caught her gently in my hands.
For the moment the panic ceased
while she adjusted
to this new sensation.

'Butterfly,' I said, 'to go out there
is certain death. It's windy, cold,
your moment's flight will end so soon.
Here in my room you can stay
and hibernate in peace all winter through.'

She stopped exploring my open hand
and seemed to sit and think
and gaze with longing
on the free-air world.

I opened the window, held out my hand
so she could just feel the wind
smell the damp earth, the rotting leaves.
'It's your decision, Butterfly,' I said.
A moment's thought, and then
she launched herself into the golden blustery day.
The breeze caught her and blew her
across the garden with the leaves
fluttering exhilarated with the uprush air
to live her last few hours riding the wind
with the sun on her wings
and the wind in her hair.

Charmian Goldwyn

My Greatest Treasure

I have a wonderful treasure
It is not made of silver or gold
But throughout the years its measure
Has increased as I have grown old.
This treasure - my precious memories,
I feel a privilege to own,
For they are mine and mine only
And mean I am never alone.
I remember my happy childhood,
With our home filled with laughter and love,
Money was scarce, but no matter
Mum and Dad did the best that they could.
Christmas now could not recapture
Those times when I was young,
The presents, the tree and the turkey
And those well-worn old carols we sung.
The family all came together, to celebrate Jesus' birth
The meaning of Christmas was foremost
When God sent His son to this Earth.
I remember my teenage years
When friends filled the house night and day,
All that came were made welcome
No one would be turned away.
When I married, my fondest memory
Is making my vows as a bride
With all of my life before me
And the one I loved by my side.
As a district nurse caring for others
I loved my working years
I met such wonderful people
And shared their smiles and their tears.
But now the years have flown by
Not blessed with a child of our own
The two of us sit in the firelight
And now we are all alone.
My husband sits in his wheelchair
And I in my comfy armchair
And I thank God for such wonderful memories
We are both now able to share.

Jackie Pearson

Mama

Before my birth, you were my protector, my cocoon,
My nativity, for you, could not come too soon,
For nine long months you nurtured my being,
You said it was worth it, when upon me your first seeing.

For the first months of my life, that ending would continue,
With a devoted dedication which came from within you,
Like with all mothers, it is a tiring task,
But made up with a cuddle, which you did not have to ask.

Then comes the crawling, the first of getting around,
Off like a shot, trying not to be found,
Whatever you were doing, had to take second place,
Because you had to chase me, it was fun, like a race.

It is a twenty-four hour job, caring for a child,
Sometimes quiet and peaceful, sometimes hectic and wild,
All children take it for granted, the service they receive,
It's only later in life, we realise, we perceive.

Sometimes I was naughty and your patience I would try,
So I was chastised, punished, I never knew why,
This kind of discipline, I did not enjoy,
But in later years, I knew it was right to employ.

I did not want for anything, during my childhood days,
Except those too excessive in so many ways,
I began to understand in the needs for a living,
Through Mama's tuition in loving and giving.

Mama, you protected me from the horrors of this world,
So to remain innocent as my young life unfurled,
The protection of an offspring can be a nervous one,
But when grown up, you can be proud of what you've done.

Thank you, Mama, for giving me life on this Earth,
Through your teachings, I now know its value, its worth,
I have been very lucky to come through that living drama,
So I owe you a great debt, with my fondest love to you . . . Mama.

Jonathan Grave

Memories

Treasured memories of our wedding day
As we stepped out together along life's way
From then our love just grew and grew
Learning together with a love so true

Memories of our first born, a lovely boy
We were filled with wonderment and joy
And also with our daughters, a brunette and a blonde
With two more sons, with each a loving bond

Happy holidays with all of the family
These live on for years in our memory
Grandchildren and great grandchildren a pleasure
These are some of the memories we treasure

Memories of my first poem published was a thrill
By Ian Walton, to carry on writing it gave me the will
To go to college I thought was beyond me
But I joined and learnt the art of calligraphy

So many lovely memories, one's never too old
To enjoy each moment as they fondly unfold
Each day and pleasure we should not miss
Living and loving memories are made of this.

E M Dowler

Childhood Days

As the wind gently blew, I turned to watch
a huge weeping willow tree
gracefully drape its leaves across the lawn
stroking the grass, bowing from side to side.
I ran between the fronds, hiding in the scented undergrowth.
A wood pigeon startled me as it flew up from its cover
beneath the tree stump.
It settled in the branches and cooed softly.
The immense oak tree beyond with its distended trunk
as large as a couch was just waiting for me
to climb and settle in its knurled lap.
If I stood very still I could hear the buzz of little insects,
honey bees on foxgloves, crickets in the wispy grass.
I loved this garden.

Beverly Maiden

Moment In A Courtyard

In the cool whitewashed curving
Of bright sun-blessed courtyard walls,
A cathedral tree, dark and tall,
Its spire aspiring, touches air,
Protects the cloistered atmosphere.
Within this quiet timeless place,
Are heard green symphonies of space.
Tall swept Japanese anemones
When gently touched, sound softly hushed,
Like wet sand when a tide is rushed.
Quiver of ivy, flicks its foliage
In tune with waving grey-green sage.
And lavender gently sways its song
As flag spears beat their metronome.
Lemon balm, like dry tinder, taps
Incessant beats on stone wall cracks.
And sedum strings its pearly beads,
Zinging the rock beds in glossy seeds.
There is a peace here that captures time
All seasons caught, an anodyne.

Janine Vallor

Suffolk Sadness

They are all there to be seen if you let your mind wander
They are all there to be heard if you let your ear be attuned
The intense images of operatic characters
And the tenor strains of musical skills can be seen and heard
Around the cold eroding sea, the shifting pebbly beach
And the wet land bird breeding reaches of the Suffolk countryside.
Now, side by side the two men lie, marked by two cold slabs of slate
Standing erect like the brave snowdrops, piercing the frigid ground
In the churchyard of the village from whence the embryo works were hatched.
The sole markings on each gravestone are the names
And life spans of the two renowned music makers.
They gave joy in their life but evoke sadness
At the stark emptiness of their last resting places.
But now, rising from the shingle and safe from the marauding tides
A soaring scallop shell - solitary and sail shaped
Offers fresh hope to the local flint faced folk from their flint faced cottages -
Weather-beaten but uncowed by the unyielding arctic blasts.
Also to the laughing holiday makers wondering and wandering
Around the monument at the lapping tide's edge.
They come to pay their respects and read with the early morning sun
Glistening through, the hammered out words along the margin of the shell -
'I hear those voices that will not be drowned'.

Robert Main

My Mum

Many things have happened throughout this life of mine.
Close friends and family have been taken over time.
I remember each with fondness, as their memory floods my mind
And I sit here for a while and gently, I unwind.
It's the little things that mean so much, the gentle word, the caring touch.
The faded photo takes pride of place and puts a smile, upon my face.
I went up to her grave
And the flowers people gave.
I looked down on the earth
And knew my memories worth.
I wasn't allowed to see her
As she lay dying in her bed.
I was banished to the outside
For something 'that I'd said'.
I may have lost my mother and 3 brothers too.
But no one can take my memories.
My age is 52.

Janice Melmoth

Bucket And Spade Holidays

Every summer after the war my mother took us away,
Each year a different part of the coast for our holiday.
Staying at 'Bed and Breakfast', they also provided our tea.
We amused ourselves making sandcastles and paddling in the sea.
Watching 'Punch and Judy' shows and riding the donkeys too,
Playing football and cricket, there always seemed plenty to do.

A band would play on the promenade in the afternoon,
All the well-known songs of the time, we sang along with each tune.
A kiosk selling toffee apples, ice cream and 'saucy' hats,
Humbugs and rock, buckets and spades, balls and cricket bats.
There was always a little café so tea was in easy reach,
Cups of hot drinks with something to eat, we would take on a tray to the beach.

You could hire a deckchair for sixpence or a shilling if you had it all day,
There were boats to have a ride in, giving trips around the bay.
At night a grand firework display was set off at the end of the pier,
We would sit and watch then write postcards saying 'I wish you were here'.
Back to our digs we would wander, you had to be in by ten.
A good night's sleep then we were ready, to start all over again.

Enid Thomas

Goodbye Dear Friend

Dear Barbara, we shall miss you,
Now you're no longer here,
We'll miss the happy times we had,
The memories we'll hold dear.
Your pain and sadness knew no bounds,
When Kenneth left your side,
Life for you was not the same,
Your grief you could not hide.
The talents that you had were many,
Musician, poet, artist too,
Accomplished pianist and conductor,
All a joy to you
And others, as you gave us all your best,
And if the songs were difficult,
We'd all rise to the test.
Life just will not be the same,
We're going to miss you so,
Memories are all we have,
But you grew tired, we know.
It's been a pleasure knowing you,
And each of us will say,
'Goodbye dear friend, until we meet
Again, somewhere, some day!'

Jasmine Grace Geddes

When We Were Young

I remember with happiness when we were both young
Days filled with laughter, adventure and fun
Out in the garden making mud pies
Or braving the sprinkler and trying to stay dry
We'd sit in the wheelbarrow while Mum raced us around
Or hide in the beech hedge until we were found
Crawling like soldiers in the long grass next door
Water-filled pistols poised ready for war!
We both had our dens, my brother and me
His near the sandpit and mine near the tree
We loved to play boardgames and whist even more
Girls versus boys and Dad would keep score
At the end of the day Mum would call us to bed
A story, then sleep, with my teddy bear, Fred
Soon morning would come and the chance for more fun
Such happy days we had when we were young

Katherine Hedison

Nostalgia

Remember the old house,
Large rooms, creaky floorboards,
Freezing in winter,
sparks up the chimney.
Remember the garden
the games we invented,
beloved pets that rest there.
The tumbledown shed
it hid many secrets.
We never suffered from boredom.
I wonder who lives there now,
Do they ever think of us?
We were not very tidy.
Remember the park and the common?
Places for adventure.
The lakes, the pagoda, the deer park,
the canal running through.
We never thought of danger,
life was for living, we lived it to the full.
I've never ventured back there.
Let it dwell in my memory -
I do have a house agent's photograph -
If only!

Ivy Allpress

A Mother's Joy

Five weeks before my baby was due
The doctor said, 'I think there are two.'
We didn't have scans in those days
And had to rely on the old X-rays.

And yes, there you were, facing each other
God, how would I cope with two and their brother?
Tho' I wanted again to be a mammy
This time I'd scored a double whammy!

What a shock, I could hardly believe
That two not one I did conceive.
First I felt panic, then feelings of joy
Would you be girls or a girl and a boy?

The day after my birthday, during the morn
You two darling girls were both breech born
And forty years on, I can truly say
Double the blessings came my way.

Marion Ward

Memories Of Bygone Days

The star that shone
In the hearts of men,
Told us that story
Of a baby born
In a stable bare.
But Mary and Joseph
Their love was gold for us all to share.

That was the first
Big memory of fame,
As we walk down memory lane.
There's a little plot
Where we sit and talk
Of birds and bees,
Even songs in the trees.

Faded memories of the frogs
Have almost gone,
We will wait one day
They will return.
As we walk up that golden stair
Millions of memories
Are on each step we share.
God tells us why they will never die.
We will be forever
With Him on high.

Elizabeth McIntyre

Homecoming

Returning, from I know not where
and there by the fireside
was my little chair;
made by my uncle
for me alone
to welcome me back
to my grandmother's home.
There was hot toast and butter.
My world was complete
as I sat on that
hard little wooden seat.
Like a queen I reigned
on my tiny throne
as the seeds of a happy memory
were sown.

Gabrielle Street

440

In The Wood

As a young girl
Every Sunday
I went to visit my
Aunt in the country
Who liked to walk
Her dog in the wood
I went too and
In springtime it
Was a hue of bluebells
Of course
And we picked a few
Summertime there
Were wild flowers too
In autumn time trees
With leaves of golden brown
Much nicer than in town
And wintertime
Amongst the snow
Holly berries all aglow
I remember it still
The wood called Bowsy Hill.

Rosalie Wells

Dear Father

Dear Father, it's a year now since you died,
How I wish you were here now!
You helped to make the world a far better place,
I miss your smile - your kindly face.
Dear Father, through my boyhood,
I looked up to you, just as any boy would
Who thought his dad an indestructible man;
Captain Marvel! Superman!
Then in my teens you showed me,
That everything in life wasn't owed me;
You gave me values that were upright and true;
My role model - my mentor, too.
Dear Father as the tears flow,
I reflect once more, how quickly the years go,
And now the chance is gone for me to convey,
All the things I didn't say.

Tony Reese

Wisps Of Time

Memories
What are they?
Wisps of time
Fragments coming back
Unexpectedly
Jogged into being
By word or deed
Scent or sound
Happy, sad,
Melancholy
Funny, bad
Or filled with laughter
Leaping about in the mind
Sometimes fading
Sometimes drawn back
Those thoughts
Our future selves
In quiet moments
Drawn on
As deposits in a bank
People, long forgotten
Actions, some regrets
Children's comic ways
Pets trusting
Cherish all memories
Impart all memories
So they may not be lost
Memories, memories
What are they?
Practice for our future lives.

Anne Codling

Youth

You only have to sit awhile, your memories to recall.
Long hot days spent playing in the park; the games of tag, hide-and-seek, until it was dark.
No boring TV sets or videos to watch,
A day out in a charabang, was a dream beyond compare.
As was that ride on the dodgem cars at the annual Whitsun Fair.
To the Lickey Hills we'd go whenever we had a chance,
Just for the thrill of riding on the tram car.

Oh! how the youthful fashions change,
No pony tails, and dirndl skirts,
no Teddy boys with DA hair cuts.
It's frizzy perms or long flowing locks,
Earring for boys and girls so it does seem.
It really makes me smile, when up at school it's out of uniform day,
So they all turn up in their T-shirts, trainers and jeans.

Unemployment! is today's youthful daunting future.
Five years apprenticeship was what you embarked on, if you wanted to learn a craft.
Today's youth struggle to their O levels just to be check-out girls at the local superstore.
We only had the radio to listen to, and when we danced; we were as a pair,
Not on the spot, alone as though we were standing on a hot brick.

The youth of today seem to have it made, they sit at desks,
No longer copying from a blackboard, with scratchy pen and ink.
But TV, computers and calculators seem to do the learning now,
Do they even have to think?

Has my own youth been so different from today's, I think not;
When I see my teenage daughter sing and dance to her favourite singer on TV.
He's number one this week, this very lucky lad.
I remember when in my youth, I sang and danced to the music of his dad.

Betty Thomas

Family Heirloom

We have a family heirloom
which we greatly treasure
It's neither porcelain or crystal
but priceless beyond measure

It stays in the garage
at our family home
and the memories it conjures up
are second to none

Now it comes in the form
of an old rusty tin
unfit for anything
except for the bin

Yet many a summer evening
it provided lots of fun
for Dad did his very best
to get a 'hole in one'

Tin can on its side
and a row of old golf balls
five in at one try
and Dad was ten feet tall

Competition was very fierce
and if ever we equalled that
we were liable for a bit of banter
or a whack on the bum with the bat (sorry club!)

All the stresses of the day
were gone as we played with the can
Quality time with Dad - you bet
we were his greatest fans

Dad has now gone
but his memory lives on
as his grandchildren play
with the old tin can.

Shelagh Gibson

444

Remembering Our Adolescent Years

Do you remember the 1st time you did things as an adult,
like giving your vote?

It might have been buying your first trendy coat, having saved hard,
knowing it could be bought using your flexible Visa card.

Or while at school, was you shown how to make the British brew,
now at that time, Buddy Holly could have been number one,
with his hit Peggy Sue.

So while being taught the best way to make a pot of tea did you use loose tea? Maybe you also remember an American TV show
'I Love Lucy'.

Nowadays it's probably quick and simple, a tea bag, with a cup or mug.

If you think back perhaps one of your parents' hobbies was learning how to make a wool rug.

Now maybe there were a few fellas, or dads who enjoyed making up treats in the kitchen also we became familiar, with our bodies' likes
and dislikes, we may have found what was ticklish, and what parts were itching.

As we became familiar with hot drinks vending machines, perhaps we enjoyed coffee from a machine rather than tea, you may also recall a female singer as in Brenda Lee.

Do you remember your first jive, your first girl or boyfriend, the pop group the Hollies singing 'I'm Alive'? Remember your first cuddly toy? Who was also likely to say while looking through their telescope, ship ahoy.

Bill Denson

The Studio Music Cat

(Dedicated to the memory of a devoted music lover without whom our monthly concerts will never be the same)

Without a word or gesture, his presence would be felt,
Green eyes a little sinister, appearance always svelte.
He never wore a bow tie, though dressed in evening black,
His cuffs and shirt front purest white, his hair smoothed slickly back.
A hauteur in his manner, with dignity he strode,
A gentleman from head to foot, politeness was his code.
He bowed his head from side to side and quietly took his seat,
Upon the softest chair or knee, or neatly, at your feet.
The largest thing about him was his quite enormous purr,
Bestowed on everyone he met who gently stroked his fur.
His passion was for music, it was fish and cream to him,
No matter what the instrument, he drank each cadence in.
On very rare occasions he would move right to the fore,
As close as he could manage to the music he adored.
He missed not one performance, loving every sharp and flat
And we'll miss our friend Sylvester, The Studio Mewsic Cat.

C D Isherwood

The Child Within

Come sing with me a lullaby
The child, he frets and wants to be out,
North Sea and wind flow in his veins,
The pull is strong at times like this.

White horses ride the waves tonight,
The lifeboat crew stands by,
Sou'westers hang ready at the door,
All watch the threatening sky.

Come quickly, how he pounds the door!
Now runs barefoot along the beach,
Gathers flotsam the tide brings in,
And feels the salt spray sting his cheeks.

Come sing with me a joyous song,
The fishing boats come home,
See how high the water line:
Full harvest in the holds.

He watches as the boats unload,
One day he'll skipper one of these,
He'll battle and weather many a storm
Before he earns that place.

His boat no longer trawls the sea
Lies idly in the bay,
Young men look far for other trades
To fill their pockets and their plates.

The fire crackles, flames burn low
Pictures fade and then are gone,
Across the room long shadows steal,
The chair, its rhythmic rock now still.

J Wilson

Remembering Days Like These

Behind an ivied wall
The rumble of heavy traffic
Passing nearby seems far away,
And a new sound,
Altogether more pleasant,
Floats gently through the trees.

Beneath a huge oak,
A school band makes music,
As other children,
Freed from adult restraint,
Play tag around a billowing marquee,
Whilst inside, their mothers make tea.

Outside, at shaded tables,
The older generation
Share a warm sun with daisies
That have evaded decapitation,
By mower,
Only a few hours before.

An infants class,
Gently prompted by teacher,
Skips lightly in intricate formation
Around a maypole,
Unaware that four runs
Have just been made.

And as the red ball
Trundles across the grass
Towards the boundary,
Up above, within the perfectly
Clear blue sky,
Time itself edges into infinity.

Andrew Farmer

Memory Scent . . .

I miss those English woodlands
Where the lily of the valley
Perfumed with subtle sweetness
An early summer's breeze
I crave again the pinewoods
Drenched with dew
And the herbal scent of
Their evergreen trees
I pine for the meadows
Where the pale moon daisies
Dusted with gold honeyed nectar
My face, hands and knees
I smell again the musty jigsaws
In their faded, dusty boxes
Untouched by human hands
Too many long years past
Their fragmented pictures
Holding yet the faint impression
Of gnarled yet nimble fingers, stilled at last
And, from once upon a Christmas,
The mingling of the peaty loam
With its icing sugar coating
Of marshmallow snow
But unbidden are my memories of
A flower-cushioned coffin
And the mingled aromas
Of chrysanthemum and rose
The problem with perfume is
That once the bottle's opened
The perfume loses potency
The scent is swiftly lost
But, dug around the lawns of life
Are my borders of experience
Into which a lifetime's memories are
Randomly tossed
Benefice is lent by tears
And the warmth of laughter's sunshine
Feeds their seedling roots
So that they flourish through the years

Sheila Sharpe

Memories Are Made This Way

Nostalgia and forgotten memories,
Memories are made this way,
Of Lydia and my broken heart,
Oh yes, of Lydia, my lady love singing besides a lark,

You haunt me like a queen inside my head,
One by one we pass this way instead,
To tell a story of forgotten memories,
Monumental bygone memories of yesteryear,

Whilst romancing a favourite restaurant,
With pleasurably dreamy moments,
Walking beside the moonlit shore,
Through a park, wood, dale and moor,

Beside the wild seashore,
While madam pens her day diary,
Romantic letters received laced with perfume,
Magical reflections uplifting,

Whilst on holiday, sojourning on the grand tour,
Watching beautiful scenery, with myriads of delightful colour,
At all the wondrous shapes of nature,
Across a meadow and yellow rape field,

And all the things that memory brings,
Where a radical poet writes you love,
Of all noble graceful things above,
To see the beauty of the world,

To have a traditional picnic,
With a special bouquet of beautiful flowers,
Where moth, ladybird and dragonfly dance awhile,
Or a butterfly, wasp and mayfly,

A passing red and orange sunset,
Besides a rolling sea, reminiscing,
Of bygone days,
O to bed and prayer,

To thank God with praise
For His beautiful creation,
Where memories are made this way,
Within the classical secret garden,

Overflowing with champagne,
With a lock of her hair,
From my childhood sweetheart,
Past the Milky Way and stars I dream,

With the gold ring upon your finger,
Aspiring with willow trees and honeysuckle,
I love you very much,
My lady and queen.

James Stephen Cameron

On Reflection

Tight-lipped in the chilling wind you stand alone,
Watching our ascent through unfocused eyes.
No cheery smile you give to greet our success,
Only an uneasy silence;
Blue and yellow clutched beside your sombre garb.
We curb our elation, sensing an aching void,
A reflex isolation,
Merely serving to cultivate the hardness of your heart.

Warm air, like the smudge of a gentle kiss brushes our cheeks,
Biting breeze briefly baffled
By cold craggy cairn:
Comfort,
As bowing, we make our meagre offerings.

Unmoved, unmoving you remain,
While we, turning, view below and behind
Fused footprints feathering soft earth,
Shadowing each measured stride;
Beckoning signposts shepherding us back to our future.

Before you there lies the lonely path of solitary descent,
Though memory be your friend, called forth,
As now, our backward glance reveals
Your misted eye unblinking, your faltering hand tenderly
Mingling with stone on stone, not soulless stone, but flowers.

H Collister

Wellington Boots

Lift up the tin cover with a handle, inhale the earthy, fusty, black ground smell.
Resting on a step stood the old black Wellington boots ready for action.

The dark black room below dug out so well by my dad was waiting to protect us.
Protect us from the sirens heralding another enemy raid and the V2s on their way.
Candles provided our light as we lay on the wooden framed bed, Mum and me.
Our little puppy Patch curled up in innocent slumber at the foot of the blanket.
Mum dare not show me her fear, she did not want me a small child to tremble too.

In the morning I awoke, Mum and puppy had gone up to the house.
I was not afraid, it was morning and I could hear the children next door.
I saw once again Dad's Wellington boots and knew he would look after us.
I lifted the lid, rubbed my eyes. The comfort of a new morning cheered me.
Our house was still standing, breakfast would be waiting for me.
We were safe.

When the war was over Dad once again wore his Wellington boots.
He toiled hard to remove the shelter in our garden.
Soon grass grew over the space, but the memories remain.

Eileen Fry

Life's Collection

Having a moment to myself
Wishing to rest an hour or two
I took out our albums of photographs
And was hooked in memories like you do
From my earliest days, as a child
A history rich in family life
To photos of weddings and babies too
When I was a daughter, mother and wife
Some could really make me laugh
While others nearly brought a tear
Holidays that I could never forget
And loved ones who are no longer here
How the children grow, how time flies past
What celebrations our family shared
it makes me proud and warms my heart
To know the family always cared
You know, I've had a lovely life
As daughter, mother and a wife
Our memories are life's true reward
And I have many, thank the Lord.

June Davies

Country Treasure

Along a winding country lane
To my great delight I found
Such wondrous beauty, there displayed
Its brilliance, quite profound
Grey cobwebs turned to silver threads
In the sunshine set alight
Laden heavy with crystal dew
Like diamonds shining bright
Each minute droplet deftly laid
Crowning each wildflower there
With darting iridescent lights
Cascading everywhere
Every leaf and blade of grass
Drenched in satin sheen
Arrayed like precious emeralds
In various shades of green
What master then could capture this
On canvas in good measure
Nature's splendid work of art
A perfect country treasure.

Patricia Whittle

Flames Of Remembrance

I light a candle,
out of darkness grows an all embracing light.
The candle glows for those so brave . . . who gave
their lives for peace . . . that wars might cease
and hatred end.

Father, uncle, brother, lover, son,
though their earthly lives are done, we love them still;
our men who left with fond goodbyes
for dark and weary lands,
and war-torn skies.

Their courage will forever shine,
they fought for freedom . . . yours and mine.

No greater gift can any man give; they died . . . that we might live.

Flames must forever burn, for valiant men who went to war,
never to return . . . again.

Light more candles,
let nothing dim their sacrifice; their selfless gift of life.
Lift up your voice, in memory of their love rejoice.
Remember their smiles on sunny days, let no one
sully memories of the brave.

Let courageous spirits live forever
warmed by eternal flames.

Yvonne Jupe

A Boy's Life . . .

Well friend here we are,
after years have flowed on far.
Adventures, from as children - where our stories began.
Though some things in our hearts always remain;
even with times passing,
and fate's mystery reign.
I remember friends off with a zest of wonder,
and a spark of awe;
out to those other worlds we made,
through stories and games, out of the back door.
In the yards and alleys - the Saturday kids . . .
Still there, when I close my eyes -
One friend who to my heart is always more.
Saturday girl. Her eyes flare in my memory now,
arcing shooting stars of prisming light.
I remember how colours kaleidoscope
and danced with exotic flashes within her pretty eyes,
spilling forth so bright.
Those wonder years now have grown.
We have changed, childhood friends,
Saturday kids - into memory you've flown . . .
Though some things remain true,
like in my heart, feelings always I will,
have of, all of you.
If fate turned the world and moved on another way,
who knows where we all might have been today . . .

Paul Holland

Countryside Childhood

I listen to the wind as it whistles and it plays,
Reminding me of long ago and golden, mellow days.
Of fields, full of barley and meadows of green.
Of waters falling softly, cool, crisp and clean.
Of rushing through woodlands with faces aglow,
Resting by trusty trees, loving life so.
The smell of wild garlic, violets and woodbine.
The days of my childhood were really sublime.

I watch the trees as they rhythmically bend.
I remember the days flowing on without end,
The frogspawn, the newts, the kingfishers blue,
The moorhens, the swallows, the woodpeckers too.
I remember with pleasure the adventures so daring.
Twisty, dank paths between bank sides so scaring
The joy of it all, the energy, the glow.
The excitement of childhood so long ago.

Christine Frederick

Reunion

What memories reunion brings
It spans so many years,
Evoking so much laughter, and sometimes tears.
Thinking back to childhood, playing in the street;
Go-carts made with pram wheels, orange box for seat.
Starting school together, joining different clubs:
Wartime years and different places; meeting up again.

Camping, Scouts and Brownies,
Church on Sundays, youth club Wednesdays -
So much to do, and then -
Came the weddings, more shared laughter;
Later christenings, noisy parties - happy times we all enjoyed.
Growing families, increased numbers, nothing stopped our unity.

Passing years and sadness joins us;
Loss of partners brings us close,
Still undaunted, friendship binds us,
Golden memories treasured most.

Ellen M Day

Shane . . . Prince Of Dogs R*I*P

I cannot sit by your fire today
But please remember me.

Don't forget that I shared your life
And your breakfast, dinner and tea.

I was your naughty rascal,
But your faithful friend, too.

Don't throw away my collar and lead
They're a link from me to you.

I cannot sit by your table today
Nor put my head on your knee.

Or lick your hand or tap your foot
For biscuits dipped in tea.

I cannot go for walks anymore
Or chase the cats up the tree.

But I am still your faithful friend
Oh, please remember me.

I cannot guard our home anymore
Nor sleep in my bed, cosily

And I cannot sit by your fire tonight
But please remember me.

Irene Nobbs

Nan's Kitchen

(In memory of my nan, Grace Fuller)

Nan's kitchen was always full of wonderful smells,
Her bread pudding was the best ever tasted -
And we never knew how she did it.
Her stews and dumplings melted in your mouth,
As the flavours lingered on your tongue.

Her evenings were spent knitting -
Cardigans and pullovers for us children
Or booties and bonnets for babies.
Above the noise of the telly, the 'clicking' of her needles,
Could be heard, as she was kept busy.

Her infectious laughter could fill a room,
As she watched something funny on the telly
Or her and Grandad began to sing their funny songs.

So now that she has departed
To the heavens above,
I'll bet she's busy in God's kitchen,
Cooking things that He will love.

Debbie Nobbs

Off To School

Here's your piece my mammy cried
As off to school I wint
Button your coat an' tie your lace
Och laddie you're aye ahint

Your pencil's in the dresser drawer
Your reader's on the stool
Put them in your bag at nicht
An' you'll be in time for school

It's earlier tae bed noo lad
Your lesson done by tea
Dinna look at me like that
But jist you listen to me

What's in your bulgin' pockets
Bools a' stuck wi' taur
Use your hankie no your sleeve
Oh man it's fue o' glaur

Say your tables doon the road
Ye might please the teacher then
I'll hae a smart wee lad
Eh och aye ye're only ten

Mary Hudson

That Special Cruise

I have such happy memories,
When I'm sitting all alone.
Things will never be the same,
Now I'm on my own.

We loved to go to Scotland,
We went there every year.
When I think of all the good times,
Makes me wipe away a tear.

We travelled all around,
Italy, France and Spain.
I know that in my heart,
I will never go again.

The most memorable of all,
Was a cruise, it was the best.
Stopping to see America,
Mexico and Key West.

We dangled our feet in the ocean,
Could have stayed all day.
Sometimes we saw the sunset,
And watched the dolphins play.

If I had one more wish,
I know what I would choose.
I would be on that ship again,
That very special cruise.

B Cotterill

Two Special People

You always were so special
You gave me my life,
And always guided me
Through this world's strife.

You would tuck me up
Snugly, every night
With a hug and a kiss
You turned out the light.

I had such sweet dreams,
The things we would do.
There was always such love
From the two of you.

The years have gone
The love is still there.
You still show me
How much you always care.

Julie Brown

Winter Remembered

The fog presses down, smothering, silent,
Forming a mushy, marshmallow world.
Wrapped up warm in wool scarf and wellies
I venture out, clutching Dad's big, strong hand.
Mysterious shapes are looming ahead,
Dragons and monsters, ghostly and strange.
But they'll not hurt me; I know they won't dare,
Not now they know that my father is here.

It's raining today, so I'm not going out,
Dad says it's blowing a terrible gale.
I'll lie on my tummy in front of the fire
And colour my pictures in purple and green.
It's still raining at bedtime. I snuggle down deep.
Something's tapping my window. Is it the wind?
I'm sure it's not ghosts. I'm not really afraid,
I hide 'neath the bedclothes just to keep warm.

No rain today, just a soft, mellow dampness,
Smelling of woodsmoke and old rotting leaves.
I tramp through the woods, glad of the freedom,
Chewing an apple, my dog at my heels.
I swing on bare branches, dislodging raindrops
That slither like snakes, ice-cold, down my neck.
I play Robin Hood with imaginary playmates,
Defeating the bad men with my trusty stick.

On November the fifth we have a bonfire,
It's lit in the evening and everyone's there.
Faces reddened with heat, backs chilled by the wind,
We cheer as the guy, that we made, catches fire.
There's whooshes and flashes; bangs echo around.
And millions of stars explode way up high;
'Tis fairyland magic in silver and gold.
Then dying embers and a cold empty sky.

Gwen Hoskins

Only The Sea

A bright sunlit day through a wooden framed window
But now the window is double glazed
The house in the distance invisible now
Obscured by the clutter of more recent times
The people of the houses in-between are gone
Like the flowers that guarded the green grass in their gardens
The bright day is gone with another in its place
But the sapphire-blue sea is still there
Waves still gently lapping the rocky shore
The rocky shore that guards the beach - and even that is changed
Only the sea never changes
Only the sea is forever and a day
Its opalescent droplets shimming like stars
Gleaming in the sun like watery diamonds
Crashing and roaring in the depths of winter
Like soft azure silk in the summer sun
From the day the first rains filled the first oceans
Through the days of the pirates and the privateers
To the day I looked through the old wooden window
And onwards and forward to the end of time.

Alasdair Cowie

A Never To Be Forgotten Memory

I shall never forget, till I draw my last breath,
The day Mark, our grandson, was stabbed to death.
Not on some wasteland in England, so grotty,
But out on the streets of Lanzarote.
His mum, our daughter, was at our house for lunch,
When a policeman came round, with her eldest son.
What a shock we all got, when he said, sad to say,
That Mark had been murdered, early that day.
He worked nights in a bar, and was on his way home,
That was all they could tell us, we felt really alone.
When we sought the cost of bringing him home,
Two thousand five hundred at least from one firm
Was quoted, three thousand or more from another.
Vast profits it seems from the anguish of others.
I can find no forgiveness for the way Mark died,
Though we're taught ours is not to reason why.
I wish that God would show me the light
And the days once more would be happy and bright.
Until that day I shall weep for my daughter,
Who lost the son whom God first brought her.

Olive Smith

Slap On The Greasepaint

Now I'm old and very arthritic
I review the lusty days of yore.
Now, as a grumpy old armchair critic,
And as a mumbling, stumbling bore,
My memory is fading fast.
But I recall a favourite rant o' mine
How I wrote, directed and helped to cast
A yearly, joyous pantomime.
Into each script the vicar pokes,
Blue pencil poised with villainous feeling
To remove all double entendres and dodgy jokes
To make the whole thing less appealing.
Cinderella, Aladdin, Babes in the Wood
All followed in glorious progression,
Poor old Jack, so misunderstood, and Red Riding Hood.
Well-known scenes, in colourful procession.
I remember the hero once, in virtuous rage,
Fired blanks when a trifle uncertain,
He got too close to the front of the stage
Singed the beautiful light green curtain.
'It'll be alright on the night,' they brayed,
With hope and fresh ardour lyrical,
I crossed my fingers, and legs, and prayed
For a really major miracle.
Those happy days are long out of sight,
But memory my fond thoughts unpeg,
Oh bliss! To hear loud on opening night,
'Good luck, and break a leg!'

Jack Scrafton

Yesteryear – A Sonnet

The hedge-lined lanes and fields have disappeared.
Gone are the little farms, the fertile ground.
The bluebell woods and ponds have all been cleared,
Where there was country, houses now abound.
Still, in the sepia photos of my mind.
I wander through the places I once knew
Remembering, whenever I'm inclined,
The way things were, nostalgic points of view,
Climb on the sandhills, watch the happy crowd,
Wave to the liners, sailing into port
Over the water, tall, majestic, proud,
Think of the picnics and the kites we brought,
Save happy memories but forget the rest.
We are alive. The here and now is best.

E Caergybi

459

Beyond The Brow

When I was a lad and the elements still
I loved to perch high upon Portsdown Hill
    And view the unravelling scene;
With cargo ships, liners and great men o' war,
By a city vibrating with nautical chore
    And surrounded by pastoral green.

But all was to change when a marauding flight
Exploded its spite on a venomous night,
    And scenes I revered disappeared;
Stout hearts would perish in rubble and flame,
With life for Portsmuthians never the same,
    When all of the debris was cleared.

Now, when I gaze at that vista below,
The Solent sweeps by in a glistening flow
    By an encroaching, urbanised spread;
Where once there were races with galloping hooves
Chimney pots sit on a phalanx of roofs
    And flora has faded or fled.

Then outward, there beckons a backdrop of Wight,
Although sometimes hazy a sight to delight
    As cross-channel ferries ply by;
There is nothing to menace those Palmerston's forts,
As yachtsmen and surfers engage in their sports
    Whilst seagulls still plaintively cry.

Yet if you look northward to guardian downs
Like a somnolent gateway to historic towns,
    In blissful serenity still;
Colourful crops from a lush tapestry
Which man has created by sound husbandry
    On God-given landscapes to till.

William Dodd

A Few Of My Memories

Playing in the cornfield on a summer day
Or climbing on a wagon load of hay.
Paddling in the stream nearby
Watching the birds flying high.
Cowslips and primroses and bluebells grew near the farm.
Playing in the woods where we came to no harm.
Riding bareback on the big handsome shire,
Then, home once again to toast by the fire.
Off to bed, our prayers are said.
Some happy memories are written here,
Memories that I will always hold dear.

Cicely Heathers

Reflections At The Close Of The Day

The busy day is hushed
Time to reflect
On the joyous fun of the day -
Children's laughter
As with bucket and spade
They gathered shells on the seashore
To adorn their castles of sand
Built with such busy hands
As if to last for evermore.

The busy day is hushed
Time to reflect
On all the wondrous beauty
We have seen -
The pulsating sea as it ebbs and flows
Crystal clear water
Mirrored like a blue lagoon
Soon to shine
With the dazzling light
Of the silvery moon.

The busy day is hushed
Time to reflect
As starlight and moonlight
Dispel the darkness of the night.
As the sun rests in the arms of the sea
So we too may rest in the arms of God
Whose vigil ever watches over you and me.
When the sunrise peeps over the hill
The dawn chorus awakens us from sleep
To another day -
New friends to meet
New scenes to greet
Thank You Lord for each memorable day.

Frances M Gorton

Boston Cream

Who'd be inspired by an old warehouse door?
Why should it mean anything more?
The door is swung back, opened wide
For a swing has been fixed to its inside.
A little girl sits there, going to and fro
The swing deliberately kept low
The reason is easy to understand
She holds a drink within her hand
It's filled with scrumptious Boston Cream
A Canadian recipe, a childhood dream!

Vera Sykes

461

School Friend

In this grammar school
the day's commonplaces -
chalk, pins, rulers, pens -
are all recreated before we wake.

We are disciplined in rows,
ink-grained chorus lines
of squirming limbs.
Each of us a dead weight

for our desks.
We are scrutinised
by an uneasy silence
and an Aegean master.

The boy in front has a cruel
haircut. He stares out
at an arthritic scarecrow
practising semaphore on Keal Hill.

Now his eyes, wet as peeled sticks,
pick the classroom walls:
for gaps to hide petitions?
Secrets drift around him.

Greek translation begins.
He stands to read from Book XI.
Archilles spoke from the underworld,
'Rather be a slave on Earth
than king of the dead.'
He stops abruptly.

Our eyes turn down
to toffee-brown stains
on the floor.
Sun-dried truth and apple cores
shrivel in my desk.

Carved on my mind:
last night's headline.
Boy's parents drowned at Torksey Lock.
Orphan: a word that sieves out
the sun for my friend.

Derek Webster

Life At A Glance

Our eyes met for a moment,
The time it takes to go out a door
And glance as you pass.
He could not have been more than nine years old;
But then, I am not a father,
And then in a wheelchair, you may look younger.
His skin was so white.
Our eyes met for just a moment.
The small legs, wasted away, useless things,
Folded together, to the right,
And white running shoes that would never wear.
Still, he glanced right up at me,
With wide-open eyes in an open face,
With interest and unafraid,
Glancing up,
But not from a lesser place.
I was ashamed of my own legs.
Why did I glance back?
There was nothing to be gained.
I was glad to see the oblique light of late afternoon,
Glad to feel the mild spring air.
Our eyes met for just a moment.

John Faucett

Memories Are Made Of This

As we journey on through life,
From childhood dreams,
Teenage screams,
Maybe a wife and mother
Sometimes another.
Memories are made of this.

Sometimes happy, sometimes sad
Days when we say,
'It's all bad.'
Then a ray of sunshine peeps through
You look up and are glad,
A child has smiled,
Someone's been kind,
Memories are made of this.

Yes, life has a way of trying us all,
Whether big or small
And in wonder we gaze,
There are yet to be happy days
And memories are made of this.

Doreen Thomson

Hard Times

Married in the sixties, times were very hard.
Rented an upstairs terrace, sharing a backyard,
No inside amenities, just an outside loo,
Freezing in the winter mornings,
Had to be a good whistler too.

Public baths had a special day, or you could
Have a good wash in the sink.
The coal-fired boilers used to roar,
So you would come out glowing pink.

Television was a luxury, and you had to pay
To view, halfway through a film the money
Ran out, so it was a good night to you.
You could hire a washing machine just for the day.
But you would hurry to get it all done
Before they took it away.

Tick on at the corner shop, something you used to hate.
They would make you wait till last, so everybody knew.
Settle up on pay day, and they would serve you front
Of the queue.

Shillings for the meter, plastic coupons for the milk,
Wouldn't like to look back when you come to think,
Times were very hard but what made it all worthwhile,
People gave you the time of day, and a friendly smile.

June Cameron

A Country Child's World

The lane was sweet with honey-filled air
Of hedges all may-blossomed white.
No pavements, but ditches so deep
That were filled with 'Lad's Love' and lush grasses there.
The beautiful blooms of the 'Nightshade' entwined
Soon to give forth their berries red, dark.
We children well knew on what we could 'dine',
And we too knew where danger could lurk.
But our 'world' filled with green of meadows and stream
Gave us sky larks and field mice and fun.
We caught minnows and frog spawn
To take home in jars and gathered daisies for chains in the sun.
When tired we rested on sweet-smelling grass,
And made 'pictures' in soft, fluffy clouds in the blue.
Our innocent world was destroyed all too soon
When the sirens of war chilled us through.
Memories like these all still fill my heart
And I'm glad of the world I once knew.

Betty Margaret Irwin-Burton

Memories Are Made Of This

Thoughts On Moments Past, And Sensations That Last

Memory, the definition in the dictionary says,
Facility by which things are recalled, stored, kept in mind,
To remember is to bring back into one's thought,
Not forget, in our 'retention system' find

From infancy we learn names, hello Jim, sorry Fred, er Martin, is it Lee?
Mathematical tables are memorised, six sevens are forty-five,
make that forty-three!
Through education, tuition, instruction, we amass a multitude of facts,
Comprehension and wisdom are attained when information with
understanding interacts.
To some this process is difficult, others with natural aptitude
find it easier,
In later years difficulty in 'knowledge banks' may come from
Alzheimer's or amnesia.

Special occasions like birthdays, anniversaries, Christmas, encourage
nostalgic mood,
Family gatherings, happy moments, fond recollection produce
cosy interlude.
The 'reservoir of impression' is a mix of good times, others
upsetting, challenging,
Thankfully, in most cases, harmony outweighs discord
When we commence deciphering.

The 'memory menu' comprises vehicles owned, precious pets,
Friends, personalities, faces,
TV programmes viewed, locations visited, products purchased,
dwelling places.
Talking to elderly folk we uncover many an interesting recounted
tale, story,
This recitation allows each individual a moment of reflected glory.

When travelling to geographical spots and buildings,
We sometimes pick up vibes, encounter 'déjà vu',
A theory exists that may explain the feelings that ensue
When we are born, we inherit facets of experience from
previous generations,
The result is a re-awakening of perception handed down from
our relations.

Though consciousness occupies the present,
We can learn from the past and what has gone before.
Ponder great thinkers, artists, benefactors, inventors, the tumult of war.
Today's actions will become tomorrow's reminiscence, photographs,
diary notes,
Who knows, in the future, from Lands End to John O'Groats,
Our musings may be resuscitated and employed in quotes
and anecdotes.

Dennis Overton

In Memory Of Bishop Henry Cecil Read

(Second Bishop of Nasik, India (1944-1959))

Bishop Henry Cecil Read
Was a man of God indeed,
A man who set Christ's word in motion
And served his Lord with great devotion.

The people loved him very much.
They called him 'Papa', and as such
His deep compassion went to all;
He loved his flock, both great and small.

My father held him very dear;
He came to visit every year;
Round the parishes he'd go
And every congregation know.

A second father, too, to me,
He sometimes paid my college fee.
Those annual visits were a joy,
When I was a little boy.

In time I made my graduation,
Then was called to ordination,
Helped again by Bishop Read,
Always in my hour of need.

To hot Calcutta off I went;
To Bishop's College I was sent;
From nineteen fifty-four to seven,
Help from Jesus I was given.

For me the climate there was bad,
It made me sick and very sad.
Many weeks I lay there ill,
Near to death in hospital.

My father came to visit me,
Fasted, prayed on bended knee,
Brought me by his prayers to life
Through those hours of bitter strife.

The bishop too prayed every day,
Till my sickness went away.
I made through ill a great discovery -
The power of prayer to help recovery.
For those who prayed when I was ill
Gave me strength that's with me still;
They built anew my faith indeed,
But most of all did Bishop Read.

Rev David Shrisunder

Driving Force

To learn how to drive, oh what a hope
To try it at 40 I felt such a dope
Thought I'd be rubbish, too nervous I guess
Why was I doing this? Pride no less.

Instructor rang the bell on that bright May day
My knees went wobbly, I stumbled and swayed
He said, 'Mrs Smith,' his smile just beamed
'Your driving lesson, my car is all cleaned.'

I relaxed at that and entered his car
His name was Ginger with a mop of red hair
He chose a quiet turning and we exchanged seats
My heart was pounding in uneven beats

Showed me the workings of wheel, brakes and gears
I'd done nothing like this in all of my years
After all my tribulation it turned out just fine
Two lessons a week for quite a long time

I enjoyed every minute, reversing round corners
Parking on steep hills, made no one a mourner
Passed my test on second try, first examiner made me sigh
It was plain to see women, made him a grizzly guy

I got my certificate, jumped feet in the air
I'd done what I intended, thanks to Ginger there
Yes, those memories stay in my heart and my mind
A better instructor would be hard to find.

The loveliest places visited when children were small
Without my old Cambridge we'd not have seem them at all.
Thirty-five years ago I ventured and gained
The good teaching I had has kept me sustained.

J Howling Smith

First Love

The east coast town of Aldeburgh I've remembered all my life,
it was there I went on holiday before the war brought strife.
the year was nineteen thirty-eight, we had no thought of war,
each day was carefree to us boys; you couldn't ask for more.

Just twelve years old I was that year, the youngest of the three,
we hoped to find adventure and were happy by the sea.
good swimming was there from the beach, you could dive from
ankle-deep; no slowly wading, creeping cold but a quick courageous leap.

Most families got there early on, to hold their chosen place
I watched a nearby family and my heart began to race.
a pretty girl about my age stood ready for a swim,
with hand on hip and cap in hand she was so very trim.

If only I could talk to her, my life would be complete;
to swim out to the bathing raft, was an act of pure conceit.
I thought it might impress her as I knew not what to say;
at twelve I was extremely shy, unlike most boys today.

I don't think I was noticed much, or so it seemed to me;
but unrequited was my love, prolonging misery.
in other ways I loved our stay, the carnival exciting,
the swimming races in the sea and fireworks delighting.

On one black Friday storm cones flew, I watched the rough seas pounding.
maroons were fired to call the crew, the quick response astounding.
the Aldeburgh boat stood on the slip, both engines then were started.
then down she went in clouds of spray, no task for the faint-hearted.

I searched for Susan in the crowd but nowhere could I find her,
then just as I was walking back, she's there with Pa behind her.
I gabbled something indistinct and felt that I was blushing,
I thought she knew just who I was, her absent face was crushing.

'Oh Susan Hickman could you know just how sweet is sorrow,
if only I could speak my mind but we go home tomorrow.'

Donald Mountain Beale

Childhood Sundays

We all went to Sunday school
Shush, shushing as we went,
And every lesson that we learned
Was truly heaven-sent.
It was such a big part of our lives
That little chapel made of tin,
The place where we were taught wrong from right,
Learned all about mortal sin.
Dressed in our Sunday best we went
A Bible in our hands,
Trying to appear so sedate,
Wondering who was on the plans.
Those childhood Sundays of my life
Seemed so gentle in a thousand ways,
And I guess that I'll remember them
All of the rest of my days.
For the little chapel stands empty now
And overgrown with weeds.
No hymn singing comes from within,
No more stories of noble deeds.
For it's fallen into dereliction
Soon it will fade away.
But memories of those childhood Sundays
Are within my heart to stay.

Joyce Hudspith

Holiday Memories

Along the seafront as we walked,
our holiday almost at an end;
The sea was calm, the air was warm,
youths skateboarding round the bend.

The evening sun gleamed brightly;
but beyond the cliff I knew
the full glory of the sunset
was hidden from our view.

And we could but recapture
the pleasure of that hour
by searching in our memory
which holds such joys forever.

Ruth Barclay Brook

Days Out With Uttin'

(In the 1940s, wandering over the Big Meadow on the outskirts of Loughborough, Leicestershire with Mrs Utting - affectionately referred to as 'Uttin' - our next-door-but-one neighbour, and a dear friend to all the children of the Canal Bank, at Meadow Lane End in my time of living there.)

Are the wildflowers on the Big Meadow still
Where 'I' used to play?
Is the background hill natural and as sweet
As was in 'my day'?

Do the long thin grasses ripple in the breeze?
Are there rook, magpie and carrion high in trees?
Does the fox stare out from his lair in the ground?
Do the hare cry on air and jump around?
Is there background echo in the wood
Where the line of budding hawthorn stood?
Is the hunting horn a distant, *chilling,* dreaded sound
With the echo of excited bloodthirsty hound?

Yes: days out with Uttin' were sweet and free
And full of joy and revelry;
For:
This was the girl who flittered with butterflies
Through wildflowers mid long grasses;
This was she who loved to play
And chased the dreams of a lovely day;
This was the girl with a magic flair,
That paddled the Summerpool brook and watched the weir;
This was the one with dreams unwound
T'would reach for the air and skim the ground;
Whose nimble feet would dance and prance
And catch the curious rabbits' glance;
And never know a moment's care
Whilst gliding wondrously through the air;
This was the special unique one
That loved 'all wild things' - every one:
Animal, fish, the bird on high,
And all the creatures mid earth and sky;
The minute being, and the great mighty beast,
She loved them most, and herself the least . . .
Wanting to protect 'all' from the hunter's horn;
And the fearful call of '*The death at dawn*' . . .
But the bad man come and taketh away
Leaving a black-shrouded 'heavy' day . . .
And the heart that skipped and danced around,
Is still and silent and grasping at ground;
With a pain so deep, a hurt so sore
For 'the life that was and is no more' . . .

There should be love and hope and joy and glory.
But for the wildlife, it's a different story . . .

A fear!

A fear - deep fear - of the hunting hound,
And the gory mess and the dreaded sound . . .

God never cried, 'Tear beast apart!
And worry them so, 'til with a beating heart,
They meet their death with a fearful pound;
And leave their young to starve at ground . . . !'

Happily the butterfly flits, as I did in my day . . .
But sadly, *the hunt and hounds never went away* . . .

Mary Pauline Winter (nee Coleman)

The School Holidays With My Grandmother

I went on the bus
Full of trepidation and fear,
I was only five
And she didn't live near.

I played in the garden
Making mud pies.
I painted and drew
And won a first prize.

We went to the art gallery
And also the zoo,
And when I was older
To concerts too.

She had a piano
And taught me to play,
And to use a sewing machine,
So I practised each day.

I do most of the things
That I did as a child,
But using a sewing machine,
That just drives me wild!

Now I go to a ceramics class
To make things with clay,
And I have kept the concert programmes
Right up to this day.

Every year I go through them,
Can I throw them away?
No, I can't, so those memories
Are here to stay.

Rachel E Joyce

Memories

Memories of days of gladness,
Memories of days of sadness.
Memories of exciting bliss,
Memories of a sweetheart's kiss.
Memories of those gone before,
Memories that we shall see no more.
Memories of walking out the dog,
In a cold night's winter fog.
Memories of many a winter's snow,
Making youthful cheeks aglow.
Memories of snowdrops and cold.
Memories of feeling so benign
At seeing spring's first celandine.
Memories of summer hay making,
The new mown grass a busy raking.
Memories of autumn's gently clime,
Of leaf fall and of conker time.
Memories of many a Christmas Day,
With Jesus in a crib of hay.
Some memories in my mind I store,
But I am sure there's many more.

David Garside

Memories Of A Holiday

The beauty of this stretch of beach
With not a soul about,
How can we say 'There is no God?'
There is, I have no doubt.
The sea, the sand and sunshine
Are here for all to see,
His handiwork is wonderful
And there for you and me.
The curve of beach, the solitude
The grandeur of it all,
Compared to pebbles on the beach
Man too is very small.
Do you see God's beauty
Sometimes spoilt by man?
He must be disillusioned
For this wasn't in His plan.
His power and might are everywhere,
His beauty we should see.
God wants us to enjoy His gifts,
That's how it ought to be.

Anne Smith

Hold My Hand Little Boy

Hold my hand little boy - walk with me
There are so many lovely things to see
Together we'll explore as you learn a little more
About the beauty of each flower and tree
And before very long, you'll recognise the blackbird's song
As we walk along little boy.

Hold my hand little boy - don't make a sound
You'll hear the voice of nature all around
In the whisper of the breeze and the buzzing of the bees
Or a tiny leaf just floating to the ground
We might see a violet shy or perhaps a butterfly
As we both walk by little boy.

Hold my hand little boy - feel the gentle rain
Then suddenly the sun is out again
We'll watch the rainbow bright till it disappears from sight
These wonders no one can explain
With skies above so blue I feel such love for you
It's too good to be true little boy.

Soon you'll grow up little boy - it has to be
And you will no longer walk with me
But treasure in your heart what you've learned from the start
Of all God's gifts so wonderful and free
Childhood goes so fast - too soon these days are past
But memories always last little boy.

Valerie Furbank

Memories Are Made Of This

When I was in Jamaica as a young boy
I had many good times going to school.
I spent some happy times going to the beach at the weekend,
Swimming with my friend.
Then in 1957 one night
After midnight in the calm of the night,
The earth started to shake and shake
People grew afraid and started to shout,
'God a cum, God a cum.'
That night God did not come,
It was a terrible earthquake that came instead.

P B James

Fishing

Waiting on the river bank
For the fish to bite:
Reflections in the water
Of a lazy kite.

Flicking line nonchalantly,
Brimmed hat shading eyes;
Lunch in a wicker basket
Safe from buzzing flies.

Fat, squirming, white maggots,
Bait in a jar, ready.
Fishing needs concentration:
Hold the rod steady!

Plop! Ever widening pool;
Silence is golden:
Silver flash in the water -
Darts under boulder.

So tense, waiting for the kill;
Swish goes rod and reel,
Line pulls taut and straight;
Digging in of heel!

Snap goes line - nearly breaks rod:
Woe betide today!
How can one tell one's folk of
The one that got away?

J Millington

Looking Back

Oh to sit here in the silence
Of our cosy sitting room
The stars up there are winking
Surrounding a peachy moon

Silken veils of wispy clouds
Passing in and out of view
special thoughts come rushing in
Of fun time spent with you

Looking at old photographs
Of the places we have been
Each one a precious memory
Of a very special scene

Turning back the pages
Of your very own story book
Reminiscing can be wonderful
Simply take your time, to look!

Ray Johnson

Memories Of World War II

The reds and blues of a gentle sunset
Slowly fading tonight in the west
Bring memories of so long ago
Flooding into my mind.

I loved running fast on the beach
When I was young and carefree
But the church caught fire mysteriously
So I stood and watched the blazing roof
Then ran back to my house
As scorching heat hit my face.

But it soon became clear to us all
That all was not well in our world
As growling masses of bombers came our way
And I did pray in my bed at night
That the bombs would not come down on us
Then next morning I went to the farm
To find the bomb holes in the fields.

Soon our small neat village was changing
It filled up with guns and soldiers too
One even rode my bike, too small for him
It was his fun, but not for me.

After a time the soldiers went
And German prisoners took their place
They all had a cycle to get them to work
And one came to our chapel every week
He was a strong but kind man to us all
So I shared my hymn book with him
And he taught me some German words.

Then at my school it was announced
The war was over, thanks to God
So we could be ourselves again
And sleep at night free from our fears.

Michael A Willsmer

School Discipline

When I was ten my teacher was Miss Scott
Typical of that age, I didn't like her a lot,
she taught us poetry and also songs
We didn't see the point but we had to sing along.

She was strict and kept us in our place
Her aim was we qualify to a high standard apace
She was small, always neat and trim
No doubt by experience she learned to look grim.

The strap was in her desk to help class obey
Which would be used without a sign of dismay
But you know when I look back on those days
I have to confess I feel nothing but praise
Although I didn't understand the poems at the time
I still remember them all, line after line
As for the songs, the same applies
I can sing them all with understanding and sighs
It would be wonderful to meet after all those years
To tell her she achieved much more that it appeared.

Helen Johnson

The Sycamore Tree

As I sit in my chair by the window
(For these days it is as far as I can go)
A new birth before me I can see
Happening in my sycamore tree.
It all started a few days ago
With two blackbirds flying to and fro
Carrying twigs in their beaks on a branch they were bound
Then one of them started weaving round and round
Until a beautiful nest was finally made
In which later eggs were laid.
Then as I eagerly sat and watched
Two little birds were finally hatched.
Their two little heads I saw moving around
Along with a gentle twittering sound
As their parents flying to and fro
Brought them food to help them grow.
But now from the nest they have all flown
Leaving me once more all alone.
Perhaps next year once more I will see
More happenings in my sycamore tree.

Doreen Yewdall

Memories

Memories of the days we left behind,
Unforgotten moments
That once were shared.
Daydreams, brief encounters,
When excitement filled the air.
Contented adoration
Of two who cared.
Heartaches which quickly passed us by,
Replaced by love and kindness
In the twinkle o' an eye.
To some these may be fantasies,
Perhaps this could be true
But these passing recollections,
Bring back my memories of you.

Alexander Hamilton

Memories

Childhood memories have I none.
From my seventies I have one:
At seventeen I always dreamt
To fly, and fly is what I meant.

No airfield near; no finance clear!
Over fifty, did I truly hear?
Gliding is not nearly so dear.
Fifty-eight switched to planes with gear.

What fun we had in every way
Until my heart refused to play,
The CAA threw my licence away.
My tears for two days had their say.

Seventies now, I had to think,
With instructors there was a link
In helicopters I could swing:
Fifteen hours saw my solo fling.

However hard life sometimes seems
Never give up, my friends, your dreams.
Tuck them away; one day who knows
They could come alive - each plan grows.

In your eighties then, as for me,
You will have happy memories.
Not a helicopter no doubt,
Just dreams come true to boast about.

Ruth Brigden

This Lucky Lad

A halfcrown postal order,
Wallpaper with floral border.
American oil cloth covered table,
Girls called Anthea or Mabel.

Bicycles with enclosed chain,
Country loos with open drain.
A ten foot mast for our radio,
Aunties called Nellie, sometimes Flo.

Uncle Fred with a very old lorry,
He'd press the horn and not say sorry.
Baby sis screamed, to her 'twould seem
Bogeyman rose out of her dream.

Pigs' feet in jelly, smelled of thyme,
Home-made marmalade with lime.
Fresh fried sprats from the pan thrown in,
Boiled cod's roe in its own skin.

Perhaps our life was somewhat rude,
Shakespeare did not once intrude.
But Mother thought it time for change,
By keeping chickens, oh so free range!

Father worked from morn till night,
To keep our small exchequer right.
And so some education filtered in,
For ignorance is mortal sin.

Headmaster lectured this wild youth,
Told me many a real home truth.
And so to life with joy and sorrow,
Hard work, good luck, what comes tomorrow?

Denis Pentlow

Unique

From out of the mists of time
Comes a memory sublime.
I boarded a train, left the Midlands behind,
Bound for the capital, famed landmarks to find.
At the Royal Opera House, now behold
The prima ballerina - such joy untold -
Margot Fonteyn! Each gifted performance
Will always my spirits lift and entrance.

Beryl Mapperley

Grandma

Ancient to me, this grandma of mine
Small and bent by the rigors of time
Crippled hands carefully held me
Close to her heart as I sat on her knee.

She could tell some wonderful stories
And would bake great cakes and pastries
Christmases with her were a happy to-do
As were the days we went to the zoo.

Through my childhood she was there
Giving me such love and care
Now she's gone, I miss her sorely
But she's earned her place, in Heaven's glory.

Jean Everest

An Evocation Of Childhood

Bees and heather, heather and bees,
the feeling of bracken brushing our knees,
the glimpse of a deer,
the sight of a hare,
a wren chit-chit-chatting,
a fox in his lair.

Blackberry juices running down chins,
our hearts in our mouths as a new day begins.
The sun always shining,
the days without end,
embraced in the warmth
of the love of a friend.

The sting of a nettle causing feelings of pain,
the leaf of a dock bringing calm once again.
The wonderful freedom
from watching the clock,
the call 'time for bed'
never ceasing to shock!

Our minds - as the skies - unclouded and clear,
a song in our hearts, complete lack of fear.
Secrets close guarded
from keen adult eyes,
no knowledge of guile
until innocence dies.

Angela R Davies

Two Lovers

When you're in love, really in love,
You can't do a thing about it,
You just want to go and shout it.
When you're in love.

Love is like the stars out at night,
By day they are gone but our love goes on,
Love shines in your face
And beauty is all over the place.

Hold me tight, we are going around this big world tonight,
When you're in love, really in love,
There is no one but us, we will see it through,
Just me and you.

Beryl Elizabeth Moore

Once More

Once more the night has come
The sun is set
Motionless I sit with hope and fear
I will keep the door ajar
And think of you in this lonesome place
Your footsteps I might hear
Or perhaps I might see your sleeping face.

Memories come back to me
Swaying and swerving like a drunken bee
Avoiding the shadows like the enemy
I shut the night away
And fade out like the stars
For each ecstatic moment
We shed a million tears.

Will I ever touch Heaven again?
Will the darkness ever pass?
I want to walk with you once more
Through soft green grass pearled with dew
Watch moonlight on a sea of glass
Rest upon a cruising cloud
Till paradise is found.

Until we meet again in a world to come
I will plod along the ground beneath my feet
Once more life will be so sweet.

Beth Izatt Anderson

My Angel

You are the sun and you are the light,
you are the stars that come out at night.
My angel, my love, my star from above,
our mum with a heart, that is so full of love.
My angel, our mum who was also a friend
and our broken hearts that would eventually mend.
Don't be sad that you left us behind,
for you will always be with us in our hearts and our mind.
I love you my precious, my angel, our mum,
who is so very special and still number one.
Our thoughts are with you, even though you have gone,
but our love will continue for our love is so strong.
Our mum who is a sister, a daughter and a wife
and all those cherished moments that she gave in her life.
Don't be sad my angel, my love,
for your mum will be waiting in Heaven above.
God bless you my angel until I see you again
and until it's my time be together again.

Clare L Pantling

How Old Was I Then . . .

Was I nine or was I ten?
It's quite hard to think back to then
nearing the end of primary school
crying over some boy - oh what a fool!
Was I four or perhaps I was three
when my Dad swam like a dolphin in the sea with me . . .
and sitting quiet on the stairs, just like my Mum had said
so that when my Dad got home -
he could put me to bed . . .
Was I twenty or twenty-one
the day that I announced 'I am going to be a mum';
a time of emotions all in a muddle
but I remember the fear of not coping -
as my baby I cuddled . . .
And now in my forties I try hard to remember
a woodland walk with my Dad, was it October or November?
for now he is no longer here -
these memories I cherish so much more
Like making marks for your child's growth upon the kitchen door
years later you notice the notches again
and you remember your child at eight or perhaps he was ten?
Priceless are our memories, a most valuable treasure
hold them close in your heart, keeping them safe forever . . .

Lisa E Bristow

Moonbeam Park

To Moonbeam Park I do tread
My very tracks do I dread,
All around are people fair
Going here, going there.

I espy a butterfly
And a babe in a pushchair
All around are people fair
Going here, going there.

I left behind another world,
A world where Heaven was unfurl'd
All around are people fair
Going here, going there.

I ventured to say 'hello'
To a lady but a while ago
All around are people fair
Going here, going there.

As I inhale some nicotine
It does swamp my bloodstream
All around are people fair
Going here, going there.

So this poem does curtail
And I draw another veil
All around are people fair
Going here, going there.

Cliff Holt

Memories Of My Childhood

Summertime warm and dry,
The birds singing in the sky.
Off to Gran's to stay a few nights,
Off we bike with all our might.
The Whitsun Fair has arrived on the green.
What a happy colourful scene
The man on the coconut shy with a very loud voice,
The swing boat all looking very nice.
The cake walk moving back and forth, and up and down.
And bumper cars all colourful and bright,
Going round and round with all their might.
The day is over, time for bed
Lots of excitement in my head.

Marion Lee

Remembering That Day You Wanted To See Me Again Because You 'Had News'

I said,
'I'm happy for you,'
Because that is what's supposed to be said,
And looking at your face,
You were so happy,
All I ever wanted you to be,
And so how could I resent? (this announcement, this event)
Well you were all I ever wanted,
And after we parted I knew,
I still wanted you all.
The fraying fronds of friendship are not enough,
But there's nothing I can do.

Later that afternoon,
I knew it was time to go
When I saw glimpses of myself in a mirror,
The lines very visible, taped together by a fixed smile,
Cracks about to split from the heaving emotion behind this face.
At our last embrace you pulled away,
Did I smell of desperation
Or did you still feel something too
And were reeling yourself in?
I walked away with a wave and cool dignity,
Then cried on the bus all the way home,
Strangers staring at the drips of my lachrymose bereavement.

So over.
So not over you.

Beverley Chipp

483

Requiem For The Lost Places

All gone . . .
The fields I walked reluctantly to school
on winter mornings; when the giant sun
contained within its fading crimson ball
the promises of all the snow to come.

All gone . . .
The places where I went to find the reeds
to make my whistles - piping my way home
in strident joy across the wooden bridge,
which spanned the stream where moorhens used to swim.

All gone . . .
The drowsy, summer - scented afternoons
spent lying in the fields; lost in the place
where children go; beneath a patch of sky
in its frame of meadow grass and daisies.

All gone . . .
All lost, and buried in a concrete tomb.
There are no fading wreaths of daisy chains,
and memories of the places that we knew
are fading;
Fading, as a dream fades in the morning . . .
and is gone.

Catherine Reay

My Great Grandma's Cottage

If I cast my memory back once again
I'm in that thatched cottage down an old lane.
Its windows were small and had seats below;
Which looked on to the garden in sunshine or snow.

There were dark oak beams in the ceiling there
And the floors had tiles which were red and square.
It was always so welcoming under that thatch
And to get through the door you undid a latch.

There were tables and ornaments and pictures of scenes
And great Grandma's baskets were hung from the beams.
Inside these baskets (although no one observed) -
Were supposed to be secrets and treasures of hers.

My great grandma's cottage was 200 years old
And was once a coaching inn, or so I was told.
There must have been ghosts there loose and abound;
But alas, like that cottage are no longer found.

Lorraine Bosworth

484

Down Forget Me Not Lane

Here are my memories of days of yore
I am nearly seventy-four,
So welcome to my memory box,
The key I'll turn and now unlock.

In the 1930s
I never knew much till five,
But I do remember one Sunday,
When I was playing outside, war!

Six long years till the mid 1940s,
Coupons, blackout, make do and mend,
When neighbours were neighbours
And friends were friends.

Jack, my dad, grew the veg,
Stella, my mum, cleaned, cooked and made beds.
Donald evacuee hated stew
And Susie our land girl,
Polished a floor or two.

Emily and I picked whortleberries in the wood,
Whort tart and custard,
Cor! That was good.

We swam in the river
And caught tadpoles in jars
And played out of doors,
For hours and hours.

Gran's feather mattress
Was luxury to me,
Chocolate pudding and custard
At five for tea.

War was now over for me as a girl,
My head was now in a kind of whirl,
Teenager, wife and a mother for me,
I will lock up the box now,
But will keep the key.

Rachel Mary Mills

Der Zeit

(The Westerkerk Church in the Jordaan Area of Amsterdam will still be ringing every fifteen minutes today as it did from its Westoren Tower over Anne Frank hiding in the 263 Prinzengracht Annexe sixty-five years ago)

I awoke to the sound of a clock
unknown to me replaced in the room,
Being and Time, Finite and Infinite.
Today Edith Stein, Rosa Stein are
Recorded in the museum ledger.

Drank Woods catching my throat
Once MOA to the SBS after all.
Drink Russian Tea that is ambiguous,
Breslau crucifixion, icons, theologians.
Thought of my own RAF Regiment
another lad killed Iraq yesterday.
Mixed up thoughts, Palestine thorns,
beautiful child's face of Anne Frank,
Auschwitz sixty-five years ago.

Nietzsche 'Beyond Good and Evil'
His prophetic transvaluation of values,
Heideggers obsession with Nothingness
Nihilism Ghost still wakes in Wales.

On that day those years ago
shielding those little ones as they choked on Cyclon B
did that genius feminist repeat to herself Finite Infinite?
'nothing can really be, or be real in the past?
I am, am only now'.

As on this day her ego shrinks from nothingness
arrives to her idea of plenitude;
to St Teresia Benedicta Patron of Europe.
I crawl to early Mass in Dukestown Tredegar.

Paul Faulkner

Memories Of An Age Long Gone

I remember the days in summers long ago drawn out and warm
With windows left wide open to sample that cool breeze at dawn
Watching horse-drawn carts delivering milk and our daily bread
Our pace of life was much slower then that's something to be said

I remember seeing the canal barges navigating the many locks
They transported everything then from coal and tar to building blocks
Those long hot days of summer lazing there with nothing else to do
Until someone suggested to break the monotony we visit our local zoo

I remember waiting in those long bus queues to visit our favourite spot
People all around me laughing and joking explaining last night's plot
Time was of little essence shuffling along in that never-ending queue
You knew once aboard the bus you could find plenty of things to do

I remember even simple journeys then, now it takes a few minutes or so
Patiently catching many buses and trains for there was nowhere else to go
Overcrowded transports would sometimes mean standing all the way
But that was the way of life back then on that long hot summer's day

I remember my journeys on a railway train now that was a real treat
Smoke pouring through the open window choking you in your seat
The old steam train chugged along the tracks at a nice leisurely pace
I've sometimes watched a car on the road as the train it tried to race

I remember the days spent by our local river it's a memory you don't forget
Watching the steamers go gracefully sailing past, fishing there with my net
You made the best of what you had for money then was in short supply
But those memories are like a treasure chest of golden days gone by

Raymond Thomas Edwards

Such Memories

My special memories go back years
With lots of fun, and sometimes tears
My very special boys in blue
They love me and I love them too

Living in a little country lane
Green fields all around, now not the same
With lovely neighbours, so good to me
We were one great happy family

Many other things we done
The farmer's apple tree was fun
Chasing animals on the farm
They caught us but done us no harm

Our dancing club was in our town
With teams competing for a crown
Gold and silver medal we did get
Those lovely days, with pals we met

Pam Chappell

Ilfracombe - Summer 1965, Devon

My husband and I decided
A holiday by the sea, would be nice
Our three young children 6½, 8½ and 13½ years said
Mum let's go! and Grandma! so August, off we set
Long hot coach ride 8am to 6pm
We had a refresher stop 2 hours then off again
We found our flat, over a wool shop
Nice, compact, comfortable and clean
Long sunny days paddling, swimming
The boat lake in the park and 'Pets' Corner'
'Charlie the chimp' a character was he
Bananas he loved and jumped with glee
Long walks, over the 'Tors' and view the sea
Lantern Hill, a haven sight for sailors
Promenade walk, beneath 'Hillsborough Hill' very high Capston and
Believed to have had criminals, rolled down its side
Chambercombe Manor, Priest Holes for a safe hide
The children loved it, warm sunny days, cream teas
We enjoyed watching, smiling faces!
Ice cream, rock pools, boat trip on the Elizabeth
Happy, sun-filled hours, when we all were young
Nanny Corbett had holiday fun and sun
Holiday Inn on Cliff Top, our son won chocolate, for the twist
Days soon sped by, sad to say goodbye
Our coach to catch, we waved a fond farewell
With memories to treasure, and saver forever!

Irene G Corbett

Above The Clouds

Excitement hangs in the air, this was the day,
    A dream to come true, in a spectacular way.
Eleven o'clock, a rush of steam, and we were off.
    A long, winding climb 3,500 feet aloft.

In unison we move, to the rhythm of the train.
    The trusty engine, pushing, pushing, taking the strain.
A collective intake of breath, as stunning views unfold;
    Rolling hills, deep valleys, all clear to behold.

Intrepid walkers wave, a solitary pony, foolhardy sheep,
    Cascading streams, grey slates, lakes dark and deep.
We pass the valley of hats, early passengers' lost head attire.
    In modern times, travelling in comfort, crawling higher and higher.

We have reached the summit, it is cold and grey.
    A different world below, with warmth from the sun's ray.
We are above the clouds, they part, but no sun.
    We still feel awe at the magic that is Snowdon.

Patricia Bannister

Wild Flowers

I can name the flowers
growing wild amongst the hedgerows.
Siberian iris
wild basil
ladies' smock
different varieties.

My grandmother taught me the names
in Latin
Iris siberica
clinopodium vulgarewe
cardamine pratensis.

We pick and press the flowers,
note the intricacy of the petals, the linear patterns of the leaves.

We press them between the pages of Genesis and
Corinthians, we press them so tightly, they can scarcely breathe.

The mattress groans and creaks as she pushes the book underneath,
the sound of metal springs, shifting and heaving like a worn out hymn.

She straightens the eiderdown, the blankets, the sheets
inspecting the surface for a single momentary crease.

'It will take a whole day and night,' she said.
You weren't allowed to look, not even a little peek.

'You will just have to wait, it takes a long time.'
She closes her eyes, 'You must learn to be patient child.'

In the early morning light, there they were
perfectly preserved petals, stalks and leaves

and in-between the sheets, you could see
the fine imprints of patterns

where the wild flowers used to be.

Rachel Burns

Reminisce

Hold on to midnight
You're here with me
And there isn't any need for fear tonight
Beautiful passion
My thoughts of you
Glow with the illuminating candlelight

Winter has put a chill in the air
But everyone says it can't last
Are they talking about the weather
Or like our time together perhaps
How can you answer for all the fears
That you haven't faced for all these years
Will you ever come around again
And will you always remember me
Distant western skies are always clear
The mountains are beautiful I hear
We can leave as soon as you say when
And we can always visit the sea

Steve V Morris

I Remember

Buses with utility seats
That were hard on the 'bott' I declare
Chemistry sets that lasted forever
Dads helped while mothers despaired
Brownie box cameras, I had one myself
Loose weighed sugar and tea
Potato picking - that was hard work
But it earned you a penny or two
'The Marx Brothers' at the pictures
A seat in the stalls was 6d
The place was always crowded with kids
At the Saturday matinee
Food and clothing rations
Two ounces of butter a week
Green Shield stamps that you saved for years
Home-made soda bread, what a treat
Hot water bottles made of delph
That kept you warm in bed
If you can remember these things and smile
You must be as old as me!

Maureen Quirey

Dream Of Childhood Days On The Farm

Alone by the fireside I'm dreaming,
In the fire quaint pictures I see,
The moon through the window is beaming,
As though she approved of my dreams.

I see the old home of my childhood,
With all the things I loved best,
Again I'm patting old Queenie dear,
Ere I leave her to her well-earned rest.

When I first rode on Queenie's back,
Oh, what a glorious thrill . . .
To canter through woodland glades
And up and down hill.

Then there was the old cow called Star,
She'd let me milk her and stand so still.
There was also Judy, Plum and Char,
Beauty and Daisy and Daffy-dill.

Again I hear dear Rover's bark . . .
As he brought the cows down the lane;
And plain I see o'er his body pass . . .
Those wheels . . . He never barked again.

How well I remember when threshing time came
And about the engine we'd crowd,
I can still feel that feeling fine . . .
When to blow the whistle were we allowed.

Oh, it seems but yesterday,
We jolly girls and boys did dance,
With ribbons around the Maypole gay,
Each with shy but happy glance.

Comes again the woodland echoes,
As we sang while gathering flowers,
I wonder where my childhood friends have gone . . .
If like me they have their dreamy hours.

At last the spell has broken,
The fire has burned quite low,
Yet . . . I'll always have my childhood dreams,
To keep my heart aglow.

I seem to hear the whispering of the trees,
Which I used to climb for play,
I seem to feel the bruises . . . when I fell,
Yet joyfully hear . . . 'No school today!'

Daisie Cecil-Clarke

Madam

You with your looks and laughing eyes
Torment me to this day;
I tried to get you for my own
But with your man you stay.

Though of ample years while you are young,
And the young men they are many,
Could it be that your one true love
Is that of the golden penny?

And many of those you he can give,
Whilst I could give but few,
And damned I'd be from your own sweet lips
To give that life to you.

Still grace you'll have from me, my dear
As know I not your reason why,
For right you have to make your choice,
And with your man to lie.

But let this poet in me speak,
With a last card yet to play,
I'll write about those laughing eyes
That just never, go away.

Alistair McLean

Bring Back . . .

Bring back the Magic Roundabout
(It'll be wrecked by lager louts)
Bring back real pop stars like Marc Bolan
Bring back winters with snow in them (maybe not!)
Bring back Lucozade with gold wrapper
You remember it tasted much better,
Bring back romance before sex,
For obvious reasons, summer of 1976
Bring back times much less frantic
Coloured by New Romantics
Bring back that long-lost friend
Swayin' in the Stretford end
Bring back landing on the moon
To a laid back spaced-out tune!
And before the planet goes for a burton
Bring back something at least a little like socialism.

Paul Reece

492

Memories Are Made Of This

My first doll that cried when I tilted her on my lap,
Her knotted long straggly hair that me and my mum washed too much,
My mum with her pink sponge rollers in her hair singing together to the latest Beatles' single,
My beautiful dresses, hair in place,
Tim's fantastic parties with red, orange and green jelly boats with sails
                                        on the top with my own name on.
Aunt Maude's divine sherry trifle and red salmon sandwiches with dainty pieces of cucumber.
Memories are made of this.

My first kiss at school in the playground drinking iced milk out of bottles.
Mr Hall the headmaster who had everyone quivering like jelly when
                                        we heard him coming up the corridor.
My first job cooking toast on the open fire.
Angela who wore her hair so high she had to have the roof down in
                                        her MGB scarf tied tight so she didn't take off.
Memories are made of this.

Going to the Locarno on Saturday night, my first pair of high heels,
My first love, the excitement, the laughter, the hugs, the being
                                                        young feeling.
Memories are made of this.

Our first house, open fires, iced up windows you couldn't see out of,
Feather mattress which was bumpy and lumpy but we loved it.
The overwhelming feeling of love I had after giving birth to our children
                                        and still have every time I see them.
Memories are made of this.

My dogs which have given so much pleasure over the years,
Long walks, dopey eyes looking with adoration,
Wagging tails as I open the door, wet cold nose nuzzling,
My beautiful grandchildren who bring so much pleasure,
Fun days making pictures, flying planes in the park,
Blowing bubbles, finding shells on the beach.

Memories are made of this

And more memories to hold soon when our next beautiful grandson is born.

Lynne Whitehouse

In Memory Of Trudy

Who says, friends are on the increase?
They're not,
Where we come from.
In fact the only ones most faithful,
Are the four-legged type
. . . What's that? I hear you say,
We're a bit of a moron.

We the 'Pet Lovers' of the nation
And within Cornwall, this pleasant land,
People who say, they're one's friend
Who welcome you, with an open hand.
They make you think you're wanted
And ask you for so much.
But! When you're unsuspected
They give you a blow in the crutch.

Why do people do it?
It's not only a shock, but a sin.
They make one's blood boil over
And you fight to the surface, from within.

Give me the love and affection
That only *pets* and *all animals* show.
And we will point out the *'B****d'*
Who's made us so red, that we glow.

Trudy! If you think, you're not missed or forgotten.
There are plenty, who still show that they care.
Not all are like the Moscato's,
Shouting loudly and polluting the air.

Les J Croft

Memories

The house where I grew up till four
                    Is not no more.
Its creepy cellars candlelit;
The harness room for stabled horse;
The pigsty and the laying hens;
The wheel-less horse-drawn bus on lawn;
The sash held shutters 'gainst the thief;
The outdoor privies still in use:
All missed the might of Hitler's war
                    Are now no more.
The next we lived in till the war
                    Is now no more,
Where babbling brook and fields of corn
And skyline trees, where rising sun
Bid me set off for city's gloom:
The school which taught me read and write
And listened to my schoolboy verse
From which I gained a grammar place:
The house where first I hugged my bride;
Where countless me's were locked inside:
                    They are no more.
My teachers' college stood the war,
                    But is no more:
The spaces sandbagged 'gainst the bomb,
The forty winks, the siren's wail,
Up all night long then out to school:
A quick goodbye then off to war.
How memories come flooding back!
                    The places are no more.
The thousand children I have taught
Their sums and writing, faith and love:
These memories are held in store
                    Now and evermore.

Owen Edwards

495

Girls' Night Out

(Or Come Dancing, 1947-style)

When we were young, I still recall,
My friend and I would go
Off to our local dance hall,
Our faces all aglow.

Dressed in our best, we whirled around
As the band began to play.
With feet that scarcely touched the ground,
We danced the night away.

Samba, quickstep, tango, rumba,
Fox-trot, waltz and palais glide.
Old time dances without number,
We calmly took them in our stride.

All the fancy steps we knew -
We practised night and day.
We really danced as one, we two
And then this boy said, 'Hey,
I think this one's an excuse me -
So may I please have this dance?
I hope that you won't refuse me,
I've waited all night for this chance.'

Then *his* friend whisked away *my* friend,
And I stood there with this youth.
You'd think this tale had a nice end,
But then came the moment of truth -
My future started looking dim,
My ego took a dent;
I couldn't dance a step with him -
I'd always danced as 'gent'!

Now 'same sex' dancers please take care -
One could end up like *me - beware!*

Anne Brown

Pennycross Dances

There were dances on Saturday nights
To a five-piece band and a vocalist;
And they saw some fantastical sights,
The five-piece band and the vocalist.

There were lads full of zest in their pressed Sunday best
Wooing girls in their marzipan dresses,
All chasing romance in the guise of a dance
By tentative, hidden caresses.
Soon the Mission Hall floor was uneven no more
But a stage on a Hollywood lot;
They all became film stars out on the town
The rest of the world they forgot.

The pair that had led were Ginger and Fred,
And behind them dancing in line:
Gable and Garbo, Cagney and Harlow,
Crawford and Andy Devine,
Farrell and Gaynor, Coleman and Rainer,
Donat and Madeline Caroll,
All playing a scene with a Berkeley routine
In a major production by Darryl.

There was Bing on the stand with the five-piece band
Now playing the Hollywood Bowl.
They puffed out their cheeks with unpractised techniques
But played it with plenty of soul.
And they blew all away till the last waltz was played
To a land where everyone sang;
Then the Pennycross skies hit them straight in the eyes,
And brought them to earth with a bang.

Now I love the music the Big Boys make,
Beethoven, Bach and Brahms,
But the music that causes my heart to break
Made those sad little tunes with their moons and their Junes
That were played as they swayed in that Picture Parade
By the five-piece band and the vocalist.

Edward Murch

A Secret Place (1940-1941)

My secret place was where the garden ended
Behind the narrow path where trellised roses grew,
They scented all the air on summer evenings
And made a private place well hidden from the view.
Tall poplar trees stretched high majestic branches,
Making the world beneath a dappled glade,
And there I acted out old stories
Or dreamed green dreams in the translucent shade.
But best of all was listening in the silence
To distance music clearly heard,
The sweet sound of my mother singing,
Better than any fledgling earthbound bird.
And while she sang the world about me
Was safe from all the sounds of war and strife,
It banished all the tumult, all the shouting,
It spoke of love and beauty, peace and life.
Though now I am no longer near that garden
And worlds of change have covered up the years,
The echoes of that time still linger
And memory brings a surge of joy not tears,
For over all I still can hear the music
And go again to where all dreams belong,
I close my eyes and in my heart with wonder,
I still can see the singer, hear the song.

D M Neu

New Year Scrambling

In our town, on New Year's Day, when I was young,
We went scrambling, undignified procedure.
A motley crew of boys and youths assembled,
Standing before each shop along the High Street,
Uttering a rousing cheer, expecting largesse from
                          benevolent proprietors,
Scuffling for the handfuls of small change they flung.
Some were niggardly, refusing to participate,
So then were roundly booed, good humoured disapproval.
No bad feeling, we moved on to neighbouring premises.

The custom is long-gone, but they were poorer, rough and ready times.
A few pence only was the sum of our reward,
Paltry to prosperous youngsters of today.
But then a penny bought a bag of chips,
And threepence opened the magic doors of the Saturday morning cinema.

Peter Hicks

498

Looking Back

A stranger passes in the street -
Was it you? I turn, yet you are lost
Amidst a bustling throng of folk
Unsympathetic to my call, stifled
Ere risen in my throat.

A snatch of conversation in my ears,
Airborne and light as any vagrant
Breath of wind across the heath,
A voice familiar to my mind - elusive,
Torn from the threads of memory - too brief.

A song, stirring a memory that lives
Among the tunes to which my footsteps
Pass through life - a tune recalling
Soft warm dusks of summer nights
And crazy stars forever falling, falling.

A footfall on the stair - could it be . . .
No. Surely it is the wind that whispers
Round the eaves, drifts crisp dry leaves
Against my door, reminding me that
Autumn for the loss of summer grieves.

Margaret Blake

Memories

My heart is filled with memories
When I walk down memory lane
Precious memories to treasure
Wondrous moments I recall
Happy thoughts without measure
Some I cherish most of all
I have known joy, sometimes sorrow
All will be revealed
In God's tomorrow
Memories are like a garden
With flowers blooming there
Proving as God does really care
He has given to me his promise
Sunshine always follows rain
So I will thank Him for each memory
One day all will be made plain

Evelyn M Lees

Memories Are Made Of This

Having pinched the school blackboard chalk,
We drew squares on pavements, where we'd walk.
Hopscotch is what it was called
Dad was always quite appalled
And used to make us wash it off,
At such behaviour he did scoff.
To spin a top was quite an art
One all ages could take part.
But glass bottle tops, the next best thing,
'Tho sometimes disaster they could bring.
As through a window they did ping.
Skipping done in ones or twos
Any age it could amuse,
So long as you kept on the move
Your circulation would improve.
Conkers, that come in the fall
Are a game for one and all.
Now marbles mostly indoors played,
In every colour, size and shade.
Swapped or sold in playing ground
With lots of cheating, I'll be bound.
Now if winter should provide
A surface on which you could slide,
The old toboggan or tin tray
Came out of hiding for the day.
For all the games kids have today
It seems their parents have to pay.
Initiative and imagination
Have gone out of circulation.
Throw out the telly, use your brain,
Don't watch the world go down the drain.

H Churchill

Christmas

At Christmas time the heart remembers,
The happiness of past Decembers,
Loving voices long since gone,
Yet their sweet echo lingers on,
Loved ones' faces seen no more,
Wishing they were at the door
To come and sing around the tree,
Like it always used to be,
But now the voices all are still,
I long to hear them and always will.
Oh Christmas, how the heart remembers
All the love of past Decembers.

Barbara O'Brien

Friends

Changing days, bussed to school,
cool in nascent uniform,
a panama against the sun
neat beret for the rain.
Heads mattered and chattered,
as bodies aproned and sleeved
bent over Bunsen and dishes.
Sewing jokes in cosy huddles,
plain and cabled wits
were pitted and knitted.
Elasticated in the gym,
balking at horses, balancing beams,
climbing ropes, sights were seen.
Lying in the grass, sports days
and house points meandered past,
while crocodiles snaked down the road
seeking water, icy cold, to swim
against the din of corrugated rain.
Acting plays and dreaming dreams,
learning lines, writing reams,
spawning artists, singers, players,
opening doors to future scenes.
Bonded in the growing years,
sharing, caring, laughter, tears,
made us what we are, friends
with memories to treasure.

Shirley Johnson

Remembering

My happiest memories are when I was young
My family together forever having fun.

We played games in the evenings
Ludo, tiddlywinks and cards
we laughed all the time
The closeness of our love and understanding
stays with me, memories are mine.

Holidays were special travelling by train
arriving with the family, sandcastles to make
swimming in the sea.
Playing with other children, lots of games on the beach
how happy, that was me.

Schooldays were special, my sports days were best
the worst being arithmetic and taking a test.

I never forget the ice cream van, the music was very loud
we all queued for our ice cream cornet
frozen lollipops, my what a crowd.
Our grocery man came with his horse-drawn cart
supplying everything from a pin to a tart.

The coalman came with his sacks full to the top
with his coal and nutty slack,
the tradesman called at our door with lemonade
and dandelion and burdock in stone jars
empty ones to take back.

I need to relive my memories even more
no one can take away my youth,
remember having ration books 'd's and 'e's
for sherbet fountains and liquorice
even with a sweet tooth.

Playing hopscotch, spinning a top and skipping
all the things we did for fun
scrumping and door knocking was naughty
my parents said never should be done.

My most vivid memories were at Christmas
we all took part in that
shopping Christmas Eve for our tree, a turkey
and my dad's six and seven eighths hat.

We cannot go back to that wonderful time
but can remember forever these memories of mine.

Joan Marrion

Memories Of Olive

Olive was a gracious lady you couldn't fail to love.
Now, she has left this earthly life to live with God above.
Her faith in Him was strong and deep. She trusted in His Word
And listened to that still, small voice which in her heart was stirred.
She faced the challenges of age in such a cheery way
That she encouraged other folks to balance work and play.

How carefully she dressed herself - so elegant she'd look!
Often, we'd pay her compliments. Pride in herself she took.
Olive had a humble spirit, rejoicing in the Lord.
Each day she offered up her thanks to the God she adored.
She was always filled with wonder at the Lord's Creation,
While her heart was greatly saddened by Man's degradation.

Kindness mingled with compassion, but there was justice too.
Olive had a sense of duty - the rights and wrongs she knew.
So many years had come and gone. Such changes she had seen.
The pattern of life was diff'rent from how it once had been.
Here, in this modern age she lived, with all her memories.
That's how we remember Olive, who had so much to give.

A lady, strong in character though fragile with her age,
Who was always full of laughter and amazingly brave.
Someone who tried to follow God, seeking Him out each day,
Putting the needs of others first, till she was called away.
How peacefully she left us all. No further words were said.
We simply said, 'Goodbye!' to her, on that hospital bed.

Jenny Stevens

Wartime Childhood (Sept 1939)

At six the world's a happy place,
No worries marred this child's face.
Until a man called Hitler tried
To conquer all who him defied.

My childhood changed from sheer delight
To being grown up overnight.
No more playing on the beach,
Those tempting waves were out of reach.

Barb wire prevented sand and sea
From touching any part of me.
We'd only just arrived by train
When we returned back home again.

The dreadful war had been declared,
Now everyone was running scared.
Our holiday was not to be,
For my mum and dad, my gran and me.

Heather D Feetham

Random Memory

I'm searching through my photos
To find a special one -
A laughing, happy picture
Of someone who has gone.
And as I turn the pages
There are others that I find
In all their radiant beauty
That brings so much to mind.

See here, four fair-haired moppets
Just sitting on a wall -
My niece and her three brothers
When they were very small.
Holidays in sailing boats
Or skiing in the snow,
Rowing on the River Thames -
The friends I got to know.

Swans serenely swimming
With families afloat.
Festivities of every kind
Deemed worthy of some note.
Christmas decorations
With presents round the tree;
My darling opens his
And here, he took one of me.

The glory of our garden
Developed by my Joe;
Glowing maze of fruit and flowers
He always got to grow.
Home, away, granddaughters play -
Now long since grown and gone -
Dolls and games and swinging high,
Painting, having fun.

Wedding days and lovely gowns,
So many happy faces!
Sea and mountains, sunsets too;
Many different places.
Tombstones, yes. Funeral flowers;
Of sad things quite a few.
Yet through it all such happiness
And glory shining through.

Random search through photo-land -
All that was way back when,
But leafing through my albums,
I live it all again.

M Vidler

My Son

I'm sitting quietly in my room, and thinking in the evening gloom,
Of all the years that we have had, together you and I my lad,
I think of how on that spring eve, we found it hard just to believe,
That Dad and I now had a boy, for whom we thanked our God, with joy.

Later, when six weeks had passed a group of young mums had been asked
To get together to discuss the future, what it held for us
And for our children, all our schemes, the hopes and rosy tinted dreams,
Mental prowess was debated, educational hopes were stated,
Occupations and degrees, many hoped for some of these.

Me, I sat and thought a while, gazed at the baby with a smile,
Said the future held no dreams of jobs, positions, power or schemes,
Just the thought expressed in word, of a prayer I hoped my God had heard,
That when my child a man became, a Christian he would still remain.

Yet now the years have passed away and middle-aged you are today,
A husband, father, grandpa too, loved by the family surrounding you,
We know that time is going by - the passing years oh how they fly,
The words I said long years ago, how a Christian son I'd be proud to know
Are fulfilled in my ears, and my thanks wend above,
I am proud of you dearest, my son and my love.

Margaret Grice

Long Afternoons

A summer's day
The smell of hay -
And two blond heads among the billowing grass -

The lazy hum
Of insects' swarm
Behind the quivering joy of a dear dog's bark -

My mother's hat
A snoozing cat
And the promise of fruit cake borne on a rattling tray -

The call to Dad
Reluctantly heard
'Cut a lettuce for supper and come up for some tea!'

Oh the lovely ways
Of long-lost days
Are never forgotten and easy to find -
For they're always around in my brimming mind
On tap to recall, to share and replay
Wherever, whenever, how often I may.

Phillipa Giles

Children At War

Do you remember little brother
The old tin tub
That hung on a hook in the yard,
Friday nights full of dread
Blackout curtains pulled tight,
Smoky lamp that scattered the dark?

You were the smallest
And shed the least dirt
So you were first in the queue
For ritual immersion
A slip'ry pink squirm
That emerged baptised, squeaky new

On to the fire
More buckets of warm
The next shouted into the bath
Much crying and wailing
'There's soap in my eye'
while I toasted bread on the hearth

When we all had been washed
And shampooed and dried
Put in freshly baked linen and parked in a line
With soft Celtic cursing
Scummy water tipped out
To nourish the garden outside

Then we'd sit down with scissors
And pieces of string
To contribute to Hitler's downfall,
The 'News Of The World'
Neatly cut six by six
To hang from a nail in the wall

Upstairs with a candle
To soften the night
Hurl into the goose feather bed
Listening to miners return from their shift
Ebon faced,
Rheumy eyes rimmed with red

In your two-bathroomed house
Little brother you live
Velvet windows and heavy oak door
Neatly pressed lawns
Lead down to the pool
But the children of war are still here.

Elisabeth Ware

506

Fairground In The Rain

The empty stalls
Where throwing balls
The coconuts
Are never won
For no one comes
To try that fun.

Behind the tents
The generators
Power the lights in vain
All because of the rain.

The rides are dripping wet
No customers to get -
And the grass all soggy
As the light gets foggy.

Fairground in the rain.

Roger F de Boer

Memories Can't Be Redeveloped!

Some houses were Victorian, trees large in avenues.
The shops were ye olde worlde, where'er I looked I loved the view.
For ten years I lived so far away, my home was out of mind.
One day I decided to return and my home I thought to find.
Where was my olde worlde towne, where the avenues and trees?
I couldn't walk where I used to walk could no longer shoot the breeze.
No rambling ivy, no twisting vines, what I knew could not be seen.
Rows of glass and bricks and plastic where my olde towne had been.
All that's left is the olde towne's name, all too modern, all so new.
All that's left are the memories which 'thank God' they can't undo.
So I took a walk down memory lane, had an apple in my hand.
The olde horse was standing by the gate and green was all the land.
I saw me walking with my pals, innocent and safe were we.
This lane cannot be scarred by Man where my memories will always be.
I would not have known the process if I had never gone away.
Ten years' absence had made it obvious and it had filled me with dismay.
All the children now are gone, 'tis the children's children now I see.
There is no one here with whom to reminisce for the new means nowt to me.
I had returned to what I knew, the change was not expected.
The town has lost its friendliness and thus I feel dejected.
Believe I've been so silly, had thought the town would wait.
I've returned to what I no longer know, I'm sad I came too late.
Shamrock has his field in memory lane, there I can pat him and rub his nose.
He's always there as he was before and from there he never goes.
Now when I go to my olde towne I go via memory lane.
That way can't be redeveloped so will the same remain.

Rosie Hues

My Memories Are Many

Many memories come from childhood days
Some good, some happy they come in so many ways
I remember the house where I was born with ivy on the wall
We gathered cowslips, Mother made cowslip wine for us all
We had paraffin lamps and candles when it was dark
A lovely feather bed, but often up with the lark
We started school when we were five walking over a mile to Beesby
Till a new school was built at Alford going by bus was easy
One moment I always remember scoring a goal
Playing in school football team, a cup final oh wrong goal
Happy moments can fade with age but some will last forever
A joyful moment in 1945 when I came home on leave
After service abroad I woke my parents banging on the door
When Father opened the door we hugged like never before
It's always sad to lose someone in your family
Three, I always remember brother Tom when he was seven
My father who died in 1957 on Boxing Day
Eight years later my mother died on Christmas Day
My memories go back nearly eighty years
So many I've forgotten, happy, funny and tears
I do not remember my first day at work
But I do remember the new bike I bought
The first car I got was a 1929 Morris Minor
I remember passing my driving test a second timer
Many cars I've had in years gone by
And I'm pleased I'm still driving but not very far
So many things I remember in the life I've had
Many are happy, funny, some disappointments and some are sad

Harry Skinn

Distant Memory

Why was she taken
When we were both so young
The mother/daughter bond was broken
Broken, before it had really begun

There she lies in a lonely grave
Memories of her are few
She was the mother that I loved
But never really knew

Even as my life moves on
And I am growing old
My need for her doesn't lessen
As the years unfold . . .

Deirdre Wise

Memories

Save up all your memories
That's what we are told
They are the things to comfort you
Later when you are old
So store them up and treasure them
And keep them in your mind
Hoping that in future days
There comfort you will find
But as the years go rolling by
And your bones begin to creak
You don't know whether it's today
Or the middle of next week
So you try so hard to recall
The times of long ago
And discover that your memory
Is the very first thing to go

Ian Russell

The Whole Tooth

Oh why didn't I listen to my mum when I was a lad
She said too many sweets and your teeth will be bad

Also to clean them after breakfast and dinner
The reasons I could not see
'After all' they would only get dirty again when I had my tea

I just could not see the reason for this tiresome chore
After all 'my teeth' were not sore

To all you young kids please don't suffer my fate
And end up with a false top and bottom plate

The moral of this story children is quite easily seen
It only takes two minutes to brush your teeth clean

To end this poem, up the whole thing I will sum
'Yes' I should have listened to my dear old mum

Robert Whyte

My Manderley

(Inspired by the first chapter of Rebecca)

Last night I dreamt
That I returned to my old home

The garden that I had once cared for
Had been allowed to let nature roam
Overgrown and wildly sown
Whichever way the wind has blown
The garden is now nature's home

I pass through the old iron garden gate
Where bold red roses congregate
Never tiring of conspiring
To climb ever higher
And yet higher still
And hanging over
The top until
They flop and drop
Their flaming faces of fire

Foxgloves grow tall and proud
All along the perimeter wall they crowd
With nature's permission allowed

The magnolia tree
Can be found just where it used to be
And on the ground its seasonal carpet
Of pink and white petals fallen, loose and free

Flowers I recognise
Appear full grown in size
Rebelliously they rise
Through cracks in the pavement patio
Where they are not meant to grow

The grapevines for making wine
Have climbed becoming entwined
And fruit in the orchard is over ripe
From time and sunshine combined

Everything is weaved together as one
Threaded and embedded and overrun
Fastened, laced up, sown and spun
Nature's work cannot easily be undone

The stone bench where I once used to sit
Is now covered and smothered
With moss, slime, lime and grit
No longer inviting me to sit down on it

While milk thistles crowns
Rule all around as they claw
The garden away from me
Up-rising under nature's lawless laws
And nettle barriers bar me
From further entering the grounds

Memories Are Made Of This

Only this time I am free
To let it be itself, to let it be
In wild abandon and disorder
From border to border
The garden is no longer mine
To control and order

My dream is but a homesick remedy
Returning me on an invite
To a wishful memory
Destined to expire
At the end of the night

For when daylight
Takes over from the dark
My visit is over
And once again
My garden is paved over . . .

To become a concrete car-park

Jane Air

The Best Days

When I was young the world was so inviting
The supersonic age would set us free,
The vibrant halls, the arcades so exciting
Were neon lit in violet just for me.
Within the cafes frothy coffee whirring
Behind the pretty teenage girls in blue,
But I preferred banana milkshakes stirring
Then slid along the melamine for you.
Our walks along the promenade are blazing,
The sea, the sand, the sun, the surf and shore
Come tripping back through eons of past gazing
And echo on to what might be once more.
To cross the world I thought would be amazing
But love was found in simple things of yore.

Fraser Hicks

The Bike

There it was . . . my lovely pink bike.
My nanna had asked me what I would like
For my birthday that year. I was going to be ten.
I didn't think twice. I knew what I wanted . . .

And there it was . . . My very own bike,
Gleaming and shiny and ready to ride.
It took lots of practice. My hands were all sticky.
I wobbled and teetered, to balance was tricky.

At last I had got it. Or so I thought . . .
It was time for an outing; To Nanna's, of course.
Off I went gingerly down the hill,
Just a bit nervous and shaky still.

My brother zoomed past. His scooter was fast.
But then he slowed down and I thought I might hit him.

How do I stop? The bike's gaining speed.
The brake wasn't something I thought I would need.
I put my foot down; I hit the ground
The bike fell on me, the wheel spinning round.

Nanna rushed over, 'You'll be alright, dear!'
But my arm was broken, all bent out of gear
My outing was just to a hospital bed,
Where they plastered my arm . . . and that was the end

Of my bike riding exploits.
Oh what a shame!
That lovely pink bike, all shiny and bright
Was never ridden by me again.

And fifty years on I have to agree
That I don't think bikes were meant for me!

Christine Polson

Childhood Memories Of The Thirties

At school our tables we learnt by heart,
We stood when Teacher came to start;
'Twas 'Sir' or 'Miss' whenever you spoke,
The stove in classroom you never did poke.

When visitors came we knew what to do,
We did not talk until spoken to;
Mum and Dad were proud of both of us,
They cared and loved but made no fuss.

The village policeman walked his round,
The fox was chased by a pack of hounds;
If you picked an apple and you got caught,
The policeman came and your parents sought.

We sat at the table for all of our meals,
Mum always made sure that we had a good deal;
We ate pheasants and rabbits and rook pie as well,
Our puddings were superb but tapioca was hell.

The Rector made a visit to each and every house,
So pleasant and so friendly, quiet as a mouse;
Each night before bed we knelt down to pray,
We thanked God for his help throughout the whole day.

We helped in the fields with harvest and hay,
We cut thistles and hoed mangolds for a long tiring day;
We learnt to catch horses out in the field,
We did harrowing and ploughing to increase the yield.

We loved our dear childhood, it was so full of praise,
We had encouragement and guidance, our standards did raise;
We pray for all children of primary age today,
Let's hope they get good memories to help them on their way.

John Paulley

Casualty Of War

'He's a Polish soldier,' she explained,
crossing the road and dragging me away.
But I was fascinated. I couldn't understand
what he was doing there, so far from home,
far from his wife and kids, his mum and dad,
running amok and dancing naked
on Burntisland High Street,
our comfortable, cosy little town
where nothing ever happened.

He stood, head down, a raging bull,
pawing the tarmac and festooned in barbs,
shot through like St Sebastian,
skewered, cornered, mad with drink,
baying defiance at the moon
after the pubs had tossed him out.
Stood, cursing us in Polish
for the war, his absent wife,
and the wind snell off the Forth.

Then he peeled off his uniform,
hurled it behind the Bank of Scotland's
sober ironwork ornamental grill,
peeled off his sad grey underpants and socks
and, solo, mimed a disconsolate mazurka,
an *a cappella* dance of death,
before the gathering crowd.
So far from Wroclaw,
sixty-three years ago, or more.

I wondered then,
have often wondered since,
if Willie Gregor, our local bobby,
who steamed up,
wearing his helmet and his cycle clips,
was able to get him back into his clothes,
help him to get back home again,

back to his mum and dad, his wife and kids,
huddled together, far away, in distant Wroclaw,
beneath the softly falling snow,
beneath the snowflakes falling steadily,
all over Poland.

Norman Bissett

514

True Love

We met when we were young
My love and I
There in a country church
'Neath August sky
He, tall, dark and handsome
Eyes so brown
Offered a lift to dance
In local town

We, innocents, engaged
The five stone ring
A wedding planned for June
The bells would ring
To settle on a farm
Two babies born
Spring into harvests went
Reaping the corn

Seasons sped by swiftly
The years just flew
Schooldays, exams, careers
Our children grew
From Santa Claus to teens
Our middle years
When some grey hairs appeared
We cried no tears

Wonderful our marriage
With no regret
Love through all the days
No cause to fret
Through worries, joy we went
United . . . on . . .
Keeping our marriage vows
Dedication

So to give, to cherish
My love and I
Forty-four years have gone
Our hopes held high
The steps along life's path
Jesus our guide
Future days, older ways
In Him abide

Margaret Carter

(Un) Familiar Haunts

The house I knew was very small
In the centre of a row
'Twas hard to tell which one was ours
Though the letterbox was low.
The front door opened in a room
Which had a couch and chairs
The next room - where we used to eat
Had a door that housed the stairs.
Three small rooms were up above
The smallest for our brother
The next one was for Mum and Dad
We five girls had the other.
It's sixty years since we lived there
I doubt if it's still standing
I guess the road has changed so much
I won't know where I'm landing.
I take the plunge and walk along
This end seems bright and new
It's nothing like it used to be
A wholly different view.
This looks a bit more like it was
At least the pub's still here
And next there are those heavy gates
That means the farm is near.
I thought of all those nights we spent
Crouched on our window seat
To watch those drunks all leave the pub
And stagger down the street.
The farmer was the worst of all
Much drunker than the rest
He'd dance around in pouring rain
His 'hijinks' were the best.
Around the back should be our school
It's now a block of flats
Further down our sweet shop stood
That's now chock full of hats.
While down the end are lots of homes
All crammed in that small space
When we were young 'twas open land
Where we could always race.
It's sad that things must change so much
And youth gets lost in mist
Yet lovely memories still remain
Like that first lover's kiss.

Elsie J Sharman

Balti Gosht

At half-past five every Friday
I telephone the Balti Ranch Takeaway
I order kebabs and curry
from the friendly young man there
a chicken karhai for me and balti gosht for you.
We both drink wine
and watch a television detective
and I feel deeply content
observing this domestic tradition
bonding us together
and strengthening the ties between us.

And so tonight I have ordered
kebabs and curry from the friendly young man
a chicken karhai for me and balti gosht for you.
I am drinking wine
and watching a television detective.
But you are half a world away
with another friend
and your meal lies uneaten in the fridge.
Even so, I observe our tradition
bonding us together
strengthening the ties between us
in a melancholic solitude.

Nicholas Howard

Come On Grandma

(Dedicated to my own Grandma, Albert's sister Carrie)

'Come on Grandma, you're never too old'
Albert said as he whisked her around and she'd scold,
'Ooh, Albert, you bad boy! Sid, put that thing down!'
She'd add to his brother with a humorous frown.

'I'm still in me pinny, me hair's all awry,
Me teeth ain't in' she'd laugh till she'd cry
'And if Sid takes that picture, I'll box his ears'
Sid took it and ran! She'd fulfil his fears!

Their ma watched on in her best party titfer,
Not knowing that shortly they'd all sorely miss her,
She died in the Bethnal Green crush with her youngest,
He lived but suffered the grief the longest.

She'd often said, 'If anyone's to die in this horrid war,
I'll go, not Carrie, the boys or me ma.'
She got her wish, that no one denied,
But those of us left, how we cried and cried

So the picture of her with her mum and a son
The memory of the day, the laughter lives on
Reminds us of the need to all take a chance
Whatever life brings, it's important to *dance!*

Anna Reid

Waltz Of Valeta

Tinkling those sounds of a tambourine
Its music was played in school,
Girls all gathered to form a ring
As they danced within the hall.
The teacher narrated of coming from Spain
Those elegant steps were in triple time.
Reversing back then begin again
With heel and toe let arms entwine.
Trip or tripping round and round
The tuneful ragtime twirling about,
Wearing silk dresses sheer to the ground
Waltz of Valeta charmed the night out.
Thus swayed the music of delirious time
Violins sighed when lights were turned low.
Chapel bells chanted as in a rhyme
And the town hall clock chimed below.

Tom Cabin

Things From The Past

Friends and family meeting together,
Do you remember this, do you remember that?
I loved The Beatles, do you remember
Lady Madonna? I still love it.
I even like Freddie and the Dreamers
He made me laugh so much,
Did you have a Rubik cube?
I could never do them, they were impossible.
Hula hoops and skipping ropes, keeping kids so fit.
Kids now watching videos, playing on Game Boys,
Kids not so fit.
Things have changed for the better, for the worse,
With minds on free flow we can choose what to remember,
What to forget.
Bring back our memories with rose-tinted specs
And let's just see the good memories.

Barbara Stoneham

Fifty Years Ago

I spent some time in New York City,
Fifty years ago.
The rum was cheap and the girls were pretty,
Fifty years ago.
The usual things were in the shops,
In a town where living never stops.
The place was full of Irish cops,
Fifty years ago.

I wandered down Fifth Avenue,
Fifty years ago,
Called in a bar and had a few,
Fifty years ago.
Manhattan's 'scrapers stood so tall,
Long Island's fairgrounds thrilled us all.
The Bronx was heading for its fall,
Fifty years ago.

Old New York City had a spark,
Fifty years ago.
I had a girl in Central Park,
Lying in the snow.
Her hair was long and made of gold
We kissed and cursed, we tossed and rolled . . .
We didn't seem to mind the cold,
Fifty years ago.

We strolled down Broadway in a dream,
Fifty years ago.
Her blue eyes had a certain gleam
They said . . . Well, y'know!
Life of course is never fair
Duty called and brought despair
And I had to leave her there,
Fifty years ago.

Bob Shelcot

Summertime In England

She flits where an angel sits
In the languished meadow fields of England
On a bright ebullient summer's day
The heat hangs heavy
Like a burnt offering to the sun gods
As the gentle rain falls
The rainbow eliminated despair
At the mellow yellow fields of grain
Crops and oast houses mix and match
Nature's bounty of the land
The tiller of the soil is no long present
His comrades lost to great wars
The horse plough no longer to be seen
Replicated by mechanisation and dislocation
Of England's sacred fields
As the sun sets on a warm day
One prays that the soil will yield its lay

Finnan Boyle

Past Memories

Past memories are precious,
They live within our heart,
We look back on those long past years,
Where memories all start.
Our fun when we were children,
And how we felt secure,
In the love and care of Mum and Dad,
That made us strong and sure.
Then when we grew up once more,
The memories all changed,
A young woman or a man stood up,
Our lives we then arranged.
We met the partner of our dreams,
A whole world lay ahead,
We could not live without them,
So then we both were wed.
Children then just came along,
And things were different too,
But they brought their blessings,
And we cared and loved them true.
So now they are all grown up,
And grandparents we became,
What a wonderful, precious gift,
We started all over again.
Now when we look back in life,
And all the love we gave,
We received it all right back,
Now we have memories to save.
So when we go out from this world,
And return once more to Heaven,
God will let us keep our memories,
For memories are God-given.

Janette Campbell

522

Memories Are

Memories can be forgotten about,
They can be far away and out of reach
Or be closer than our hands and feet.
They can last a long time or just for a short while.
They can be old or new, be about everything or
Just about you.
They strike without any asking, coming out of the blue.
Sometimes they just won't leave you, no matter what
You tell them to do.
Memories are made of happiness, sadness, fear and strength.
They will paralyse, inspire stagnate into
Your mind heart and soul.
Often destroying, enhancing, dictating to you
Your past, present and your future abodes.
Memories are just memories.
They are gathered up in many lifetimes, stored in the soul.
Being the greatest healers, comforters and spiritual growth
Teachers ever been told.

Jenifer Ellen Austin

Another Year

Another year has gone by
Where does the time go?
It feels like we've been together forever
I can hardly remember what my life was like without you
You are my best friend as well as my husband
Making me laugh when I want to cry
Tucking me in bed when I'm sick
Holding me at night as I sleep
Sharing my dreams and helping make them come true
But most of all you are there for me every day, in every way
You support me, love and protect me
And all I wish for today is to spend it with you
Looking forward to . . .
                                        . . . another year.

Jacqui Watson

Memories Of Old Jack Tar

The lapping waves around his feet
Tells turning of the tide
But still the old man keeps his seat
And scans the ocean wide

His seat, a rock well washed by foam
A necklace of seaweed draping
The endless sea he once did roam
All life on land escaping

Oceans and ships were all he sought
No wish for family or wife
Of a landlubber's life he knew just naught
The sea and a ship his whole life

Poor Jack on his rock he sits every day
Wishing he could climb one more mast,
Yearning, he watches each ship in the bay
Recalling the years that have passed

He wistfully gazes at the waves as they foam
And knows when he no longer will be
His restless ghost forever will roam
On the deck of a ship out at sea.

Olive Woodhouse

Theme Tune

Visions, swathed in time,
Swish back the curtains of my mind,
And memories take centre stage.
Then, as one holds a dream,
I live the scene:

My image, or a stranger?
I feel pain, sharp, intense.
Reaching out for what used to be,
Longing for what cannot;
Time dances by, inexorably.

The tableau changes. Light. Animation.
Laughter from the shadows.
Bouquets and heartaches,
Entwined forever.

Unalterable moments,
People and places,
To remember with love,
At the end of the play.

June Holmes

Remnants Of A Village

The old village used to smell
Of fresh fish and sea lettuce,
Of sea water stored in barrels
Where fish was cleaned and washed.

The fishing boats are all departing
But not on fishing trips
To catch *lampuki,*
But on harbour cruises for tourists.

Ports are no longer made
From ageing pebbles where crabs
Used to build their den,
And little prawns tickled
Children's toes as they cooled
Their feet in the warm summer sea.
It's all luxurious yachts,
Reserved for only those who could afford
Flooded by artificial lights.

When the wind angers
The rest of the elements,
It's no longer like it's blowing kisses,
Rather it's like it hisses
'The past has passed,
No place for the past . . .'

When the first rain falls
The poppies and clover
Will be gone from the fields
Where new apartments stand,
More trophies for the millionaires:
The red and green is only in traffic lights.

Raymond Fenech

Last Sky Of Summer

The days begin to shorten
As summer makes way for autumn
Departure tinges the air
Her exit is a sad affair
Just as the regrets we all share
But before she goes she waves
Her colours for one last show

In the skies the swallows weave
Travelling light they turn tail and leave
The birds begin to beckon
As the winds start to threaten
They move among the reeds and rushes
They call in whispers and hushes
Upon the wings of dragonflies

Last sky of summer above my head
The blue of the heavens above
Now wears a paler wash and shade
As if some vision wrapped in veils
Of wispy strands of cloud across the face
Out across the waters from the shore
The watery hazy sun lays a rippled path

Here in the fields of harvest
Lying in the shadow of the hills
That stand shrouded with the mists
There's a chill cutting into the heat
Of those bending to reap and gather
To leave the soil to the flames and plough
Beneath the last sky of summer.

Richard Gould

My Sussex Retreat

A tree-lined street, with white-wood fronted houses
An old church to pray in and garden to sit in,
Overlooking the valley
Gleaming in splayed sunshine
Pleasing to the eye and bringing peace to the mind.

The Bear Inn with motel, boasting four-poster beds and scenic view
With antiques and old tea shop
For cream teas and staff to please

Not far from the coast, it can boast
Of its famous inhabitant from the past
Rudyard Kipling no less
And in his house, one can bless
Its history and air of mystery
Open to all who care to call

My Sussex retreat, I'll never tire
It has everything I require
To sit and meditate is my aim
And this small village I reclaim
To fill up my senses now and then
To ease my tension
And other cares I'll not mention.

Wendy Andrews Nevard

Thanks For The Memories

Memories are different thoughts,
Depending on the person's arts,
Some are colourful and bright,
Others, grey or darkest night,
Happy, sad or just don't care,
Some are secrets, some we share.
Yet they all have the same effect,
Stirring up thoughts we all neglect,
A warmest glow, a tender touch,
Memories that mean so much,
Tear-felt moments lost in time,
Surfacing into this rhyme,
As I lay my pen aside,
I've laughed, I've loved, I've lost, I've cried.

Kathleen Townsley

Memories

As you get older and time slips away,
you're left with your memories at the end of the day.
Sometimes it is like a faulty video recorder,
the playback is all misty and not in the right order.

I remember my maternal grandfather, he was a big man,
gentle as a lamb with a baby budgie in his hand.
With his corduroy trousers and his brown overall,
he seemed like a giant to me, when I was small.
He was a coal miner, as tough as need be,
also very kind-hearted and loving as could be.

Then there's my father, a handsome young man,
with his rugged smile and cheeky ways, a real lady's man.
When he was young, he was jack of all trades,
but he was only at his best in the company of maids.
A bit of a joker with his mates at the club
he met them there more often than on the job.

I close my eyes and see my mother standing there
always at the kitchen table, fresh baking everywhere.
Ever smiling, no sign at all of the strain
whatever happened she never showed the pain
A lot of things happened to her in her life
still she kept smiling, a brilliant mother and wife.

Your memory can be a very strange thing
all it takes is a piece of music or maybe some other thing
to set the playback in motion to replay the past
most memories are pleasant, the nasty ones don't last.

David I Muncaster

The Meadow

The meadows where we used to play
and while away the hours.
With poppies in the unmown grass
amongst so many flowers.

The cowslips in the hedgerow,
wild orchids dewy spot.
With vetch and bobtail grasses
it was our secret plot.

We loved those fragrant flowers
their heady summer scent.
This wild and natural beauty
for our childhood it was lent.

Blue cornflowers and pale scabious
and yellow buttercups.
The harebell, lords and ladies
all fascinated us.

Now land is left untended
and meadows thrive anew.
Now dandelions and coltsfoot
they all come into view.

So time can surely find a way
to even out the score.
As dormant plants and seeds return
all fresh from nature's store.

Alan J Vincent

Beautiful Thoughts

When one becomes very old
You are apt to look back to the past
And the things that last.
One's children when they were small and sweet
And now grown up and standing on their own feet.
Now it's your grandchildren who have grown up
And are bringing much joy and interesting things
One feels like singing
Loving them with all your heart
Each in their own way.
In your eyes they can do no wrong
Although it may not be so easy for their mum and dad
Dealing with them every day.
But life's hard and it's not always easy growing up
Sometimes lack of confidence holds them back
Until they learn more about the things that they lack.
So we must never forget
They need all the encouragement they can get.
Now I'm nearly 93,
I try to imagine how it must be these days
With all the technology and complexity of life.
How is it growing up?
Not very easy I would say.
So we must be with them all the way!
Bless all our dear children near and far
May God's good guidance see them through life
Free from too much trouble and strife!

J W Wight

My Grandad

My grandad is a storyteller.
He is a hot water bottle on a cold winter's night.

My grandad never lets me down.
He is a cup of hot cocoa in front of the fire.

My grandad is a rabbit searching for a carrot.
He is a knight in shining armour.

My grandad is a map through a dark and dangerous wood.
He is the sun looking down on everyone.

Tom Wells (12)

Contentment Villanelle

Silence is golden, helps one to concentrate
our minds making melody singing
for joy my heart doth contemplate

The dawn chorus interrupts to confiscate
precious moments, in rhapsody singing
silence is golden, helps one to concentrate

Memories are made of this to consummate
befits the family cycle ensuing enduring
for joy my heart doth contemplate

Some are given sign language to gesticulate
also love, peace, trials, tribulations, long suffering
silence is golden, helps one to concentrate

In our autumnal years, time to dedicate
taking stock, improving, forgiving, ensuring
for joy my heart doth contemplate

The perfume of *Christ* may permeate
given the chance He may beholding
silence is golden helps one to concentrate
for joy my heart doth contemplate.

Jennifer Margaret Hudson

The Magic Of Nature

From the cool spring to hot summer
Spins the green clad mummer
Then autumn rains to frosty winter
Comes the icy sprinter
Green lush grass growing
Fields that need sowing
To nature all knowing
A dream of Jack in the Green
Making a pastoral scene
Trees' arm-like branches
And green leaf avalanches
The earth of fertility
Leads the animals of all abilities
A world of nature explodes
Echoing over ear lobes
Vibrancy with some slowness
Mingle with order and aloneness.

Tim Sharman

A Young Boy's First Holiday

He had never been on holiday before.
Oh! To have a look at the shore.
What a change from his front door.
His parents could not send him before.

The journey was exciting.
Seaside dreams were inviting.
Many things to do and games to play.
Will be packed into every day.

Will the weather be sunny?
Has he been given enough money?
Will the sea really be blue?
Are stories of holidays true?

He arrives but where to start,
Quick let's have a go on that go-kart.
That was wonderful, let's do it again.
And look there's a toy train.

Come on to the house that's haunted.
With a ghost to be taunted.
There are sandcastles to make
And pictures to take.

Now he has got a kite to fly.
Well, he will try.
It goes high into the air.
Shall he release it for a dare?

He has been to sea in a boat.
He swam and found he could float
Oh why could he not come before?
Can they afford to send him next year?

J V Ford

Shall We Call Him Frederic?

They often meet when walking the dog
She (that is Beth) has a cropped poodle bitch
He (that is George) strolls a randy old mix up
And as the dogs circle to sniff
They pause, smile, then pass on
Beth often thinks of George
As pinned silent neath her grunting husband
(Shall we call him Frederic?)

Thomas Cobley

Memories

Even when someone's gone,
Your memories linger on,
When your mum's no longer there
You still can smell her hair!
You remember how she looked,
Of the lovely things she cooked.

I remember my dad, a good pal.
My childhood days
Never a minute to spare.
My dad always cutting hair,
A barber's shop we had
Those days were both sad and glad.

War time when I was born.
One thing you don't forget
Sitting on a cellar step.
Air raids, as a child
Wondering if you would stay alive.

But happy times as well
Picnics at Matlock Bath
With my brother, sister, mum and dad.
Our trips to Malery Park
Motorbikes, the smell, the excitement of the day.

Things you never forget
Fishing trips with my dad
He sold all this in our shop:
Maggots, nets, even a license
You could get.

My dancing days I loved the best.
They stood out from the rest.
I just loved to dance.
I wasn't the best
But I never thought of it as a test.

When my two sons were born,
Nothing could compare!
To bath and put them to bed,
The smell of talc, to see them rest,
It really is the best.

Now my grandchildren are here,
Four girls, a set of twins and two boys.
They give me so much joy!
We go to Notts, where I live.
They love those trips.

I just hope I see them grow.
Then my life will have been worthwhile
And I can say, goodbye with a smile.

Pamela Hawksley Blackburn

My Father

(This poem is in memory of my dear father,
the late Louis Freeman, who died on 3rd March 1968)

My father was a good man,
He had a heart of gold,
He was always helping people,
The young and the old,
He called it 'shepherd enterprise',
Be a good shepherd every day,
Help the poor and needy,
And those who have gone astray.
My father enjoyed poetry and politics,
He wrote to government ministers and his MP,
In the hope they would take his advice,
For people's plight to ease.
Memories of my father,
Are always on my mind,
So when people ask me for help,
I know I will be kind.

Stephen L Freeman

Past Moments

Our lives revolve around memories
We hold them close to our hearts
Happiness and sadness are part of them
Remembering the joy that they bring

Fond memories when I was a child
Playing in the woods with my friend
The steps that led to a secret place
Temptation was just too much

We climbed the steps and opened the gates
Beautiful gardens, lawns so luscious and green
Tables lay out across the lawns
With wonderful things to eat

Unaware of our presence
The ladies laughed and chatted
Enjoying each other's company
In beautiful dresses never seen before

But for two little girls who would never forget
The memories of yesteryear
Of the days they spent in their secret garden
Memories they would never forget.

Doreen Cawley

Lover Come Back

Oh were it that I might recall those memories sublime?
That I could lay aside these mental ravages of time!
Once more - to see rapport with all those ghosts of yesteryear,
To stroll again down Lovers' Lane with those I held so dear.
But age has shown no mercy, as I slump here by the fire.
And although mind can't envisage, yet the heart still holds desire.
And maybe one golden day in time, when hold on life is slack.
An angel will my brow caress, 'twill all come flooding back?

Anthony William Roberts

Memories

What are memories? I was once asked.
They are precious moments from the past
They can be good, or can be bad
Make you happy, or make you sad

They are a gift to you and me,
Ours to choose what we see
A chronicle of past life spread out
For your eyes only, there is no doubt

They are filed away for another day
And can be recalled without delay
Summoned up at any time
All labelled and waiting in line

I remember when my sister bit our dog
That time we got stranded in the fog
The dance lessons I took in the village hall
The window smashed by kicking the ball

The holidays we had by the sea
Aunts and uncles, one big family
Playtimes in school, not a pretty sight
Always someone looking for a fight

Thinking of excuses to tell my dad
Why my school report was so bad
My first interview left me feeling sick
Was I really that stupid and thick?

My first date I was nervous and shy
He kissed me and I started to cry
He took me home, Dad opened the door
Needless to say, I didn't see him anymore

I've so many memories stored in my head
I pick and choose them when I go to bed
Some make me smile and gently sigh
Some are so poignant they make me cry.

Anne Jenkins

Broughton-In-Furness

When we were young we often went to Broughton,
That place, for me was full of many joys,
We lodged with Stephen Fry, the village postman,
His buxom wife and their two bright-eyed boys.

There was Braid Street to explore the very first day,
And then the square with all its lovely trees.
I recall the village shop, so aromatic,
Aladdin's cave of coffee, spice and teas.

I remember with nostalgia those bright mornings
When we walked with Stephen on his postman's round
To Althurstside, and other lonely farmsteads;
The mushrooms that we picked on dewy ground.

And sometimes at high noonday we would wander
To find a place of quiet green retreat
And see the timely warning, 'Watch for ye know not',
The village church so compact and so neat.

I recall the very warmest of Whit Mondays,
When old folk sought to find some place of shade,
And the Crier with his 'Oyez, Oyez, Oyez'
And the children's annual fancy dress parade.

Once I saw Lord Cross so well accoutred, finely mounted,
As he cantered down a lane till gone from sight,
And later, as my adventures I recounted,
It seemed so very English and so right.

There were warm September days just made for nutting,
How soon the pockets bulge and then, to fill,
In a narrow lane, with hazel branches jutting,
Where a man wove oval baskets, called a swill.

There were evenings spent in happy conversation,
A congenial ring around the kitchen fire,
With tales of far off war and men in trenches,
And my excitement mounting ever higher.

Stephen never said why one coat sleeve was empty,
Or why it hung down useless by his side,
But he spoke of his companions with great humour
Recalling all their exploits with some pride.

And though no word by him was ever spoken
Of sanctimonious reasons for that war,
If he loved Broughton in full measure, just like I did
He knew that it was well worth fighting for.

Stella Shepherd

Timely Thoughts

Recollections may be precious, like gems in a vault.
Tragic events which are seldom forgot.
Romantic occasions leading to long term joy.
An immediate attachment to an unexpected toy.

Like movements of tide, mem'ries come and go.
Bringing floods of tears, or laughter which flows
And ripples through time, resembling pebbles on a beach.
Inward t'ward land, then retreating beyond reach.

Mixed reminiscences, degrees of thought.
Meaningful to individuals who've experienced a lot.
Satisfaction, strains, contentment in senior years.
Considering past days, we're fortunate to be here.

'Tis a privilege to recall the Creator's role
In forming the earth. A mystical 'bell'.
Man's chief end is to glorify God.
Have we remembered to explore and obey His word?

Annie R Harcus

Port-au-Prince By Moonlight

Bright lights bathing the pavement,
Wiping out the starkness of dusk.
Soft music coming from everywhere,
Enchanting those milling around.
A one-arm man directing a martial group,
Delighting passers-by with its harmonious blend.

Balmy Sundays find lovers stretched on the grass,
Listening to the sounds of the waves.
Nothing pierces the absorption of first love,
Enchantment brought about by contemplation.
Looking into eyes that reflect pure adoration,
Oh that we could love God as much!

The morning sunlight reflects upon a blue sea,
That has nothing of the nocturnal view.
Something magical has gone away,
As if lost in the bustle of the daytime.
But once we return to the wharf at night-time,
Port-au-Prince welcomes us in all its glory.

Gladys Bruno

No More Rainbows On The Flowers

Long, long ago - so long ago! -
    When I was a schoolgirl small,
I loved to play in the garden
    With our dear dog, Jack, and a ball.

When Jack was tired, he'd lie and rest,
    Flopped out on the grass so cool,
And I would smell the flowers
    That grew around the pool.

After a while I'd hop and skip
    The flowery paths along,
And Jack would wag his tail to hear
    Me sing a childish song.

But loveliest, most wondrous
    Of all things beauteous there
Were the drifts of rainbow butterflies
    Which filled the sunny air.

Thousands - yea, ten thousand,
    Or so it seemed to me,
Which brushed against my face and arms,
    And made me laugh with glee.

Children today can never know
    The joy which once was ours,
For modern chemicals have killed
    The rainbows on the flowers.

Sometimes in dreams I still can feel
    Their satin wings caressing
My face, and hear our dear Jack's bark . . .
    Kind memories are indeed a blessing.

Marjorie Piggins

Time Was Short, Life Was Harsh

Dark winter, shivering days
Saturday night
Farm chores done
Friends and family gather
Around the glowing paraffin lamps

Sipping last October's liquid harvest,
Its fresh bouquet merging with
The scent of the wood fire
The aroma of pancakes or waffles,
Some play cards
Others play pallets on a wooden board

An accordion squeezes jolly notes
They all sing
Old, young, they all sing
Local lore
Funny rhymes
Bawdy songs
Time's so short, life's so harsh

Christenings, weddings
They're causes for celebration
Funerals also
To die's part of life
No more no less
Urban hypocrisy has not yet encroached on rural life
There's no pretence
Time's too short, life's too harsh

They enjoy what they have
Food on the table, simple but wholesome
Wine to share with friends
Food, good food is the credo
That unites folks
Though insulting nutriments
Are creeping slyly
Looks and names more important than taste

A home is to live in
Not an investment
Greed and envy
The two ugly siblings
Are slowly becoming icons
People believe in

But for real folks
Work's hard, time's short
But life's satisfying

J-C Chandenier

Confirmation - My Life In God's Hands

Great God, great King
maker of Mankind
how kind You are
merciful and wise

We love Your look
although we cannot
see You. We see
You everywhere.

Your presence we feel
so tender, strong and full
of care

You surround us, hold us
embrace us and care
for our every being is held
in Your tender care.

You speak to us
guide, provide our
every need
want for
nothing with
You as our
guide

You uplift us, sustain us
guide and guard us
support us, encourage us
love us and please us.

Giver of life, true Father and friend
we owe You everything
as You made us, created
and care for us as Father
and friend.

What a God, the maker of
all, creator of people
nations, the
universe and all.

You gave us life
You gave us the Earth
You gave Your Son
once to forgive us
our sins.

You, our ruler though
King of all Kings
Maker, Creator
defender, miracle maker
and friend.

What a friend we
have in You
to share our
troubles
leave us
without a care.

You take our troubles and
sort them out
and leave us more time to
praise and rejoice

You know what we are
going to do before we
do it and have everything
mapped out for us and
every time and situation
well in hand.

What a king, dressed
in majesty, diamond
ring You wear
rich and royal
You truly are
what a
sight for
us to stop and stare.

I give You my life
my time, my home
they all belong to
You anyway and me

Lord when will you come

Your ever loving daughter
Daniela.

Daniela Morbin

Lost

The cat that came in from the cold -
it was thinner but it was not old.

The cry at the door, the scratching
paw, meant she was home. But at
first no one came, then a step,
then a smile from a familiar face
as the door flew open and up
jumped Mandy into loving arms
and she cried no more.

Robert Wynn-Davies

Spring Flowers Around The Lake – 1943

When first I was dumped on the magic carpet
I threw out my arms
with a yell of delight:
I stretched,
leaped, danced, somersaulted
and looked at the world still once again.
This was my day!
I grabbed a fistful of green,
tore it gleefully into snippets,
crushed petals and stalks between hot palms,
sniffed, licked, nibbled,
lapped up, spat out
the tight, stringy pellet that had been flower -
All in a tumble
of young spring.

Then I grew quite still.

Living life.
It was too much
and I so small -
wading through waves of anemones,
clustered primrose galaxies,
yellow, pink, white and mauve.
I floundered in a sea
of brilliant,
carolling coronets
which lured in mermaid fashion.
Fragrance caressed my toes,
hugged the crocodile skin of grandfather tree-boles,
spread a crown of glory,
an immense Hawaiian necklace,
around the lake
and its darkness.

Françoise de Pierpont

Memories

I had a lovely mum and dad
Who are now at peace in Heaven,
So hard they worked from morn till night
To wash, feed and clean us all
I was one of the seven.

We were taught to help each other.
To get ready for school each day.
Buttoning our gaiters up with a hook
And carrying our satchels with our books.

We had a lovely policeman who crossed us over the road.
We were so happy with him, we had such fun,
Especially when he climbed the tree
And picked us all a plum.

We had to hurry to reach the school gate.
The bell would be ringing for us not to be late.
We marched into our classroom to attention
We would stand and say good morning to our lovely teacher.
Her name was Miss Sands.
She sang with us a lovely song
Before we went home for dinner which went like this.

'Thank you for the world so sweet
Thank you for the food we eat
Thank you for the birds that sing
Thank you God for everything'.

Winifred Brasenell

My Rabbit Hole

Slipping, sliding out of control.
Falling into the bowels of the earth.
Tripping over the fragments of my life.
Incredible feelings of deep despair.
Alone in an unknown place.
As walls close in upon me.
Heaviness covers me as a cloak.
I am consumed with my suffering.
Hear my still small voice cry out.
Show me a flicker of hope.
Lead me through the gloom.
Out into the light of day.

Deborah Grimwade

My Memories Are Made Of This

We were happy, young and wed
We were overseas from home
Never knowing - no one said
We were destined now to roam

No sweet babies would I hold
When cancer struck inside
But I survived and we went on
With my man still at my side

I tried hard to fill the void
Giving all I had to give
But I saw the hurt he felt
I hid my own and learnt to live

Each smile he gave - I kept
In my secret hiding place
I would watch him as he slept
And so loved his sleeping face

I knew that he would go
Yet I held his hand so tight
So that when he'd gone, I'd know
He'd still be there in my heart

Then one day he met the girl
With 3 darling little 'men'
I knew then that he would go
The boys were 4 and 6 and 10!

So I didn't fight divorce
We retained what we survived.
He remarried - had the boys
Then 2 darling girls arrived

I became Godmother to
Those lovely little girls
How I loved them as they grew
With their smiles and tossing curls

The years passed by so slow
But my love has never waned
Each year I feel it grow
Never failing - always gained

Then one day I heard the news
The lovely lady she had gone
Leaving him a broken heart
Plus the children - him alone

So we were happy but not wed
Many places I've called home
I still love him - more instead
Even though we're both alone

Memories Are Made Of This

No longer young, we still survive
Constant contact warms me still
I still love him while I live
And beyond - I always will

I am filled with memories
I would do the same again
He still has got the keys
To a heart that loves in vain

So my memories are made of this
Nothing's perfect in this world
But our memories are bliss
When you've lived and loved as told.

Moby Bowery

First Day At School

There, how do I look Mum?
In my uniform all new.
I've waited for this day to come
Of the children I know a few.

Into the playground we go,
Children running, kicking a ball,
I am worried, don't want it to show,
Oh look at Fred, he's had a fall.

The bell rings, the playground stops still,
I look around, don't know if I want to go.
All of a sudden my tummy feels ill,
We all line up now, six lines in a row.

In we go, I feel a little safer
On our hooks we hang our coats,
The shelf above we put lunch boxes for later,
Around the classroom chatter floats.

I sit on the rug,
The register is called, silence falls,
My fingers twist my hair, now I have a lovely lug,
Then off to play with bats and balls.

The day has come to an end,
My tummy settled down in time,
Today I made one new friend,
My first day at school was fine.

C Paxton

Home Of My Childhood

Our village was known as the 'British', it lay at the top of the hill
And though houses have crumbled and people have gone
The memories linger there still.

The village was built for the miners, their cottages stood row on row
And although they were poor, you could eat off their floors
And the men worked the pits, down below.

They were really great people, those miners.
Kind-hearted, warm, gentle and 'black'
Trouble shared, trouble halved they would tell you.
They'd give you the shirt off their backs.

Aye, though oft' times they were broke, they enjoyed a good joke.
The women all washed on a Monday.
Every cot' had a piano, be it tall, short or narrow
And they went twice to chapel on Sundays.

There was Muriel, Christine and Morfydd,
'Our Joan, Ivor, Billy and Ben.
There is Kate whom I love,
And many more now above'.
And Lillian and Gwynth and Ben.

There was old Mrs Mags and her daughter,
They delivered fresh milk to your door.
'A pint or a quart?' they would ask with a smile
And they'd be there come rain, hail or snow.

I could name many others who lived there.
They laughed, cried, laboured and loved.
In a death they all mourned, in birth they rejoiced
And sang hymns to His praises above.

On vacation we made for the mountain,
The fern and the mossy, green dell.
Left behind were the miners' cottages
And Ty-Ffynnon, 'the house of the well'.

Meandering down through the valley.
A stream tripped and fell on its way.
As a pool it now stands, dammed by our busy hands
Reflecting God's heavenly rays.

Picking berries that grew on the hillside,
We'd eat them then tackle the 'slip'.
Dangers grew deeper as we lay across sleepers.
Dropping stones through the cracks, down the pit

Those were the days, dead and gone sad to say.
And the people, you'll ne'er see their likes.
Yet while I'll remember, there'll be no September.
'Twill remain the springtime of my life.

The hearts of the people still dwell there.
So few were prepared to leave.

Now scattered north, south, east and westward.
Yet some for the 'British' still grieve.

I went back to the 'British' last summer.
Where I walked, houses lay there at rest.
On the hillside I paced.
Doors, walls, footpaths I traced.
As they lay 'neath the earth's silent breast.

Diane Lavery

A Precious Memory – Christmas 1939

It was a Christmas long ago, remembered to this day.
A family altogether, with our gran and grandad,
Mum and Dad, us children six, and the war far, far away.
Or so it seemed for a while, such a good time we had.

The Christmas tree was lovely, as it stood there so tall.
With sparkling tinsel and baubles, presents tied all round.
A beautiful fairy on top, I feared she might fall.
Who put her up there, so far from the ground?

Warm and cosy the room, a log fire burning so bright.
And the dining table with scrumptious food was laid.
Trifles, mince pies, Christmas cake, a kiddie's delight,
Also crackers, but 'specially Mum's home-made lemonade.

We were so happy playing games and we had lots of fun
With squeak piggy squeak, blindman's buff and many more.
The grown-ups joined in, made sure no one felt glum.
Gave us a Christmas to remember, knew what was in store.

Time came for our presents from off the tree so grand.
We all sat down, and each child in turn, would have a go.
Blindfolded, turned round, a wand was placed in our hand.
Then reached out, had what we touched, knew what I wanted so.

I longed for that fairy, high on the Christmas tree.
My turn. On my toes, stretched, reached as high as the sky
Tapped something with the wand, sure the fairy it must be
It wasn't. She stayed there. Never understood why.

This is a memory I've kept through all of my days.
Last happy time with Dad, before he was sent to war.
A telegram came. Changed our lives in so many ways.
Gone. Christmases with Daddy. They were to be no more.

Monica Tompsett

Memories

In memories I can travel far
And need no train or plane or car.
To see again each much loved scene
Familiar places where I've been.
I can walk down a Devon lane
See springtime's violets bloom again,
See once again primroses sweet
Away from any city's street.
I stand once more beside the sea
In places well beloved by me.
In childhood on that much loved shore
I can revisit ever more
And call, make echoes in a cave
In summer by the sparkling wave.
At Christmas I can go again
To my home town by Memory Lane,
Hear carols sweet played on church bells
Near to the house wherein there dwells
Grandmother and the family
All these are very dear to me
My husband, my true love has gone
To join them, now I am alone.
'Til time will take me and I'll be
With them in Land of Memory.

Margaret B Baguley

A Child, 70 Years Ago, On The Cliffs Of Dover

Nothing can ever take away
The joy and wonder of many a day -
I could wander the chalk path of old,
With companion, Billy - my bold, fox terrier -
A young girl exploring fields of wild flowers
And the grasses and gorse,
Being enchanted, Spring, Summer and Autumn days,
When allowed on my wandering ways -
All common names I got to know,
Of wonderful leaf and flowers too,
Grasses, many in dancing crowds.
The screaming gulls,
The cushion-like clouds -
The wash of the sea
The background music, a symphony -
That stays with me.

Muriel Jean Golding

The Lonely Gardener

I worked so hard, one week, to build a garden.
From dust and sweat I fashioned trees and pools;
A million, rainbow-coloured, flowering pictures.
When this was done, I put away my tools.

I rested, well content with my creation,
I gave it to my sons and went away
To journey forth on Time's unending pathway,
Then, longingly, with joy, returned one day.

I looked around, with hope, to see my garden;
I sought its peace, with patience, but in vain.
Of all those magic gifts I'd freely given,
No single sign could I discern again.

I gazed at scenes of bloody devastation,
I sought and found my long-discarded tools,
I stumbled over frantic, mangled creatures.
Had I, unwisely, shared my world with fools?

My horror grew as I surveyed each fragment;
A dream of beauty, blindly torn to shreds.
Was this the garden where, with love, I'd laboured;
This blackened hell where millions now lay dead?

Thus is the gift returned unto the giver,
Destroyed, diminished till there is no trace,
By thoughtless, thankless, stupid, selfish people,
Who crushed it up and flung it in my face.

'Ah! God alone knows why!' their souls cry to me.
Yes, God alone, who dug that shovel deep;
Who chose to fashion beauty and to share it.
And God, alone again, will sadly weep.

A M Atkins

The Long Road Of Memories

The whole of one's life
Is a long road of memories,
Some happy, some sad,
And funny ones, that made us all glad.

The first memories are of our childhood days
When we were happy, just learning to play,
Growing up was great fun, on sports days we'd run
Sometimes we were last, but we'd all have a laugh.

As we grow older life becomes harder
And sometimes the fun disappears.
Then look back through the years
And I'm sure you will find
Dozens of memories of all different kinds.

Some may bring a tear to your eye,
Many will bring a smile,
That's what memories are for
To sit back and recall for a while.

Mollie Carter

Twenty Years Ago

Sitting in the park, watched young mum pushing pram past,
Reminded of myself, my how time's flown so fast.
Seems like yesterday, double buggy was pushing,
Extremely heavy uphill with two children in.

In those days, of my youth, I used to walk for miles,
With husband in fields, lifted buggies over stiles.
We did not own a car back then, still did not drive,
But what we did have was four children under five.

Saw mum had reached a bench on other side of park,
She fed baby, I noticed toddler clothes all dark.
By mother's feet he contentedly played with toys,
Recalled similar time when with my own two boys.

Twenty years ago, all four from home have flown,
And settled into family lives of their own.

S Mullinger

Freedom

In my childhood, I recall,
The countryside was free for all,
Open gates, easy stiles,
Fields of green, for miles and miles.
Climbing trees, picking flowers,
Here were passed happy hours.
Sometimes on our backs we'd lie,
Hear the insects, watch the sky,
Round the hedges we would race,
Scattering rabbits in our haste,
Jam jars dip in pond and stream,
Or just sit around and dream.

Nature's harvest we would plunder,
With no fear of farmers' thunder.
Elderflower and the sloe,
Sunkissed blackberries fresh and ripe,
Stained our mouths and fingers striped.
Down lanes and byways wander,
Exploring what lay yonder.
Home we'd trek at the appointed hour,
No irate parents to fuss and glower.
My love of nature, I am sure,
Stems from those halcyon days of yore.

Sue Cann

For Uncle Col

(Dedicated to Colin Moorhouse (1957-2007))

Memories are precious and dear to your heart
Memories of times before we were apart
You'll be loved forever
And forgotten never

I remember the times we went to a match
Supporting Leeds United - not a grey patch
Billy was our meeting place
Took a photo - it was ace.

You always loved to be outdoors
Wandering around, exploring the moors
Your love for nature from spring to fall
Has inspired us all

These are the things that stop me from being sad
Remembering the happy times that you have had
Your fighting spirit, strength, love and care
Is special to you and also very rare

Jessica Teggart (15)

Happy Memories

When I think about my schooldays, I break into a smile,
some small thing jogs my memory and I'm transported back for a while.
It seems then all that mattered was meeting boys and having fun,
when all we talked about was music and what song had reached number one.
I had many different friendships that seemed to change from year to year,
but the one friend that I recall the best, the one I still hold dear,
Is a girl called Beverley, who though at first did not impress.
She appeared to be unapproachable with an attitude of 'I couldn't care less'.
She faced life with whatever it brought and she was no one's fool,
and for this fact she was well-known among the pupils round the school.
Forty years on we still can giggle about the silly things we did,
remembering how we ate cold toast in the classroom as behind our desks we hid.
She has such a fond place in my memory that I'm smiling as I write
and I've discovered the woman she's grown up to be is still positive and bright.
She still takes on life as it comes with an attitude I admire.
I think it's true to say such friends motivate and inspire.
I'm having strong and happy flashbacks as I now relate this verse,
but of all my friendships in the past she comes to my mind first.

Eileen Wilby

Travelling Companions

Liberty bodices . . .

Siren suits and ration books
Free school meals and
Hollywood
Inoculations and free eye glasses
Cod liver oil and
Free school classes
Orange juice and bluebell woods
But - no kisses.

An era that has long since past
Whose leaving leaves us
No regrets
No regrets that it has gone
But leaving leaves a memory
Clear tho' distant
Travels with us
As we move on.

Opal Innsbruk

My Favourite Sweets

What's happened to all the sweets,
    I loved when I was young,
Like the 'liquorice belt', I used to suck,
    That blackened all my tongue?
There were also, 'Penny Lucky Bags',
    And 'Lucky Tatties', too,
And if you were really lucky,
    They'd contain, another halfpenny for you.
Then there were 'marzipan tea cakes',
    Also 'choc-o'-mels', as well,
And sweets, shaped like 'the alphabet',
    That helped you, how to spell.
A 'Peg's Bar', or a bar of 'Highland Toffee',
    Or a bar of 'Double Six',
Also, they even had sweets, to give to Mum,
    If you asked for some 'cough mix'.
But now you have to spend, one pound,
    To buy a bag of sweets,
Yet years ago, a penny's worth,
    Was one of my weekly treats.

Jean Hendrie

Sunday Best

Our roads and streets
dressed in their early summer casuals
of lace-like mists and grey uniforms
of well measured suits of hard-core.
As it was in the days of a young moon
treated like a newborn child with its
parents glorifying in all its basic behaviour
and how youths played truant
from art college and decorated
the outside of the pubs and cafes
with extracts from The Beatles' Sgt Pepper cover
as I ran through the sixties
like a runner who never quite reached his destination,
and as I slowed down I could see
various wallpaper and interior design
made from society's hates and loves
displayed in the qualities that separate
us from the animal kingdom
although a beast often discovers depths
to his being that he never comprehended he had
and is immediately dismissed by Man as being mere instinct.

Laurence DE Calvert

Uncle Adolph's Birthday Present

When I arrived in the world he thought to celebrate
That's the little German painter Uncle Adolph the Great
Decreed in my honour as if it was the second coming
He'd send us a firework display after the droning and humming

Cockney land was aglow with bright light, smoke and fire
I was able to watch from the Anderson in my nightly attire
Mind I'd been dragged from my cot with no chance to retire
Into those dreams of milk flowing teats and heavenly choir

Isn't that just like a German to this day it's well known
See a deckchair on a beach they're like a dog with a bone
That I enjoyed all his effort is maybe too strong a word
But for five noisy years the crashing and banging was heard

I'm five by this time and he's called it a day
Mind there's plenty of open space now to discover and play
I know it sounds ungrateful but five years and never a card
Even the presents arrived broken, I still find bits in our yard

Charles Keeble

Early Days

At the age of five I can clearly recall
Being with a group of children in the school's assembly hall
Having been left by my mother, who was a little upset
And left in a situation, I would never forget.
Be a good boy, and do as you're told
So said my mother as she let go of her hold.
None of us having ever been left before
Started crying as they closed the door.
No amount of cajoling, and oh children what's this
Could make up for the mothers we would miss.
But like all good stories, it all comes good in the end
For days at school became a happy place in which to spend.
Thinking back now to a time of change
A happier place where innocence reigned
A time of contentment, a feeling of being secure
The world has moved on, and to where I'm not sure.

Charles Trail

Times Past (A Scottish Widow)

A bonnie salmon, that it is
upon the kitchen table,
caught by a cleek in the river
but not for poor folk's diet.
Some smart hotel, for it will trade
milk, bread and old potatoes,
if feeling sort of kind
a pair of smelly kippers.
So when you sit to wine and dine
think of us from not long past,
when being a widow was a disgrace
and thank god, those days no longer last.

Elizabeth Murray Shipley

The Wedding Of The Year

Eee, it were a right grand thrash
And nobody seemed short of cash.
Eee, everybody came
The fit, the able and even the lame
At Sonia Wainthrop's wedding of the year.

Eee, we didn't have octopus and squid on the menu
Just fish and chips wrapped up in newspaper would do.
Eee, we didn't have a stately home
Or fly our guests into Rome
At Sonia Wainthrop's wedding of the year.

Eee, champagne bought direct from the grower we didn't have
Just stout and ale to fill the bath.
Eee, we danced the night away to Grandad Charly's solo saxophone
And nobody was alone
At Sonia's Wainthrop's wedding of the year.

Eee, we all made it to the church
And at the altar nobody was left in the lurch.
Eee, the skies were always blue
Church bells rang and confetti threw
At Sonia Wainthrop's wedding of the year.

Philip Loudon

A Thing Of Beauty

The snow comes twinkling downwards from the heavens,
And makes the landscape glisten virgin white,
The children wake to greet a frosty vista,
Which looked so green and brown the previous night.

They dress up warm like little woollen parcels,
And dash outside, exploding with delight,
They build a snowman, pelt their friends with snowballs,
And play on sledges, what a happy sight!

Their tiny cheeks are rosy, as they gambol
And tumble in the white and fluffy mess,
And afterwards, they warm up by the fire,
And Mum dries out their wet clothes while they rest.

But when she tries to make them mugs of Oxo,
The tap gives out a rumble and a squeak!
The water's frozen up inside the pipework,
So Dad goes up the loft to take a peek.

The water tank and all the pipes are splitting,
The ice inside them swells up more and more,
Dad's face goes sickly green with apprehension,
He knows what's going to happen, come the thaw!

The plumbers all charge thirty quid a call-out,
Plus parts and labour (twenty quid an hour),
This little lot will set Dad back a fortune,
The morning's fun and laughter turning sour!

He'd go and buy some pipe to try and fix it,
Providing he could get inside his car,
But all the doors are stuck. His only option
Is smash the window with an iron bar!

And even if he chanced to get inside it,
And made his frozen engine come alive,
It wouldn't really help his keen endeavours,
There's fifty tons of snow stuck in the drive!

So all the world is pretty as a picture,
All white and peaceful, like a Christmas card,
And on the telly, holiday commercials
Rub salt in wounds, and make life twice as hard!

The snow that lit their faces up with smiles,
Has made them go all miserable and dour!
A thing of beauty is a joy forever,
Or there again, perhaps for half an hour!

Mick Nash

Anxious For Lost Things

I often mourn
Things I've lost.
Books friends borrowed thirty years ago,
'Well,' I say, 'Tree and Leaf was my favourite present.'
Clothes abandoned to jumble sales.
'Well, that fine voile, it's back in fashion now.'
Things I threw away,
I used to throw away the lids of things
If I thought they didn't fit just so.
Now I've got so many pots with no lids
Incomplete.
'Well, they could be worth something now.'
I'm not sure
Why those lost things
Are more precious to me,
'My treasures',
Than the things that still remain.
I suppose it's perversity
Makes me grieve so.

Chris Madelin

Your Smiling Face

You have a smile that warms my heart
And make me long for you when we're apart
I'm truly blessed by God's good grace
And I often think of your smiling face

You've shown me love from deep within
You've given me your trust and been my friend
You've given me a love on which I can depend
And your love I'll cherish until the end

I've seen your beauty outwards and within
I prayed for your body that would not mend
I saw your pain upon your face
And I prayed for a miracle by God's good grace

You've left me with memories time can't erase
In my heart I'll remember your smiling face
I'll think about the suffering you went through
And I'll cherish the time I spent with you

William Lacewell

Memory

I only loved
You from a distance.
It was love
In the first instance.
Never felt a love
So true,
Until the day
I met you.
And as each day
Passed by,
My love for you
Just grew and grew.
I just loved you
More and more
With a strength
I never knew before.
Now I have only
My precious words
To remind me
Of a love
That was never meant to be.

C A Keohane

Never Again

(For Bob)

Will the sun shine, as it does now,
Burnishing the treetops in the same way?
Never again.
Will you stand by my side, as you do now,
To watch the swallows dip and swirl
Across the sky?
Soon they will wing to warmer chimes,
Never again to return to us
To see them as we do now.

Shafts of golden light tip the hedgerow's jewels
Of berries - hips, and twisted bryony.
Never again shall we walk along the path
And hear the crackle of straw under our feet,
Just so . . .

Our thoughts wrap around us
To enrich these moments for our store of memories:
Together we share this moment of happiness
Never to return,
Never again.

K Merle Chacksfield

A Place To Be

Tales of time
Tales of life
Tales of worry
Tales of strife.

For no tomorrow
Love me today
Live for now
Not yesterday.

Thoughts in mind
A ticking clock
Memories to search
Key to unlock.

Down memory lane
A place to be
Please move in
Right next to me.

Geoffrey Meacham

Carols On Milk St

On Milk Street with frozen hands.
Ears red-tipped,
And noses that dripped,
We sang.
Songs of good cheer,
Of this pure time of year,
Songs the missus asked to hear,
And gave us pennies in our fists
And warm mince pies of melting bliss.
No cold caroller could resist
Kind onslaught of neighbours' Christmas wish.

Then, 'We wish you a Merry Christmas,'
And with breath-clouded faces
And snow's soft embraces
Went singing on our way.
Our pockets a-jingle with pennies from Heaven.
Carolling on Milk Street
This Christmas Eve day.

Miki Byrne

559

If

I sit alone and wonder
As you rest upstairs in bed,
And all these funny, weird thoughts
Keep going round my head.

If we'd shared our lives together more
Right from the very start,
Would we now be facing
Time; close by when we must part.

If I'd shown you what you meant to me
And you'd shown me the same
Would I feel so guilty now,
As if I were to blame.

If I could turn the years around
And start again from new,
I'd make it so that we would live
You for me and me for you.

If I could do so many things
To take away this pain
We'd start afresh, and never do
What'ere we'd done again.

If I could only tell you,
You are my perfect man,
But some higher being
Has made another plan.

No matter what the world may think,
I've loved you for so long
And if I show my feelings now
Would that be very wrong?

If I can find the courage
I'll be brave and I'll not cry
When you finally close your eyes
And say your last goodbye.

Farina May Jenkins

The Old Farmhouse, How Times Change

For hundreds of years this farmhouse has stood, the test of time, as the farmer knew it would.
It had been handed down for generations, and in times had helped a troubled nation.
To feed the people and the services, who had relied on the farmer for food surpluses.
To feed an army plus the RAF, even the Navy and the rest of the growing army of a million souls
Who had pledged their troth, their country to salve,
Now, now it seemed to the farmer, who had fallen on hard times, was this to be the ever last time.,
That they would sit at a polished table and have their tea as they were able to.
What of the china on the welsh dresser, was that to be lost as well as the heifer
That lived in the barn with the mother cow, and seem doomed too - destruction
And yet somehow he thought there must be a way to keep the farm
And the house that had always sheltered him from harm, but *oh how the times change!* Is this the end?
Tight-wedged, between the factory wall and imposing homes of betters long since gone
The fragile farmhouse peeped across its new made urban gate
A lifeless cobbled yard no lovely clip of hoof within
No light betrayed, its honest purpose done
Awaiting execution exigency of state
Oh how times change!

Rosemary Peach

I've Never Been 50 Before

I've never been 50 before.
My middle has spread to the floor.
HRT is a pain, but I've nothing to gain
From hot flushes again and again.
People nod and say I look swell, then pause and say well,
For a middle-aged woman. (It's hell.)
My arms are too short, I can't read a thing.
It's glasses I have everywhere.
I'm not laughing at lines that dare to appear.
They've never been funny before.
Grey hairs do resist the colours I found, and insist to sprout everywhere
Talking of hairs that grow everywhere.
A beard I seem to have found.
I pluck and I shave, and to my added shame,
People talk to my chin all the same.
To be honest I know, no one is to blame.
It's the birthdays that come round too quick.
I'm forced to admit, I'm no longer a spring chick.
An old boiler it's not fair to say, I'm not ready to call it a day.
My head held up high, about my age I will lie.
Slap more cream on my bum and thighs.
After all, I don't wet the bed; I'm not funny in the head.
It's just.
I've never been 50 before.

Jacqueline Ibbitson

Nostalgic Yesterdays

My childhood years have blown
In the blink of an eye
But all my memories are stored
In the subconscious of my mind
Things were so different then
How frantically they've changed
From a time that was heaven-sent
To a stressed out - express train

It all crackles with electricity
So I can feed and digest
Savouring the era that lives in me
As it slowly begins to manifest
I love my nostalgic yesterdays
But progress - and time moved on
Wouldn't it be nice just to stay
Where your best dreams - all come from.

Frank Howarth-Hynes

The Old Music Box

I came across a music box, while clearing Granny's room.
Just a broken black box, on her dresser, near her stale perfume.
It had been her most treasured possession
But it also held a few confessions,
As inside were the secrets of her heart.

There were some old scraps of paper with faded ink,
Granddad was not the writer, so it really made me think.
Was the writer a long-lost lover
Who I had just discovered
In her broken black music box.

I would not read those letters from her past,
I just tore them up and let Granny rest at last.
No wonder she would not let anyone
Hear her musical box song
And from my eyes I shed silent tears.

Doreen E Hampshire

Those Were The Days

Something that you hear
It is a common phrase
Take a look back in time
Because 'Those were the days'
When tin baths were used
One washed, who was next?
Hand-me-down clothes
No talk about sex
'Run for the shelter!'
The siren is crying
Hiding in the darkness
Whilst the soldiers are dying
No video players
Hardly ever saw a car
No expensive posh pets
Just a tadpole in a jar
There were marbles and jacks
Porcelain dolls, hopscotch too
A seat in the flea pit
Cost a shilling or two
Mrs Dale's Diary on the wireless
Bag of coal for the fire
Squeeze the washing through a mangle
To the launderette for a washer and dryer
Chicken once a year at Christmas
Plain crisps with a bag of salt
There were steam trains and trams
Kodak box cameras - front doors without bolts
Black polish on hobnailed boots
No GCSEs, for us - Eleven Plus
Pack of ten Woodbines
A conductor on the bus
A guinea or a threepence
Quill pens you dipped in ink
Bets clothes on a Whitsun
Pigtails with ribbons of pink
An annual trip to somewhere
It was all we could afford
Bag of chips and some scrumpy
We were happy, never bored
No talk of the ozone layer
We had lots of the sun's rays
Families were big and we were poor
We didn't care because those were the days!

Joanne Hale

563

Super Southsea

Southsea is a wonderful place to be
It's a fun-loving place right by the sea
So much to do there and so much to see
When you visit there I know you will agree
If you like a nice stroll along the prom
You'll find it flat, even and very long
Joggers use it to keep themselves fit
When you are tired there are plenty of places to sit
The D-Day Museum is a must to be seen
Or fly a kite on the common so green
Visit the castle, it's a thrill to behold
To climb to the top you must be bold
The pier for the fishermen is sheer delight
Spend all day there hoping for a bite
Restaurants are there to suit every taste
Eating at leisure for there is no haste
Candyfloss and ice cream are all found there
Lots of amusements and, of course, the fair
The hovercraft is noisy as it slips into the sea
Southsea is wonderful, come along and you'll agree

L A G Butler

Someone Special

The days slowly pass since you passed away,
we will remember you each and every day.
You were so generous in every kind of way,
but even in prayers you were unable to stay.

You have certainly left a big impact behind,
and a huge gap in our lives, always in our mind.
You would always listen to everything we did,
and always loved to cook lifting the saucepan lid.

You were young at heart amongst your family,
holding a cigarette made you happy.
We feel you are still close by and at peace at last,
always remembering fond moments of you from the past.

We had many telephone calls when you felt well to speak,
with your unique humour, you would throw in a cheek.
Your sister in the States would call all of the time,
leaving us with much more to offer, still in your prime.

We would learn of your progress over a brew,
and pleased with your planned kitchen, oh! so new.
Organising everyday things when it was too much to do,
you were extremely brave and we are all proud of you.

Adrian Bullard

564

Friend Susan

Form 1R had the general science lab,
smelling of formaldehyde and rats in cages.
alphabetically arranged: Kent, Ketley, Kitto,
we sat on wooden stools at benches.
Through registration Susan mumbled behind cupped hands
about the ballet lessons she was taking.

At her birthday party in October
after the matinée of Coppelia,
I was one of the three
to taste her mother's baked Alaska.

Rosemary Benzing

The Thirties - A Penny Worth Of Chips

A 'pennuth' of chips, salt and vinegar please
I don't have enough for faggot and peas
Which I must admit is my favourite treat
But a hot bag of chips can hardly be beat
That's my pocket money all gone in one go
But I'm making them last, for I'm eating them slow
I suck the newspaper, when my feed is done
And feel a bit sad - my money has gone

Gordon Andrews

Lancashire Life

The thirties was a time of smoke -
Cough, cough, splutter and choke.
A pall of smoke hung over all
Houses, buildings, low and tall.

The time when cotton was the king -
Sometimes one could not see a thing.
It was a wonderful childhood.
Life was extremely good, good, good.

The crime rate was really low,
When no meant no, no, no.
A carefree time was had by all -
We played tig, marbles and football.

Or is only with hindsight
We really missed the light.
Darkness brought the blackout
When lights had to go out.

Ina J Harrington

565

Keep On Dreaming

Your dreams, are they good or bad,
Do they raise your spirit,
Or only make you sad,
And where do they come from?

It seems there are many ways
For dreams to make such displays,
Memories play a part,
Chance remark might light a spark.

Anger too can enter the theme,
Remorse and guilt, not a pleasant dream,
But on the opposite side,
Love can take a ride.

Most dreams occur in the early morn,
Some creative, others forlorn,
While colours too enter the score,
Choice may determine if a bore.

For action, the colour is red,
While with blue calm is spread,
Black is associated with fear,
It's in your mind that you must be clear.

How long do these memories remain?
With most, it is far from plain,
Making a note when you wake,
May be all the help you need take.

We long for those happy ones,
Where we can add up the sums,
With creativity and peace,
So best memories may release.

George Beckford

Inheriting The Present

Everything that we have now is due
To something that happened in the past,
The bad things and the good it is true.
With more kindly tolerance - no means the last,
And a warm sympathetic point of view
Toward the other man's needs today
Marking the future whatever we do
In much the same old repetitive way.
Unceasing the story unfolds anew:
Life in Britain so much better than before
Does not mean that it still cannot be
Greatly improved and designed to endure
When all may have input whereby we,
Teamed with that vital helping hand
Can improve things as always planned.

Betty Bukall

I Sit Upon A Lonely Hill

I sit upon a lonely hill,
waiting, waiting,
sitting still;
I think of the world I follow round,
listening, listening,
to the oncoming sound;
I sit upon this lonely hill,
under cloud,
upon a window sill;
I search the ground below,
waiting for,
well you know;
I sleep forever on this hill,
silently dreaming of the thrill,
I know my time,
will have to wait:
looking towards the heavenly gate;
I sit upon this lonely hill,
with all my heart and my will:
searching for evermore,
until I see the heaven's door.

Gareth Culshaw

Memories Are Made Of This

Way Back Then!

Way back in the years of fifty-six and fifty-seven,
it must have been a fashion designer's heaven!
As men, and boys, took on a new approach, to the way they look,
which opened up a whole new fashion book!

With thin bootlace ties, no frills, no bows,
brothel creeper shoes with thick crêpe soles!
Fluorescent socks they wore on their feet,
which set the look off to a treat.
Drainpipe trousers as tight as can be,
black drape jackets down to their knee!

There was one more thing to make the look complete,
before they stepped out onto the street,
Tony Curtis was their hair *icon,*
he was who they modelled their DA hair style on!
It was the fashion statement that took the country by storm,
and that was how the *Teddy Boy look was born!*

Saturday night, they would all go into town, where in the coffee bars they would all sit around,
having a coffee, and in the jukebox money they would put, to hear
their favourite sound!
Like Bill Haley and 'Rock around the Clock',
but the one they played the most was the *master of rock!*
Elvis Presley was then at that time the *king,*
making all the coffee bars in the country *swing!*

In fifty-six *Heartbreak Hotel* was his record debut,
but that only got up the charts as far as number two.
Another hit in fifty-six, was *Love me Tender,*
but the one in fifty-seven is the one that all Teddy Boys will remember,
All Shook Up made it all the way
and that's why people still love his music to this day!

Teddy Boys changed the face of fashion and the music scene, that can't be any clearer,
they also changed the course of history, *way back then,* in the *Teddy Boy Era!*
Sue Dancey

Memories Are Made Of This And That

Memories can be the sweetest thing
Or are they only fact
I never know quite what is what
Or fathom what's exact
I wake up in the morning
Vivid on my mind
Things that have nothing to do with me
Nothing I can find
Have I regressed a former life
Or am I going mad?
Could be due to stress and strife
Or just a silly fad.

Enid Hyder

East Lancashire Railway – A Dream In Steam

Thank you Polly and Max too, we shared a lovely day with you.
The clouds stayed white, no sign of black, we picnicked by the railway track.
We shared our food and Polly's sweets, that was the first of many treats.
A lovely village, full of charm, no speeding cars, I felt its calm.
I heard the babbling river sound, in Irwell Vale such peace I found.
We hurried down to get the train, my heart raced as once again
I heard the hiss of white hot steam and saw the sight this child had seen.
My dad drove the trains back then, behind our house and back again
Diesels and electrics were quite new, far inferior thought Dad and I still do.
The lady on the train was full of facts, about the village by the tracks
Of how it used to be in days gone by, a harder life than we have, you and I.
Next stop we had was Summerseat, we walked and had some fruit to eat.
Polly waved each passing car carrying folk from near and far.
We're on the steam train once again for our journey home and then
We climbed upon the footplate Max and I gazed upon the fire with wondrous eye.
At Rawtenstall we found at last another blast from my past
A temperance bar, the only one, the others have drunk up and gone.
Sarsaparilla was my choice, Dandelion & Burdock you said with one voice.
Polly likes my favourite sweet, a piece of fudge, another treat.
Then in the cars we all sat, chauffeur driven, bliss, thought Pat.
To Edenfield we wend our way a perfect end, a perfect day.
A meal of fish and chips so good, we all had just no room for pud.

Thank you Louise and Nigel too, it was for me a dream come true.

Patricia Eves

569

The Memories Of A Short Homecoming . . .

From Australia, the rugged land of huge deserts,
    the golden sandy beaches and the deep blue skies,
famed for creatures - 'roos, wombats, snakes, koalas,
    mozzies and great multitudes of pesky flies,
came word that two of our daughters, residents of
    that legendary land that's so far away,
were coming home, here, soon, after many
    years, on a two month holiday.

Hence a veritable feast of deep emotions, moist eyes,
    choked throats, impatience . . . then the Day!
They arrive with luggage galore and commence
    non-stop conversations in verbalic disarray . . .

Divulging family news, visitings and visitors,
    renewing relations and meeting many an old friend.
Postcards written hastily, phone calls made,
    including some email messages to send.

Then - too quickly - came the Black Day when
    their booked returns to Oz looms,
flurries of activities, suitcase packings and
    desperately weighing luggage in their rooms.
Oh God. Noting miserably how the time has flown
    and . . . once again to say farewell to our own.

Bodies held stiffly in control, watching
    carefully with teary, blinking eyes,
the sadness as we looked longingly as the
    car slowly departs . . . all are waving goodbyes . . .

Once again, the house is tranquil and so empty again,
    but many happy memories overwhelmingly remain.
Both daughters returned to the sunny days and blue skies,
    the 'roos, wombats, mozzies and multitudes of pesky flies . . .

J Fred Jackson

Memories Of A Lost Love

You have a very special way
of adding joy to living,
You have a most unselfish way
of love and cheerful giving.

It's really just the little things
that to me mean so much.
A smile across the room,
the gentleness of your touch.

I very often wonder -
what you saw in me.
I never fail to wonder
just what it could be.

I lie awake and think of you
and wonder what you're doing now.
I miss you very much you see,
if you were here I'd know, and how.

I suppose you also think of me,
at least I hope you do,
Because things aren't quite the same
when not shared with you.

Ted Brookes

At Home

How nice the green today
As our friends arrive to play,
The mats are out
One on each rink, fresh cut,
And woods away
Eighteen ends are done
And we sit down in the sun,
Tea is served, we gather round,
Keen bowlers everyone.

Back on the green again
All hoping it won't rain,
Till evening light
Begins to fade,
Then tired, we call it game,
And so goodnights are said,
It's such a happy sound
All good friends, all ages blend,
When bowlers are around . . .

Joan Hammond

Past And Present

(To my friend Pat on her 70th birthday)

Very many years ago,
'Twas nineteen forty eight -
We moved into the prefabs
And thought it simply great!
We really were excited -
When we received the keys,
Our first real home
Just we alone -
The kids and Selb and me.
I didn't really know you then,
Until we moved up there,
And as the years went swiftly by -
The many hours we shared.
We had our daily gossip -
And talked of this and that,
We always shared a secret -
Do you remember Pat?
We moaned about the menfolk -
and also 'bout the kids,
The things we sought
And sometimes bought
If only for a quid!
We always went to 'Ton' to shop -
And always at the Co-Op!
Excitement! when the word got round -
I think the Divi's back!
Those summer nights, we used to sit -
Outdoors and have some fun,
With you and Dan, Iris and Bill,
And Betty and Eddie too -
There was Olwen and Cy
And Selby and I,
Some laughs we had too true!
Then came television,
With work for the women,
In factories, and elsewhere too!
Things were never the same -
Once TV came -
We were stuck to the telly like glue!
There was a time though -
When down came the snow,
And we and the neighbours had fun,
Going up on the hill,
It was such a thrill,
To ride down on the sleigh -
What a run!
Things really did alter -
When you made a move

Memories Are Made Of This

To the place where you're living today,
You really were glad -
But we were quite sad,
Because you were moving away.
We just carried on -
And then later on -
We, like you, decided to go,
We're not very far -
From where you are -
It'll just take a minute or two!
This 'gadabout', will pass your house,
And you will hear me shout,
If you are in, you'll see me grin -
And wave my arms about!
Forever in a hurry,
Just going to and fro,
'No time to spare, I must get there'
I really have to go.
On very rare occasions
I'll call in to have a chat,
'Bout you and me, and those and them,
And always this and that!
And in-between the fleeting years,
The sadness, we both shared,
The sudden, tragic shock we had,
Of poor old Dan and Selb.
Now they are gone -
We carry on - with thoughts of days gone by,
Those happy days that made us smile,
Now make us want to cry.
I never will forget the days -
We shared so long ago,
The days we went out shopping
The fun out in the snow!
And now that you are seventy
I can't believe it's true -
But when you get to eighty,
We'll still be friends we two!

Rose E Selby

When Mourning Comes

Whenever I look around me,
I see the many traces of you:
And now you've gone, I visualise,
the life that I once knew.

The dreams and the pulsing memories,
are my companions along the way,
and the ghostly shadow of your smile,
still haunts me - to this day.

Free, my love, from the ties that bind,
in a world of endless pain;
for the lord of mercy, beckoned you,
from the portals of a higher plain.

I've seen your shape, in the swirling mists
of the golden autumn days,
but you are always out of reach,
when I follow in the haze.

I see your face, in the setting sun,
sinking slowly in the sky;
and the heartache, all consuming,
is just the echo, from a mourning cry.

I've heard your sigh, in the summer wind,
as it lingers on my face,
but those longed for words - 'I love you!'
are now lost, in time and space.

You come and go like the April rain,
through the windmills of the mind;
for death, the mournful reaper,
left showers of grief behind.

Reclining in our upper room,
I recall your presence here;
and the memory of encircling arms,
is as fresh, and ever dear.

The ebb and flow of your haunting stance,
inspires the memory;
for words that flow, will bring relief,
from mournful reverie.

The memory of you will forever remain:
I've known this right from the start:
And I'm always prompted to mourn for you,
by the skipping beat of my heart.

Patricia-Mary Gross

A Whisper On The Wind

Whisper to me softly
a whisper in the wind
may the warm breeze
that blows at night
a kiss blown in the wind

may all the past be memorised
a whisper from your lips
a breath of sweet soft scentedness
caress my presentness

address my waking hours
and stay with me always
I'll listen to that breath of wind
that shows to me you care

creep softly around me always
that gentle breeze that blows
the passing clouds
and the midday hour
from Earth to Heaven goes

sleep not our yesteryears
let not the past grow dim
remember to me gently
a breath blown on the wind

Margery Rayson

Cross Reflection

Reflects on life
worry and strife.

People you like dead and gone
you to carry on.

Suffer loss and pain
Glory and gain.

Thorns to His head
Saviour to the *Lord* he led.

He saves from our sins and to heal
Strong abundance love to feel.

Pierced in His side suffering until dying
what pain He had?
We have none we should be glad.

Think of *Jesus* on the cross
offered for our cause.

Raised up to Heaven
with love and forgiving.

Marie Coyles

Reflections

From flesh and bone my mirror framed,
reflects a face gone by,
so fresh, so young, so full of hope,
such bright and twinkling eye.

The living image mocks and taunts,
yet loves and draws you near,
to wipe away lost hopes, lost dreams,
each torn and wasted year.

The shattered spirit strong again,
the flame of life grows bright,
my mirror lives, in heart, in soul,
its brave young heart gives flight.

The fire that courses through those veins,
the same that burned in mine,
I stand again as though reborn,
my heart, my spirit thine.

When years subdue and image fades,
when heart and will are done,
may you in turn your mirror find,
my life, my hope, my son!

Sullivan the Poet

Childhood Memories

As I wandered slowly down the lane
With memories by my side
I thought about the happy times
When I was but a child

I remembered how you held me
I remembered how you smiled
I remembered how you kissed me
When I was just a child

You taught me how to fish and swim
And showed me boxing in the gym
Kicking footballs in the park
And hide-and-seek in the dark

You taught me what was right and wrong
And helped me grow up fit and strong
I try to do goodly deeds
By fulfilling other's needs

I remember how you held me
I remember how you smiled
I remember how you loved me
For I was your only child.

Diana Daley

The Cupboard Under The Stairs

(Evacuation from Dover to Clevedon)

Looking over the banisters in Grandma's house
She could see a short passage. It looked a bit gloomy
By flickering candlelight. Maybe, just maybe
There were treasures at the end.

She found the passage led to a very large cupboard,
With a door with a stiff latch. It was secret really,
No one ever seemed to go in there. The
Inside was dusty, dim and had a musty smell.

When all was quiet she ventured in again.
What treasure there was, a jointed doll with
A pretty wax face. Oh! how she grew to
Love her, secretly and all alone.

There were so many things untouched on the shelves of
The secret cupboard, but one day
She was discovered loving the doll.
Such a pandemonium and a good telling off.

When her aunt married the wax doll went away.
Never to be cherished again. It was
Wrecked years later by her two small girls who
Did not realise the value of the beautiful doll.

Grown up. The cupboard was empty now.
She had cleared her mother's house, too big now.
Her aunt seemed to want all of its contents,
No matter anymore.

Hilary Moore

December Twilight

When fog and dusk
merge into gloom
my heart fills with
a sense of doom . . .

Then festive scenes
through windows bright
cheer me with thoughts
of summer's light!

David Hancock

From Old To New

Work, work seemed to
be my life
not a lot of money left in sight
my shoes were a shocking sight
worn from hard work
from morning to night
a knock came on the door
a parcel in sight
opened it up
a brand spanking pair
of new shoes
in sight
my feet seemed to
smile and
so did I with
delight
what a wonderful
sight

Denise McDonald

We Will Remember Them

The patchwork quilt lying on Gran's bed
Was like a favourite book, we often read.
Each patch told a story of its own
As by loving hands the quilt was sewn.
Yes the white was Grandma's wedding gown
the blue, the little flower girl's dress,
It was a wonderful day for the wedding
For which they were thankful - I guess.
Yes that was my first long evening dress
I really wanted red,
But it ended up with Mother's choice -
A dainty pink instead.
Christening gowns, school uniforms
They all have a tale to tell
And bring the memories flooding back -
Some happy, some sad - ah well.
It's years since Grandma stitched the quilt
It has given us lots of pleasure
The memories it holds, the tales it tells
I know we'll always treasure.

Constance Vera Dewdney

No One Can Take That Away

Farmers in their fields,
Freshly cut hay,
Trailers taking the corn and seed away,
Sun beating down on a summer day,
All of us children happily at play,
Chasing butterflies as they flutter away.
Winter on her way, it all turns white,
Making snowmen, having a snowball fight,
Let's see who can make an igloo.
Mum wants to know where are your socks?
On my hands to keep them warm.
Then comes Christmas, Santa's on his way,
I hope I get the elephant, the soft cuddly toy,
I fell in love with the other day.
Night after night in the shop,
Every time I saw you my heart felt as if it would stop,
Then one night the tears, you were gone.
Christmas Day it was here, down the stairs I went,
What was that present all wrapped up?
I opened it, it was my elephant,
Thanks Mum.
You know still to this day
I have my Elle the Elephant
And no one can take that away.

Leeanne Shires

A Bench At Wazeley

Here is a song that waits for you on apple blossom hillsides
Where cows and sheep wait, a-whistling in the tree's breeze.
Look for me upon the view that stretches a-yonder
Beside the dreams are memories of people and places.
The Malvern Hills stand at distance now where once we stood.
A dog races round the cows and into the past now.
Here, are my memories of childhood, see how clouds race by.
Friend's name on a bench, tells me soon all must decay or die.
Here is a whisper upon a lonely summer day.
Grass and mind sets to wonder, far outstretched played.
That soft birdsong a memory, a butterfly carved into the hillside.
Where is my belief in life as I sit with the cows?
Here in my heart, my memories as the sun sets over Wazeley.

Barry Powell

No Regrets

How simple, to just turn around,
and find yesterday once more,
to wander back, to childhood days,
through memory's sweet door.

To see again, my mom and dad,
remember all they used to do,
two little brothers,
up to tricks,
but very loving too.

The happy years, we all shared,
the lessons we were taught,
the love, that never went away,
such memories, can't be bought.

Christmas time, birthdays too,
treasured more as time goes by,
sunny smiles, always blue skies,
at least in my mind's eye,

and if sometimes, my days are grey,
memories, take the grey away,
and as I walk down memory lane,
once more, I am a child again.

Jacqueline Claire Davies

Rhine Cruise

As we sailed the gentle Rhine
true peace I felt was really mine.
Fast flowing water and gentle breeze,
stirring grass and bankside trees.
Musical boxes and cuckoo clocks,
freight barges waiting at the docks.
Many castles to feast the eye,
vineyards flourishing under a summer sky.
We heard the tale of the Lorelei,
and the wave rolling wild and high,
taking sailors away to the deep,
their date with 'Lorelei' to keep.

Joyce Shinn

Summer In The Sixties

The sixties were a haven
Of happy times, some not
Friends played in the park with me
While the sun shone from above
Happy time was had by all
Lemonade in the garden
Ice cream was on tap
Hot and heady summers
Parents were not about
Just good friends one and all
Some now forgotten
Some still keep in touch
School days were so clever
Some of us bright
Others where the light didn't shine
But now we're older
And time has passed by
Now we are all married
And have children of our own
I hope their memories will be as good
As ours were from long ago.

Elaine Day

Childhood Memories

We moved to the country when I was three
Mum, Dad, my sister and me
Plenty of space to run and play
Lots of things to do each day
When I was five I went to school
It was small and select, I thought it was cool
When I grew up in my teens
I'd go out dressed in a sweatshirt and jeans
I was a tomboy, a Jack the lad
So on the farm I'd help my dad
Life in the country was really good
I have happy memories of my childhood

Wilma Barrett

The Broken-Hearted Parish

Tonight in fancy, come with me
And take a trip to see,
Our own beloved companions
In a place we'd love to be.

It lingers in our memories
The times we used to know
Oh! just tonight, step back in time
To the long, long, long ago.

Through bygone streets, with friends long-gone
We'll take a stroll once more
And meet with fine, hard-working folk
We knew in days of yore.

We'll saunter to St Marie's church
Then over to the hall,
Remembering those joyous times
In the days of sweet recall.

Back in church, the choir will sing
The Benediction hymn.
At the door stands Tommy Monaghan
We all remember him.

Then as the boys and girls come out
And o'er the street we go.
To live again, those dancing hours
Of the long, long, long ago.

They're going to pull it, brick by brick
And tear the place apart.
The powers that be, don't care a jot
Whilst stepping on your heart.

Sign the cross, while Jesus weeps
A river of tears will flow,
In a barren field, where a church once stood
In the long, long, long ago.

Monica Doyle

Our Love

(Dedicated to my darling husband who died in January 2006)

'I promise to love you now and forever
This ring is the circle that binds us together'

This is the inscription on our new rings of gold
And this is our love story I think should be told

When we first fell in love I was only fifteen
He wore a smart leather coat and rode a shiny machine

We rode out on rallies in the rain and the sun
We won lots of trophies and had lots of fun

It was April '55 that we got wed
We bought a house, table and chairs and a bed

We couldn't afford more furniture or even a shed
So we kept the bikes in the front room instead

The children came along in due course
Then the bikes had to go cos they wanted a horse

We kept lots of horses over the next thirty years
We had lots of laughs and shed a few tears

When the kids all moved out the last horses were sold
So let's have a new bike, we're not too old

We bought this gorgeous 'Race Replica' - almost new
Had matching helmets and leathers in white, red and blue

So forty years on we're riding again
But only in the sun and never the rain

This year we've been wed for fifty years
The family came round and we had a few beers

We've sold the bike now but we miss the speed
A nice open sports car is what we need

So we're searching the ads for something we like
But will it ever be as good as the bike?

So this is our first fifty three years together
And we've promised to love now and forever

Audrey Amphlett

The Cat And Man Church

It's a story in rhyme with family in mind,
About a bank holiday - the busiest kind,
The weather was fine - but where to spend the time?
Dad had planned our day out of doors to unwind.

We would be back for tea, Dad assured, we agreed,
Out on the main road the hill slowed our feet,
On our left towered the pit shaft and black slag heaps,
Where Dad worked below ground to earn his and our keep.

Look over this side, in the shade, under the trees,
We all turned our heads and had to agree,
The contrast was soothing and beautiful to see,
Dappled young deer nibbled at the bark on the trees.

At the top of Hickleton Hill, we entered a churchyard path,
In the lynch gate wall a skull encased in glass,
'Today for me - tomorrow for thee,' I read aloud and aghast!
Spooked children - we ran to join Mum and Dad on the path.

On the Barnborough Road we sheltered in a barn during heavy rain,
And Dad told us a true story when we set off again,
A man on a horse was attacked by a wild black cat,
Into Barnborough Church he ran to ward off attack.

A stone monument of a man and a large cat,
To this day, can be seen in the church alcove, in fact,
As the man stretched out in his dying breath,
With his feet he killed the cat and this brought death.

Kathleen McBurney

The Worst Of Times

I remember,
            I remember that cold November,
when snow fell
            and war clouds gathered:
the world prayed
            as death wandered free.
The streets were dark
            only burning buildings
lit up the night sky
as the Devil rode out
to challenge the Spirit of Man . . .
I remember,
            I remember that time long ago.

Arthur Pickles

Watching From Darkness Rise The Dawn

Everyone has wonderful pieces of reflection
Also things they'd rather not reflect on
Good and bad down to the mood's selection
Times spent, but within the memory never gone
Looking back at youthful days from old age
The distance is measured in pleasure and pain
Warm and cold memories occupy our skull cage
Both can cause tears to fall like rain
The heart is pulled in many a direction
Thought travels over ground smooth and rough
The living of your life needs closer inspection
Remember, every one of us finds getting it right tough
But when a memory lifts the soul
Causing fallen lips to turn up into a smile
It fills in that wistful thinking hole
Makes you feel you can go that extra mile
It's all about mind over matter
It matters what's in the mind
The herd of good memories, don't let them scatter
Sometimes the bad can be too easy to find
They can choke the future with the past
Where they can hold you bitter and dark
Reality's good times they just don't last
But lighting a positive memory they're the spark
It's easier said than done
But it's something to work upon
Getting it right will stun
Like watching from darkness rise the dawn.

Mark Tough

In The Gentle Glow Of Candles

In marbled ancient churches
that echo the prayers of time
Lord, as we light candles
let our thoughts entwine.
With memories, we keep close by us
to embrace, yours and mine.

May we ask a blessing
to give us strength, a sign!
That precious times remembered,
within this peaceful domain.
In the gentle glow of candles
beguile, a smile again . . .

Joanne Manning

585

Silent Innocence

Eyes framed against the harshness of decaying wood
Thoughts deep
Staring
The eyes behold
No need for speech
Her hair as thistledown blowing in the wind
Yet she cannot wander as the down
Her girlish elegance of purity against the filth and ugliness of her surroundings
She indulgently watches immersing herself in the street
Her large brown eyes possess a sadness of the realities of her existence
Silence sanctifies, her posture a vulnerable one
Submissively intimate with her surroundings for she is acquainted with every nail and piece of
wood making her wooden window
Her intense stare liberates her from her window
In her mind she is free, her mind images hold no resistance
She wanders, awakening thoughts of paradise for a little girl
Silent innocence

Hilary Jean Clark

Dog Who Knew

During the war, when sirens sounded, we had to move fast,
No matter, how rapidly we always were outclassed.
My brother's dog was always in the shelter shivering there,
Terrified when sirens sounded, knew just to go in that lair.
We'd stroke his head, whisper words in gentle loving tones,
Still he'd lay there shivering, making funny little moans.
We'd offer him some titbits, he did not want to know,
He'd just lay there shivering from top of head to toe.
Then suddenly all-clear would sound very, very loud,
The difference it made to that dog would stand out in a crowd.
He'd shoot off out of that room like a black coloured splash,
Across to his food dish, clear it in a flash.
Through all the war he did this, until the war was over,
Then contemptuously he'd have a nap, *inside lair* he'd sleep,
Until the day box was put away for keeps.
He had been so scared just like human Man,
Then he'd shown us he *could* do it when must, like we can.

Barbara Goode

Memory Lane

I've been looking through my albums of photographs galore,
Of albums I have twelve all told, and really need some more.
Memories came flooding back, remembering past years,
Of holidays and outings, happiness, sometimes tears.
Donkey rides and candyfloss, ball games on the sands,
Lilos in the shallows, paddling with our hands.
Walks along the cliff tops, stunning scenery,
Sometimes we had a pub lunch, sometimes a picnic tea.
Lazing in the deckchair soaking up the sun,
Kids splashing in the ocean, having so much fun.
Visits out to theme parks, and visiting the zoo,
Sometimes we were spoilt for choice, so many things to do.
A ride out in the country, gathering blackberries was fun,
Filling high our baskets, and taking them home to Mum.
Who made us lovely puddings, with apples from our tree,
Gave some to the neighbours, we liked to share you see.
Although I'm almost eighty-one, I remember vividly,
Our trips out in the country, and days out by the sea.
I can no longer travel to places far and near,
But I do have all my memories and all these I hold most dear.

Brenda Hill

HD Rediscovered

I got a lovely train set, when I was just a boy;
'Twas made by Hornby Dublo; it filled my heart with joy.
A little black tank engine, with coaches red and cream,
Some grey coal trucks, a guard's van - about them I did dream.

Then, in the later fifties, 'eleven-plus' was passed,
So Mother's precious angel became her 'top of class'.
She promised me an engine, whichever one I chose,
And so, of course, it had to be the 'Duchess of Montrose'!

The sixties brought me pretty girls and horses, motorbikes;
Then GCEs and starting work, my first car and such likes.
The trains got sold to raise some cash and make a bit more room,
So thirty years skittled by, just like a rocket - zoom!

I drove around in classic style, in shiny Jaguars;
The pretty girls seemed drawn to me - or was it just my cars?
Somehow, the years have added up, whilst slipping all away;
I've had a smile for everyone, through all my work and play.

And now, retired, I ride around with my cousin - she's so fair;
We cycle, (somewhat slower, now, . . . because of my grey hair).
Old photographs and sixties' tunes help us forget the rain,
Whilst on a track, in my spare room, is a Horny Dublo train.

Gareth Wynne Richards

A Memory

(Acriedu'coeur)

What is a memory?
Something remembered, once forgotten,
A smile, a touch, a caress,
Oh - what memories to possess.

I love to sit and think back
Thro' the annals of my life,
To days of youth and innocence,
To recall a certain person's presence.

Yes it is good to now remember;
It fills the weary days of age
With sparkles of youthfulness,
To recall promises of His faithfulness.

I found a loving husband,
And bore him four children far apart;
We lived and served in a foreign land
The stress there broke my heart.

But God persisted in love,
He brought us back to England,
And my mind and heart recovered.
I even forgot the desert sand.

They are all grown and married now.
There has been pain through these years.
O God please help us in our memories.
To gather the grain and throw away the useless chaff.

A rainbow in the rain and storm,
A sunrise and a sunset.
Yes I'm getting on but in good form,
There may be many years yet.

Who knows, but God our Creator;
He gave us all the facility to remember.

Anne B Simms

Memories

You can never lose your memories
They are with you every day
The good things that you have done
As through your life you sway.
You can never lose your memories
The good, the bad, the sad
They are part of what makes you and me
So let's all just be glad.
You can never lose your memories
You make new ones every day
And each one's very special
In its own sweet little way.

Linda Francis

A Wealth Of Memories

Often at night, when sleep won't come,
I relive my past memory store,
Eighty years of changing life,
With all, that has gone before.
Childhood, family, friends long ago,
Tears and laughter galore,
Coping with bombs, fire and rationing,
Teenage, stolen by a world war.
The aftermath, losing loved ones,
Regret, relief, thanks for peace,
Building a new life as best we could,
Would rationing ever cease?
Marriage, children, the wonder years,
Love, that conquers all,
Father rejoining the RAF,
Years of moving house, to recall.
New places, new faces, new people to meet,
New schools for children to find,
We lived in Germany for 6 years,
Great memories, got left behind.
Retirement, to open a tropical fish shop,
Proved fantastic satisfaction,
Terry and I, did it, mostly alone,
Father had bowls, as a distraction.
The sadness of widowhood, living alone,
Makes memory, a happy past time,
Imagination, runs riot at times,
But I'm grateful for memories of mine.

E M Eagle

Thanks For A Memory

Hey, hey, hey, let the church bells ring
Joining in a tribute to the one they called 'the king'
He was one with an enormous charm
Some think drugs may have caused him harm
But for most it was to be a tribute still
To he who the millions never failed to thrill
As slick as the hair that adorned his head
We all were stunned to hear that he was dead
About convention he did not give a toss
Now every mention reactivates the loss
Always prepared to strum the odd refrain
For twenty-odd years at the top did reign
This world has changed not always for the best
You are better off where you now rest
Time's stood still - it is now two thousand and seven
Gone through Hell ever since you went to Heaven
From humble beginnings you did go far
You had your 'innings' and became a 'star'
We are aware that we have lost a friend
May the inspiring that you started never end
You changed the world with enchanting song
Dear, dear Elvis we all for you still long
You have gone away and there is no trace
Gone from Graceland to a land of grace
Sweet dreams lover in your bed there curled
Hearts go out from all over this world
Strum, strum, strumming on your old guitar
Our love goes to you wherever you are
Elvis Presley a self-made man
Remember us - please - whenever you can!

John L Wright

49 Headcorn Road

I am the gate at which we met
I am the look that we exchanged
I am the shy smile which you gave
I am the thrill when our hands touched
I am the stars under which we stood
I am the years we spent together
I am the despair when you died
I am the hope we'll meet again
I am the gate where it all began.

John J Allan

Six Summers And Ten

Remember Wullie, we thought we were men
That sunny day, we were but six summers and ten.
The empty harbour, 'Selina' beached for repairs,
Blue sky, no breeze, just gentle airs.
Leather sea boots above the knees, murder in this heat,
Standing in wooden tub, tap running, cooling our feet.
Thumping crash of maroon, lifeboat engine dub a dubbing,
Waiting cox'n's anxious look, no running feet, thud thudding.
'You two, you've crewed fishing for a couple of year,
This is a Bobby's Job. Go! Get some gear!'
The yellow coat almost brushing the ground,
Sleeves rolled back, life jackets fastened around.
Down the channel, past the breakwater, over the bar,
She lurched, bucked, twisted, we hadn't gone far.
My head ached, I sweated, I heaved up over the side,
My pie and chips, but, most of all my pride.
Seasick, never, never, live it down,
Long coat, life jacket touching knees, indeed felt a clown.
The anchor puffer was lucky, the tide was high,
Ebb tide on Adwick Reef, she'd be high and dry,
Towed her into Shallock Bay, sandy floor,
Tug arrived, relieved us of our chore.
Cox'n let us take the wheel, explained,
Lifeboat differently built, needs crew trained,
To deal with her idiosyncrasies in different seas,
You were sick, don't bother about the tease.
Pleased if you signed for talks, training, exercise sailings,
To test your fitness, maybe failings.
Remember Wullie, indeed we were men.
E'en tho' we were but six summers and ten.

A Quinn

Summer Holiday

In that year, one perfect week of summer,
When all spring had blossomed and blown away
And autumn slept as soundly as winter
In the petal drop heat of the still day.
When children ran barefoot on castled sand
Between the white sailed sky and foamy run
Of the resting sea, soft mouthing the land,
Happy in the golden lap of the sun,
And in gardens of pinks and hollyhocks
And the bright umbrella leaved nasturtium,
Lavender, mullion, night scented stocks,
Lobelia and red geranium.
The time of the runner bean and sweet pea,
The blackbird, butterfly and bumblebee.

Susan Wren

Ballet Flutter

Feast the eyes on wings of grace
A Tchaikovsky note completes the pace
Tender emotion frames the face
Beauty abounds on wings of lace
Ballerina crying let me dance
A story well told in motion

Dance, jump and pivot free
Joy of emotion exudes from thee
Beauty cascades all around
In tender high emotion

Love eternal the ongoing dance
With perfect precision enhance
A story well told in motion

Fly in harmony thou beauty for thee
Gives great pleasure for all to see
Flutter your colourful wings free
To defy the cloak of constraint
Before catastrophe
And fly away to pastures new
For others to see
A story well told in motion

Jean Bald

Childhood Memories

Now I am facing sixty,
it's time to reflect
of times in the past
not to forget.

From being born prematurely
along with my twin.
It was quite a struggle . . .
of which we did win.

We have been close
as far as I know . . .
except when the time came
he trapped my finger in a door.

We shared great holidays
in England and Wales,
camping and caravanning
in sun, rain and gales.

We have had laughs
and lots of tears too,
especially on losing Mum and Dad.
Life 'goes on' as they say,
and we are glad of the life we've had.

We now have children and grandchildren
to give us life anew,
and from our early struggle
we know we will get through.

Elizabeth Anne Gifford

Remember, Remember

All round the fire on Bonfire night.
Paraffin to make it light.
Dad's old trousers, stuffed with straw.
That jacket that he hardly wore.
Tied round a sack of Evening Standards,
Crosswords started then abandoned.
A mattress that we found somewhere -
(We always seemed to have a spare)
That should make the fire burn on,
Long after fireworks are all gone.
We have to keep the fire alight,
So we can stay up late tonight.

Del Isaacs

My Memories

Memories are of things
that happened in the past,
Good times and bad times
and some that have gone too fast.

Memories of good times
can also be sad,
Some that you remember
can also be glad.

Those events that have gone by
being years or just days,
They have all happened
new ones are on the way.

Why do good times never last?
They only last for a short while,
Bad times are always there
they gnaw big in the pile.

Memories of being young
of being children with no cares,
Then we grow older
and we all have our fair share.

Memories of being loved
for someone to care,
But when it doesn't work
we say it isn't fair.

You look back on your life
and sometimes you think,
Where has it all gone?
It's gone in a blink.

But never mind
our memories bring it all back,
Of the things that we have said and done
the memories, 'it's a fact'.

Niall McManus

When I Was Seven

Quietly as I sit on the banks of the slow moving stream
Shaded by trees on either side with sunlight breaking through
The chinks in the canopy of green
Shafts of light dancing on the water like spotlights on a dance floor
Picking out the good and the not so good dancers
From water boatman, midges, gnats, mayflies and butterflies
All doing their best to please as the light hits them
Slowly the time ticks by as if it really wants to stand still
With eyes starting to shut listening to the music of the stream
And its co-habitants
A gentle rippling sound as a branch dips in and out of the water
On the warm summer breeze
With the buzzing of bees endlessly searching for pollen,
From crows to song thrush all trying to out do one another
With their own songs to sing
Branches of the trees rustling and swaying so gently not trying
To out do others
Long pleasant summer days spent listening and dreaming of days
Long-gone and years yet to come
Not knowing what tomorrow will bring, just to lie with no worries
Of now and the rest of the day
I still return to the stream some fifty years on, it still holds all its magic
Now, as then its not changed and as I sit under the trees
I am seven again
With no worries or cares, just how long will the day last this time.

Christopher Bean

Memories

Our memories never fade,
They're with us all our days,
Some behind us we have laid,
Some give light like the sun's rays.

Some good, some bad, all around us,
Some locked in our hearts we've sealed,
Some make us happy, some sad,
But in truth we always feel.

At peace when we remember
All the good times we have had,
From January till December,
They keep us from feeling sad.

From us they can't be taken,
We relive them if we choose,
From slumber till we waken,
Our memories we'll never lose.

Suzanne Joy Golding

In Loving Memory Of My Grandparents, The Jacksons And The Wrights

Grandparents are our link with the past,
They are very special people who we grow to love.

We appreciate the wisdom of their words,
Their words ring out loud and clear,
Ring out loud and clear in our ears.

As we grow older it all makes sense,
Each of us has talents to offer
As we learn from one another.

Grandparents are 'the pillars of society',
They work to hold 'the family' eternally together,
They gave their love and their devotion to their family.

And so,

It is through their hard work and sacrifice,
Our love grows stronger and deeper for them
As the years go by.

Toni Fowler

Thanks Mum

Patiently you smiled, each and every time,
Telling me I was doing 'just fine',
With tired legs and scraped knees,
I wouldn't give up, I wanted to succeed.

One minute I was on,
The next I was off,
Eventually my legs peddled but I forgot how to stop,
You simply encouraged me no matter what.

Without my stabilisers I'd been so excited,
I wanted to please you, make you delighted,
You watched me constantly with such love and care,
Even now I can still see you there.

Some while later, I was riding shakily,
Instantly forgetting the pain, I was so happy,
Your smile went from ear to ear,
I felt so proud when you gave me a big cheer.

Julie Marie Laura Shearing

Sweet Cradled Brightness Back-Dropped

Such coloured fish and sky feathered finery
All dashed by this ugly pattern
Streaking through the vapours rattling coloury
As rifted wrack tossed breakers whiten
Mob noise drills through - now and histories highway
To renew passions flown
Unwilling our dialogue from hysteria
Through tall grass unclouded blue
Under the twelve o'clock dazzling solaria
As creeks and inlets sparkle too
Or when the inward hour overlaps
In the special sunshine cloud tattoo
Caught in the soft swathed bubbling champagne flowers' scent trap.

Edward Tanguy

Memories

An old man closed his eyes to find,
Life's hidden treasures in his mind.
Beautiful pictures flashed in his mind's eye,
'Reliving the past', Yes! for you and I.
Mother Nature telling the same old story,
A harvest field full of golden glory,
My father saying, do good, never bad,
I've kept to his words, since I was a lad.
So! Be honest and true,
Then nothing you will rue.
Be kind to everyone in need,
That was my father's creed.
I've followed these good intentions,
And some of my own inventions
So progress like a pilgrim,
Smile, be happy, never grim,
Be cheerful and kind,
Then peace you will find,
Turn away from the devil,
Think grand thoughts, ne'er evil.
Help your fellow man
In any way you can,
Do a good deed each day,
You'll feel better in every way,
Try singing lovely, old, melodies
'They'll bring back cherished memories'!

Alfred Smirk

Garden Swing

As I tread my way through the damp overgrowth
to the bottom of the garden
a swing of many years stands,
rusty chains, a wooden seat of green,
creaking back and forth with light breeze
bringing memories of long ago.
The broken gate weighted down
by the old blackberry bush can just be seen.
Happy and innocent you rock to a lullaby
although alone, feeling protected in your dreams.
It seems like yesterday as suddenly you hear
your mother calling your name.
You run into her open arms,
feeling loved and safe inside
as thoughts of her will stay with me
in my heart forever.

Vera Jones

Rutherford Rhyme

On Silk Mill Road, of 'Cookridge' fame
A range of buildings stand
Some people call them shabby which
I don't understand!

They wear the dirt of duty years
And proudly take command
Of anyone who enters,
Into this unknown land.

Angels walk these corridors and
Angels take your hand . . .
They don't make fancy promises
They have no magic wand
Just the best the NH offers
. . . They won't build on sand.

Jack Ellison

Our Judd

My son George, affectionately known as Judd
    The name's appropriate, it rhymes with good
A hole in his heart was brought to light
    At the age of four he fought his first fight

Our joy turned to heartbreak
    When his heart valve was found to be weak
This couldn't be treated in one so young
    We had to wait when he wasn't so young

At the age of eighteen he faced his next fight
    A pig valve was put in place
I still marvel at his incredible fight
    His handicap he thought light

Twelve months went by the valve gave out
    Replaced by a manmade valve
His medication to thin his blood
    Finally proved to be not so good

Judd your courage and bravery still lives on
    Emotions still run deeply
God help me I never got round to round to tell you
    I loved you very deeply.

John Morrison

The Thousand-Yard Stare

They all had it, those Yanks
I remember, as if
They had flown into space
And walked on the moon.

They had not, they had walked
In the sweltering jungles
Of South Eastern Asia,
Where the only clear view
For a thousand yards
Was above them.

And like Keats' naughty boy
I wondered, I wondered,
I stood in my shoes
And I wondered.

But of course! They did not
Stare a thousand yards out
They stared in, at the things
They could never forget
If they lived
For a thousand years.

J C Fearnley

Restless

Lisbon has stolen my heart away
With her narrow cobbled streets where urchins play
And quaint little cafes to dream awhile,
Where Gypsy singers enchant and beguile,
With songs of love - the joy and sorrow
'Neath starlight and moonlight with hopes of tomorrow.
Where fishermen unload their catch at dawn
For quayside markets in the early morn
And almond trees so elegant and bright
With blossoms pastel-pink and snowy-white
Sway and murmur in a cool summer breeze
Embraced by the fragrance of eucalyptus trees.

I close my eyes and recall once more
The sun on the ocean as it lapped the shore
And I am ever restless - by night and by day
For Lisbon has stolen my heart away.

Jean F Mackenzie

Foolish Pride

Our guilt filled eyes have overflown with tears
As refuge, from those grim and sorry years,
When hardened hearts refused to budge
In memory, of a long-held grudge.

How silly can be misplaced pride.
Foolishness, undignified.
Yet this alone keeps us apart,
So why not make a brand new start?

The feud between we two should now be ended
Unkind words, once said could be amended.
Statements that were never really meant
Have often echoed like a sad lament.

The years have passed no time left for delay.
There are so many things we have to say.
Our families have grown yet grown apart,
It's time for us to make a brand new start.

Enlightened gossip, this and that,
A cup of tea, a cosy chat,
Will break the ice and tears may fall . . .
With willingness we'll conquer all.

Stan Taylor

Above The Cumulus

When you gaze into the heavens what do you see?
Billions of stars looking back infinitely
And each one of those stars that burn so bright
That flicker like diamonds, in the deep of the night
What secrets do they hold in their gravitational snare?
As planets pirouette with the sun's glare
Is it not a sight wonderful to behold?
Yet all this happens in a universe so dark and cold
Our minds cannot imagine the vastness of space
Huge distances between galaxies is hard to embrace
Will we one day travel to the far reaches of the void?
Using means of transportation not yet employed
What wonders could await those intrepid explorers?
As they venture to a distant star systems borders
Out there could there be other civilisations?
On Earth like planets in other constellations
So when you look up into the darkness above the blue
And stare and wonder, what if? Could it be true?
Are other eyes searching for answers like us?
But from a distance far far above the cumulus

Dave Mottram

Memories

I'm living in a memory,
A memory so true,
Reminding me of that day,
That day that I met you.

That day tho' far gone by
Still seems so very near
And like some precious photographs
I treasure them so dear.

When I sit alone at night
Before a frosty fire
And listen to the howling wind outside
I have but one desire,
To dream and live those happy days once more
O how I really miss them
And wish they would return,
But alas, this will never be
So all I do is yearn

Gordon West

Memories

I remember the farm, where as a boy,
I spent my leisure time.
The woods and fields I roamed with joy,
the trees I used to climb.

I remember the games we used to play,
the tricks we used to do.
I smell the scent of new mown hay,
I hear the first cuckoo.

I remember the work we used to share
of taking milk around.
Where is the fun that we found there
that cannot now be found?

I remember the days when it would rain
and in the house we stayed.
I still recall the old refrain
of records that we played.

I remember the fights we used to have
when sticks and stones would fly.
But you were always tough and brave,
I never saw you cry.

I remember all those things and more,
no matter where I roam.
Come let us seek the joy of yore,
come let us both go home.

Robert Hogg

Multi-Cultural Day, 2nd March 1994

The booths around the theatre foyer
Were a blaze of colour and life
From all corners of the world
Its children had arrived.
Sweet meats, flags, pictures, artefacts
Everything was there, waiting and ready.
In they came, Corfiots, mainland Greeks
Ex-patriots of all countries
Who are part of this tiny island's life.
Music, dance, songs and sketches
From every land.
One world, a world of colour, of joy and laughter
Shared in a final song 'We are the children of the world'
Applause from the great crowd,
Strangers now friends, *shalom* my friend,
Shalom.

Shirley Ludlow

Memories II – School Holidays

How many sitting there remember when
from up the lane, around the bend,
beyond the thorny thicket hedge
the jangling school bell beckon'd all?
And who, when its strident note had ceased
for that long summer school release
remembers then?
I recall -
with furtive gait from Mother's glance
stalking forth,
cloaked in holiday romance.
No thought those days of
Shakespeare plays or mathematic ways;
For me the quarry,
its life trapped underfoot,
frozen tight between the sandstone rock.
The dips, the sapling copse,
the secret paths I'd explore -
or perhaps the old mill shed
in whose cool, dim bowels
the bails stacked high,
and smelling sweet of damp'd dye
became a den.
But of all, a vision lingers;
A scene of once my favourite spot
when high the sun, blazing hot,
along the Navigation bank I'd step
to languish quiet, all serene,
half submerged,
in some clear, tranquil lock
till homeward bound I'd make my way
conscious of the ending day.

Alan Whitworth

The Awakening

I said
> You were only a few hours old,
> I held you, a welcome stranger. Suddenly
> You opened your eyes for a second's stare -
> A glance so brilliant, intense, aware,
> Laser beam sealing the bond -
> Before they closed a while.

He said
> Yes, I remember thinking
> Let's see what sort of a mother I've got then,
> Just my luck - she's incredibly ugly,
Trying not to smile.

Nowadays
> I ask his advice and sometimes
> Take it. Much has changed.
> But that first waking moment
> Is with me
> Always.

Anne Filkin

Sea Shirley

Down the shady lane: tree tunnel
clinging Mother's arm
five-year-old feet fumbling
on pobbly pebbles.

Sun-filled round end
a sound like angels' breath . . .
feet feel sand . . .then
Bright . . . everlasting water
from sky to land
> . . . with white waves.

Mother left she runs along
putting up gulls
into the foam which leaves
and then returns higher to knees

She runs along
arms up to sea-reflecting clouds
splashes in cloud reflecting sea

They looked for her
she looked for them
but who could see in a bucket and spade crowd.
she turned again to the sea.

Shirley Beckett

Our Childhood Games

(Of my sister and I)

The Fowlers' little son and daughter
  Had plenty of fun
  Playing in the sun
Making mud pies and splashing water.

They played table farmyards
  Had good games
  Guessing names
And happy families playing cards.

They sure had lots of fun
  Indoors,
  Outdoors
Whatever the weather, rain or sun.

Pirate ships they played
  Large cranes
  Long trains
And hospitals too they played.

In bed they played motorcars
  Motorbikes
  Pushbikes
And rocket ships to the stars.

They cracked jokes before sleep
  In the bed
  Dolls overhead,
One doll beside me, rest in a heap.

They enjoyed a game of I spy
  Jolly times
  Reading rhymes
My sister Millicent and I.

Stuart Fowler

To Joe - My Dear Brother

(Recalling happy days when we were young before and just after, the Second World War)

Do you remember those heavenly days
on Epsom Downs? We took our kites
and sometimes found a breath of air
that didn't respond to a fervent prayer
and wouldn't puff and wouldn't blow
until the clouds came trundling by.
And then, and then, and then, how high
your aeroplane and my butterfly
went flying up to tug at the strings -
while we pulled hard to tip their wings.

We didn't know then that cousin Clyde
would be quite famous because of Epsom.
He met the Queen, walked by her side,
escorted her into the New Royal Stand -
built to specifications he had planned.
His taking part in the opening ceremony
was a real privilege and a lovely memory.
A feather in the *top hat* of our cousin!
Not the only one - but the first of many
to embellish annals of the Malby family!

And what about a fortnight by the sea
when we were young? Yes, we *were* young.
But not too young to enjoy our stay
in a boarding house for our holiday.
Each years, most families boarded a train
to a lovely resort. Remember the rain?
Remember the pier, the jolly bandstands,
the cliffs, the rocks, the golden sands?
Never a dull moment! Ice cream and chips,
bright shining eyes, sea-salt on the lips.

And then we reached our teenage years,
learning to adapt to grown-up ways -
dancing and romancing - innocent times -
for boys and girls and midnight chimes!
The Streatham Hill Theatre, ice-skating rinks,
the milkshake bars for healthy drinks,
the Gaumont stage-show and cinema,
the Rex at Norbury, Streatham Astoria . . .
and for popular ballroom dancing pursuits,
girls wore long dresses and boys wore suits.

Remember our holiday at Clacton-on-Sea
at Oulton hall? - more classy than Butlins,
but offering the same sort of activities
that began to be fashionable in the thirties.
Our parents and all our close friends came
and so our holiday turned out to be
quite wonderful - an outstanding spree -

shortly before the Second World War . . .
The end of an era, when your life and mine
had to move on - signposted in time.

Our shattered world mended after the war
and things that had slept, woke up again.
New faces, new learning, new aspirations,
grown-up desires and new occupations.
Sadlers Wells, art galleries, Covent Garden,
opera and ballet at the Davis, Croydon . . .
the Royal Albert Hall, and on and on . . .
And after the black-out every light shone . . .
brilliant and alive - so we started to unwind
and sent our kites flying to culture the mind.

Rosemary Watts

Disposable

When I was boy the gypsies came
To peddle wooden pegs to pin
Our dripping clothes on line to dry.
Today they're made of plastic, in
A gaudy range of colours. But
The sun destroys them, bit by bit,
Until the hinge becomes too weak
To hold. It can't be past the wit
Of man to make enduring peg.
Today the greed for profit rules
That products not be made to last
For years. They count on craven fools
Who don't complain or else ignore
Them when they do. The same applies
To microwave that's dead for want
Of part that no one now supplies,
Or so they claim. But when abroad,
In 'undeveloped' land, they used
Their nous, and odds and ends, to fix
And mend a range of goods abused
By years of wear and tear. The same
Applies to youths who've gone astray.
We write them off without attempts
To guide them back to narrow way.

Henry Disney

Memories Of Our Haven

We have a Haven down by the sea,
that is where we long to be.
It's a place to relax and enjoy each day,
no need for a watch as the hours slip away.
Sunshine and sand and lovely salt air,
seagulls flying everywhere.
A walk on the sand with shells all around
and lovely smooth stones on the ground.
Down on the beach the dogs run free
enjoying the sand, the wind and the sea.
Dogs walk home they're ready for food,
we walk back feeling good.
After we've eaten we wash and get dressed
and go out for the evening with friends we like best.
We laugh and talk and enjoy cabaret
and before we know it time has slipped away.
Back to our Haven cosy in bed
we close our eyes for a good night's rest.
Then in the morning we open the door
and start to plan a day once more.
The people are friendly if you go for a walk,
you're sure to find someone who'll stand and talk.
The caravans, some large, some small,
with pots of flowers around them all.
Some have patios with chairs where they sit
especially when the sun comes out for a bit.
They enjoy the sun, cool wind and the smell of the sea,
so thinking it over I'm sure to be found
down in our Haven next to the sea,
where the people are friendly that's the place to be.
Enjoying the wind, the sun and the smell of the sea.
Memories to treasure in years to come
of our little Haven next to the sea.

Jean Adam

608

A Weekend With Nan

When I was just a little girl
She taught me to knit and sew
She took me on trips by train
Guessing where we would go.
We sang the songs she taught me
As we walked for hours on end
Pretending to be millionaires
With pockets full of money to spend.
She scrubbed my hair on Sunday
With green carbolic soap
Read me bedtime stories
And laughed at all my jokes.
She shared her love for flowers
And importance of family life
Taught me how to lay the table
Each spoon and fork and knife.
Mind your Ps and Qs she'd say
With a cuddle and a smile
Sharing in all the little things
That made the stay worthwhile.
On Saturday afternoons
An awful mess would be made
Digging in the garden
With my very own fork and spade.
We'd dig and pick the vegetables
Potatoes, runners and peas
Wash them, salt and cook them
To serve for Sunday tea.
She'd brush my hair a hundred times
Each night before bedtime
Sit with me to say my prayers
Then kiss me and tell a nursery rhyme.
She'd tell me of all the things
My father did as a lad
Each tale she'd tell with a smile
Whether he was good or bad.
These memories are mine to hold
To remember and give me pleasure
To have this woman in my life
Is a true and loving treasure.

Sheleen Hems

Many Years Ago

When I was five, and my sister was seven
Mother hired a cottage somewhere in Devon.
I remember the windows and white lacy curtains
Lovely flowers on the table, primroses they were.
We found country delightful, as we lived in a town
Mountains and hills in the country surrounds,
Near the end of this holiday one bright sunny day
All our family were climbing on a hill far away.
A picnic was called as a break from the climb
Mother noticed, my sister, had fallen behind,
Then just at that moment, down came the mist
Like a ghoul in the darkness and a terrible hiss,
All of us frightened my mother did say,
'Let us drop on our knees, to Heaven we'll pray,'
We all said a prayer for my sister now missing
I asked for daylight and that my sister be living,
The mist did evaporate in front of our eyes
God and my sister had heard all our cries
Then my sister appeared, our family amazed
From that day to this I give God my praise.

Joan Prentice

The Precious Present

Feeling sexy wearing my Christian Dior,
That thrill of my lover's sweet kiss,
Knowing I was precious in my lover's eyes,
Memories are now made of this.

The confidence that came with being young,
Feeling you are entitled to bliss,
Believing your love helped the world turn around,
Only memories are now made like this.

But this didn't happen to me in my dotage,
In my twin set and muted crimplenes,
I was dynamic, ambitious, had so much to live for,
I was in the last year of my teens.

Picture life without this, I ask you to try it,
For all that is past you now miss,
Muddles and mishaps, the sound of strange shadows,
Amnesia is now made of this.

Sally E Owens

610

Honey

My mother said, 'I want a dog.
The children need a guide.
A noble dog, a giant dog,
He'll never leave their side.'

Of dogs I only knew one kind,
The name stayed in my head.
'I want a dog. Mum, you must find
A poodle, please,' I said.

She was gentle, she was funny,
There was poodle in her - some.
Loving, laughing, sweet as honey,
Gazed adoringly at Mum.

Honey was my sheep-like sister,
Doggy tail, lop-sided grin.
Many times I hugged and kissed her,
Laughed when Mum gave her a trim.

She sat by me at the table,
Snuffled out the titbits well.
'Dogs must not be fed at table!'
'I didn't feed her; it just fell!'

Honey was my dog of childhood:
I'll remember all my days.
Happy through the years of childhood,
Honey romps and barks and plays.

She was little, silly, funny,
The child that never really grew.
Not a guard dog, not our Honey,
But a sweet heart, ever true.

Miriam Wood

The Past

The past
Passes
The time
Becomes
An ordered
Reference
With a
Lasting name.

The past
Grows
Like a
Flower
Into an
Album,
A framed,
Faded,
Treasured,
Picture.

Nicola Barnes

If He Were Around Today

If he were around today
he would remember when 'twas safe
to leave his front and back doors unlocked,
and when 'twas safe to walk the streets after dark.
He would also be sickened reading in the papers
about our gun and knife culture. Britain now rife
with terrorists, murderers, paedophiles, rapists,
bank robbers, muggers, drug dealers and heartless yobs
targeting the vulnerable and the elderly.
He would also agree with Sir Elton John
calling for the closure of the internet
responsible for the destruction of the music industry
and the arts in general.
And if his father were now at his dying height;
he would now tell him - to go gentle into that good night,
and not to . . . rage, rage against the dying of the light.

Fran Hughes

Child's Play

As young children in a village
We lived an outdoor life.
Few homes had television sets
And those were black and white.

Simple play was our great pleasure;
Football with a tennis ball,
French cricket on the garden lawn,
Were games that I recall.

Hide, seek and tag in local woods
Or climbing up a tree,
Sledge racing down a snowy hill
And all completely free.

If kids today would exercise,
Walk, run, swim, skip and hop;
With less TV and computer,
Obesity would stop.

Brian M Wood

Sweet Memories

Those days gone by, when I was young
The world seemed new, now songs are sung
About the days that went before
The life we led up to the war
Childhood memories - children's dreams
So little by today it seems
Sixpence then, went very far
A comic, peardrops, chocolate bar
A sweet shop, one we couldn't pass
With noses pressed against the glass
So many 'naughties' caught our gaze
Gobstoppers, Mars bars - Milky Ways
Sherbet dabs and liquorice laces
Aniseed balls to blow out faces
I loved it all, and would do still
But most of it would make me ill
'All of it' so says my wife
And so I lead a sweet-free life
Well nearly, though I must admit
I sneak a chocolate, just one bit
Well, maybe two - but who's counting
Forget the avoirdupois that's mounting!

Derek H Tanton

The Rickety-Rackety Road

I remember the rickety-rackety road,
that bumped itself over the land;
it wandered round corners and climbed over hills,
in a tractor the feeling was grand!
It was great to be tossed and jolted around,
sitting high on top of the hay,
looking over the hedges,
through broken down fences,
at lambs as they gambolled in play!

I often went strolling along the old track,
with my fishing gear over my back;
down to the stream that meandered along,
looking sluggish and sullen and black.
I tiptoed along, not making a sound,
in the hope of seeing a fat vole;
I heard a loud splash!
Saw a little brown flash!
Silver bubbles led to its hole.

Sometimes I was lucky to see him,
nibbling without any pause;
chewing away, not a care in the world,
as the food disappeared in his jaws.
A furry wee chap, often spurned as a rat,
children chased him with sticks and with stones;
but quickly he'd dash,
with a hop and a splash,
to vanish with no broken bones!

Now down to the fishing I untied my jars
I lowered them into the stream.
They sank to the bottom, to rest in the mud,
until only the rim could be seen!
The stickleback shoals would shimmer and dart,
then one rushed into the jar.
I tugged at the string,
to trap him within,
he's the best I had caught - oh by far!

I set out with my quarry along the farm track,
with the skylarks proclaiming it's spring.
They shattered the air with their urgent refrain,
the notes keeping pace with their wings.
The rooks in the trees were feeding their young,
calling hoarsely high up in the sky;
I was making my way,
intending to play,
with my friends in the farmhouse nearby.

We met in the barn, Pat, Jessie and June,
we climbed high up in the hay,

we tossed it around, we scrummaged and clowned,
we fought each other in play.
We jumped from great heights, in a dangerous way,
the hours slipped happily on;
it was time to go back
for the afternoon snack,
on our road that passed the mill pond.

The pond that we passed, supplied the old mill,
that was white like the clouds in the sky.
It bleached the lace, from far distant lands,
and prepared it for others to dye.
It had a great chimney of rusty red brick
the tallest for many a mile,
that belched out black smoke,
which made us all choke,
it blotted the sun's radiant smile.

I had come to the end of my day with my friends,
on the rickety-rackety road.
The story I've told was of years long ago,
when the war had its terrible hold.
I've been back just to see the road once again
the country is still much the same,
But the friends that I knew
have all said adieu!
But the road will remain a good friend!

Robert Neill

Bristol Fashion

They stand in all their glory, overlooking College Green.
Two of the finest unicorns that you have ever seen
No one can remember, from where or whence they came,
But regally majestic, they stand there just the same.

These are not the only unicorns that Bristol proudly boasts,
There's another 'band of unicorns' renown from coast to coast.
They are Bristol's sons and daughters and they proudly bear
the name
'Band of the Bristol unicorns', for there's no one quite the same

Their music is the music that stays forever green,
Their marching and deportment the finest ever seen.
They play their music fiercely, you can *feel* the pride and passion
And when you have heard them you will know, what's meant by . . .
. . . Bristol Fashion

Tony Fuller

That Happy Woman

She lives on one floor, 'cause she can't climb the stair,
But her mind's very active, 'neath the fluffy grey hair.
She still love to dress, in colours that tone
And she cheerily chats, for hours on the phone.
Although she is housebound, her dreams of the past,
Nourish her mind, with pictures that last.
She likes to sit, in a straight high-backed chair,
By the wide open door, to get some fresh air.
Planting a bulb, in a pot full of peat,
Her heart's in the country, though she lives in a street.
She strums a guitar and sings with strong voice,
You'd think that each day, was her special choice.
Though he is long dead, her own unique man,
Lives every day in the heart of his Anne.
Strangers are welcomed, with biscuits and tea,
Some apple tart and a slice of Dundee.
She pours out concern, like tea from the spout,
Her heart is sincere, there isn't a doubt.
She's mastered the art of cheerfully giving,
A recipe for a whole lot of living,
From all the centuries, I'd pick no other,
Than that happy woman, to be my mother!

Mary Lefebvre

A Secret Place

Cat

is my favourite. Who lives
in the half-lights of secret places,
in slim poses. Is a poem,
swift, light and graceful. So subtle
and designing. Yet

so richly comic. Who can
communicate without words. You hear
him purring, with happiness overflowing,
to please himself,
only showing content.

Mysterious little-great being
with glaring night-lit eyes that smile,
yet burn in thickets, projecting
fear that stills and
quells small creatures

resting. Cat is a dramatist
prancing, darting at nothing at
all. On hind legs with ridiculous
agility and zeal. There's beauty in

his fluid body. In the reign
of the dog, cat comes with
contempt. Spitting, clawing, flashing
paws, vicious teeth bared. For
cats are mercurial. Never

can be fully tamed, like my
unconscious. Cat is the
mystical, spiritual, intuitive
and emotional me, which
lies in a secret place:

Am a cat - am a cat - am a cat.

Ellen M Dunn

Ready For His Rendezvous

The young ones wade towards a rock.
Which they have made their mounting block.
The rules they must abide,
Or be refused their special treat
Where only two each time can ride.
Behind the girl,
Who owns the Appaloosa.

A predetermined pattern
The gentle giant picks his way
Wading through the water.
Winding his way, fetlocks covered,
Withers splashed with saline spray,
Ears pricked.

Time to go!
For children and a horse who loves to play.
To gambol in the sun,
Have fun.
Now gone away.
Until tomorrow, when the laughter
Hidden with the echoes,
Deep in the crevices
Will come alive again,
As little people and a horse return to play,
On yet another summer's day.

Ann Wardlaw

Where Can I Go?

I ask myself
as I gaze into the mirror
my face looked back
all is quiet
the world has changed
we are now at peace
alone I decided to travel to town
what now is my future?
shall I climb the hill
I ask myself
my head turned around
across the road
a handsome airman
gave me a smile
then came and spoke
we joined together smiling
loneliness gone we shared the evening
the war ending brought me love
marriage and four children
How I wish I could relieve those days.

Elizabeth Cowley-Guscott

Lorna

I had read the novel
then I saw you in the ballroom -
'My' Lorna Doone.

So young, slender and full of grace;
your face radiated innocence.

Slowly, you waltzed towards me
as if I had the remote control
and you were responding.

I remember that coral dress
caressing your curves - complementing
the flush on your cheeks.

You drew close - noticed me.

Who can explain the mystery?
That moment of enchantment and exquisite delight.
The captivating magnetism -
the meeting of eyes.

You smiled
and snatched my heart -
the sun broke through the clouds.

Jonathan Bryant

Childhood In Nottingham

I remember my childhood in Nottingham
As if it were yesterday
In Bunbury Street in The Meadows
Is where I used to play.
In those days people were far happier
With a smile upon their face.
There was no keeping up with the Jones's
No being caught up in a mad rat race.
Everyone it seemed had more time to spare,
If ever our neighbour was in need
If we had it, then we would share.
We all knew one another, so we didn't lock the door.
We didn't have anything to pinch,
For nearly everyone was poor.
I don't know why, but people were friendlier
More helpful and nice.
Although they had to work much harder
For there was no labour-saving device.
We had to boil every drop of water
Each washday was a chore.
Dirty clothes piled up in the scullery,
You could barely open the back door.
For Mam would be very busy
No wash powder could she afford
Hot water in dolly tub and Sunlight soap
And a well-worn rubbing board.
Then into a gas copper boiler,
Everything in a tangle
Then carry it into our backyard
To put them through the mangle.
Until they were ready, to hang on the washing line,
Or round the fire on the clothes horse,
If the weather wasn't fine.
In my early years, we had no electric light,
But only a dim gas mantle,
Some people had an oil lamp,
Or, failing this, a candle.
Mam would send me to Pinders,
our tiny corner shop
Telling me 'and please be quick',
No money, but small red book,
For nearly everyone was on tick.
I would often wonder as I grew up
How Mrs Pinder was still alive
For if folk didn't have money to pay the bill
Then how did she survive?
Saturday night, Mam got Derbac soap,
With which to wash our hair,
Then we would bathe, in the old tin bath

Memories Are Made Of This

Splashing water everywhere,
Yes, pleasures were few, and life was simple,
But very happy in many ways,
You could get real value for money
And, things would last longer in those days.
Our lavatory wasn't warm or cosy,
For it was out the back
Squares of newspaper for toilet roll,
Hanging from a tack.
It would ice up in winter,
If the weather turned cold and bleak,
And when it thawed it would drip on us
For the lavatory roof did leak.
On Mondays word would get around
That the rent man was on his way,
Poor Mam would hide outside in the lavatory
For she didn't have any money to pay.
In the 70s I moved to Wales
I heard they had knocked our old house down
All our neighbours had moved to council estates
A good bus ride out of town.
They were very nice, with all mod-cons
But I bet that they do miss,
All the fun of those childhood days like me
And often reminisce.

June Power

Fragile Butterfly

Butterfly you're so fragile so graceful,
you flutter where your country companions are so playful,
you flutter in summer's new dimension,
summer's beauty draws your attention,
you love being summer's party guest,
nature fills you with so much interest,
you flutter in the dale and up the grassy hill,
on a flower you rest ever so still,
you flutter in summer's colourful presentation,
you love the flowers' sweet temptation,
you flutter in the warm sunny days that are so still and calm,
where spring and summer go arm in arm.

Joanna Maria John

Memories Are Made Of This

Treasure Trove

How wondrous is God's gift of memory.
A treasure trove of experiences.
Some lie half-forgotten until ignited
By a certain sight, sound or smell,
Which transports us back to that place again.

Seeing your first rainbow,
Trying to catch it,
To touch its elusive beauty.

Post-war austerity, with rationing throughout the land
But as a child I was too young to understand.

Paddling in the sea, squealing with delight,
As the cold water covers your toes sinking in the sand.

Servicemen adjusting to civilian life again.
In my innocence I was unaware of their pain.

Building a snowman in the garden
Until your fingers were numb with cold.

Women mourning the loss of those who did not come home,
Nursing their silent grief, hiding their sorrow
From children apparently too vulnerable to know.

The joy of watching a raindrop shining on a rose.
Is it a sparkling diamond, or a teardrop? Who knows.

A M Drever

The Home

I used to visit a residential home,
To see an old lady who could no longer roam
Her eyes were slowly growing dim
And she had a clot in her left limb.
A stroke she took some time ago,
Had left her feeling very low.
I knew that she could hardly hear,
And many's a time she shed a tear.
Life took more than she could give,
I think she lost her will to live.
A silver haired grandma that was stooped and bent,
I prayed to the Lord to make her content,
I loved that wee lady like no other,
For she just happened to be my mother.
So if you have a mother trust she keeps fine
And pray that she doesn't end up like mine.

Ina Higginson

The Road Ahead By A Day Out

We like to see the road ahead.
Sometimes we see it as an open road.
With enticing views of beauty on ahead
Or warming sunshine that cheers and makes the flowers bloom.

Then sometimes it disappears to a windy, hidden,
Unending, depth, with road closed signs,
Where unexpected hindrances take their toll,
Sometimes in life and limb.

But then I see the sea.
A vast expanse of space.
No road is laid out there,
Where wheels and tarmac meet.

And yet,
The ships their way do make.
Because they set their course,
By compass, sun, pole and star.

That's how a way is made,
Where none was seen to be.
So in life, The Road Ahead,
Is set through word of God and thought.

I know the Bible's old,
It tells of roads all trodden before.
Now covered with dust of time,
But rediscovered bit by bit.

By those who trust and know,
The truest compass reading of all,
Not all by sight, but bit by bit in faith,
Even when the roads seem closed.

The sea of life, comes from above,
By choice of deed or will for as I learn,
'Tis not so much the road that counts,
As the vehicle in which we trust or choose to ride.

The scenery may change.
Like the Road Ahead,
Sometimes like the sea,
Where the road is always made for ships to pass.

The passage of the ship
Is guided not by road, but by compass set,
When way is always made through the deepest storm
So life is built, and ways revealed, and harbour made, from word
and Bible page.
All set by the Captain, Guide, and maker of us all.

A V R Cracknell

Strangers' Meeting

He stood erect . . . so tall . . . so strong.
Grey hair belied by youthful face
And sky blue eyes that shone.
He took her hand in bands of steel,
His accent curled around her ears,
Making her senses reel.
With language strange . . . softly as gentle waves
Ever rolling . . . breaking . . . echoing through caves.
Without a word he poured his soul
In every glance . . . in every touch . . .
Until her heart he stole.
His love was ice cold fire, burning deep.
Warming . . . awakening . . . lovingly embracing
Her body close in sleep.
So came the dawn and parting sweet.
He to his far distant isle.
Oh when again to meet?
Whispered words upon the shore . . .
Tumbling softly . . . hearts gently breaking . . .
Never . . . never more.
Last kisses warm on silver sand . . .
A touch so fleeting.
Never forgotten . . .
Strangers meeting . . .
In a foreign land.

Heida

Bloodstock

A stallion raced through an open lea
then cooled himself beneath a tree

A mare that once bore his seed
witnessing his turn of speed

Called to him just in case
he fancied one more chase

Her attention made his nostrils flare
and he nipped the neck of the brazen mare

And rises up to make her heed
his desire for them to breed

So she submits to his control
pleased again, to bear his foal

Proudly then each hold their head
assured the foal will be well bred

Peter Cullen

Pause For Thought

It came by post, that little
Book of poems
Mostly blank verse, but some rhymed.
Blank verse or prose? Who knows?
Too deep for me, a simple soul.
I was as a little child at her
Mother's knee, learning.
And in that learning,
Should I write the lines: 'and
The black cat pounced and tore
The robin, and licked the blood'?
I think not! It gave me
  Pause for thought!

So I read, listened, and tried to
Learn. What was to be learned?
Blank verse! Rhyme or prose? Who
Knows! This child with library books
And cassette tapes, would a poet make?
Maybe! We will see. In time,
If she should find the words
To catch the imagination of
The minds of others, will they
Listen? A book of poems. Not
Very big. Forty-one pages, and
Reading through, it gave me
  Pause for thought.

Doreen Williams

6th August 1994

The flower girl's playing football
And the vicar has peddled away.
The flashlight and clicking has ended
And the lens no longer holds sway.

We gathered in places appointed
And offered a toast 'All the best'.
Boxes and packets with cards of all kinds
To help fill the gaps in 'The Nest'.

We laughed with friends new acquainted
And waived to life on its way.
So many good folk came together
For a much-loved pair on their day.

Mary Biggs

My First Fish

A bamboo stick, a length of twine,
A cork and feather quill for float,
A hook and tin of garden worms,
Off on my bike to marshland reen.
Upon the bank I bait the hook,
Cast in and watch my float with bated breath:
It bobs and starts to run - a bite!
I strike and fight and there upon the bank
A slimy, slippery, wriggling eel.
A few more hours and two more eels,
Then home with 'Fish for tea!' I speed
'They look like snakes,' my mother said
'I'll not cook those,' and in the bin they went.
It mattered not, naught could suppress my joy
No cloud could dim the brightness of the day:
I'd caught three eels - a noble catch!
No experience could match,
Nor fade within my mind the memory
O'er three score years and five,
Not of a tasty dish,
But just the thrill of catching
                                    My first fish!

Michael Hewlett

The Way We Were

I find myself reflecting on Christmas times gone by
When Woolworth's was Aladdin's cave - for sixpence we could buy
The dearest item in the store - with wonderful selections
The self same things are priceless now in modern day collections.

When poultry was a luxury - tasted better that's a fact
And Christmas puds had 'thrupenny' bits and crackers really cracked.
When flame licked logs blazed in the grate the bars of which were loaded
With chestnuts near the roasting stage - once roasted they exploded.

TV, computers, microwaves and 'chips' were all unknown
The magic of the music world - a wind-up gramophone.
The postage rate was three halfpence - that's all we had to pay
Some letters posted in the morn would reach their goal same day.

No staff box on the counters - no 'take it leave it' air
Some grocers gave folks Christmas boxes filled with festive fare.
The milk came in a gleaming churn - a horse-drawn trap conveying
No battery hens - just happy hens - contented to be laying.

Eric E Webb

To The Highwayman!

Once upon a Sunday drive, given to an exploring mode,
Two travellers in their stalwart Mini Minor, christened 'Mr O',
Much marvelled at a landmark just beside a twist of ribbon road.

A stroppy stallion wildly stood high-hoofed, unsaddled, free of load,
Alert and eager for the moor where wanted men in haste should go.
A highwayman, notorious was, when he upon the stallion rode.

A Mother Goose-rhyme pitch-roofed shoe,
Stood blackened, worn and high windowed . . .
Concealed inside the giant's boot, a slide exiting out the toe.
Now what, the travellers pondered (but to this day, no one knows)
Did betide each child of the said shoe, who there within had once abode?

A hut of twin oak barrels, from whose shrouded windows dimly glowed
Two coaches' lanterns burning oil so clear and brightly just below,
Stood proudly hooped, grey iron 'round wood; a portly pair so smartly bowed.

The travellers, peering through a door,
As if into a coach they strode,
Encountered buttoned seats so fashioned in the antique coach,and lo,
In mirthful conversation, sat they, face to face and pigeon-toed.

As inn host and hostess Jones's hearty greetings were bestowed,
So these and other travellers have also fondly come to know
This inn, such as no other in existence, on the ribbon road.

Mark Van Warmer

Woolly Jumpers

It was just like hugging a bear,
My dad's big brown jumper.
Lovingly crafted by my resourceful mum.
I'm sure he hadn't had it forever,
But to me it was eternal.

I was five when I remembered it first,
Being given a big comforting hug
After falling down and bumping my knee.
An enveloping embrace that made everything right again
Something I always found
However old I became.

My dad is gone now and so is the jumper
But I never forget the love that made it
Or the love that inhabited it
Or the love that was embraced by it.

Bye, Dad.

Georgina Wilson

Sundays

We climbed over the stile, where the grass was mown
and we walked, in the meadow, where the flowers had grown.
The sun shone down, as we walked through the field
and we saw some cows and the church bells pealed.

There weren't any clouds - only blue, blue sky
and the birds wheeled round, calling softly, on high.
The bees were droning. The butterflies danced
and I gathered some flowers, at times quite entranced.

We walked on, then, to my aunt's house, nearby,
where Dad had some coffee and a slice of pie.
She gave me a sixpence, to buy an ice cream
and paper, to draw on - she had lots, it would seem.

My auntie and uncle would both kiss my cheek
and say, 'Hope to see you, again, in a week.'
And then, home to dinner, which Mom had been making,
with beef, on the table, and apple pudding baking.

Now, in my memory, I jump over that stile
and there's strong arms, to catch me, and I see his smile.
But, at that time, I just couldn't know
how sweet were those Sundays of long, long ago.

Linda Blakey

The Day Has Come

So many mixed emotions and manifold thoughts stirred in my mind.
Abiding love, immeasurable pride, a hint of nervous fear together
with an unsuspected sense of achievement.
Apprehension, a forced laugh, butterflies in the stomach
at the prospect of the inconceivable parting -
A separation, but only for a little while!
How I would miss his laughter, his sense of humour, his warmth,
his kindness, his unreserved love.
It was over, too soon, time to say goodbye.
A kiss, a last hug, weak smile, a whispered, 'Love you' - a wave -
And silence!
So many mixed emotions and manifold thoughts as I sat near
the phone, longing for it to ring.
At last.
I smiled, so happy as I heard his voice saying,
'Hi Mum. Uni's great, made lots of new friends . . . '

Maureen Watson

Untitled

Pension book arrived, joy or sad,
independence at last, all mine.
Off to shops, come past office,
over to the butchers, joined queue,
feeling embarrassed, bright red too.
Gave my list, to save me more.
He was a wicked Dewhurst,
calling out my list.
The young lad saw my embarrassment
and told him to read the list, and not talk.
Thirteen years have gone by,
when, my list contained this,
2oz of lambs' liver, steak and kidney,
mincemeat, plus two sausages,
two rashers of streaky bacon
and two small eggs. Bisto.
My ears, didn't seem the same,
Lady behind, asks for the same,
telling friend follow her.
Greengrocer's scuffed box ready,
two pounds of spuds, one large carrot,
one onion too, nearly forgot sprouts.
My tail still copying, third lady following,
got to supermarket,
one cheap loaf, three pounds SR flour,
Echo is the cheapest, cheap lard will do.
I've left some for ground rent,
gas man, electric, rates to follow,
so much for big ideas
what I'd do, with my pension.
But I got more joy, in giving than
receiving house-keeping money.
Hubby's now seventy-three,
so with his pension, he treats me too,
my fresh fruit, chocolate milk.
November, December, January,
all the rest of months, I paid gas,
electric, rates, ground rent. But now,
my own pension is all mine. God bless.

Mabel Clark

Memories Are Made Of This

Memories, how precious they can be
When we think of life as it used to be
When we were but a child
And the sun seemed always to shine.
When we knew nothing of worldly strife
And we were safe to play anywhere
In the street or mountainside.
The grass seemed always greener
And there was peace that was shared in our home
And there was laughter when you
Went to bed by the light of the moon.
And we had neighbours who cared
Money and food the parents went without.
I was rich if I had a penny for sweets
Sixpence, well we could go to the pictures
And if I had a shilling
That would be kept for collection
For chapel at the top of the street.
Sunday really was a day of rest
When I wore that special dress.
I can still remember it, it had frills all around
And I stood to recite in the anniversary
In front of a crowd.
That was my memories of long long ago
And they go back almost eighty years.
That's a long time for sure.

Lily Williams

To My Dear

To my dear husband.
I still remember when you held my hand.
It is still OK.
From that first date,
Do you remember the first date?
And in those days Branson had no mate.
Do you think.
That it happened so fast, like a blink.
All those years ago.
And all the memories still flow.

TS

Yesteryears

When we lived in a pinafore
And poked the coal fire
And shovelled the ashes into the mire.
When we wore fleecy knickers
And knitted woollen socks
And sat our bare bottoms
On the cold closet box.
When we warmed the bed
With the hot oven shelf
And used a potty underneath
To relieve ourselves.

Candles and gaslight lit the rooms
Hand pegged rugs covered
The stone cold floors:
Washing was done in a galvanized tub
Whisked with a Peggy leg
And scrubbed on a rubbing board.
An old wooden mangle
Squeezed out the drops;
Clothes hung from the ceiling
On wooden pulley props.

Now I'm a relic of the past;
Left to dream and wonder;
If and when I have to die;
What is waiting there up yonder?

Hetty Launchbury

Dilemma

A perfect world with so many thoughts
Yet reality alone is out of sorts
Denial! Is the word that I search for
Intellectual hopes - but my eyes are sore
So many times, I sit waiting for answers
But heart and soul never give me chances
And each definitive word in which I hear
I must admit that I shed many a tear
And remembering things my father said
Through the years, at the back of my head
Each word brings emotions - from the past
And as I grow - ideals run out fast
So thank you, Dad, for all of your ideas
From this one so weak - now with no fears
Yes, I will gain a future within your name
And hope that my kids will do the very same.

Lee Connor

I Remember, I Remember

I remember, I remember,
On a beautiful summer's day
Cows and horses out in the fields
And all the little lambs at play.
A small boy fishing in the brook
I rested in a shady nook.
White billowy clouds rolled overhead,
O'er all the world God's beauty shed.

I remember, I remember,
On a beautiful summer's day
Green grass, trees in a leafy glade,
Sunlight glistened on all that God had made.
Twigs that crackled, birds on the wing,
It was such joy to hear them sing.
Insects tiptoed around my feet
And all the flowers smelled so sweet.

I remember, I remember
On a beautiful summer's day
Waves that rippled over the sand,
As on a sunlit beach I lay.
Shells and pebbles glistening bright,
Children laughing with all their might,
Building sandcastles just nearby,
Their turrets raised towards the sky.

I remember, I remember
On a beautiful summer's day
Sight and sound of the tidal sea
Rolling back its great waves to me,
Seahorses riding upon its back,
Small crabs and fishes in their track.
Fishing boats out upon the waves,
Small inlets, mysterious caves.

I remember, I remember,
Those long beautiful summer days
Of long ago and far away.
My hair is grey and old my ways,
My eyes are dim, I cannot see
The beauties that there used to be,
But in Heaven I'll open my eyes
To God's beauty above those skies.

E Squire

Eddie The Eagle The Human Cannonball

(As it was, the way the little man became the star of the 1988 Winter Olympic Games)

Zoom zoom zoom! Boom boom boom!
Here comes ski jumping Eddie the Eagle!
You may have seen other ski jumpers so much faster;
But you've never seen anything like our Eddie! the Cheltenham ski jumping plasterer.

The Winter Olympics may come and go: but you've never seen anything like our Eddie giving it a go!
Zoom zoom zoom! Boom boom boom!
Here comes ski jumping Eddie the Eagle!
The other ski jumpers thought that Eddie wouldn't fit in the groove:
But our Eddie knows how to take the rough with the smooth.
Five six with ginger hair and large pink glasses,
Eddie brought a new meaning to scoring top with bottom passes.

Zoom zoom zoom! Boom boom boom!
Here comes Eddie the Eagle on full power;
He may not look a James Bond, but he's certainly the man of the year and the hour.
The girls love the way he goes all out on full tilt:
For Eddie isn't the kind of guy to wilt!

No one's ever seen anything like our Eddie soaring where only eagles dare;
And from Cheltenham to Calgary, the girls all love the way he shows his own true sporting flair!
Just look at our Eddie go! Look at him soar;
Our Eddie certainly knows how to hit top score!

The smooth-talking guys tried to make our Eddie look small;
They hadn't reckoned with the human cannonball;
He may not know much about being the King of the Ice Mountain!
But when Eddie gets going, he sure makes others look as wet as a water fountain.

When Eddie got to the Winter Olympic games, he never gave up the ghost:
He showed how to finish last, yet become first past the post.
Now our Eddie is the most famous ski jumper of all time!
A man of the moment forever, and the real King of the Ice Climb!

Here comes Eddie the Eagle the Cheltenham ski jumping plasterer;
Many may mock him, but he's definitely his own ski jumping master!
Just to see him speeding down the ski jumping slope with ease,
Makes other ski jumpers shiver and quake at the knees!
No one's ever seen anything like Our Eddie soaring where only eagles dare!
And from Cheltenham to Calgary the girls all love the way he shows his own true sporting flair.

Just look at the way Eddie goes! - Look at him soar!
Our Eddie certainly knows how to hit top score!
Now our Eddie is known the whole world over;
For though he can't jump far: he's not a metre less bolder!

Zoom zoom zoom Boom boom boom!
Eddie the Eagle the girls all cry;
Zoom zoom zoom! Boom boom boom!
Eddie the Eagle you're their kind of guy!
Johnnie J Docherty

A Message From My 'Ronnie'?

I know you did
I know you do
I know you will, my sylou, love me
For your ever. . .

There, in oblivion there is not much I can do.
So, permanently I dream of you . . .
Of our special days and nights
And our pretend fights.

It was only tickles
But I loved to hear you giggle.
Oh! How sweet were your embraces
Oh! The lovely smile on your face.
I tell you all of this my sweetheart
To bring some balm into your aching heart.

I know . . .

It's only . . . via: *'You'* that I speak
But another option makes me sick.
(I don't want you to be dead too for I would die myself twice.
You see? Now I still live through you darling).
I want you in my arms again . . .
I want to sing with you in the rain?

I want, I want, in 2008 for you to catch a train which destination
Will bring you by my side into . . . oblivion.
Then our stay on Earth will be but a fiction
In the world of humans' imagination.
This planet will go on and on without us darling
Till its day of reckoning?

Hush don't be sad, smile for your Ronnie
Who's trying to erase some agony.

Ronnie XXX

Sylvette Gilbert-Sivieude

634

Love Is A Many Splendoured Thing

'Love is a many splendoured thing'
That's what the lyrics say
And if it is long lasting
It changes on the way

You like his air, the way he looks
And he has such a lovely smile
You enjoy the things that he says
Your relationship becomes more tactile

You dream of him holding you in his arms
And giving you such a loving kiss
Your body tingles at the thought of his touch
And it's right that you feel like this

Without the sex the human race
Would not continue to survive
The thrill of his embrace
Makes it good to be alive

The years go on and you survive
Children can bring joy and bring strife
You both have 'edges' rounded off
To fit together for the rest of your life

When you are older there's still his smile
And the comfort of his loving arms
You both have changed but with good luck
You are still aware of his charms

Your hair is grey, you start to feel old
Just be glad if your friend is still there
And as he holds you in his arms
The depth of his love makes you a pair.

Mary Williams

Snapped

The winter nights darken
Oh what can we do? Santa's gifts are beginning to pall
Mum says 'I know what will please you'
Gather you round one and all.

Let's take out the well worn old suitcase,
And settle ourselves by the fire
We'll open the lid, as our grandparents did,
Of the contents we never will tire.

There's a snapshot of Dad as a baby
Curled up on a rug in the nude,
One of Mum as the May Queen, or maybe
We little ones begging for food.

Is that old Auntie Mabel with Dad there?
Why her skirts are right down to the ground.
There's old Uncle Bert in his collarless shirt,
Surely she didn't want him around.

We titter at hairdos old fashioned,
Poke fun at the sepia tints,
But each generation loves snapshots
Despite lack of colour on prints.

The fire it is waning, the lid is tight shut,
The time has gone quickly alas.
Old suitcase returns to the attic
With its memories that we all amass.

Hilda Hazlewood

Life's Blessings

To have a spring in your step as you go through the day,
Brings to mind the blessings we can have on the way.

To have an eye to see the beauty of a tree,
Flowers, nature, as it's meant to be.

The family, a smile on a grandchild's face
Brings happiness to outdo any pace.

To win that ambition, so important to youth,
Does it really matter who wins it on foot?

To look to the heavens, the cumuli in the sky,
Fills one with pleasure and joy for that sky.

When one is young and ambition draws near
These things are forgotten, such a pity I fear.

But when one is old, ambition is spent,
So count your blessings and feel content.

Elsie Woodward

The Best Party Ever

My best party I'll always say, was our road party on V Day.
At the time I was ten years old,
some gifts we had seemed more than gold.
The sweets we had brought so much joy,
to every little girl and boy.
The tables that were laid out there,
made younger children really stare.
Bananas they'd not seen before,
those tables had them by the score.
Our parents all worked very hard
and all saved up their ration card.
We sang and played, without the fear,
that planes of enemies were near.
The fun went on till the set of sun,
with one great thought, *England had won.*
No such a party have I since known,
in the last fifty years that I have grown.
And I don't think I ever will,
while I'm alive on this Earth still.

Nita Garlinge

The Guided Tour

Now - first we'll see the birthplace, destroyed in sixty-one.
Please ignore the wider street, they couldn't know those quickening feet
Might challenge Tennyson.

Day two: the school remains, its shelter's grassy mound
Recalls for you, on audio, the bombs that landed there below;
Her books were never found.

Day three: we'll tour the farm on foot, I hope you've brought good boots?
The horse is dead, its cart remains, pushed underneath that shed.
Ignore the thistle roots.

Day four: I hope you're rested? In cities sleep is rare.
You see that place of glass and stone? Work kept our subject up alone in antithetic glare.

Day five: the house has some additions, completed by herself.
You'll note the builder's rubble, preserved to show the trouble in straightening a shelf.

Day six has been a tough one, you've travelled through the night,
But this doleful dereliction is a visible prediction of our victim's coming plight.

Day seven: were you warned? You should return to base alone.
This tour is never circular, its route is quite peculiar,
So if you feel you've gained from the knowledge we have feigned,
We welcome your donation.

Judith Thomas

My Childhood

The freedom of childish
games such as catch;
running the town after
boys and girls.

Sliding on hard ice
and later trying to warm
tingling fingers.

Saturday when the
farmers came to do
their shopping - the
busyness and bright
lights

The annual fair and
many goodies to
delight.

The smell of apple pies
father made and
joy of sharing the
eating of hot food.

Entering the travellers'
caravan and retrieving the
coloured basket! Only
to be sent back with it -
fear of being caught.

Making the daisy chains
with friends in the
sun. Sister got
stung by a bee.

Marie McCarthy

Tony And The Tramp

When Tony entered the garden gate
The wind blew chill, the cloud were grey clouds.
Old Peter trailed along behind
As Tony put his scooter away.

A tramp was Peter, ragged and thin.
He wandered all around the street,
Searching in every rubbish sack
For things to sell, to keep, to eat.

I held two steaming coffee cups,
Prepared for Tony and me alone.
'Give one to Peter,' Tony said,
And I just stood there, turned to stone.

Tony noted my fear of Peter,
Dripping nose and dribbling chin.
'Give him my cup,' he quietly said,
'Take sugar, Pete?' I watched Peter grin.

His shivering quieted as he drank,
His smile lit up the gloomy night
As Tony found a pair of boots
To warm his feet in winter's blight.

The memory will never fade
Of Tony's kindness on that day.
Abu Ben Adhem I had wed.
An angel smiled, and flew away.

Mary Robertson

Memories Of A Short Stay In Oxford - Oxford Streets

Down and out in draughty doorway,
Dossing down on rubbish sack.
No ambition, self-respect - there you lay,
Object of derision - a broken hack.

What cruel twist of fate
Brought you to this dreadful state?
Once you must have enjoyed your life,
Did you succumb to the daily strife?

Wino now, scavenger of hotel bins,
Oft jailed no doubt to reflect on your sins
And when released, still half-crazed,
You return to your former ways.

Unencumbered with a sense of sin,
You will never win,
You have no hope,
You will never cope.

Charity you accept, but scorn,
A burden of society,
Oh, wretched tramp, why were you born -
A victim of impropriety?

Though disillusioned and downcast
Forever bear in mind
And blotting out the painful past,
You are still the gift of mankind.

Created in His image by the Lord above,
An endearing object of unfailing love,
But belief and faith you never knew,
So what is to become of you?

In spite of these features,
You are one of His creatures.
So, if you determine to follow your Lord,
You will surely reap your reward.

Reg Windett

Food For Thought

Freshly baked scones and cakes,
You certainly had what it takes
To entrance a child.

Apple pies topped with crust,
Rhubarb crumble always a 'must'
For Saturday lunch.

Shortbread shapes, sponge with cream,
Gingerbread men. Every child's dream
Of home-made heaven.

Fairy cakes, almond slice,
No one ever had to ask twice
If you would like one.

A special tin for each,
Which you stood on a chair to reach
Down from the cupboard.

Memories still remain
Although for many years have lain
Undisturbed 'til now.

Angela Pritchard

The Way We Were

As I sit here by the firelight glow
Thinking of the times we used to know
The morn we met at the swimming pool
There was just the two of us, I can recall

He asked to meet me outside the building
Upon, a lovely bright Saturday morning
The blackbirds sang out their notes of ecstasy
As our eyes met it was like electricity

Thinking now, as the years have gone by
How our love blossomed, I sometimes now sigh
He was travelling from London, from the Barracks Square
Throughout the weekends, such love we did share

Although so innocent, how our love grew
Such memories are still there, the way we knew
A guards man was he, and always in uniform
I will always remember his appearance, and form

Like the thunder that roars from the skies
Or the beauty of the birds that sing and flies
Like the lightning that flashes, fast and sudden
Or springtime, when flowers and daffodils blossom

Like the winds' whistling down the chimney breast
Or the leaves whisper, as birds lay on their nest
Like the swallows that spread their strong wings
Through the summer nights as the nightingale sings

So, drawing the curtain together once again
Still the cold icicles lay upon the windowpane
Just feeling the warmth, through this cold night
Till it's nearly time to turn out the dim light

God knows each memory, through His mighty power
The times spent together, and the way we were

Jean McGovern

Swung To Higher Rung

(Memory of early life)

That was a big step
To venture to use a swing
Seen from afar (so far) as yet,
One of the favourite joys
Of much older boys.

That giant swing hung twixt
Trees with tops quite
As high as the poplar's height.

The traverse of the rope was immense,
Staggered the sense
Of the adventurer;
Who nevertheless
Took the great step (no less).
Effort intense
Brought the fight
To success.

To attain the greatest height
And bask in one's prowess
Besides exult in the bird's-eye view
And suppress sensation of stomach in a stew!

But look wider still
Distant to the hill
And there appearing
Like magic horse rearing
In many hues aglow
a rainbow.

An extra sensation,
What a revelation!
Bow of beauty
Bands of ribbons
Breathtaking
Confection:
Bounded by earth and sky -
Delight for the eye.
Product of sun and rain
Made multi-faceted challenge for the brain.

Alas, a sadly disappearing rainbow
As swing sinks low
As sun draws into its glow
Produces developing sense
Irretrievable
Lifetime memorable
Experience.

Alec Burton

Memories Of Childhood

Looking back on my childhood
When I was just a girl,
I used to skip and hopscotch
And give my dress a twirl,
Play tick and hit, and kiss chase
And all those playground games,
The innocence of children
In those happy childhood days.

Looking back on my childhood
When I was still at school,
Playing hide-and-seek, and statues
I'd always be the fool,
And hula hoops at playtime
They were the latest craze,
The innocence of children
In those happy childhood days.

Looking back on my childhood
The laughter and the tears,
With memories of friendships
That lasted through the years,
The long, hot days of summer
You wished would last always,
The innocence of children
In those happy childhood days.

Maureen Reeves

A to Z of Authors

Forward Press Information

We hope you have enjoyed reading this book - and that
you will continue to enjoy it in the coming years.
If you like reading and writing poetry drop us a line, or give
us a call, and we'll send you a free information pack.
Alternatively if you would like to order further copies of this book or
any of our other titles, then please give us a call or email us at
info@forwardpress.co.uk

Forward Press Ltd. Information
Remus House
Coltsfoot Drive
Peterborough
PE2 9JX
(01733) 898101